THE KING'S MUSICK

Da Capo Press Music Reprint Series
GENERAL EDITOR
FREDERICK FREEDMAN
VASSAR COLLEGE

THE KING'S MUSICK

A Transcript of Records Relating to Music and Musicians, 1460–1700

EDITED BY

HENRY CART DE LAFONTAINE

DA CAPO PRESS • NEW YORK • 1973

Library of Congress Cataloging in Publication Data

De Lafontaine, Henry Cart, ed.
  The king's musick.

  (Da Capo Press music reprint series)
  Reprint from the ed. of 1909, London.
  1. Music—England—History and criticism.
2. Chapels (Music)—England. I. Title.
ML286.8.L5D3   1973   780'.942   70-169648
ISBN 0-306-70269-X

This Da Capo Press edition of *The King's Musick*
is an unabridged republication of the 1909 edition
published in London.

Da Capo Press, Inc.
A Subsidiary of Plenum Publishing Corporation
227 West 17th Street, New York, New York 10011

THE KING'S MUSICK

THE KING'S MUSICK

A TRANSCRIPT OF RECORDS

RELATING TO MUSIC AND MUSICIANS

(1460—1700)

EDITED BY

HENRY CART DE LAFONTAINE, M.A.

(FORMERLY INCUMBENT OF BERKELEY CHAPEL, MAYFAIR.)

" Wee must not brave it as some doe
that there was never good musick
in England but in our time."—
NORTH'S MEMOIRS OF MUSIC.

LONDON: NOVELLO AND COMPANY, LIMITED.

DEDICATED

BY GRACIOUS PERMISSION

TO

HER MAJESTY

QUEEN ALEXANDRA

PREFACE.

It is, I think, but fair and seemly, to express in the very forefront of these pages my most respectful gratitude to the Queen's Majesty for allowing me to dedicate to her this work. It appears to me most fitting that these records, which in a sense are Royal Records, should go forth as it were under Royal protection and patronage. When we consider how much our beloved King and Queen, as also the Prince of Wales and other members of the Royal Family, do to foster and encourage the gentle Art of music, we should indeed as a nation be proud and heartened to have such rulers and patrons.

I ought next to mention that these Records are published (and I fancy it is the first time that most of them have been brought under public notice) by kind permission of the Lord Chamberlain, which permission I value exceedingly.

Having discharged these two most pleasing obligations, it now remains to consider briefly what the work really is. One has only to turn a few pages of the text to discover that we have here a collection of documents, arranged in chronological order and classified under the various reigns, all coming from the Lord Chamberlain's records, as now preserved in the Record Office. Those selected treat for the most part of the maintenance and ordering of musicians attached to the English Court, but we gather up by the way many details concerning their lives which ought to be of much interest to students of music and musical history. These records commence in 1460-1, and are carried up to Michaelmas, 1700. It was thought that such date would be a convenient stopping-place; had investigations been carried further it would have made too bulky a volume, and this is more than sufficient for a first instalment.

It may be interesting to give some little account of the inception of such an undertaking, and the reasons which led to publication. The idea was first set in motion by Mr. Hardy, a well-known and able authority on all that concerns antiquarian subjects. We went to the Record Office, and looked at some volumes of the Lord Chamberlain's accounts, and thereby gained some idea of what the task really meant. As I had not sufficient leisure, Mr. Hardy undertook the searching of the various volumes for any entries pertaining in any degree whatsoever to matters of music, and much time elapsed before this could be finished. However, at its completion, a small and friendly dinner was arranged at which a small committee met (a good deal of the business of Englishmen seems to be accomplished at dinners), and we afterwards adjourned to Mr. Hardy's offices in the vicinity of Chancery Lane, and surveyed the formidable mass of type-written slips which met our alarmed gaze. Various suggestions were made, all of them having as basis the absolute gain that there would be to musical history by the publication of facts selected out of this monument of paper. It was resolved that we should meet again, and we did so on two occasions, at Sir Frederick Bridge's delightful old-world abode in Westminster Cloisters. A third meeting was held after some interval in Mr. Hill's rooms in Bond Street. From that time till now the work has been carried on by Miss Stainer, the daughter of Sir John Stainer, and myself.

I daresay Miss Stainer would wish that her name should not be mentioned, but I regard her as so intimately associated with this work that I am impelled to speak of her labours on its behalf. Fearing that any errors might have crept into the copied slips, Miss Stainer re-examined (a formidable task) the whole of the documents; she also revised all the proofs, and they were afterwards subjected to a second revision (if necessary) at my hands; she further compiled the index, her only assistance being a rough form I sent to her, and which served as a basis. Out of this rough copy she had to evolve an alphabetical sequence, and at the same time to add the descriptions of the posts held by the various musicians. I can unhesitatingly say that had it not been for Miss Stainer's valuable aid, this work would never have been brought to a satisfactory conclusion. I therefore take this opportunity of expressing my obligation to her, not only for so aiding me, but also for rendering—and I think all will confess she has so done—signal service to musical literature.

I cannot say how many times I have turned and re-turned the leaves of the text, sometimes with a sense of disappointment that information was here so meagre, sometimes with a sense of thankfulness that such a detail or such an event was there brought to light. It seems to me that the work cannot be without effect on our musical history ; it opens out many possibilities for the musical historian, and gives indeed at times curious sidelights on the doings at Court and in the town during the Tudor and Stuart reigns. But during this frequent thumbing of the page, I thought it might be an aid if I collected certain particulars and classified them under the individuals to whom they belonged. I know from experience that it is very convenient to have everything " sous main," and much loss of time and temper may be avoided by this expedient. Hence the notes that I have written on certain musicians, and placed at the end of the text. Of course they bear a very small proportion to the whole number, and they mostly concern only leading names, so far at least as our present knowledge is concerned. In looking through the various volumes of Grove's " Dictionary of Music " we find but few of the names that are met with in these records, and in many instances, as I have premised, the information in our text will not help us to knowledge. This is matter requiring research, painstaking and accurate, whilst it is also possible that no particulars now exist of many of these old-time worthies. All I can do is in the main to present the skeleton ; and though before it leaves my hands it has begun to put on flesh, such flesh must grow and acquire firm consistency by others' labours, and it is for the skilful and experienced to impart the breath of life. In the notes on Masques I have given many particulars respecting the Whitehall masque of 1674, as it is a prominent feature in the actual text, and it was, I believe, the last of these entertainments given at the English Court. I would fain see a revival of such artistic productions in these days, and many of our noble families might thereby give a great impetus to the poetic and melodic tastes of the painters and musicians now amongst us. The notes on Costume are somewhat meagre, but I have only inserted these as an explanation of many words that have passed out of use ; to my thinking, the most interesting is the note which treats of the livery or actual clothing given to musicians. " Originally ' livery ' meant the allowance in provisions and clothing made to the servants and officers of great households, whether of baron, prelate, monastery or college. Certain survivals of livery in this original sense still linger in the rations supplied to Fellows in the colleges of the older universities. The term was gradually restricted to the gift of clothing as a badge of service and of protection." In the notes on references in the text, I have collected together various items, a sort of literary hotch-potch. But these, if carefully looked over, will show of how many matters these records treat; and how, from being essentially musical at a first point of view, they branch off into tributaries which may be pursued with infinite profit and amusement.

The Index has been subjected to many revisions, and I hope will be found correct; but it is quite possible that errors may still exist. If any should be discovered, I trust the hypercritical mind will look on them with gentleness, though I am not of those who look on honest criticism as an unmixed evil. Stinging as it at times may be, it acts, when taken at its proper value, as an educator and an incentive to more painstaking and accurate work. I have in some few instances in the Index enclosed certain of the references in brackets, meaning thereby either that I regard it as doubtful whether such references apply to the names under which they occur, or that they may be set down to two persons of the same name.

It is well to bear in mind in reading the text that the Chapel Royal establishment was mainly connected with the Palace at Whitehall, as, from the time of Henry VIII. to the reign of William and Mary, Whitehall was the principal residence of the Sovereign. The Chapel Royal, as a building, was destroyed in the great fire which raged in the Royal buildings at Whitehall in 1698, and William III. then removed to St. James's Palace. The Chapel Royal at St. James's Palace had been for a considerable period used as a guard-room, but on the accession of Charles I. it was furnished anew for Divine Service.

The following note, taken from Delaune's "Angliae Metropolis" (1690), may be useful in setting forth somewhat of the composition of the Chapel Royal establishment in those days: "By the Dean are chosen all the other officers of the Chapel—32 Gentlemen of the Chappell, where 12 are Priests; the other twenty, commonly called Clerks of the Chappell, are to perform, with the said Priests, the office of praying, singing, etc. One of these, being well-skilled in music, is chosen Master of the Children, whereof are 12 in ordinary, to instruct them in the Rules and Arts of Musick, for the Service of the Chappell; 8 others are chosen to be organists, to whom is joined, upon solemn Days, a 'Consort' of the King's Musick, to make the musick more full and compleat." It links us on to those dear old days when we reflect that the Children of the Chapel Royal still have their livery from the Great Wardrobe—unless any change, of which I have not heard, has been made lately.

Dr. Rimbault, writing in 1893, gives the strength of the Chapel Royal staff as 9 Gentlemen, 10 Children, a Serjeant and Yeoman of the Vestry, a Groom of the Vestry, an Organist who is also Composer, and an Organ-blower. The posts of violist and bell-ringer have been abolished. It was the duty of the bell-ringer to attend at the Chapel at every stated hour of prayer, and to go round a certain part of the Palace with his handbell, in order to give notice that the time for Divine Service was approaching.

It will be observed that these records are in the commencement merely lists of names, and though these have their value, yet their frequent reiteration is apt to become monotonous. But as we go on these tiny rivulets broaden out like an ever-increasing stream, and in the voluminous details which mark the reign of Charles II. we are in full flood, and on our way to the open sea of clear knowledge. May the frail barque which we have launched on this stream, in the shape of our own small labours, ride to a haven of safety, there to encounter many nobler vessels that will bring rich stores of light and learning to create another chapter of our nation's history.

H. C. DE LAFONTAINE.

49, Albert Court, *March* 1, 1909.
Kensington Gore.

THE KING'S MUSICK.

[1460-1.]

Account for robes and liveries given at the King's coronation :—livery for John Dowett, William Hown, John Broder and 22 other minstrels of the King.

L. C. Vol. 424, *folio* 1*d.*

[1483.]

Accounts for the King's coronation :—account for twelve "trumpet banners made of sarsynett, with the King's armes." £14 16s. od.

L. C. Vol. 424, *folio* 24.

[1483.]

Account for "betyng and gylding of forty trumpetts banners, beten with the kyng's armes."

L. C. Vol. 424, *folio* 55.

[1483.]

Coronation liveries for William Herte the younger and Edmond Trumpet, mynstrals ; John Hert, William Hert the elder, William Mayhue, James Hylle, Thomas Freman, William Wright, Edward Scarlet, Robert Trumpett, William Scarlet, John Bulson, John Browne, John Marshall, John Talbot, Henry Swan, Watkyn, Palvyn, William Davy, William Scarlet the younger, Rauf Hubert, William Wortley, Richard Dalamare, Henry Gyles, and Janyn, taberetts and trumpetts.

Livery for John Crowland, marshal of the mynstrals ; also for Richard Hylles, John Pryoure, John Paynell, Thomas Paynter, John Hatche, William Elyston, Nicholas Dennis, Peter de Casa noua, Saunder Marshall, Robert Grene, Thomas Mayhue, William Barley, Johannes William, mynstral, Lyefart Willerkyn, Walter, minstrel, and Gylkyn Couper.

L. C. Vol. 424, *folio* 101, 101*d.*

1503-4, *February* 23.

Liveries for the king's household, for the funeral of Queen Elizabeth, wife of Henry VII.

Gentilmen of the King's chapell.

Edward John	John Petwyn
William Newerk	Thomas Sexten
John Sidburgh	William Sturton
Thomas Bladesmyth	Robert Penne
John Penne	John Fyssher
Henry Wilkyns	John Venner
John Cornysh	John Fowler
John Prate	William Tebbe
Robert Fairfaux	William Browne

L. C. Vol. 550, *folio* 68d.

Mynstrell.

John Buntaunce.

L. C. Vol. 550, *folio* 70.

Sakbusshes and shalmoyes.

John de Peler	Hans Naille
William Burgh	Edward Peler
	Adryan Wilmorth

L. C. Vol. 550, *folio* 70d.

The king's trumpettes.

Peter de Casa noua	Domonys
Thomas Freman	Adryan
John Gece	Fring
Jaket	John Decessid
William Freman	

L. C. Vol. 550, *folio* 71.

Mynstrells to the prince.

Steven Delalaund

Pety John

Hakenet Delmers

Mynstrells to the Quene of Scottis.

Gabriell

Kenner   *L. C. Vol.* 550, *folio* 74.

1509.

Liveries for the household for the funeral of King Henry VII.

Mynstrells.

Hakenett de Lewys

Stephyn de Lalaunde

L. C. Vol. 550, *folio* 124d.

Mynstrells of the Chambre.

Gyles
Buntanes
Barbram

L. C. Vol. 550, *folio* 125*d.*

Seykebuds and Shalmeys.

Johannes
Guyllam Borrow

Edward John
Alexander Massu

The kyng's trompytts.

Jakett
Peter
Domynye
John Beale
Frank

Christopher
Adryan
John Broune
John Blank

L. C. Vol. 550, *folio* 126.

Chyldryn of the chapell.

William Colman
William Maxe
William Alderson
Henry Meryell
John Williams
John Graunger

Arthur Lovekyn
Henry Andrewe
Nicholas Ivy
Edward Cooke
James Curteys

L. C. Vol. 550, *folio* 131.

Trumpets.

John Hert
Thomas Wrey
John Scarlet

John Frere
John Strutt
Robert Wrey

L. C. Vol. 550, *folio* 135.

The Mynstrells.

John Chambre, marshall
John Furnes
Thomas Spencer
Thomas Grenyng

Thomas Mayre
John Abys
Richard Waren
Thomas Peion

L. C. Vol. 550, *folio* 142.

Tabretts with others.

Marquesse Loreden
Janyn Marquesyn
Richard Anows

L. C. Vol. 550, *folio* 142*d.*

[1509?]

Gentilmen of the king's chapel.

Robert Feyrefax
John Sudburgh
William Cornysshe
John Petwyn
John Weyver
William Sturton
Robert Penne
John Fyssher
William Dobeney

William Newark
William Broun
Edward Johannes
William Crane
John Penne
John Smythe
Thomas Sexton
Henry Stevynson
Henry Prentyce

Children of the chapel.

William Colman
William Maxe
William Alderson
Henry Merell
John Williams

Arthur Lovekyn
Nicholas Ive
John Graunger
Edward Coke
Henry Andrewe

L. C. Vol. 424, *folio* 202*d*, 203.

[1509.]

Liveries at some Coronation, probably that of Henry VIII.

The styll shalmes.

John Chambre, marshall
John Furneys
Thomas Mayow
Richard Waren
Bartram Brewer, mynstrell

Thomas Spencer
Thomas Grenyng
John Abys
Thomas Pegion

Sakbudds and shalmes of the Privee Chambre.

Johannes
William
Alexander
Edward
} (*sic*)—no surname

The kyng's trompytts.

Peter, marshall of the kyng's trumpetts

Jakett
Franke
John de Cecill
Domynyk
Andryan
Christopher
John Broun

John Banke
John Hert
Thomas Wrethe
John Frere
John Scarlett
John Strett
Robert Wrethe

L. C. Vol. 424, *folios* 207*d*, 208.

[1510-11, *February.*]

Liveries for the funeral of Prince Henry, son of Henry VIII. Died 22 February, 1510-11, aged 7 weeks.

Gentlemen of the Chapel.

Mr. Doctor Farefax	John Fissher
Edward John	Robert Pende
Mr. John Lloidd	Henry Stevenson
John Sidborough	William Dawbeney
William Browne	Henry Prentisshe
William Cornysh	Thomas Farthyng
William Sturton	John Gyles
William Crane	Robert Hawkins
John Pende	John Petwyn
Thomas Sexten	Davy Burten
John Wever	

L. C. Vol. 550, *folio* 170d.

[1525-6, *January.*]

Orders by the king as to his household.

" It is ordered for the better administration of divine service that the Master of the children of the King's Chapell with six of the same children and six men with some officers of the vestry shall give their contynuall attendance in the King's Court, and dailie to have a masse of Our Lady before Noone and on Sondaies and Holly Daies, masse of the day besides our Lady Masse and an antempe in the afternoone."

Wages and fees of the king's household :—

Sergeant of the minstrels, Hugh Woodhouse, £6 16s. 10½d.

L. C. Vol. 590, *p.* 50.

The increase of charge in the king's household. The boardwage of 18 minstrels at 4d. each by the day, £109 10s.

The boardwage of 16 trumpeters at 4d. each by the day, £97 6s. 4d.

L. C. Vol. 590, *p.* 89.

[1546-7, *February* 20.]

Account of liveries, etc., at the Coronation of Edward VI.

Gentilmen of the Chapell.

John Fisher	Thomas Byrd
Henry Stevinson	Richard Bower
William Hochins	Richard Pigott
Thomas Bury	John Perrye
Robert Phelipps	William Barbor

Robert Richemountt   Thomas Tallis
John Allen   Nicholas Mellowe
Richard Stephin   Richard Kenricke
Thomas Wayte   Thomas Wrighte
Robert Okelaund   William Poope

> L. C. Vol. 426, *p.* 84 ; *see also Vol.* 425.

Trumpettors.

Benedict Browne, sergeant. John Tucke
Peter Frauncis   John Pytches
John Fryer   Richard Frende
Thomas Newman   Thomas Browne
Arthur Skarlett   William Frende
Edmond Fryer   John Warren
Robert Copley   Richard Lane
Henry Ryve   John Hall
Stephen Medcalf   John Graunge

Musicians.

Lewes   Anthony Symon
John   Albertt
Antony   Marc Antony [*sic,* twice]
Gasper   Vyncentt
Baptist   Ambrose
Marc Antony   George
Nicholas Andrewe   Fraunces
Antony Mary

> L. C. Vol. 426, *p.* 90.

The Flutes.

John de Severnacke   Piero Guye
Guillam Troche   Nicholas Pewell
Guillam Deventt

The Vialls.

Peter Vanwilder   Hans Aseneste

Harper.
Barnard Depont

Bagge piper.
Richard Woodwarde

Syngers.

William Browne   John Temple
Richard Atkynson   Arthur Kellyn

Singinge men undre Mr. Phelips.

Thomas Kentt
Thomas Bowde
Thomas Browne
Thomas Lichefelde
Robert Mantell

John Johnes
William Bradbury
George Pygge
John Edmound

L. C. Vol. 426, *p.* 118.

The king's majesty's musicians.

Hugh Pollard
Edward Lake
Thomas Lye
Thomas Cursson

Robert May
Allen Robson
Thomas Pagington

The king's harper.

Mr. Moore

L. C. Vol. 426, *p.* 119; *see also Vol.* 425.

1547-8, *February* 21.

Account for liveries for the Household for the burial of Henry VIII.

Gentilmen of the Chapell.

John Fisher
Henry Stephinson
William Hychyns
Thomas Burye
Robert Phelipps
Thomas Byrde
Richard Bower
Richard Pigott
Robert Perrye
William Barber

Robert Richemound
John Allen
Richard Stephin
Thomas Whayt
Robert Hockland
Thomas Talys
Nicholas Mellowe
Richard Barwyck
Thomas Wrighte
William Poope

Trumpettors.

Benedict Browne, sergeant
John Tuke
Peter Frauncis
John Pytches
John Frere
Richard Frende
Thomas Newman
Thomas Browne
Arthur Skarlett

William Frende
Edmond Frere
John Warren
Robert Copley
Richard Lane
Henry Ryve
John Hall
Stephin Medcalfe
John Graundge

Singing men and children under Philips.

Thomas Kempte
Thomas Boude
Thomas Lyfelde
Thomas Bram
Robert Mantell

John Jones
William Bradbury
George Pyge
John Edward

Mynstrells.

Hughe Wodhouse, marshal
Thomas Mayewe
John Webbes
Thomas Pigen

Robert Strachon
Hugh Grene
Robert Norman

Musytyans.

Alinso Bassani
Zuani Bassani
Anthony Bassani

Gespero Bassani
Baptista Bassani

Shackebuttes.

Marck Anthonio Petala
Nicholas Dandre

Anthony Syma
Anthony Maria

Vyolls.

Albertt de Venyce
Marcke Anthonye
Zorzi de Cremona

Ambrose de Myllan
Frauncis de Vyzenza
Vizenzo de Venetia

Fluttes.

John Syvernacke
Guillam Trochies
Guillam Puett

Nicholas Puvall
Pietro Guy

Vialls.

Piero Wylder

Ans Aseneste

Fyfer.
Olyuer Fyfer

Drume player.
Allexaunder

Harper.
Bernardo

Bage piper.
Richard Edward

[1549, *May* 22.]

Warrant for livery for Thomas Kentt lately admitted to the vialls in place of " greate Hans " deceased.

L. C. Vol. 811, *p.* 24.

[1553, *December* 8.]

Warrant for liveries for John Temple, Richard Atkinson, Thomas Kente and William Maperleye " sewers of our Chambre and oure four ordinarye singers."

L. C. Vol. 811, *p.* 62.

1553 (?)

Warrants signed for liveries for :—

Henry Vanwilder, musician ⎞
Richard Pike   ,,   ⎬ durynge pleasure.
William More   ,,   ⎠
Thomas Browne   ,,   during lyfe.

L. C. Vol. 791, *pp.* 16, 17.

[1554], *December* 23.

Warrant for livery for Thomas Browne, one of the vyalls, admitted in the roome of Hans Harsneste, deceased.

L. C. Vol. 811, *p.* 70.

[1554], *December* 29.

Warrant for livery for Richard Pyke, one of the musicians.

L. C. Vol. 811, *p.* 69.

[1555], *December* 7.

Warrant for liveries for Anthonie Bassanie, Jasper Bassanie, John Bassanie, John Baptista Bassanie, and Augustine Bassanie, musicians ; Nicholas Andrewe, Anthonie Marie, Nicholas Coteman, Edward Devis, John Peacocke, Richard Welshe, Alyn Robinson, and Robert Maie, sackebutts ; John Severnake, Guillam Troche, Guillam Dovett, Piro Guye, and Thomas Pagington, flewtes ; Albert de Venice, Ambrose de Millayne, Frauncis de Venice, George de Cremona, Mark Anthonie, Pawle Gayerdell, violons ; Innocente de Comas, and Piro Wilder, vialls ; Richard Woodwarde, another musician : Alexander Pennax, John Hutchins, and Robert Brewer, dromslades ; Henry Bell and Thomas Curson, fyfers ; Barnard, and Edward Lake, harpers ; and Anthonie de Countie, lewter.

L. C. Vol. 811, *p.* 260.

[1555], *December* 12.

Warrant for livery for William More, harper.

L. C. Vol. 811, *p.* 91.

[1556], *July* 11.

Warrant for liveries for Peter Frauncis, John Hall and Robert Turreyn, three trumpeters attendaunt upon the Earl of Pembroke into the parts of France.

L. C. Vol. 791, *p.* 70.

[1556], *December* 18.

Warrant for liveries for Richard Pyke, and Richard Woodwarde, musicians.

L. C. Vol. 811, *p.* 102.

[1556-7], *February* 20.

Warrant for livery for Henry Vanwilder, musician.

L. C. Vol. 811, *p.* 97.

[1556-7], *March* 16.

Warrant for liveries for 25 musicians :—

Nicholas Andrewe, Anthony Mary, Nicholas Coteman, Edward Devis, John Peacocke, Richard Welshe, sackebutts; John Severnake, Guillam Trochie, Guyllam Dovett, Piro Guye, Thomas Paginton, Alyn Robson, flutes; Albert de Venice, Ambrose de Myllayne, Frauncis de Venice, George de Cremona, Innocente de Coma, Mark Anthonie, Paul Gayerdell, vialls; Piro Wilder, vial; Henry Bell, fyffer; Alexander Pennax, Robert Brewer, dromslades; Edward Lake, harper; and Anthonie de Countie, leweter.

L. C. Vol. 811, *p.* 96.

[1557], *April* 23.

Warrant for liveries for Benedict Browne, sergeant of the trumpeters, John Tucke, Peter Frauncis, John Pitches, Arthur Skarlett, Thomas Browne, John Warren, Henry Reve, Richard Lane, Stephen Medcalf, John Hall, Edward Eliott, Richard Frende, John Winke, Robert Turren, and Thomas Westcrosse, trumpeters.

L. C. Vol. 791, *p.* 44.

See also p. 102 [22 *April,* 1558] *with the addition of John Iryshe, also p.*127 [10 *April,* 1559] *with Edmond Lynsey instead of John Iryshe.*

[1557], *May* 18.

Warrant to deliver white and green cloth " for cassocks and maryners sloppes " to Stephen Medcalf, Richard Frynde, Thomas Westcrosse and Peter Farewell, four trumpeters appointed to attend Lord William Haward of Effingham, high admiral of England, upon the seas.

L. C. Vol. 791, *p.* 50.

[1557], *July* 25.

Warrant for livery for Stephen Medcalf, trumpeter, attending the Earl of Pembroke to France.

L. C. Vol. 791, *p.* 70.

[1557], *August* 22.

Warrant for liveries for John Wynke, and Thomas Westcrosse, trumpeters.

L. C. Vol. 791, *p.* 71.

[1557-8], *January* 22.

Account for livery for John Hall, trumpeter, in attendance upon the Earl of Rutland towards the parts of France.

Account for liveries for two trumpeters:—Edward Elyott and Thomas Westcrosse, attending the Earl of Westmorland to the north parts.

L. C. Vol. 1 ; *see also Vol.* 791, *p.* 83.

[1558], *April* 10.

Warrant to deliver to John Grene "coffer-maker," "as much grene velvett as will suffice for the covering of one pair of virgynalls and as much grene satten as shall serve to lyne the same, with passamayne lace of silver for the garnishing and edginge of the same. And that ye paie unto the said John Grene as well for two cases of tymber covered with lether and lyned, th' one being for the aforesaid virgynalls."

Payment also to be made for " a newe key for the aforesaid virgynalls, also for mendynge the iron worke and gildinge of eight squyers to the same. Item for one locke, a pair of hendges, two handles, two hooks, with nailes for the case of the same virgynalls."

L. C. Vol. 791, *p.* 50.

[1558], *April* 24.

Account for liveries for Benedict Browne, sergeant of the trumpeters, and sixteen other trumpeters of the Queen.

L. C. Vol. 1.

[1558], *May* 6.

Account for liveries for Stephen Metcalf, and John Hall, trumpeters.

L. C. Vol. 1 ; *also Vol.* 791, *p.* 101.

[1558], *June* 30.

Warrant for liveries for Anthony Bassanye, Jasper Bassanye, John Bassanye, John Baptista Bassanye, and Augustine Bassanye, musicians.

L. C. Vol. 811, *p.* 108.

Accounts ending Michaelmas, 1558.

Account for livery for William More, harper, by warrant dated 12 December, 1555.

Account for liveries for Richard Pike and Richard Woodwarde, musicians, by warrant dated 18 December, 1556.

Account for livery for Henry Vanwilder, musician, by warrant dated 20 February, 1556-7.

Account for liveries for twenty five musicians :—Nicholas Andrewe, Anthony Mary, Nicholas Cottman, Edward Devis, John Peacocke and Richard Welshe, sackebutts ; John Severnake, Guillermo Trochie, Guillermo Dovett, Pyro Guye, Thomas Pagington and Alan Robson, flutes ; Alberto de Venis, Ambrosio de Myllan, Francisco de Venis, Georgio de Cremona, Innocent de Coma, Marco Anthonie, Paul Gayerdell, vials ; Piro Wilder, vial ; Henry Bell, phifer ; Alexander Pennax and Robert Bruer, dromislades ; Edward Lake, harper ; and Anthonio de Countie, lewter ; by warrant dated 16 March, 1556-7.

Account for liveries for five musicians :—Anthony Bassanie, Jaspero Bassanie, John Bassanie, John Baptista Bassanie and Augustino Bassanie, by warrant dated 30 June, 1558.

Account for livery for Thomas Browne, musician, by warrant dated 23 December, 1554.

L. C. Vol. 1.

[1558.]

Account for liveries for the Household for the coronation of Queen Elizabeth.

List of 17 names of trumpeters, the same as in the 1557 list, with the addition of Edmond Lynsleye.

L. C. Vol. 3, *p.* 110.

Ordinary Musicians.

Marten Kaynell, John White, Thomas Elles, John Small.

L. C. Vol. 3, *p.* 111.

Musicians.

Anthony Bassany, Jasper Bassany, John Bassany, Baptiste Bassany, Augustine Bassany, Lodovike Bassany.

Sackebutts.

Nicholas Andrewe, Anthony Mary, Nicholas Coteman, Edward Devis, John Peacocke, Robert Maie.

Vyalls.

George Comyn, Peter Vanwilder, Thomas Browne,

Drommes.

Alexander Pennax, Robert Brewer.

Fyffers.

Henry Belle, Thomas Curson.

Violons.

Albert de Venice, Ambrose de Myllayne, Frauncis de Venice, Mark Antony, Paul Gayerdell, Innocente de Coma.

Musicians.

Richard Woodwarde, Richard Pike, Robert Woodwarde.

L. C. Vol. 3, *p.* 112.

Flutes.

Guyllam Trochie, Guyllam Dovett, Pyro Guy, James Fonyarde, Thomas Paginton, Alane Robson.

L. C. Vol. 3, *p.* 113.

[1558], *November* 19.

Warrant to deliver banners of damask to sixteen trumpeters :—Benedict Browne, sergeant of the trumpettes, John Tuck, Peter Frauncis, John Pitches, Arthur Skarlett, Thomas Browne, John Warren, Henry Reve, Richard Lane, Stephen Medcalf, John Hall, Edward Elyott, Richard Frende, John Wynke, Robert Turren, Thomas Westcrosse and Edward Lyndseye.

L. C. Vol. 791, *p.* 118.

[1558], *November* 19.

Warrant for livery for George Come, musician for the vialls.

L. C. Vol. 811, *p.* 120.

[1558-9], *February* 3.

Warrant for liveries for Albert de Venice, Ambrose de Myllayne, Frauncis de Venice, Mark Antony Gayerdell, Paul Gayerdell and Innocente de Coma, vyalls.

L. C. Vol. 811, *p.* 113.

[1558-9], *March* 2.

Warrant for liveries for Alexander Penax and Robert Brewer, dromes, and Henry Bell, fyfer.

L. C. Vol. 811, *p.* 115.

[1559], *April* 18.

Warrant for liveries for Guyllam Trochie, Guillam Dovett, Piro Guye, Thomas Paginton, Alane Robson and James Fonyarde, flutes.

L. C. Vol. 811, *p.* 114.

[1559], *July* 15.

Warrant for liveries for Anthony Bassanye, Jasper Bassanye, John Bassanye, Baptiste Bassany, Augustine Bassany and Anthony Maria, musicians.

L. C. Vol. 811, *p.* 121.

[1559], *December.*

Warrant for liveries for two trumpeters, Stephen Medcalf and Thomas Westcrosse appointed to attend upon the Duke of Norfolk in the north parts.

L. C. Vol. 791, *p.* 166.

[1559], *December* 14.

Warrant for liveries for five sackbuts:—Nicholas Cottman, John Peacocke, Robert Maye, Edward Petalay, and Robert Howlett.

L. C. Vol. 811, *p.* 131.

[1559], *December* 23.

Warrant for livery for Edmond Linsye, trumpeter.

L. C. Vol. 791, *p.* 166.

[1559], *December* 23.

Account for livery for Edmund Lyndseie (also Lynseye), one of the Queen's trumpeters.

L. C. Vol. 4.

[1559], *December* 30.

Account for livery for John Wynke, trumpeter.

L. C. Vol. 4.

[1559-60], *January* 22.

Warrant for liveries for Richard Pyke and Richard Woodwarde, musicians.

L. C. Vol. 811, *p.* 136.

[1560], *May* 28.

Warrant to deliver to William Treasorer, " maker of our instruments five yards of crimson velvett, to cover one payre of regalls, and one yarde of purple satten to line the same. Item for the iron worke of a case for a paire of virginalls aforesaid, covered withe crimson velvett."

L. C. Vol. 791, *pp.* 189-190.

Accounts ending Michaelmas, 1560.

Account for liveries for six flutes:—Guillermo Trochie, Guillermo Dovett, Piro Guye, Thomas Paginton, Alano Robson and Jacobo Funyarde.

Account for liveries for Stephen Medcalf and Thomas Westcrosse, trumpeters.

Account for liveries for six musicians :—Anthonio Bassany, Jaspero Bassany, Johannes Bassany, Baptiste Bassany, Augustino Bassany and Anthony Mary.

Account for liveries for Alexander Pennax and Robert Brewer, drum-players, and Henry Bell, fiffer.

Account for liveries for five vialls :—Ambrose de Millayne, Francisco de Venice, Marco Anthonio Gayerdell, Paul Gayerdell and Innocent de Coma.

Account for George Come, musician for the vial, for his livery.

Account for liveries for five sackbuts :—Nicholas Coteman, John Peacock, Robert Maie, Edward Petley and Robert Howlett.

L.C. Vol. 4.

[1560], *November* 9.

Warrant for livery for John Thomas, drum-player, in the room of John Hitchens.

L. C. Vol. 811, *p.* 140.

[1561], *May* 8.

Warrant for liveries for 17 trumpeters :—Benedict Browne, sergeant of the trumpettors, Peter Frauncis, John Pitches, Thomas Browne, Arthur Skarlett, John Warren, Henry Reve, Richard Lane, Stephen Medcalfe, John Hall, Edward Eliott, Richard Frende, John Winks, Robert Turrin, Thomas Westcrosse, Edmond Linsey and John Restan.

L. C. Vol. 811, *p.* 137.

Accounts ending Michaelmas, 1561.

Account for liveries for Richard Pyke and Richard Woodwarde, musicians.

Account for liveries for Alexander Pennax and Robert Brewer, drumplaides, and Henry Bell, fyfer.

Account for liveries for six flutes :—Guillermo Trochie, Guillermo Dovett, Piro Guye, Thomas Paginton, Alano Robson and Jacobo Fonyarde.

L. C. Vol. 5.

Account for liveries for seventeen trumpeters :—Benedict Browne, sergeant of the trumpets, Peter Frauncis, John Pitches, Thomas Browne, Arthur Skarlett, John Warren, Henry Reve, Richard Lane, Stephen Medcalf, John Hall,

Edward Eliott, Richard Frende, John Winks, Robert Turrin, Thomas Westcrosse, Edmund Linsye and John Restan.

Account for liveries for five sackbutts:—Nicholas Cotteman, John Peacocke, Robert Maye, Edward Petalaye and Robert Howlett.

Account for liveries for five vialls:—Ambrosio de Millano, Francisco de Venice, Marco Anthony Gayerdell, Paul Gayerdell and Innocent de Coma.

Account for livery for George Come, musician for the vialls.

Account for liveries for six musicians : — Anthonio Bassanye, Jaspero Bassanye, Johannes Bassanye, Baptist Bassany, Augustino Bassany, and Anthony Mary.

L. C. Vol. 5.

[1561], *December* 11.

Account for livery for William More, harper.

L. C. Vol. 6.

Accounts ending Michaelmas, 1562.

Account for liveries for five vialls:—Ambrose de Millan, Francisco de Venice, Marco Anthony Gayerdell, Paul Gayerdell and Innocenti de Coma.

Account for livery for George Come, musician for the vialls.

Account for livery for Thomas Browne, one of the vialls.

Account for liveries for six musicians :—Anthony Bassany, Jaspero Bassany, Johannes Bassany, Baptist Bassany, Augustino Bassany, and Anthony Mary.

Account for liveries for Richard Pike and Richard Woodwarde, musicians.

Account for liveries for Alexander Pennax and Robert Bruer, drum plaiers, and Henry Bell, fifer.

Account for liveries for five flutes :—Guillermo Dovett, Piro Guye, Thomas Paginton, Alano Robson and Jacobo Fonyarde.

Account for liveries for seventeen trumpeters :—Benedict Browne, sergeant of the trumpets, Peter Frauncis, John Pitches, Thomas Browne, Arthur Skarlett, John Warren, Henry Reve, Richard Lane, Stephen Medcalf, John Hall, Edward Eliott, Richard Frende, John Winks, Robert Turrin, Thomas Westcrosse, Edmund Linsey, and John Restan.

Account for livery for John Thomas, drum-player.

Account for liveries for five sackbutts:—Nicholas Cotman, John Peacock, Robert Maie, Edward Petaleye, and Robert Howlet.

L. C. Vol. 6.

[1562], *October* 12.

Order for materials for liveries for Stephen Medcalf and Edmund Linsey (also Lindeseye), two of the Queen's trumpeters, appointed to attend upon the Earl of Warwick.

L. C. Vol. 795, *pp.* 2 *and* 21 ; *also Vol.* 2.

[1562-3], *February* 12.

Warrant for livery for Anthonie de Countie, lewter.

L. C. Vol. 811, *p.* 143 ; *also Vol.* 2.

[1563], *July* 13.

Warrant for a trumpet banner for Henry Hewes, trumpeter, appointed to attend the Earl of Warwick at Newhaven, and for his livery.

L. C. Vol. 811, *p.* 145 ; *also Vol.* 2.

Accounts ending Michaelmas, 1563.

Account for George Come, musician for the vialls, for his livery, by warrant dated 19 November, 1558.

Account for liveries for Alexander Pennax and Robert Bruer, drumme plaiers, and Henry Bell, fyffer, by warrant dated 2 March, 1558-9.

Account for liveries for seventeen trumpets :—Benedict Browne, sergeant of the said trumpets, Peter Frauncis, John Pitches, Thomas Browne, Arthur Skarlet, John Warren, Henry Reve, Richard Lane, Stephen Medcalf, John Hall, Edward Elyott, Richard Frende, John Winks, Robert Turren, Thomas Westcrosse, Edmund Lindseye and John Restan, by warrant dated 8 May, 1561.

Account for livery for John Thomas, drum-player, by warrant dated 9 November, 1560.

Account for liveries for six musicians :—Anthonio Bassany, Jaspero Bassany, Johannes Bassany, Baptist Bassany, Augustino Bassany and Anthonio Mary, by warrant dated 15 July, 1559.

Account for liveries for Richard Pyke and Richard Woodwarde, musicians to the lady the Queen, by warrant dated 22 January, 1559-60.

Account for liveries for five flutes, to wit :—Guillermo Dovett, Piro Guye, Thomas Paginton, Alano Robson and Jacobo Fonyarde, by warrant dated 18 April, 1559.

Account for livery for Thomas Browne, one of the vialls, by warrant dated 6 July, 1561.

Account for liveries for five sackbutts :— Nicholas Cottman, John Peacocke, Robert Maye, Edward Petalaye and Robert Howlett, by warrant dated 14 December, 1559.

Account for liveries for five vialls :—Ambrose de Millan, Francisco de Venice, Marco Anthony Gayerdell, Paul Gayerdell and Innocent de Coma, by warrant dated 3 February 1558-9.

L. C. Vol. 2.

[1563], *November* 26.

Warrant for livery for Joseph Lupo, one of the vialls.

L. C. Vol. 811, *p.* 146. *See also Vol.* 7.

[1564], *April* 14.

Warrant for livery for John Laneer, one of the musicians sakebutts.

L. C. Vol. 811, *p.* 147. *See also Vol.* 7.

Accounts ending Michaelmas, 1564.

Account for liveries for four vialls :—Ambrosio de Millan, Francisco de Venice, Marco Anthonio Gayerdell, and Innocentio de Coma.

Account for livery for George Come, one of the vialls.

Account for livery for Henry Hewes (also Hues), trumpeter, by warrant dated 13 July, 1563.

Account for livery for Anthonio de Countie, luter, by warrant dated 12 February, 1562-3.

Account for livery for Thomas Browne, one of the vialls.

Account for liveries for five flutes:—William Dovet, Pyro Guye, Thomas Paginton, Alano Robson and Jacobo Fonyarde.

Account for liveries for sixteen trumpeters (tubicinars):— Benedict Browne, Peter Frauncis, John Pitches, Thomas Browne, Arthur Skarlet, John Warren, Henry Reve, Richard Lane, Stephen Medcalf, John Hall, Edward Elliot, Richard Frende, John Winks, Robert Turren, Thomas Westcrosse and John Restan.

Account for livery for John Thomas, drum-plaier.

Account for liveries for six musicians :—Anthony Bassany, Jaspero Bassany, Johannes Bassany, Baptist Bassany, Augustino Bassany, and Anthonie Mary.

Account for liveries for Alexander Pennax and Robert Bruer, drum plaiers, and Henry Bell, fifer.

Account for liveries for Richard Pike and Richard Woodwarde, musicians.

Account for liveries for four sakebutts :—John Peacocke, Robert Maie, Edward Petaley and Robert Howlet.

L. C. Vol. 7.

[1565], *September* 1.

Warrant for trumpet banners for Richard Smith, John Newman, and Thomas Royston, now appointed to be trumpeters.

L. C. Vol. 811, *p.* 152.

Accounts ending Michaelmas, 1565.

Account for Richard Smith, John Newman and Thomas Roiston, trumpeters to the Queen, for three banners, and for their livery for this year, by warrant dated 1 September, 1565.

Account for livery for John Laneer, one of the sackbuts, by warrant dated 14 April, 1564.

Account for livery for Henry Hewes (also Hues), trumpeter.

Account for livery for Anthony de Countie, luter.

Account for livery for Thomas Browne, one of the vialls.

Account for liveries for five flutes :—Guillermo Dovett, Pyro Guie, Thomas Paginton, Alano Robson and Jacobo Fonyarde.

Account for liveries for Alexander Pennax and Robert Bruer, drummers, and Henry Bell, fifer.

Account for liveries for Richard Pike and Richard Woodward, musicians.

Account for liveries for sixteen trumpeters :—Benedict Browne, serjeant, Peter Frauncis, John Pitches, Thomas Browne, Arthur Skarlet, John Warren, Henry Reve, Richard Lane, Stephen Medcalf, John Hall, Edward Elliot, Richard Frende, John Winks, Robert Turren, Thomas Westcrosse and John Restan.

Account for livery for John Thomas, drum-player.

Account for liveries for four sackbutts :—John Peacock, Robert Maie, Edward Petaleie and Robert Howlet.

L. C. Vol. 8.

[1565], *October* 31.

Warrant for livery for Mark Anthony Bassany, one of the musicians sackbutts.

L. C. Vol. 811, *p.* 154.

[1565], *November* 10.

Warrant for livery for Radulpho Grene, one of the musicians sackbutts.

L. C. Vol. 811, *p.* 155.

[1566], *April* 30.

Warrant for livery for Nicholas Layner, one of the flutes.

L. C. Vol. 811, *p.* 157.

[1566-7], *February* 1.

Account for banners for seventeen trumpeters :—

Stephen Medcalf, sergeant

John Pitches	John Winkes
Thomas Browne	Thomas Westcrosse
Arthur Skarlet	John Roiston
John Warren	Henry Hewes
Henry Reve	Richard Smythe
John Hall	John Newman
Edward Eliot	Thomas Roiston and
Richard Frende	William Lindseie

L. C. Vol. 793, *p.* 11.

[1567], *May* 14.

Warrant for livery for William Lindsey, trumpeter.

L. C. Vol. 811, *p.* 165 ; *also Vol.* 10.

[1567], *May* 24.

Warrant for livery for William Garson, drum player, appointed in room of Robert Brewer, deceased.

L. C. Vol. 811, *p.* 162 ; *also Vol.* 10.

Accounts ending Michaelmas, 1567.

Account for liveries for Richard Smythe, John Newman and Thomas Roistan, trumpeters to the Queen.

Account for livery for John Laneer, one of the sackbuts.

Account for livery for Henry Hewes, trumpeter.

Account for livery for Marco Antonio Bassany, one of the sackbutts, by warrant dated 31 October, 1565.

Account for livery for Radulpho Grene, one of the sackbutts, by warrant dated 10 November, 1565.

Account for livery for Nicholas Laneer, one of the flutes, by warrant dated 30 April, 1566.

Account for livery for Antonio de Countie, lewter.

Account for livery for Thomas Browne, one of the vialls.

Account for liveries for five flutes :—Guillermo Dovet, Pyro Guye, Thomas Paginton, Alano Robson and Jacobo Fonyarde.

Account for liveries for 12 trumpeters :—John Pitches, Thomas Browne, Arthur Skarlet, John Warren, Henry Reve, Stephen Medcalf, John Hall, Edward Eliot, Richard Frende, John Winks, Thomas Westcrosse and John Restan.

Account for livery for John Thomas, drum-player.

Account for liveries for Alexander Pennax and Robert Brewer, drum players, and Henry Bell, fifer.

Account for liveries for Richard Pyke and Richard Woodwarde, musicians.

Account for liveries for three sackbuts:—Robert May, Edward Peteley and Robert Howlet.

L. C. Vol. 9.

[1567], *October* 10.

Warrant for trumpet banners and liveries for Robert Westcrosse and Thomas Holdworthe, trumpeters.

L. C. Vol. 811, *p.* 166 ; *also Vol.* 10.

Accounts ending Michaelmas, 1568.

Account for liveries for Richard Smythe, John Newmanne, and Thomas Roiston, trumpeters to the Queen.

Account for livery for Radulpho Grene, one of the sackbutts.

Account for livery for Nicholas Laneer, one of the flutes.

Account for livery for Marco Antonio Bassanio, one of the sackbutts.

Account for livery for John Laneer, one of the sackbutts.

Account for livery for Henry Hewes, trumpeter.

Account for livery for Antonio de Countie, luter.

Account for livery for Thomas Browne, one of the vialls.

Account for liveries for five flutes:—William Dovet, Piro Guye, Thomas Paginton, Alano Robson and Jacobo Foniarde.

Account for livery for John Thomas, drum-player.

Account for livery for Alexander Pennax, drummer, and one fifer [no name].

Account for liveries for Richard Pike and Richard Woodwarde.

Account for liveries for eleven trumpeters:—Stephen Medcalf, sergeant, John Pitches, Arthur Skarlet, John Warren, Henry Reve, John Hall, Edward Eliott, Richard Frende, John Winks, Thomas Westcrosse and John Restan.

Account for liveries for three sackbutts:—Robert Maye, Edward Petalaye and Robert Howlet.

L. C. Vol. 10.

Accounts ending Michaelmas, 1569.

Account for livery for Marco Antonio Bassany, one of the sackbutts.

Account for livery for William Lindsey, trumpeter, by warrant dated 14 May, 1567.

Account for liveries for Robert Westcrosse and Thomas Holdworthe, trumpeters, by warrant dated 10 October, 1567.

Account for livery for William Garson, drum-player, by warrant dated 24 May, 1567.

Account for livery for Richard Smythe, John Newman and Thomas Roiston, trumpeters to the Queen.

Account for livery for Radulpho Grene, one of the sackbutts.

Account for livery for Nicholas Laneer, one of the flutes.

Account for livery for Henry Hewes, trumpeter.

Account for livery for Antonio de Countie, luter.

Account for livery for Alexander Pennax, drummer, and one fifer [no name].

Account for livery for Richard Woodwarde, musician.

Account for livery for Thomas Browne, one of the vialls.

Account for liveries for four flutes:—Guillermo Dovett, Piro Guy, Thomas Paginton and Jacobo Fonyarde.

Account for liveries for eleven trumpets:—Stephen Medcalf, sergeant, John Pitches, Arthur Skarlet, John Warren, Henry Reve, John Hall, Edward Eliot, Richard Frende, John Winks, Thomas Westcrosse and John Restan.

Account for livery for John Thomas, drum-player.

Account for liveries for three sackbutts:—Robert Maie, Edward Petaley and Robert Howlett.

Account for livery for John Laneer, one of the sackbutts.

L. C. Vol. 11.

1570, *October* 6.

Warrant for livery for Peter Dorosell, trumpeter.

L. C. Vol. 811, *p.* 172; *also Vol.* 12.

1570, *November* 28.

Warrant for trumpet banners for Stephen Medcalf, sergeant of the trumpettours; John Pitches, Arthur Skarlet, John Warren, John Hall, Edward Eliot, Richard Frend, John Winks, Thomas Westcrosse, John Restan, Henry Hewes, Richard Smyth, John Newman, Thomas Royston, Robert Westcrosse, Thomas Holdeworthe, William Lindsey, and Peter Dorosell, trumpettours, and to Humfrey Spark, trumpettour of Barwick.

L. C. Vol. 811, *p.* 173.

Accounts ending Michaelmas, 1571.

Account for livery for William Lindsey, trumpeter.

Account for liveries for Robert Westcrosse and Thomas Holdworthe, trumpeters.

Account for livery for William Garson, drum-player.

Account for livery for Nicholas Laneer, one of the flutes.

Account for livery for Marco Anthonio Bassany, one of the sackbutts.

Account for liveries for Richard Smyth, John Newman and Thomas Roiston, trumpeters to the Queen.

Account for livery for Radulpho Grene, one of the sackbutts.

Account for liveries for ten trumpets :—Stephen Medcalf, serjeant, John Pitches, Arthur Skarlet, John Warren, John Hall, Edward Elliott, Richard Frende, John Winks, Thomas Westcrosse, and John Restan.

Account for liveries for three sackbutts :—Robert May, Edward Petaley and Robert Howlet.

Account for livery for John Thomas, drom player.

Account for livery for Alexander Pennax, drome player.

Account for liveries for four flutes :—Guillermo Dovett, Piro Guye, Thomas Paginton and Jacobo Fonyarde.

Account for livery for Thomas Browne, one of the vialls.

Account for livery for Anthonio de Countie, luter.

Account for livery for Henry Hewes, trumpeter.

Account for livery for John Laneer, one of the sackbutts.

Accounts ending Michaelmas, 1572.

Account for livery for William Lindsey, trumpeter.

Account for liveries for Robert Westcrosse and Thomas Holdworthe, trumpeters.

Account for livery for William Garson, drum-player.

Account for livery for Peter Dorosell, trumpeter, by warrant dated 6 October, 1570.

Account for livery for Nicholas Laneer, one of the flutes.

Account for livery for Radulpho Grene, one of the sackbutts.

Account for livery for Marco Anthonio Bassanie, one of the sackbutts.

Account for liveries for three sackbuts :—Robert May, Edward Petaleie and Robert Howlet.

Account for livery for John Thomas, drum-player.

Account for liveries for ten trumpets:—Stephen Medcalf, sergeant, John Pitches, Arthur Skarlet, John Warren, John Hall, Edward Elliott, Richard Frende, John Winks, Thomas Westcrosse, and John Restan.

Account for livery for Alexander Pennax, drome player.

Account for liveries for four flutes :—William Dovet, Piro Guye, Thomas Paginton and Jacobo Fonyarde.

Account for livery for Thomas Browne, one of the vialls.

Account for livery for Anthony de Countie, lewter.

Account for livery for Henry Hewes, trumpeter.

Account for liveries for Richard Smythe, John Newman and Thomas Roiston, trumpeters to the Queen.

Account for livery for John Laneer, one of the sackbutts.

L. C. Vol. 13.

Accounts ending Michaelmas, 1573.

Account for livery for Peter Dorosell, trumpeter.

Account for livery for William Lindsey, trumpeter.

Account for liveries for Robert Westcrosse and Thomas Holdworth, trumpeters.

Account for livery for William Garson, drum-player.

Account for livery for Nicholas Laneer, one of the flutes.

Account for livery for Marco Anthonio Bassani, one of the sackbuts.

Account for liveries for Richard Smythe, John Newman and Thomas Royston, trumpeters to the Queen.

Account for livery for Radulpho Grene, one of the sackbuts.

Account for livery for John Thomas, drum-player.

Account for liveries for three sackbutts :—Robert Maie, Edward Petaley and Robert Howlet.

Account for liveries for ten trumpets :—Stephen Medcalf, sergeant, John Pitches, Arthur Skarlet, John Warren, John Hall, Edward Eliott, Richard Frende, John Winkes, Thomas Westcrosse, and John Royston.

Account for liveries for four flutes :—William Dovet, Piro Guye, Thomas Paginton and Jacobo Foniarde.

Account for livery for Thomas Browne, one of the vialls.

Account for livery for Anthonio de Countie, luter.

Account for livery for Alexander Pennax, drum-player.

Account for livery for Henry Hewes, trumpeter.

Account for livery for John Laneer, one of the sackbutts.

L. C. Vol. 14.

1573-4, *February* 1.

Warrant for liveries and trumpet banners for Francis Bourne and Benedict Browne, trumpettours.

L. C. Vol. 811, *p.* 181.

Accounts ending Michaelmas, 1574.

Account for livery for Peter Dorosell, trumpeter.

Account for livery for William Lindsey, trumpeter.

Account for liveries for Robert Westcrosse and Thomas Holdworth, trumpeters.

Account for livery for William Garson, drom player.

Account for livery for Nicholas Laneer, one of the flutes.

Account for livery for Marco Anthonio Bassani, one of the sackbutts.

Account for liveries for Francis Bourne and Benedict Browne, trumpeters, by warrant dated 1 February, 1573-4.

Account for liveries for Richard Smyth, John Newman and Thomas Roiston, trumpeters to the Queen.

Account for livery for Radulpho Grene, one of the sackbutts.

Account for livery for Henry Hewes, trumpeter.

Account for livery for Anthonio de Countie, lewter.

Account for livery for Thomas Browne, one of the vialls.

Account for liveries for three flutes :—Pyro Guy, Thomas Paginton and Jacobo Fonyarde.

Account for liveries for ten trumpets :—Stephen Medcalf, sergeant, John Pitches, Arthur Skarlet, John Warren, John Hall, Edward Eliott, Richard Frende, John Wynks, Thomas Westcrosse and John Restan.

Account for livery for Alexander Pennax, drumplayer.

Account for liveries for three sackbuts :—Robert Maie, Edward Petaley and Robert Howlett.

Account for livery for John Thomas, drom player.

L. C. Vol. 16.

Accounts ending Michaelmas, 1575.

Account for livery for Nicholas Laneer, one of the flutes.

Account for livery for Marco Anthonio Bassani, one of the sackbutts.

Account for liveries for Francis Bourne and Benedict Browne, trumpeters.

Account for eighteen standards for trumpeters :—Stephen Medcalf, sergeant, John Pitches, Arthur Skarlet, John Hall, Edward Eliott, Richard Frende, John Winks, Thomas Westcrosse, John Restan, Henry Hewes, Richard Smythe, John Newman, Thomas Royston, Robert Westcrosse, Thomas Holdworthe, William Lindsey, Peter Dorosell, and for Humphrey Sparke, trumpeter of Barwicke.

Account for liveries for Richard Smyth, John Newman and Thomas Roiston, trumpeters to the Queen.

Account for livery for Radulpho Grene, one of the sackbutts.

Account for livery for Peter Dorosell, trumpeter.

Account for livery for William Lindsey, trumpeter.

Account for liveries for Robert Westcrosse and Thomas Holdworth, trumpeters.

Account for livery for William Garson, drum-player.

Account for livery for John Thomas, drum-player.

Account for liveries for three sackbutts :—Robert Maie, Edward Petelay and Robert Howlett.

Account for livery for Anthonio de Countie, luter.

Account for livery for Henry Hewes, trumpeter.

Account for livery for Alexander Pennax, drum-player.

Account for liveries for ten trumpets :—Stephen Medcalf, sergeant, John Pitches, Arthur Skarlett, John Warren, John Hall, Edward Eliott, Richard Frende, John Winks, Thomas Westcrosse, and John Restan.

Account for liveries for three flutes :—Pyro Guie, Thomas Paginton and Jacobo Fonyarde.

Account for livery for Thomas Browne, one of the vialls.

L. C. Vol. 17.

[1576], *May* 23.

Warrant for livery for Gawin Smith, drum-player, in place of William Garson, deceased.

L. C. Vol. 811, *p.* 183.

1576, *July* 12.

Warrant for liveries for William Tuson and Robert Hune, trumpettours.

L. C. Vol. 811, *p.* 192.

Accounts ending Michaelmas, 1576.

Account for livery for Radulpho Grene, one of the sackbutts.

Account for liveries for Richard Smyth, John Newman and Thomas Royston, trumpeters to the Queen.

Account for liveries for Francis Bourne and Benedict Browne, trumpeters.

Account for livery for Marco Anthonio Bassanie, one of the sackbuts.

Account for livery for Nicholas Laneer, one of the flutes.

Account for livery for William Garson, drum-player.

Account for liveries for Robert Westcrosse and Thomas Holdworth, trumpeters.

Account for livery for William Lindsey, trumpeter.

Account for liveries for eight trumpets:—Stephen Medcalf, sergeant, John Pitches, Arthur Skarlett, John Hall, Edward Eliott, Richard Frende, John Winks and John Restan.

Account for liveries for three flutes:—Piro Guye, Thomas Paginton and Jacobo Fonyarde.

Account for livery for Thomas Browne, one of the vialls.

Account for livery for Anthonio de Countie, lewter.

Account for livery for John Thomas, drum-player.

Account for liveries for three sackbuts:—Robert Maie, Edward Petaleie and Robert Howlett.

Account for livery for Alexander Pennax, drum-player.

Account for livery for Henry Hewes, trumpeter.

Account for livery for Gawyn Smythe, drum-player, by warrant dated 23 May, 1576.

L. C. Vol. 19.

[1576-7], *January* 28.

Warrant for livery for George Langdale, trumpettour.

L. C. Vol. 811, *p.* 194.

1577, *May* 12.

Warrant for livery for William Nash, trumpettour in the place of John Newman, deceased.

L. C. Vol. 811, *p.* 193; *also Vol.* 24.

Accounts ending Michaelmas, 1577.

Account for livery for William Garson, drum-player.

Account for liveries for Robert Westcrosse and Thomas Holdworthe, trumpeters.

Account for livery for William Lindsey, trumpeter.

Account for livery for Nicholas Laneer, one of the flutes.

Account for liveries for seven trumpeters:—Stephen Medcalf, sergeant, John Pitches, Arthur Skarlett, John Hall, Edward Eliott, John Winkes and John Restan.

Account for livery for Marco Anthonio Bassanie, one of the shagbutts.

Account for liveries for Francis Bourne and Benedict Browne, trumpeters.

Account for liveries for Richard Smythe, John Newman and Thomas Roiston, trumpeters to the Queen

Account for livery for Radulpho Grene, one of the shagbutts.

Account for livery for Gawin Smythe, drum-player.

Account for livery for John Thomas, drum-player.

Account for livery for Alexander Pennax, drum-player.

Account for liveries for three flutes:—Piro Guy, Thomas Paginton and Jacobo Fonyarde.

Account for liveries for two shagbutts:—Robert Maie and Edward Petaleie.

Account for livery for Henry Hewes, trumpeter.

Account for livery for Anthonio de Countie, lewter.

Account for livery for Thomas Browne, one of the vialls.

L. C. Vol. 21.

Accounts ending Michaelmas, 1578.

Accounts for liveries for :—

Thomas Browne - - -	vn de lez vialls
Pyro Guy - - - -	flute
Thomas Paginton - -	*"*
Jacobo Fonyarde - - -	*"*
Nicholas Laneer - - -	vn de lez flutes
Edward Petaley - - -	vn de lez shagbutts
Marco Anthonio Bassany -	*"*
Radulpho Grene - - -	*"*
Anthonio de Countie - -	lewter
Alexander Pennax - -	drum-player
John Thomas - - -	*"*
Gawin Smythe - - -	*"*

Trumpeters.

Stephen Medcalfe, sergeant	Richard Smythe
John Pitches	Thomas Roiston
Arthur Skarlett	Robert Westcrosse
John Hall	Thomas Holdworthe
Edward Eliott	William Lindsey
Thomas Winks	Francis Bourne
John Restan	Benedict Browne
Henry Hewes	

L. C. Vol. 22.

1579, *March* 29.

Warrant for liveries for John Smyth and William Elyott, trumpettors.

L. C. Vol. 811, *p.* 195.

[1579], *September* 20.

Warrant for sea liveries for William Lyndsey and Thomas Holdworthe, trumpettours appointed to searve on the seas under Admiral Sir John Parrot.

L. C. Vol. 794, *p.* 188.

Accounts ending Michaelmas, 1579.

Accounts for liveries for :—

Thomas Browne	- -	vn de lez vialls
Pyro Guy -	- -	flute
Thomas Paginton	- -	"
Jacobo Fonyarde -	- -	"
Nicholas Laneer -	- -	vn de lez flutes
Edward Petaley -	- -	vn de lez shagbutts
Marco Anthonio Bassany	-	"
Radulpho Grene -	- -	"
Anthony de Countie	- -	lewter
Alexander Pennax	- -	drum-player
John Thomas	- - -	"
Gawin Smythe	- - -	"

Trumpeters.

Stephen Medcalf, sergeant	Henry Hewes
John Pitches	Richard Smyth
Arthur Skarlett	Thomas Royston
John Hall	Thomas Holdworthe
Edward Eliott	William Lyndsey
John Winkes	Francis Bourne
John Restan	Benedict Browne

Account for thirteen banners for all the trumpeters :—

Stephen Medcalfe, sergeant	John Restan
John Pitches	Henry Hewes
Arthur Skarlett	Richard Smythe
John Hall	Thomas Royston
Edward Eliott	Thomas Holdworth
John Winks	William Lindsey

Humphrey Sparke (trumpeter of Barwick)

L. C. Vol. 23.

Accounts ending Michaelmas, 1580.

Accounts for liveries for :—

William Lindsey	}	trumpeters attending upon
Thomas Holdworth	}	Sir John Parratt, admiral.
Thomas Browne	- -	vn de lez vialls
Piro Guy	- - -	flute
Thomas Paginton	- -	"
Jacobo Fonyard	- -	"
Nicholas Laneer	- -	vn de lez flutes

Edward Petaley - - -	vn de lez shagbutts
Marco Anthonio Bassany -	"
Radulpho Grene - -	"
Anthonio Countie - -	lewter
Alexander Pennax - -·	drum-player
Gawin Smythe - - -	"

Trumpeters.

Stephen Medcalf, sergeant	Francis Bourne
John Pitches	Benedict Browne
Arthur Skarlett	William Tuson
John Hall	Robert Hunne (also
John Winkes	Hune)
John Restan	George Langdall (also
Henry Hewes	Langdale)
Richard Smythe	William Nashe
Thomas Royston	John Smyth
Thomas Holdworth	William Eliott
William Lindsey	

L. C. Vol. 24.

Accounts ending Michaelmas, 1581.

Accounts for liveries for :—

Thomas Browne - - -	vn de lez vialls
Piro Guye - - - -	flute
Thomas Paginton - -	,,
Jacobo Fonyard - - -	,,
Nicholas Laneer - - -	vn de lez flutes
Edward Petaley - - -	vn de lez shagbutts
Marco Anthonio Bassany -	"
Radulpho Grene - - -	"
Alexander Pennax - -	drum-player
Gawin Smythe - - -	"

Trumpeters.

Stephen Medcalf, sergeant	Thomas Holdworthe
John Pitches	William Lindsey
Arthur Skarlet	Francis Bourne
John Hall	Benedict Browne
John Winks	Robert Hunne
John Restan	George Langdale
Henry Hewes	William Nashe
Richard Smythe	John Smythe
Thomas Royston	William Eliott

L. C. Vol. 25.

[1582], *April* 6.

Warrant for livery for Thomas Kinge, drum-player, in the place of Thomas Shingwell, deceased.

L. C. Vol. 811, *p.* 203.

[1582], *August* 4.

Warrant for livery for Robert Benson, trumpeter.

L. C. Vol. 811, *p.* 205.

1582, *August* 20.

Warrant for livery for John Brewer, trumpeter.

L. C. Vol. 811, *p.* 201.

Accounts ending Michaelmas, 1582.

Accounts for liveries for :—

Thomas Browne	Vialls
Piro Guy	flute
Thomas Paginton	*"*
Jacobo Fonyard	*"*
Nicholas Laneer	vn de lez flutes
Edward Petaley	vn de lez shagbutts
Marco Anthonio Bassany	*"*
Radulpho Grene	*"*
Alexander Pennax	drum-player
Gawin Smythe	*"*

Trumpeters.

Stephen Medcalf, sergeant	William Lindsey
Arthur Skarlet	Francis Bourne
John Hall	Benedict Browne
John Winks	George Langdale
John Restan	William Nashe
Henry Hewes	John Smyth
Richard Smyth	William Eliott
Thomas Royston	John Brewer
Thomas Holdworth	

L. C. Vol. 26.

Account ending Michaelmas, 1582.

Warrant for the delivery of crimson velvet for covering, lining and ornamenting divers of the Queen's "regalls and virginalls," and for the payment for covering with velvet four pair of regalls and virginalls and for ornamenting the same with gold and silver lacquer; for covering and ornamenting divers virginals with green velvet, and levant leather, and for iron work for the same; for a wooden box lined with velvet for a pair of virginals, etc., etc.

L. C. Vol. 26.

[1582-3], *March* 21.

Warrant for liveries for John Parkin and Patrick Owen, trumpeters.

L. C. Vol. 811, *p.* 204.

Accounts ending Michaelmas, 1583.

Accounts for liveries for :—

Piro Guy - - - -	flute
Thomas Paginton - - -	"
Jacobo Fonyard - - -	"
Nicholas Laneer - - -	vn de lez flutes
Edward Petaley - - -	vn de lez shagbutts
Marco Anthonio Bassany -	"
Radulpho Grene - - -	"
Alexander Pennax - - -	drum-player
Gawin Smythe - - -	"

Trumpeters.

Stephen Medcalf, sergeant	Benedict Browne
Arthur Skarlett	George Langdale
John Hall	John Smyth
John Winks	William Eliott
John Restan	John Brewer
Richard Smythe	Robert Benson
Thomas Royston	John Parkin
Thomas Holdworth	Patrick Owen
Francis Bourne	

Account for eleven banners for all the trumpeters :—

Stephen Medcalf, sergeant	Henry Hewes
Arthur Skarlett	Richard Smythe
John Hall	Thomas Royston
John Wynks	Thomas Holdworthe
John Restan	William Lyndsey

Humphrey Sparke, trumpeter of Barwick.

Account for livery for Thomas Kinge, one of the drum-players, in place of Thomas Shugwell, deceased.

L. C. Vol. 27.

Accounts ending Michaelmas, 1584.

Accounts for liveries for :—

Pyro Guy - - - -	flute
Thomas Paginton - - -	"
Jacobo Fonyarde - - -	" .
Nicholas Laneer - - -	vn de lez flutes

Edward Petalley	-	-	-	vn de lez shagbutts
Marco Anthonio Bassany	-			"
Radulpho Grene	-	-	-	"
Alexander Pennax	-	-	-	drum-player
Gawin Smyth	-	-	-	"
Thomas Kinge	-	-	-	"

Trumpeters.

Stephen Medcalf, sergeant	Benedict Browne
Arthur Skarlet	George Langdale
John Hall	John Smyth
John Winks	William Eliott
John Restan	John Brewer
Richard Smyth	Robert Benson
Thomas Roiston	John Parkin
Thomas Holdworth	Patrick Owen
Francis Bourne	

L. C. Vol. 28.

Accounts ending Michaelmas, 1585.

Accounts for liveries for :—

Piro Guy	--	-	-	-	flute
Thomas Paginton	-	-	-	"
Jacobo Fonyard	-	-	-	"
Nicholas Laneer	-	-	-	vn de lez flutes
Edward Petaley	-	-	-	vn de lez shagbutts
Marco Anthonio Bassany	-			"
Radulpho Grene	-	-	-	"
Alexander Pennax	-	-	-	drum-player
Gawin Smythe	-	-	-	"
Thomas Kinge	-	-	-	"

Trumpeters.

Stephen Medcalf, sergeant	Benedict Browne
Arthur Skarlett	George Langdale
John Hall	John Smyth
John Winks	William Eliott
John Restan	John Brewer
Richard Smythe	John Parkin
Thomas Royston	Patrick Owen
Thomas Holdworthe	Robert Benson
Francis Bourne	

L. C. Vol. 29.

[1585], *November* 2.

Warrant for liveries for Henry Martin, John Jucks, Robert Benson, and Thomas Fyssher, trumpettours.

L. C. Vol. 811, *p.* 209.

1586, *May* 18.

Warrant for livery for Thomas Jackson, trumpettor.

L. C. Vol. 811, *p.* 220.

Accounts ending Michaelmas, 1586.

Accounts for liveries for :—

Piro Guy — — — —	flute
Thomas Paginton — — —	//
Jacobo Fonyard — — —	//
Nicholas Laneer — —	vn de lez flutes
Edward Petaley — —	vn de lez shagbutts
Marco Anthonio Bassany —	//
Radulpho Grene — — —	//
Gawin Smythe — — —	drum-plaier
Thomas Kinge — — —	//

Trumpeters.

Stephen Medcalf, sergeant	George Langdale
Arthur Skarlet	John Smyth
John Hall	William Eliott
John Winks	John Brewer
John Restan	Patrick Owen
Richard Smythe	Robert Benson
Thomas Royston	Henry Martin
Francis Bourne	John Jucks
Benedict Browne	Thomas Fissher

L. C. Vol. 30.

Accounts ending Michaelmas, 1587.

Accounts for liveries for :—

Piro Guye — — — —	flute
Jacobo Foniarde — — —	//
Nicholas Laneer — —	vn de lez flutes
Edward Petaley — —	vn de lez shagbutts
Marco Anthonio Bassany —	//
Radulpho Grene — — —	//
Gawin Smythe — — —	drum-player
Thomas Kinge — — —	//

Trumpeters.

Stephen Medcalf, sergeant	George Langdale
Arthur Skarlett	John Smyth
John Hall	William Eliott
John Winks	John Brewer
John Restan	Robert Benson
Richard Smyth	Henry Marten
Thomas Royston	John Jucks
Francis Bourne	Thomas Fyssher
Benedict Browne	

Account for banners for eight trumpeters :—

Stephen Medcalf, sergeant	John Restan
Arthur Skarlet	Richard Smyth
John Hall	Thomas Restan
John Wynks	

Humphrey Sparke, trumpeter of Barwick

L. C. Vol. 31.

1588, *August* 18.

Warrant for livery for Nicholas Watts, trumpettoure.

L. C. Vol. 811, *p.* 221.

Accounts ending Michaelmas, 1588.

Accounts for liveries for :—

Piro Guy - - - -	flute
Jacobo Fonyarde - - -	"
Nicholas Laneer - - -	vn de lez flutes
Edward Petaley - -	vn de lez shagbuts
Marco Anthonio Bassany -	"
Radulpho Grene - - -	"
Gawin Smyth - - -	drum-plaier
Thomas Kinge - - -	"

Trumpeters.

Stephen Medcalf, sergeant	George Langdale
Arthur Skarlett	John Smyth
John Hall	William Eliott
John Wynks	John Brewer
John Restan	Robert Benson
Richard Smyth	Henry Marten
Thomas Royston	John Jucks
Francis Bourne	Thomas Fyssher
Benedict Browne	

L. C. Vol. 32.

Accounts ending Michaelmas, 1589.

Accounts for liveries for :—

Piro Guy - - - -	flute
Jacobo Fonyard - - -	"
Nicholas Laneer - - -	vn de lez flutes
Marco Anthonio Bassany -	vn de lez shagbutts
Radulpho Grene - - -	"
Gawin Smith - - - -	drum-player
Thomas Kinge - - -	"

Trumpeters.

Stephen Medcalf, sergeant	George Langdale
Arthur Skarlett	John Smyth
John Hall	William Eliott
John Winks	John Brewer
John Restan	Robert Benson
Richard Smyth	Henry Martin
Thomas Royston	John Jucks
Francis Bourne	Thomas Fissher
Benedict Browne	Thomas Jackson

L. C. Vol. 33.

Accounts ending Michaelmas, 1590.

Accounts for liveries for :—

Piro Guy - - - -	flute
Jacobo Fonyarde - - -	"
Nicholas Laneer - - -	vn de lez flutes
Marco Anthonio Bassany -	vn de lez shagbutts
Radulpho Grene - - -	"
Gawin Smyth - - -	drum-plaier
Thomas Kinge - - -	"

Trumpeters.

Stephen Medcalf, sergeant	George Langdale
Arthur Skarlet	John Smyth
John Hall	William Eliott
John Winks	Robert Benson
John Restan	Henry Marten
Richard Smyth	John Jucks
Thomas Royston	Thomas Fyssher
Francis Bourne	Thomas Jackson
Benedict Browne	Nicholas Watts

L. C. Vol. 34.

Accounts ending Michaelmas, 1591.

Accounts for liveries for :—

Piro Guy - - - -	flute
Jacobo Fonyard - - -	"
Nicholas Lanier - - -	vn de lez flutes
Marco Anthonio Bassany -	shagbutt
Radulpho Grene - - -	"
Gawin Smythe - - -	drum-plaier
Thomas Kinge - - -	"

Trumpeters.

Arthur Skarlett	John Winks
John Hall	John Restan
Richard Smyth	Robert Benson
Thomas Restan (also Royston)	Henry Marten
Francis Bourne	John Jucks
Benedict Browne	Thomas Fyssher
George Langdale	Thomas Jackson
John Smythe	Nicholas Watts
William Eliott	

Account for seven banners for all the trumpeters :—

Stephen Medcalf, sergeant	John Restan
Arthur Skarlett	Richard Smyth
John Hall	Thomas Restan
John Winks	

L. C. Vol. 35.

Accounts ending Michaelmas, 1592.

Accounts for liveries for :—

Piro Guy - - - -	flute
Jacobo Fonyard - - -	"
Nicholas Laneer - - -	vn de lez flutes
Marco Anthonio Bassanie -	vn de lez shagbutts
Radulpho Grene - - -	"
Gawin Smithe - - -	drum-plaier
Thomas Kinge - - -	"

Trumpeters.

John Hall, sergeant	John Smith
Arthur Skarlett	William Eliot
John Winks	Robert Benson
John Reston	Henry Marten
Richard Smithe	John Jucks
Thomas Roiston	Thomas Fissher
Francis Bourne	Thomas Jackson
Benedict Browne	Nicholas Watts
George Langdale	*L. C. Vol.* 36.

1593, *September* 5.

Warrant for liveries for Thomas Kellway and Francis Hall, trumpetours, in room of other trumpetours, deceased.

L. C. *Vol.* 811, *p.* 227.

Accounts ending Michaelmas, 1593.

Accounts for liveries for :—

Piro Guy - - - -	vn de lez flutes
Nicholas Lanier - - -	"
Marco Anthonio Bassany -	vn de lez sackbutts
Radulpho Grene - - -	"
Gawin Smithe - - -	drum-plaier
Thomas Kinge - - -	"

Trumpeters.

John Hall, sergeant	William Eliott
Arthur Skarlett	Henry Marten
John Winks	John Jucks
John Reston	Thomas Fissher
Richard Smith	Thomas Jackson
Thomas Roiston	Nicholas Watts
Francis Bourne	Robert Benson
Benedict Browne	Thomas Kellway
George Langdale	Francis Hall
John Smithe	

L. C. *Vol.* 37.

Account ending Michaelmas, 1593.

Warrant for the delivery of certain black velvet, black satin, blue (glaucus) velvet, scarlet cloth and gold and silver lacquer, for covering, ornamenting and repairing the Queen s virginals.

L. C. *Vol.* 37.

1593.

A list of all in the offices in England, with their fees.

Musicions and Players.	£	s.	d.
Sergeant trompetor - - - -	24	6	8
Trompetors 16, fee amongst them - -	389	6	3
Sagbuttes 6, fee to 5 of them - - -	24	6	8
" to one - - - -	20	0	0
Vyalls 8, fee to 6 of them a peece - -	30	8	4
" one - - - - -	20	0	0
" and the other - - -	10	5	0
Drumslads 3, fee to every of them - -	18	5	0
Players on the flute 2, fee to eyther of them	18	5	0

	£	s.	d.
Players on the virginalles 3, fee to every of them - - - - - -	50	0	0
Musicions straungers 4, to the 4 brethren Venetians, amongst them - - -	183	6	8
Players of enterludes 8, fee to every of them per annum - - - -	66	0	0
Makers of instruments 2, fee to one per annum - - - - - -	20	0	0
Fee to the other - - - - -	10	0	0

L. C. Vol. 617, *folio* 19*d.*

	£	s.	d.
The Chappell.			
Mr of the children - - - fee	40	0	0
To the children at highe feastes, largess	9	13	4
Gentlemen of the Chappell 32, fee to every of them per diem - - -	0	0	7$\frac{1}{2}$

L. C. Vol. 617, *folio* 24*d.*

Accounts ending Michaelmas, 1594.

Accounts for liveries for :—

Piro Guy - - - -	vn de lez flutes
Nicholas Laneer - - -	" "
Marco Anthonio Bassany -	vn de lez shackbutts
Radulpho Grene - - -	"
Gawin Smith - - -	dromplaier
Thomas Kinge - - -	"

Trumpeters.

Arthur Skarlett, sergeant	Henry Martin
John Winks	John Jucks
John Reston	Thomas Fisher
Thomas Royston	Thomas Jacksonne
Francis Bourne	Nicholas Watts
Benedict Browne	Robert Benson
George Langdale	Thomas Kellway
John Smith	Francis Hall
William Eliot	

L. C. Vol. 38.

Accounts ending Michaelmas, 1595.

Accounts for liveries for :—

Piro Guy - - -	vn de lez flutes
Nicholas Lanyer - - -	"
Marco Anthonio Bassany -	vn de lez shagbuts
Radulpho Grene - - -	"
Gawin Smyth - - -	drum-player
Thomas Kinge - - -	"

Trumpeters.

Arthur Skarlett	Henry Martin
John Winks	John Jucks
John Restan	Thomas Fysher
Thomas Royston	Thomas Jackson
Francis Bourne	Nicholas Watts
Benedict Browne	Robert Benson
George Langdale	Thomas Kelleway
John Smyth	Francis Hall
William Eliott	

Account for banners for four trumpeters :—

Arthur Skarlet	John Restan
John Winks	Thomas Restan

L. C. Vol. 39.

1595-6.

Warrant to pay for " 14 yards of carnation velvet and eight yards of wrought velvet black and ash colour, employed and spent in covering of our virginals, and for twelve yards of grene velvet to cover a greate instrument, all being garnished with lace of gold and silver and silke riben and sowing silke to them."

L. C. Vol. 797, *p.* 183.

Accounts ending Michaelmas, 1596.

Accounts for liveries for :—

Pyro Guy	-	-	-	- vn de lez flutes
Nicholas Lanyer	-	-	-	"
Marco Anthonio Bassany			-	vn de lez shagbuts
Radulpho Grene	-	-	-	"
Gawin Smith		-	-	- drum-player
Thomas Kinge	-	-	-	"

Trumpeters.

Arthur Skarlet	Henry Martin
John Winks	John Jucks
John Reston	Thomas Fisher
Thomas Royston	Thomas Jackson
Francis Bourne	Nicholas Watts
Benedict Browne	Robert Benson
George Langdale	Francis Hall
John Smythe	Thomas Kellaway
William Eliott	

L. C. Vol. 40.

1597, *May* 2.

Warrant for liveries for John Relie, Anthony Denham, Griffin Martin, and Robert Wrothe, trumpeters.

L. C. Vol. 811. *p.* 232.

Accounts ending Michaelmas, 1598.

Account for livery for Nicholas Warde, trumpeter, in place of John Winks, deceased, by warrant dated 15 March, 1597-8.

Accounts for liveries for :—

Piro Guy - - - - -	one of the flutes
Nicholas Laner - - -	"
Marco Anthonio Bassany -	- one of the shackbuts
Radulpho Grene - - -	"
Gawin Smith - - - -	timpanist
Thomas Kinge - - - -	"

Trumpeters.

Arthur Skarlet	John Jucks
John Reston	Thomas Fisher
Thomas Royston	Nicholas Watts
Francis Borne	Robert Benson
Benedict Browne	Francis Hall
George Langdale	John Reyle (also Reley)
John Smith	Anthony Denham
William Eliott	Griffin Martin
Henry Martin	Robert Wroth

L. C. Vol. 41.

Accounts ending Michaelmas, 1599.

Accounts for liveries for :—

Petro Guy - - -	- one of the flutes
Nicholas Lanyer- - -	"
Marco Anthonio Bassany -	vn de lez shagbutts
Radulpho Grene - - -	"
Gawin Smith - - -	drum-player
Thomas Kinge - - -	"

Trumpeters.

Arthur Skarlet	Thomas Fisher
John Reston	Nicholas Watts
Thomas Royston	Robert Benson
Francis Borne	Francis Hall
Benedict Browne	John Relie (also Reley) .
George Langdale	Anthony Denham

John Smith	Griffin Martin
William Eliott	Robert Wroth
Henry Martin	Nicholas Ward
John Jucks	

Account for three banners for all the trumpeters :—

Arthur Skarlet	John Restan
Thomas Restan	

L. C. Vol. 15.

1599, *October* 18.

Warrant for livery for Mark Bateman, trumpeter, in place of John Royston, deceased.

L. C. Vol. 811, *p.* 237.

Accounts ending Michaelmas, 1600, *and Michaelmas,* 1601.

Accounts for liveries for :—

Petro Guy - - - -	one of the flutes
Nicholas Lanyer- - -	"
Gawin Smyth - - -	drum-player

Trumpeters.

Arthur Skarlet	John Jucks
Thomas Royston	Thomas Fysher
Francis Bourne	Robert Benson
Benedict Browne	Francis Hall
George Langdale	John Relie
John Smyth	Anthony Denham
William Eliott	Griffin Martin
Nicholas Watts	Robert Wroth
Henry Martin	Nicholas Ward

Account for livery for Mark Bateman, trumpeter, in place of John Royston, deceased, by warrant dated 18 October, 1599.

L. C. Vol. 18 *and Vol.* 20.

[1602], *July* 13.

Letters patent granting the office of trumpeter to Thomas Reston, trumpeter extraordinary, upon the surrender of Thomas Reston, his uncle.

L. C. Vol. 792, *p.* 123.

Accounts ending Michaelmas, 1602.

Accounts for liveries for :—

Petro Guye - - - -	one of the flutes
Nicholas Lanyer - - -	"
Gawin Smyth - - -	drum-player

Trumpeters.

Arthur Scarlet	Nicholas Watts
Francis Bourne	Robert Benson
Benedict Browne	Francis Hall
George Langdale	John Relye
John Smyth	Anthony Denham
William Eliott	Griffin Martin
Henry Martin	Robert Wroth
John Jucks	Nicholas Ward
Thomas Fisher	Mark Bateman

L. C. Vol. 42.

1603, *June* 22.

Warrant for liveries and banners for seventeen trumpeters:—

Benedict Browne, sergeant, William Ramsey, Francis Borne, Robert Dromane, John Smyth, Nicholas Wadoll, John Jewkes, Archibald Sym, Robert Benson, John Ramsey, John Reyley, Anthony Denham, Griffen Marten, Robert Wroth, Henry Marten, Nicholas Ward, and Thomas Underhill.

L. C. Vol. 811, *p.* 242.

Accounts ending Michaelmas, 1603.

Accounts for liveries for :—

Petro Guy	-	-	-	- one of the flutes
Nicholas Lanyer	-	-	-	"
Gawin Smyth	-	-	-	drum-player
Arthur Skarlet	-	-	-	trumpeter
Nicholas Warde	-	-	-	"

Thomas Restan, nephew of Thomas Restan, trumpeter.

Seventeen Trumpeters by warrant dated 22 June, 1603 :—

Benedict Browne, sergeant	John Ramsey
William Ramsey	John Reelie
Francis Bourne	Anthony Denham
Robert Dromond	Griffin Martin
John Smyth	Robert Wroth
Nicholas Woddall	Henry Marten
John Jewks	Nicholas Ward
Archibald Sym	Thomas Underhill
Robert Benson	

L. C. Vol. 43.

1603.

Allowance of mourning liverie to the following Gentlemen of the Chappell :—

Doctor Bull	John Stephens
Nathaniel Giles	John Howlett
William Birde	Thomas Gold
Richard Canwell	Richard Plumley
Drue Sharpe	Peter Wright
William Randoll	William Lawrence
Edmond Browne	James Davis
Thomas Woodison	John Amery
Robert Stone	John Baldwell
George Buck	Francis Wilbroughe
Henry Oveseed	Arthur Cocke
Robert Allison	George Woodison

Children of the Chappell 12.   (Names not given.)

Gentlemen of the Chappell extraordinary.

Edward Peers	George Greene
Edmund Hoop	Peter Hopkins

L. C. Vol. 554.   *Funeral of Queen Elizabeth.*

1603.

Allowance of mourning to the following singing men at Westminster :—

Mathew Holmes	Thomas Godinge
Richard Baker	Robert Forrest
John Searell	John Gregorie
John Thorogood	Henry Northedge
William Murrey	Richard Bently
William White	James Hoop
William Heather	John Estey
John Stone	

L. C. Vol. 554.   *Funeral of Queen Elizabeth.*

The Quiristers of Westminster.

John Hoop	Marmaduke Feild
Walter Porter	John Clarke
Richard Warren	Richard Hutchins
Samuel Brown	William Chambers
Thomas Pee	Thomas Case

L. C. Vol. 554.   *Funeral of Queen Elizabeth.*

1603.

Allowance of certain mourning livery to the following musicians for the funeral of Queen Elizabeth.

Violins.

Joseph Luppo
Peter Luppo
Cesar Galliardillo
Thomas Luppo, sen.

William Warren
Thomas Luppo, jun.
Anthony Coomes

Recorders.

Augustine Bassano
Arthur Bassano
Andrea Bassano
Edward Bassano

Jeromino Bassano
Alphonso Lanier
Robert Baker

Flutes.

Peiro Guy
Nicholas Lanier
James Hardinge
Anthony Bassano

Peter Edney
Innocent Lanier
Petro Guy, jun.

Hoboies and Sagbuttes.

Henry Troches
Samuel Garshe
John Snowsman

Thomas Mason
Jerom Lanier
John Lanier

Lutes and others.

Walter Peirce
Robert Hales
Alphonso Forobosco

Thomas Cordall
Henry Porter
Robert Henlocke

Trumpetors.

Benedict Browne, sergeant
Arthur Skarlett
Francis Borne
George Langdale
William Elliatt
John Smyth
Robert Benson
Henry Marten
John Jucks
Thomas Fisher
Nicholas Watts

Francis Hale
John Kelley
Anthony Denham
Griffen Marten
Robert Wrothe
Nicholas Warde
Mark Bateman
Thomas Royston
John Dale
William Hunte
Raphe Smythe

Drums and Fiffes.

Gawine Smyth	George Polliard
John Singwell	William Gossone

L. C. Vol. 554. *Funeral of Queen Elizabeth.*

1603.

Allowance for mourning livery for Mr. Mathias, lute of the privie chamber.

L. C. Vol. 554. *Funeral of Queen Elizabeth.*

Bellringers.

Richard William	John Chapple
Hugh Edwards	Lewis

L. C. Vol. 554. *Funeral of Queen Elizabeth.*

1603-4, *January* 9.

Warrant for the allowance of a yearly livery to Richard Thorne, drumplaier, appointed in the place of Gawen Smith.

L. C. Vol. 812, *p.* 10.

1603-4, *January* 12.

Warrant for the allowance of a yearly livery to Pyro Guye, one of the musytian flutes.

L. C. Vol. 812, *p.* 8.

1603-4, *January* 12.

Warrant for the yearly allowance of a livery to Nicholas Lanyer, one of the musytian flutes.

L. C. Vol. 812, *p.* 9.

1604, *August* 30.

Warrant for the allowance of a livery to John Smith, the younger, appointed trumpeter to Prince Henry.

L. C. Vol. 812, *p.* 25.

1604-5, *February* 8.

Warrant for the allowance of a livery to Robert Ramsey, appointed trumpeter in the place of William Ramsey, his father.

L. C. Vol. 812, *p.* 34.

1605, *October* 7.

Warrant for holland for shirts, etc., "for James Cutler, a Chappell boy gone off"; also for the twelve Children of the Chappell.

L. C. Vol. 804, *p.* 222*d.*

1606, *August* 12.

Warrant for the allowance of two liveries due to William Peirson, dromeplayer to Prince Henry, for "two years last past."

L. C. Vol. 812, *p.* 45.

1606, *August* 12.

Warrant for the allowance of a yearly livery to Adam Smitheman (also Smetheman), appointed as trumpeter to Prince Henry.

L. C. Vol. 812, *p.* 46.

1606, *September* 9.

Warrant for two curtains for the organ loft in the Chapel.

L. C. Vol. 805, *p.* 167.

Accounts ending Michaelmas, 1606.

Accounts for liveries for :—

Piro Guy - - - -	one of the flutes
Nicholas Lanyer - - -	"
Richard Thorne - - -	timpanist

Sixteen trumpeters.

Benedict Browne, sergeant	John Ramsey
Francis Bourne	John Relie
Robert Dromond	Anthony Denham
John Smithe, senior	Griffen Marten
Nicholas Woodall	Robert Wrothe
John Jewks	Henry Marten
Archibald Sym	Nicholas Ward
Robert Benson	Thomas Underhill

Robert Ramsey, trumpeter in place of William Ramsey

John Smithe, junior, trumpeter to the lord the prince, by warrant dated 30 August, 1604.

William Peirson, timpanist, by warrant dated 12 August, 1606.

Adam Smetheman, trumpeter to the lord the prince, by warrant dated 12 August, 1606.

L. C. Vol. 44.

1607, *May* 18.

Warrant for the allowance of a yearly livery to Randolph Floud, appointed trumpeter in the place of Archibald Syme, deceased.

L. C. Vol. 812, *p.* 50.

1607, *August* 3.

Warrant for the allowance of a yearly livery to Josias Broome, appointed trumpeter to Prince Henry.

L. C. Vol. 812, *p.* 53.

Accounts ending Michaelmas, 1607.

Accounts for livery for :—

Nicholas Lanyer	-	-	- one of the flutes
Richard Thorne	-	-	- timpanist

Trumpeters.

Benedict Browne, sergeant	John Relie
Francis Bourne	Anthony Denham
Robert Dromond	Griffin Martin
John Smyth, senior	Robert Wrothe
Nicholas Wodall	Henry Marten
John Jewks	Nicholas Warde
Robert Benson	Thomas Underhill
John Ramsey	Robert Ramsey

John Smyth, junior, trumpeter to the lord the prince.

William Peerson, timpanist to the lord the prince.

Adam Smytheman, trumpeter to the lord the prince.

Reginald (Ranulpho) Floud, trumpeter, in place of Archibald Symme, deceased, by warrant dated 18 May, 1607.

Josias Brome, trumpeter to the lord the prince, by warrant dated 3 August, 1607.

L. C. Vol. 45.

1609, *April* 17.

Warrant for the allowance of a yearly livery to Humphrie Floud, appointed trumpeter in the place of Robert Dromond, and also to Richard Pitocke, appointed trumpeter in the place of Francis Bourne, deceased.

L. C. Vol. 812, *p.* 72.

1609, *December* 10.

Warrant for the allowance of a yearly livery to Samuel Smithe, appointed trumpeter in the place of Nicholas Woodall, deceased.

L. C. Vol. 812, *p.* 79.

1609 (?).

The following names occur in a list of allowances for liveries to servants of the Prince, in the account of the Great Wardrobe, for one whole year ended Michaelmas, 1609 :—

Trumpeter John Smith- ⎫
 ″ Adam Smetheman ⎬ £19 14s. 4d. each per annum.
 ″ Josias Broome -⎭

L. C. Vol. 812, *p.* 303.

[1610-11.]

The names of the Prince's servants of the Chamber with their wages and board wages.

Teacher of musique, Walter Quinn £50 (wages only).

Allowance of wages and liveries to be now yearly paid to divers of his highness's servants, formerly paid in the King's Majesty's Treasury Chamber and Great Wardrobe :—

Drumplaier William Peerson - ⎫ £20 each in wages and
Fyfe -   - Abraham Hardy - ⎭   £16 2s. 6d. for liveries.

Trumpeter John Smithe -   - ⎫
    "   Adam Smitheman - ⎬ £20 each in wages and
    "   Josias Broome   - ⎭   £19 14s. 4d. for liveries.

    "   Nicholas Stransham ⎫ £13 6s. 8d. each in wages
    "   William Arnett   - ⎬ and £13 2s. 10d. for liveries.
    "   Roger Burfeild   - ⎭

1612.

Mourning allowed for Mr. Giles, Master of the children of the Chappell, and for 12 children.

1612.

Allowance of mourning for the following trumpeters of the late Prince Henry of Wales :—

Adam Smetheman	Josias Broome
William Arnold	Roger Barfeild
Nicholas Tramsom	John Smith

Trumpeters of the King.

Henry Marten	Griffin Marten
John Smith	Robert Wroth
John Jewks	Thomas Underhill
John Reelie	Robert Ramsey
Anthonie Denham	Randolph Floud

Dromplayers.

William Peirson	Robert Drought

Phyfe.
Abraham Hardie

Doctor of Musicke to the Kinge.
Mr. Bull

Teacher of Musicke to the Prince.
Mr. Quin

Musicians.

John Ashbie	Thomas Day
Mr. Ford	Valentine Sawyer
Mr. Myners	Mr. Jonas
Mr. Cutting	Mathew Johnson
Signeor Angello	Edward Wormeall
Mr. Stirte	

Norman Lister, Musician to Prince Charles

L. C. Vol. 555. Funeral of Prince Henry of Wales.

Gentlemen of the King's Chappell.

Mr. Hooper	Mr. Henlie
Mr. Harke	Mr. Bathe
Mr. Cooke	Mr. Gibbons
Mr. Wybroughe	Mr. West
Mr. Jones	Mr. Wright
Mr. Stephens	Mr. Baldwyn
Mr. Frost	Mr. James Davies
Mr. Woodson	Mr. John Woodson
Mr. Wade	Mr. Sheffield
Mr. Emerie	Mr. Eveseede

L. C. Vol. 555.

1612.

The Queene's Majestie and her Officers.

Liveries of mourning for Prince Henry of Wales, allowed to the following musicians :—

Five Dutch musitians	Buckan
Four French musitians	Oliuer
Mr. Daniell	Isaake
Mr. Littleboy	

L. C. Vol. 555. Funeral of Prince Henry of Wales.

1613, *November* 18.

Warrant for the allowance of a yearly livery to Robert Westcott, appointed trumpeter.

L. C. Vol. 812, p. 103.

Accounts ending Michaelmas, 1614.

Accounts for liveries for :—

Nicholas Lanyer	-	-	-	one of the flutes
Richard Thorne	-	-	-	timpanist

Trumpeters.

John Smith, senior	Robert Wrothe
John Jewks	Henry Marten
Robert Benson	Nicholas Ward
John Ramsey	Thomas Underhill
John Reelie	Robert Ramsey
Anthony Denham	Ranulpho Floud
Griffen Marten	

Humphrey Floud and Richard Pittocke, trumpeters, by warrant dated 17 April, 1609.

Samuel Smith, trumpeter, by warrant dated 10 December, 1609.

Robert Westcott, trumpeter, by warrant dated 18 November, 1613.

L. C. Vol. 46.

Accounts ending Michaelmas, 1615.

Accounts for liveries for :—

Nicholas Lanyer -	-	-	one of the flutes
Richard Thorne -	-	-	timpanist

Trumpeters.

John Smithe, senior	Nicholas Ward
John Jewks	Thomas Underhill
Robert Benson	Robert Ramsey
John Ramsey	Ranulpho Floud
John Reelie	Humphrey Floud
Anthony Denham	Richard Pittocke
Griffen Marten	Samuel Smith
Robert Wrothe	Robert Westcott
Henry Marten	

L. C. Vol. 47.

1616, *December* 6.

Warrant for the allowance of a yearly livery to William Allen, appointed trumpeter in the place of Nicholas Ward, deceased.

L. C. Vol. 812, *p.* 129.

1617, *October* 17.

Warrant for the allowance of a yearly livery to John Holeman, appointed trumpeter in the place of Robert Westcott, deceased.

L. C. Vol. 812, *p.* 133.

1618, *September* 20.

Warrant for the allowance of a yearly livery to Andrew Lanier, appointed musician for the flute, in the place of his father Nicholas Lanier, deceased.

L. C. Vol. 812, *p.* 141.

1618.

Accounts for the funeral of Queen Anne. List of servants of the late Queen.

Trumpettors.

Henry Martin, sergeant
John Smith
Robert Benson
John Jewkes
John Rily
Anthony Denham
Griffith Martin
Robert Wroth
John Ramsey
William Allen
John Hollman
John Smith, junior
Humphrey Floyd
Adam Smithman

Nicholas Transam
William Arnold
Roger Barfeild
Josias Broome
Christopher Harman
John Pendre
Samuel Booth
Robert Beath ·
William Baylie
William Broome
Mark Bateman
George Longdon
Richard Stock
Martin Seacoe

Musicians.

Lewies Richard
Camille Provoste
John Chauntred
Claud Oliver
Peter de la Mare
Christopher Harwood,
    tuner of instruments

Jehan Savage
William Le Graund
Malcum Grate
Daniel Hayes
William Treshey
Gilbert Johnson

The Kings Chappell.
Nathaniel Giles, Master of the Children.

Gentlemen of the Chappell.

Crewe Sharpe
John Stevens
John Amery
George Woodson
Edmond Hooper, organist
Orlando Gibbons, organist

Humphrey Bath
John Froste
George Sheffield
William Crosse
William Heater
Thomas Day

John Woodson	Martin Otto
James Davies	Peter Hopkins
William Weste	Walter Porter
George Cooke	William Bird
John Clarke	Anthony Kerkbye
Robert Bickner, bellringer	

Twelve children of the Chappell.

L. C. Vol. 556.

1619, *June* 23.

Warrant for allowance of a yearly livery to Daniell Farrant, appointed a viall, in the place of Thomas Browne, deceased.

L. C. Vol. 812, *p.* 143 ; *and Vols.* 148 *and* 149.

1619, *September* 27.

Warrant for a yearly livery to Silvester Ramsey, appointed trumpeter in the place of Robert Wroth, deceased.

L. C. Vol. 812, *p.* 145.

1619, *December* 28.

Warrant for a yearly livery to Richard Stocke, appointed trumpeter in the place of Robert Benson, deceased.

L. C. Vol. 812, *p.* 149.

1620, *December* 24.

Warrant for a yearly livery to Peter Jones, appointed trumpeter in the place of John Jewkes, deceased,

L. C. Vol. 812, *p.* 151.

1620-1, *February* 16.

Warrant to the Treasurer of the Chamber to pay "fortie marks by the year" to Thomas Lupo, appointed "composer for our violins, that they may be the better furnished with variety and choice for our delight and pleasure in that kind."

L. C. Papers, Bundle 75.

1620-1, *March* 19.

Warrant for a yearly livery to Robert Beech, appointed trumpeter in the place of Samuel Smith, deceased.

L. C. Vol. 812, *p.* 153.

1621.

Accounts for liveries and banners for the trumpeters :—

John Smith	Humphrey Floyd
John Ramsey	Richard Pittocke
John Reely	John Hoeman
Anthony Denham	William Allen
Griffin Martin	Silvester Ramsey

Henry Martin	Richard Stock
Thomas Underhill	Peter Jones
Robert Ramsey	Robert Beech
Ranulph Floud	

L. C. Vol. 165.

1621.

Payment for liveries to the following :—

Andrea Lanier, musician ⎫
Daniell Farrant   *"*   ⎬ £16 2s. 6d.
Richard Thorne, drummer ⎭

L. C. Vol. 812, *p.* 272.

1622, *April* 1.

Warrant to pay to Thomas Lupo, composer for the violins, £16 2s. 6d. yearly for his livery.

L. C. Papers, Bundle 75.

1622, *September* 28.

Warrant for a yearly livery to Edward Juckes, appointed one of His Majesty's trumpeters in the place of Richard Pittocke, deceased.

L. C. Vol. 812, *p.* 161.

1622, *October* 11.

Warrant to the Treasurer of the Chamber :—" Whereas we have thought fit to disburden our privy purse of certain payments used of late to be made out of it, and to assign the said payments to be hereafter made by you our treasurer of our chamber ; " amongst the payments so assigned are "payments to our musicians, for cornets, lutes, violins and other instruments of musick, and for strings and repairing of them," etc.

L. C. Papers, Bundle 75.

1622-3, *February* 6.

Warrant for a yearly livery to George Porter, appointed trumpeter in the place of Silvester Ramsey, deceased.

L. C. Vol. 812, *p.* 163.

1623, *March* 25.

Warrant for a yearly livery to Serle Perkins, appointed trumpeter in the place of John Smith, deceased.

L. C. Vol. 812, *p.* 163.

Accounts ending Michaelmas, 1624.

Accounts for liveries for :—

Richard Thorne	- -	king's drummer
Andrea Laniere	- -	musician
Daniell Farrant	- -	*"*

Trumpeters.

John Ramsey	John Hoeman
John Reley	William Allen
Anthony Denham	Richard Stocke
Griffin Martine	Peter Jones
Thomas Underhill	Robert Beech
Robert Ramsey	Edward Jewks
Randulph Floyd	Serle Perkins
Humphrey Floyd	George Porter

L. C. Vol. 48.

1624-5, *March* 7.

Warrant for a yearly livery to William Marr, appointed trumpeter in the place of Thomas Underhill, deceased, and also to Cuthbert Collin, appointed in the place of Humphrey Floyd.

L. C. Vol. 812, *p.* 170.

1625, *May* 25.

Warrant for liveries and banners to be delivered to the trumpeters :—

John Reyley	Edward Jurkes
John Horman	Cuthbert Collin
Peter Jones	

L. C. Vol. 813, *p.* 7.

1625, *May* 25.

Warrant for liveries and banners for four trumpeters to the King, at £19 17s. 8d. each :—

John Ryleigh (Ryghleigh)	Edward Juckes
Peter Jones	Cuthbert Collins

L. C. Vols. 148, 149 *and* 150.

1625, *May* 28.

Warrant to provide liveries and banners to eight trumpeters at £19 17s. 8d. each :—

Josia Broome	Richard Stocke
Robert Ramsey	Charles Perkins
Randulph Floyd	George Porter
William Allen	William Marr

L. C. Vols. 148, 149 *and* 150.

1625, *May* 28.

Warrant for liveries and banners to be delivered to the following trumpeters :—

Henry Martyn, sergeant	Robert Ramsey
Josias Broome	Randolph Floid
Nicholas Stramsome	William Allen

William Arnold	Richard Storke
Roger Barfoote	Robert Beeche
Robert Broome	Charles Perkins
Anthony Denham	George Porter
Griffin Martyn	William Marr
John Ramsey	

L. C. Vol. 813, *p.* 10.

1625, *June* 6.

Warrant for livery for Nicholas Lanier, luter to the King, at the cost of £16 2s. 6d.

L. C. Vols. 148, 149 *and* 150.

1625, *November* 8.

Warrant for livery for Henry Farrabosco, musician to the King, at the cost of £16 2s. 6d.

L. C. Vol. 148.

1625, *November* 28.

Warrant for livery for Andrew Laneire, one of the musician flutes.

L. C. Vol. 813, *p.* 15.

1625, *November* 28.

Warrant for livery for Andrea Lanier, one of the musicians to the King, at the cost of £16 2s. 6d.

L. C. Vols. 148, 149 *and* 150.

1625, *November* 28.

Warrant for livery for Henry Ferabasco, one of the musician flutes.

L. C. Vol. 813, *p.* 16.

1625, *December* 15.

Warrant for livery for Humphrey Jenkinson, appointed trumpeter in the place of Anthony Denham, deceased.

L. C. Vol. 813, *p.* 19.

1625, *December* 15.

Warrant to provide livery and banner for Humphrey Jenkinson, trumpeter to the King, at the cost of £19 17s. 8d.

L. C. Vols. 148, 149 *and* 150.

1625, *December* 19.

Warrant for livery for Jerome Lanier, musician to the King, at the cost of £16 2s. 6d.

L. C. Vols. 149 *and* 150; *also Vol.* 813, *p.* 20.

1625, *December* 19.

Warrant for livery for Clement Lanier, musician to the King, at the cost of £16 2s. 6d.

L. C. Vols. 149 *and* 150; *also Vol.* 813, *p.* 23.

1625.

Account of the funeral of James I. List headed "The Chamber of our late Sovereign Lord King James."

Trumpettors.

Henry Martin, sergeant
Edward Juckes
John Reileighe
John Hoeman
Griffin Martin
George Porter
Anthony Denham
Serles Perkins
Christopher Hopkins
William Allen
John Pendry

Humphrey Jenkins
William Lesom
Mark Bateman
Richard Ballard
William Broome
William Marr
Cuthbert Collin
Peter Johnes
John Ramsey
Robert Beech

Drums and Phife.

William Gosson
Henry Pullyard

Peter Pullyard
Jeoffrie Crews, phifer

Musitions for Violins.

Caesar Galliardello
John Hooper
Anthonie Come
Thomas Lupo, composer
Davis Mell
Thomas Lupo
Leonard Mell

Thomas Warren
Richard Dorlin
John Heydon
Alexander Chessam
Adam Vallett
Horatio Lupo

Musicians for windy Instruments.

Edward Harding
James Harding
Jeronimo Bassano
Nicholas Guy
Jerome Lanier
Andrea Bassano
Robert Baker, senior
Peter Guy
Andrea Lanier
Thomas Mason
Henrie Bassano

Jacob Froches
John Snowsman
John Hussey
Clement Lanier
Richard Blagrave
William Gregorie
Robert Baker, junior
Samuel Garshe
William Noakes
Thomas Mell

The Consorte.

Charles Coleman	John Dowland
Francis Cozens	Daniel Farrant
Maurice Webster	Timothy Collins
Philip Squire	John Friende
Robert Johnson	Nicholas Lanier, singer
Robert Major	

The Chappell.

William Heather, Doctor
Nathaniel Giles, Doctor and Master of the Children
John Stephens, gentleman, recorder of songes
Thomas Tompkins, organist

Gentlemen of the Chappell.

George Cooke	William West
Crew Sharpe	Richard Giles
Peter Hopkins	Nicholas Rogers
John Woodson	Thomas Peirce
Thomas Day	John Clark
Walter Porter	William Crosse
George Sheffeild	John Frost, junior
John Crocker	Francis Sennock
George Woodson	John Cooke
Humphrey Batche	

Orlando Gibbons, privy organ
Sampson Rowdon, bellringer
12 Children of the Chappell.

Singing men of Westminster.

John Frost, chantor	Richard Giles
Orlando Gibbons, organist	Adrian Batten
Thomas Peirce	Richard Patrick
Edmund Nelham	Richard Sandie
Daniel Taylor	Robert Willis
Robert White	John Croker
Thomas Day, Master of the Choristers	John Clarke
George Greene	Robert Williams
Henrie Northedge	Two Shagbutts
James Hooper	Two Cornitors

Choristers of Westminster.

George Heath	Abraham Langton
Owen Adamson	Andrew Scriven
James Trie	Thomas Kealish
John Harding	Thomas Finche
John Jewill	Hercules Geeringe

Bellringers.

John Richardson	John Stockdall
James Chappell	Francis Towson

L. C. Vol. 557.

1625.

List headed " The Chamber of King Charles."

Trumpeters.

Josias Broome	William Arnold
Nicholas Transome	Roger Barrfeild
Robert Broome	

Drumes and Phife.

Robert Tedder	Robert Droute

Thomas Hearne, phife.

Musicians.

Innocent Laneir	James Graye
Edward Wormall	Norman Lesley
John Lanier	Angelo Notarie
Thomas Fourd	Alphonso Bales
Robert Bourman	John Drew
Jonas Wrench	Alphonso Ferabasco
Abraham Coates	John Coperario
Thomas Hassard	Thomas Day
John Daniel	Robert Taylour
John Coxall	Robert Marshe
John Ballard	Sebastian Lopier
Gilbert Johnson	Tymmothie Collins

L. C. Vol. 557.

1625.

List of the Queen's servants who came over with her; to have black cloth for liveries.

Musicians.

Francis Richard, the elder	Robert Roane
Lewis Richard	Simon de la Gard
Francis Richard, the younger	Nichola du Vall
	Peter de la Marr
Camille Prouott	Andrew Mawgard
Marturine Marye	John Garnier

Singing boys:—To 3 little singing boys to each of them 5 yards.

L. C. Vol. 557.

1625.

" Tickets double served."

Trumpettor.

Will. Browne.

L. C. Vol. 557.

[1625] (?).

Extract from a book of orders given by and signed by King Charles I.

" Our express pleasure is that our Chappell be all the year through kept both morning and evening with solemn musicke like a collegiate church : unles it be at such times in the summer or other times when We are pleased to spare it."

" These Orders shall stand in force not onely at our Chappell at Whitehall but wheresoeuer We come to service or sermon in Chappell."

[*This book was probably drawn up on the King's accession.*]

L. C. Vol. 591.

1625-6, *January* 4.

Warrant for livery for Alphonso Ferrabasco, one of the musicians.

L. C. Vol. 813, *p.* 27.

1625-6, *January* 4.

Warrant to the effect that the livery allowed to Daniel Farrant, one of his Majesty's musicians, by the late King James, is to be continued.

L. C. Vol. 813, *p.* 305.

1625-6, *January* 14.

[Warrant for livery for Alphonso Farabosco crossed out with the memo.—since deceased.]

L. C. Vol. 148.

1626, *March* 28.

Petition of Roger Nott against Thomas Lupo, debt of £40, " answered of course."

L. C. Vol. 648.

1626, *May* 8.

Warrant to provide livery and banner to William Ramsey, trumpeter to the King, at the cost of £19 17s. 8d.

L. C. Vols. 148, 149 *and* 150.

1626, *May* 8.

Warrant for livery for William Ramsey, trumpeter, in place of John Ramsey, deceased.

L. C. Vol. 813, *p.* 36.

1626, *May* 25.

Warrant for allowance of £20 by the year to be made to Thomas Day, musician, for the custody and teaching of a singing boy for the service of the King according to the like allowance made to him when the King was Prince of Wales.

L. C. Vol. 813, *p.* 61.

1626, *May* 25.

Warrant to pay £20 a year to Thomas Day, musician, for keeping and teaching one singing boy, in quarterly payments of 100s. each.

L. C. Vols. 148, 149 *and* 150.

1626, *June* 6.

Warrant to provide livery for Nicholas Lanier, luter to the King, at the cost of £16 2s. 6d.

L. C. Vol. 813, *p.* 37.

1626, *June* 6.

Warrant for payment of £59 13s. 4d. to Andrea Lanier, musician to the King, for the summer and winter liveries of two boys committed to his keeping for the purpose of being instructed in the art of " Lez Flutes et Cornetts."

L. C. Vols. 148, 149 *and* 150 ; *also Vol.* 813, *p.* 37.

1626, *June* 13.

Warrant to Francis Gaulle, esquire, one of the clerks of the Signet, to prepare a bill to be directed to the master of the great wardrobe for providing liveries for the following musicians :—

Nicholas Lanier, master of the music

Alphonso Ferabosco	Thomas Day
Robert Johnson	Richard Deering
Thomas Foord	John Drew
Thomas Lupo	John Lanier
John Laurance	Edward Wormall
John Kelly	Angello Notarie
John Coggeshall	Jonas Wrenche
Robert Taylor	Alphonso Bales
Robert Marshe	

L. C. Papers. Bundle 1.

1626, *June* 22.

Warrant for liveries for eighteen of the ordinary musicians :—
Nicholas Lanier, master of the music

Alphonso Ferabosco	Richard Deeringe
Robert Johnson	John Drew
Thomas Ford	John Lanier

Thomas Lupo	Edward Wormall
John Lawraunce	Angello Notary
John Kelley	Jonas Wrench
John Coggeshall	Alphonso Bales
Robert Taylor	Robert Marsh
Thomas Day	

L. C. Vol. 813, *p.* 40.

*The same list, but endorsed " A copy of Angelo Notarie's Warrant"
in L. C. Papers, Bundle 17. In Vol. 148 only fifteen names are
given, Ferabosco, Lupo and Wrench being omitted ; in Vol. 149
the list diminishes to thirteen, Deeringe is omitted and the name
of Robert Marsh is crossed out with a note " dead " ; in
Vol. 150 the number is reduced to ten, Johnson, Lawrence and
Bales being omitted.*

1626, *August 8.*

Warrant to admit Henry Bassano as musician to his
majesty for the wind instruments, in the place of Andrea
Bassano, surrendered, and to grant him the fee of 1s. 8d. per
day, and £16 2s. 6d. yearly for livery, during his life, in such
manner as was formerly granted to Andrea Bassano.

L. C. Vol. 648.

1626, *September 13.*

Warrant to admit Edward Juxe, trumpeter at half wages
to whole wages, upon the death of John Holman.

L. C. 485 (*opposite end of Vol.*).

1626, *October 5.*

Warrant to admit Cuthbert Collins, trumpeter in ordinary
at half wages, to whole wages on the death of Robert Broome,
deceased.

L. C. Vol. 485 (*opposite end of Vol.*).

1626, *October 14.*

Petition of Mary Vallett, widow, against Richard Darney,
musician. " Answered of course."

L. C. Vol. 648.

1626, *October.*

Warrant to swear William Smyth a trumpeter in ordinary
at half wages in the place of Robert Broome, deceased.

L. C. Vol. 485 (*opposite end of Vol.*).

1626, *November 3.*

Warrant for livery and banner for William Smith,
trumpeter to the King, at the cost of £19 17s. 8d.

L. C. Vols. 148, 149 *and* 150.

1626, *November* 18.

Warrant for twenty-four surplices of fine holland cloth for the children of the Chappell; and for three score and four for the Gentlemen of the Chappell.

L. C. Vol. 798, *p.* 65.

1626, *December* 18.

Warrant for livery for Anthony Robertes, appointed ordinary musician in place of Jonas Wrench, deceased.

L. C. Vol. 813, *p.* 48.

1626, *December* 18.

Warrant to provide livery for Anthony Roberts, musician to the King, at the cost of £16 2s. 6d.

L. C. Vols. 148, 149 *and* 150.

1626, *December* 19.

Warrant for livery and banner for John Pendre, trumpeter to the King, at the cost of £19 17s. 8d.

L. C. Vols. 148 *and* 149.

1626, *December* 29.

Warrant for livery for John Pendre, appointed trumpeter in place of Nicholas Transome, deceased.

L. C. Vol. 813, *p.* 49.

1626, *December* 29.

Warrant for livery for Christopher Hopkins, appointed trumpeter in place of Robert Beech, deceased.

L. C. Vol. 813, *p.* 49.

1626, *December* 29.

Warrant to provide livery and banner to Christopher Hopkins, trumpeter to the King, at the cost of £19 17s. 8d.

L. C. Vols. 148, 149 *and* 150.

1627, *March* 29.

Warrants to swear Alfonso Ferabosco, a musition to his Majesty for the Violls and winde Instruments in the place of his father Alfonso Ferabosco, deceased ; and Henry Ferabosco a musician in ordinary to his Majesty for the voices and wind instruments, in the place of his father Alfonso Ferabosco, deceased.

NOTE :—" Their father enjoyed four places, viz., a musician's place in general, a composer's place, a violl's place, and an instructor's place to the prince in the art of musique. The benefit of all which places did descend unto his sonnes by his Majesty's special grant."

L. C. Vol. 738, *p.* 3.

1627, *April* 18.

Petition of Edmund Nelham, gentleman of his Majesty's Chappell, against Thomas Hale, " answered of course."

L. C. Vol. 648.

1627, *April* 18.

Petition of Ralph Tuggy against Henry Bassano, debt of £9, " answered of course."

L. C. Vol. 648.

1627, *May* 20.

Warrant to pay Andrew Miller for making fifteen long gowns for musicians, for the Queen's masque performed at Christmas, 1626.

L. C. Vol. 798, *p.* 108.

1627, *June* 1.

Petition of Roger Nott against Mr. Thomas Lupo. Answered, the sum of £20 to be paid to him.

L. C. Vol. 648.

1627, *June* 7.

Warrant for allowance of £20 a year to be made to Thomas Day, musician, for keeping and teaching a boy to sing, beyond the like sum formerly granted for keeping another boy.

L. C. Vols. 148, 149 *and* 150.

1627, *July* 15.

Petition of Thomas Lupo, composer of his Majesty's Musick against a former petition of Roger Nott, who upon wrong allegations had procured an order for the receiving of £20 at one entire payment out of the Treasury of the Chamber, the said Lupo never consenting to it.

L. C. Vol. 648.

1627, *November* 28.

Warrant for liveries for Stephen Nau and John Woddington, (musitian violins), musicians to the King, at the cost of £16 2s. 6d. each.

L. C. Vols. 148, 149 *and* 150; *L. C. Vol.* 813, *p.* 56.

1627-8, *February* 27.

Warrant to provide livery for Henry Bassano, musician to the King, at the cost of £16 2s. 6d.

L. C. Vols. 149 *and* 150. *Also Vol.* 813, *p.* 69.

1628, *April* 26.

Warrant for the payment of 40 marks per annum to Estienne Nau, composer of music for the violins, in the place of Thomas Lupo, deceased; also £16 2s. 6d. yearly for livery.

L. C. Vol. 738, *p.* 13.

1628, *May* 6.

Warrant for the allowance of £16 2s. 6d. for yearly livery to Henry Ferabosco, and two liveries of the same value to Alphonso Ferabosco.

L. C. Vol. 738, *p.* 13.

1628, *June* 20.

Warrant to grant Theophilus Lupo, one of his Majesty's musicians in ordinary in the place of his father Thomas Lupo, deceased, the sum of £40 yearly as wages, etc., and £16 2s. 6d. yearly as livery.

L. C. Vol. 738, *p.* 25.

1628, *June* 28.

Warrant for twenty-four surplices of fine holland cloth for the children of the Chappell ; and for three score and four for the Gentlemen of the Chappell.

L. C. Vol. 798, *p.* 116.

1628, *June* 30.

A list of his Majesty's Chappell :—

Gentlemen of the Chappell.

Nathaniel Giles, Doctor of Musick

John Stephen	Thomas Day
George Woodeson, senior	Walter Porter
John Woodeson	Thomas Peirce, junior
William West	Thomas Tomkins
Humphrey Bathe	Richard Boughton
George Cooke	Thomas Warwicke
John Clarke	George Woodeson, junior
John Frost, senior	Henry Lawes
George Shofield	John Tomkins
William Crosse	Richard Sandy
	Thomas Laughton

L. C. Vol. 738, *p.* 27.

1628, *July* 15.

List of musicians who are discharged from paying the five subsidies lately granted by the Parliament :—

Musitions for the recorders.

Jerimino Bassano	Anthony Bassano
Robert Baker, senior	John Husty
Clement Lanier	William Noke

For the flutes.

Andrea Lanier

Peter Guy

Nicholas Guy

Alfonso Ferabosco

Henry Ferabosco

William Gregory

For the hoboies and sackbuts.

Jerom Lanier

John Snowsman

Richard Blagrave

Henry Bassano

Christopher Bell

John Mason

Robert Parker

Edward Bassano

Robert Baker, junior

For the violins.

Thomas Lupo

Anthony Comy

Thomas Warren

John Haydon

Leonard Mell

John Hopper

James Johnson

David Mell

Nicholas Picart

Estienne Nau

Richard Dorney

John Woodington

For the lutes and voices.

Nicholas Lanier, master of the music

Robert Johnson

Richard Deering

John Coggeshall

John Lanier

John Kelly

Robert Taylor

Alphonso Balles

Robert Marsh

Maurice Webster

Philip Squire

Danyell Farraunt

Timothy Collins

Anton Roberts

Thomas Foord

John Drew

Angelo Notary

Edward Wormall

John Laurence

John Friend

Robert Dowland

Robert Kindersley

Charles Coleman

Theophilus Lupo

Trumpettors.

Josias Broom, sergeant

John Riley, sergeant

William Allen

Richard Stocke

George Porter

Charles Perkins

Peter Jones

Edward Juxe

Robert Ramsey

Randall Flood

Cuthbert Collins

William Marre

Humphrey Jenkins

William Ramsay

William Smith

John Pendry

Christopher Hopkins

Drummes and fiffes.

William Gosshen, drum major   Henry Pullyard
Peter Pullyard   Jeoffrey Cruse
William Allen   Robert Tedder

Keeper of the Organs.
Edward Norgate

L. C. Vol. 738, *p.* 37.

1628, *October* 10.

Warrant to swear John Rudd, a drummer extraordinary.

L. C. Vol. 738, *p.* 51.

1628, *October* 21.

Warrant for livery for Alphonso Farabosco, musician violin (musitian for the violls), at the cost of £16 2s. 6d.

L. C. Vol. 148, 149 *and* 150, *and L. C. Vol.* 813, *p.* 62.

1628, *October* 31.

Warrant for livery for Henry Farrabosco, one of the musicians for the voices to the King, and musician for the windy instruments.

L. C. Vol. 149 *and* 150, *and L. C. Vol.* 813, *p.* 71.

1628, *November* 20.

Certificate of bill for riding, waiting and attending on his Majesty on his journies from October, 1627, to September, 1628, for Robert Ramsey, Randolph Flood, and Richard Stock, his Majesty's trumpeters in ordinary.

L. C. Vol. 738, *p.* 66.

1628, *November* 27.

Petition of Margaret Blocksieige against Edward Bassano, debt of £5 p. bond, " answered of course."

L. C. Vol. 648.

1628, *St. Andrew.*

Payment of £16 2s. 6d. to the following musicians to the King for their livery :—

Andrew Lanier   Anthony Roberts
Henry Farrabosco   Stephen Nau
Clement Lanier   John Wooddington
Jeromino Lanier   Richard Deeringe
Daniel Farrant   Alphonso Ferabasco
Nicholas Lanier, luter

Payment of £29 16. 8. to Andrea Lanier for liveries for two boys in his care.

L. C. Vol. 459.

1628, *December* 8.

Petition of Nathaniel Lauander against Henry Bassano, debt of £4 16s. "Answered of course."

L. C. Vol. 648.

1628, *Christmas.*

Payment to Thomas Day, "Mu" [sician], 100s.

L. C. Vol. 459.

1628-9, *January* 2.

Warrant directed to the jewel house and treasury chamber for a New Year's gift to Theophilus Lupo, musician for the violins in the place of his father Thomas Lupo, deceased.

L. C. Vol. 738, *p.* 72.

1628-9, *January.*

Warrant for the payment of £5 to John Coggeshall, one of the musicians for the lutes, for strings for his Majesty's lutes, for one year ended at Christmas, 1628.

L. C. Vol. 738, *p.* 74.

1628-9, *January.*

Warrant for the payment of £9 to Thomas Lupo, for strings for the violins for one year ended at Christmas, 1628.

L. C. Vol. 738, *p.* 74.

1628-9, *January* 10.

Warrant for a New Year's gift to Mons. Estienne Nau as one of his Majesty's violins, to be the same proportion of plate and money as the rest of his Majesty's musicians have received. He received his New Year's gift as composer without warrant.

L. C. Vol. 738, *p.* 75.

1628-9, *January* 10.

Warrant for the payment of £23 to Andrea Lanier, one of his Majesty's musicians for the wind instruments; *i.e.*, £20 for four setts of musique books at £5 a sett, and £3 more for two Italian musique cards to compose upon, at 30s. each.

L C. Vol. 738, *p.* 75.

1628-9, *January* 12.

Warrant for the payment of £12 to Edward Norgate, keeper of his Majesty's organs and other instruments, for repairing the organs at Hampton Court and Whitehall, for porterage, and for repairing the virginalls for his Majesty's chamber musique.

L. C. Vol. 738, *p.* 79.

1628-9, *January* 12.

Warrant for the allowance of 20 marks to Davis Mell, for a treble violin, granted upon the certificate of Nicholas Lanier, master of his Majesty's musique.

L. C. Vol. 738, *p.* 80.

1628-9, *March* 17.

Warrant to swear John Smith a trumpeter extraordinary.

L. C. Vol. 738, *p.* 102.

1629, *March* 25.

Payment to Thomas Day, " Mu " [sician], 100s.

L. C. Vol. 459.

1629, *April* 16.

Petition of John Tisser against John Lanier, debt of £3 6s. " Answered of course."

L. C. Vol. 648.

1629, *May* 5.

Warrant to swear John Rudd drummer in ordinary, in the place of Robert Tedder, who is sworn drum major in the place of William Goshen, deceased.

L. C. Vol. 738, *p.* 112.

1629, *May* 6.

Warrant to pay Theophilus Lupo, one of his Majesty's musicians, £40 due to him as wages for the year 1628.

L. C. Vol. 738, *p.* 113.

1629, *June* 4.

Warrant for payment at the rate of 3$^{s.}$ 4$^{d.}$ per diem to each man to Robert Ramsey and Randolph Flood, trumpettors, . . . for attendance on the corpse of the late Duke of Buckingham from Portsmouth to London, . . . in August and September, 1628.

L. C. Vol. 738, *p.* 118.

1629, *June* 6.

Warrant for the payment of £20 to John Coggeshall, musician to his Majesty for the lutes, for strings bought and provided by him for his Majesty's lutes and theorba for one year ended at Christmas, 1627, and another warrant for the like sum for the year ended Christmas, 1628.

L. C. Vol. 738, *p.* 122 ; *on p.* 99 *a warrant for the same payment, dated* 13 *February*, 1628-9.

1629, *June* 24.

Payment to Thomas Day Mu [sician], 100s.

L. C. Vol. 459.

1629, *July* 13.

Petition of William Marre, one of his Majesty's trumpeters, to be freed from subsidies. " Answered."

L. C. Vol. 648.

1629, *September* 29.

Warrant to grant Henry Lanier, one of his Majesty's musicians for the flutes in the place of Nicholas Guy, deceased, the fee of 1s. 8d. per day, and a yearly livery of £16 2s. 6d.

L. C. Vol. 738, *p.* 140.

1629, *Michaelmas.*

Payment of £16 2s. 6d. to each of the following musicians for livery,

Robert Marsh	John Lanier
John Coggeshall	Thomas Forde
Theophilus Lupo	Alphonso Bales
Robert Johnson	John Laurence

L. C. Vol. 459.

1629, *Michaelmas.*

Payment to Thomas Day, Mu [sician], 100s.

L. C. Vol. 459.

1629, *October* 5.

Warrant to swear Richard Dorney a musician for the violins in ordinary in the place of Anthony Comey, deceased.

L. C. Vol. 738, *p.* 142.

1629, *October* 5.

Warrant for the allowance of £16 2s. 6d. yearly as livery to Richard Dorney, musician for the violins, and the wages of 10d. per diem to Robert Parker, musician for the wind instruments.

L. C. Vol. 738, *p.* 144.

1629, *October* 11.

Warrant to swear Mons. de Flelle, " his Majesty's servaint and a musition for the harp in ordinary."

L. C. Vol. 738, *p.* 143.

1629, *December* 9.

Warrant to pay Edward Norgate, keeper and tuner of his Majesty's organs, the sum of £37 10s. due to him upon two years' bills.

L. C. Vol. 738, *p.* 156.

1629, *December* 30.

Warrant for the payment of £9 to Theophilus Lupo for strings for the violins for one year ended at Christmas.

L. C. Vol. 738, *p.* 161.

1629-30, *January* 4.

Petition of Richard Hilton against Robert Ramsey, trumpeter, debt of £7. "Answered of course."

L. C. Vol. 648.

1629-30, *January* 14.

Warrant to swear Jeremy Crews a drummer in ordinary, upon the removal of William Allen to be drum major, in place of Robert Tedder, deceased.

L. C. Vol. 738, *p.* 166.

1629-30, *January* 19.

Warrant to pay Robert Johnson £20 for strings for the year ended at Christmas 1628, and a like allowance for 1629.

L. C. Vol. 738, *p.* 168.

1629-30, *February* 18.

Warrant to swear Edmund Cooper a drummer extraordinary.

L. C. Vol. 738, *p.* 172.

1629-30, *February* 19.

Petition of Robert Ramsey against Sir William Erwin, debt of £30. "Answered of course by a letter."

L. C. Vol. 648.

1629-30, *February* 20.

Warrant for the payment of £34 to Estienne Nau for four instruments, viz.:—£12 for a base, £6 each for 2 tenors, and £10 for a treble violin.

L. C. Vol. 738, *p.* 174.

1629-30, *March* 7.

Warrant for the payment of £10 to Timothy Collins for a lute, upon the certificate of Nicholas Lanier.

L. C. Vol. 738, *p.* 176.

1630, *March* 30.

Warrant to swear George Giles a trumpeter extraordinary.

L. C. Vol. 738, *p.* 177.

1630, *April* 2.

Warrant to swear Giles Tomkins a musician for the virginalls with the voices in ordinary, in the place of Richard Deering, deceased. Also warrant dated 20 April for £40 yearly as wages.

L. C. Vol. 738, *pp.* 178 *and* 183.

1630, *May* 4.

Warrant for the allowance of £6 to John Heydon for a tenor violin.

L. C. Vol. 738, *p.* 187.

1630, *May* 6.

Order concerning the waiting of the musicians for the wind instruments :—

One company of the cornets, recorders, and howboies to wait one week - - -	} *i.e.*	{ Jerome Lanier, Clement Lanier, Andrea Lanier, Robert Baker.
The other company of cornets, flutes, and hoboies to wait the other week -	} *i.e.*	{ Jerome Lanier, Clement Lanier, Andrea Lanier, Robert Baker.

The following to wait Sundays and holidays :—

To wait one Sunday	{ Jeromino Bassano, Robert Baker, senior, Anthony Bassano, William Noke, Robert Parker Henry Bassano.
To wait the other Sunday	{ Henry Ferabosco, Alfonso Ferabosco, Richard Blagrave, Christopher Bell, John Mason, Edward Bassano.

William Gregory, who is to wait also on play nights instead of Mr. Jeromino Bassano, who is the ancientist musician the King hath.

L. C. Vol. 738, *p.* 189.

1630, *May* 6.

"*Musique Order.*"

It is ordered by the consent of all that havė here subscribed, that if any man be sick or some other excusable cause detayne him, he is to pray in time convenient some one of his fellows to wayte for him, and they are all obliged to wayte on collar days : —

Nicholas Lanier	Anthony Bassano
Jerom Lanier	William Noke
Clement Lanier	Henry Bassano
Andrea Lanier	Christopher Bell
Robert Baker	Richard Blagrave

John Mason

L. C. Vol. 738, *p.* 190.

1630, *May* 8.

Petition of Edmund Maynard against Henry Bassano, debt of £16. " Answered."

L. C. Vol. 648.

1630, *May* 15.

Warrant for livery for Theophilus Lupo, appointed ordinary musician to the King in the place of Thomas Lupo, his father, deceased.

L. C. Vol. 813, *p.* 76; *also Vols.* 149 *and* 150.

1630, *May* 28.

Warrant to pay John Coggeshall £20 for strings for the four lutes and theorba for one year ended at Christmas, 1629.

L. C. Vol. 738, *p.* 193.

1630, *Pentecost.*

List of livery fees (£19 17s. 8d. to each person) due at Pentecost, 1630, to seventeen trumpeters :—

  Mr. John Reighley (Ryleigh), sergeant trumpeter.
  Mr. Josias Broome, sergeant trumpeter
  Mr. William Allen
  Mr. John Pendrey (also Pendre)
  Mr. Edward Jukes (also Juckes)
  Mr. Richard Stocke
  Mr. William Marr
  Mr. Robert Ramsey
  Mr. George Porter
  Mr. Humphrey Jenkinson
  Mr. Peter Jones
  Mr. William Ramsey
  Mr. William Smith
  Mr. Randoll Lloyd (also Ranulpho Floyd)
  Mr. Searles Perkins
  Mr. Christopher Hopkins
  Mr. Cuthbert Collins

L. C. Vol. 799 ; *and in Vol.* 459.

1630, *June* 30.

Warrant for livery for Giles Tompkins, appointed ordinary musician to the King in the place of Richard Deeringe, deceased.

L. C. Vol. 813, *p.* 76, *and L. C. Vols.* 149 *and* 150.

1630, *Michaelmas.*

Account paid to Mr. Daye, for keeping two boys for Midsummer and Michaelmas quarters, £20.

L. C. Vol. 799.

Accounts ending Michaelmas, 1630.

Accounts for liveries for :—

Trumpeters.

John Ryleigh	Charles Perkins
Peter Jones	George Porter
Edward Juckes	William Marr
Cuthbert Collens	Humphrey Jenkinson
Josias Broome	William Ramsey
Robert Ramsey	William Smyth
Ranulph Flod	Christopher Hopkins
William Allen	John Pendre
Richard Stocke	

Andrea Lanier, musician, for two boys committed to his care for instruction in the flutes and cornetts.

Thomas Day, musician, two sums of £20 per annum for two singing boys.

L. C. Vol. 49.

1630, *October.*

A bill signed for Robert Ramsay, Randolph Flood and Richard Stock, trumpeters, for waiting and riding charges in the months of June, July, August and September, 1630.

L. C. Vol. 738. *p.* 207.

1630, *November* 20.

Warrant for payment of £12 to Thomas Warren for a base violin.

L. C. Vol. 738, *p.* 210.

1630, *St. Andrew.*

Payments for liveries due at the Feast of St. Andrew, 1630 :—

Paid Mr. Angelo Notory, musician to the King, £16 2s. 6d.

Similar payments to the musicians to the King :—

Mr. Henry Forabasco, with a payment for voyces and liveries.

Mr. Alphonso Farabasco	Mr. John Cockshall
Andrea Laneer	Mr. Henry Basanio
Clement Laneer	Mr. John Lawrence
John Laneer	Mr. Drue
Jeremy Laneer	Mr. Taylor
Mr. Balls	Mr. Lupoe
Mr. Anthony Roberts	Mr. Kellye

Mr. Wooddington	Mr. Marshe
Daniel Farrant	Mr. Thomas Daye
Mr. Woormall	Mr. Giles Tompkins
Mr. Nawse	Mr. Robert Johnson
	Mr. Thomas Ford

Mr. Laneer for a livery for John Farabasco, £16. 2. 6.

To Andrea Laneer for teaching two boys, £29 16s. 8d.

To Nicholas Laneer as Master of Musick, £16 2s. 6d.

Paid him more as luter, a livery, £16. 2. 6.

L. C. Vol. 799.

1630 (?), *St. Andrew.*

Payment to Nicholas Lanier, master of music to the King for his livery £16 2s. 6d.

L. C. Vol. 459.

1630, *December* 19.

Warrant for the payment of £16 10s. to Andrea Lanier for six cornets, viz. :—3 tenors at £3 each, and 3 trebles at 50s. each.

L. C. Vol. 738, *p.* 221.

1630, *Christmas.*

Paid Mr. Thomas Daye, a musician, being a quarterly payment, £10.

L. C. Vol. 799.

1630-1, *January* 4.

Warrant for the payment of £9 to Anthony Bassano for three mute cornets.

L. C. Vol. 738, *p.* 222.

1630-1, *January* 5.

Petition of Andrew Wanley against Theophilus Lupo, debt of £70, "answered of course."

L. C. Vol. 648.

1630-1, *January* 6.

Warrant to swear Mr. Henry Lawes a musician for the voices in the place of Robert Marsh, deceased.

L. C. Vol. 738, *p.* 223.

1630-1, *January* 10.

Warrant to pay Thomas Lupo £9 for strings for the violins for one year ended at Christmas, 1630.

L. C. Vol. 738, *p.* 224.

1630-1, *January* 10.

Warrant for payment of £20 to John Coggeshall, musician for the lutes, for strings for his Majesty's lutes and theorba, for one year ended at Michaelmas, 1630, being an accustomed yearly allowance.

L. C. Vol. 738, *p.* 224.

1630-1, *January* 15.

Warrant for livery for John Farrabosco, appointed musician for the windy instruments in place of Henry Farrabosco.

L. C. Vol. 813, *p.* 80 ; *also Vols.* 149 *and* 150.

1630-1, *February* 7.

Petition of Thomas Southwell against Mr. John Lanier, debt of £7. " Answered of course."

L. C. Vol. 648.

1630-1, *February* 28.

Warrant for a patent of £20 per annum to Mr. Henry Lawes, a musician for the lutes and voices in ordinary in the place of Robert Marsh, deceased, and an allowance of £16 2s. 6d. yearly for livery.

L. C. Vol. 738, *p.* 233.

1631, *Lady-Day*.

Paid Mr. Daye, a musician, for keeping singing boys, £10.

L. C. Vol. 799.

1631, *April* 12.

Order directed to Mr. Nau, concerning the musicians for the violins, as follows :—

Estienne Nau	treble
Davis Mell	"
Nichola Picart	"
John Woodington	contratenor
Theophilus Lupo	"
James Johnson	tenor
Leonard Mell	"
John Heydon	"
Thomas Lupo	low tenor
Robert Parker	"
John Hopper	basso
Thomas Warren	"
Richard Dorney	"
Robert Kindersley	"

L. C. Vol. 738, *p.* 242.

1631, *April* 27.

Warrant for the payment of £15 to Maurice Webster, one of the musicians, for lute strings for three years ended at Christmas 1630, being an allowance of £5 yearly.

L. C. Vol. 738, *p.* 246.

1631, *May.*

Warrant for the payment of £13 10s. to Edward Norgate, for repairing his Majesty's organs in 1629.

L. C. Vol. 738, *p.* 254.

1631, *Pentecost.*

Paid Mr. John Releighe, sergeant trumpeter, £19 17s. 8d.

Paid Mr. Josias Broome, sergeant trumpeter, £19 17s. 8d.

Paid William Allen, Edward Juckes, Richard Stocke, William Marr, Robert Ramsey, George Porter, Humphrey Jenkenson, Peter Jones, William Ramsey, William Smithe, Randall Loyd, Searles Perkins, Cuthbert Collins, John Pendree, and Christopher Hopkins, trumpeters, £19 17s. 8d. each.

L. C. Vol. 799.

1631, *St. John Baptist.*

Paid Mr. Andrea Laneere for keeping two boys, £29 16s. 8d.

Paid Mr. Daye for keeping singing boys, £10.

L. C. Vol. 799.

1631, *July.*

Warrant for the payment of £20 to Robert Johnson for lute strings for a year ended at Christmas, 1630.

L. C. Vol. 738, *p.* 262.

1631, *July* 14.

Warrant to pay William Crosse, deputy master of the children of his Majesty's royal Chappell, the sum of £25, disbursed by him from 1626 to 1630 in the execution of his office.

L. C. Vol. 738, *p.* 262.

1631, *July* 30.

Warrant for the allowance of a livery to James Nare, a child of the Chappell whose voice is changed.

L. C. Papers, Bundle 19.

Accounts ending Michaelmas, 1631.

Accounts for liveries for :—

Daniel Farrant, vn de lez violls
Andrea Lanier, musician
Nicholas Lanier, luter

Musicians.

Nicholas Lanier, master of the music

Andrea Lanier	Angelo Notarie
Robert Johnson	Alphonso Bales
Thomas Ford	Robert Mirricke
John Lawrence	Anthony Robertes
John Killey	Stephen Naw
John Coggshall	John Woodington
Robert Taylor	Giles Tompkins
Thomas Day	Henry Bassano
John Drew	Jeromino Lanier
John Lanier	Clement Lanier
Edward Wormall	Theophilus Lupo

Alphonso Farrabosco, musician violin
Henry Farrabosco, musician for le voices
John Farrabosco, musician for the windy instruments.

Trumpeters.

John Releigh	Richard Stock
Peter Jones	Charles Perkins
Edward Juckes	George Porter
Cuthbert Collins	William Marr
Josias Broome	Humphrey Jenkinson
Robert Ramsey	William Ramsey
Randulph Floyd	William Smith
William Allen	Christopher Hopkins
	John Pendre

Andrea Lanier, musician, for the apparel of two boys committed to his care to learn the science of the flute and cornet.

Account of £20 per annum paid quarterly to Thomas Day for a boy kept and taught singing for the service of the King.

Account for the same amount paid to the same for another boy.

1631, *October* 25.

Bill signed for the allowance of 3s. 4d. per diem to Josias Broome, sergeant trumpeter, and thirteen other trumpeters, for their attendance on his Majesty at Portsmouth and Rochester for sixteen days in June and August 1631, total amounting to £37 6s. 8d.

1631, *November* 2.

Letter of assignment from Henry Bassano, one of his Majesty's musicians, assigning to Ralph Hope of Lincoln's Inn, his liveries of £16 2s. 6d., for the years 1632 and 1633.

L. C. Vol. 813, *p.* 334.

1631, *November* 26.

Petition of Mr. Christopher Bell, one of his Majesty's musicians, against Walter Gray "for scandalous words and abuse of his quality."

L. C. Vol. 648.

1631, *November.*

Warrant to swear Thomas Mell as musician for the wind instruments in the place of William Noke, deceased.

L. C. Vol. 738, *p.* 272.

1631, *December* 13.

Warrant for sea liveries for Richard Stock and Christopher Hopkins, two of his Majesty's trumpeters, who had leave to attend his Majesty's service under Sir Henry Fane when he was employed in his ambassage.

L. C. Vol. 738, *p.* 278.

1631, *December* 21.

Warrant for payment of £20 to John Coggeshall for strings for the lutes for one year ended at Michaelmas, 1631.

L. C. Vol. 738, *p.* 280.

1631, *December* 22.

Warrant to pay Edward Norgate the sum of £25 for repairing the organs and virginals in his Majesty's several houses of St. James', Hampton Court, Greenwich and Whitehall.

L. C. Vol. 738, *p.* 279.

1631.

Petition of William James, against Clement Lanier: "answered."

L. C. Vol. 648.

1631-2, *February.*

Warrant for payment of £25 to Mr. John Le Flelle for a harp bought by him for his Majesty's service.

Mem.: " He is sworn a musician in ordinary for the harp."

L. C. Vol. 738, *p.* 287.

1631-2, *February* 22.

Bill signed for allowance of 2/- per diem unto Robert Ramsey, Randolph Flood and Richard Stock, riding trumpeters.

L. C. Vol. 738, *p.* 290.

1632, *May* 10.

Warrant for the allowance of 15s. per diem to Edward Norgate for " the diet and lodging of Signior Antonio Van Dike and his servants, to begin from the 1st April last," and to continue during the stay of the said Van Dike.

L. C. Vol. 738, *p.* 297.

1632, *June* 12.

Warrant for payment of £5 to Maurice Webster, one of his Majesty's musicians, for lute strings for one year ended at Michaelmas, 1631.

L. C. Vol. 738, *p.* 301.

1632, *June* 13.

Warrant to pay Edward Norgate, keeper of his Majesty's organs, £17 for repairing the organs at Whitehall and Greenwich.

L. C. Vol. 738, *p.* 305.

1632, *June* 30.

Warrant to provide livery for Daniell Farrant, musician to the King, at the cost of £16 2s. 6d.

L. C. Vol. 150.

1632, *July* 21.

Warrant for payment of £8 to Mr. John Woodington for a base violl.

L. C. Vol. 738, *p.* 306.

1632, *July* 21.

Warrant for the payment of £6 to Mr. Thomas Lupo for a tenor violin.

L. C. Vol. 738, *p.* 306.

1632, *July.*

Warrant for payment of £15 to Mr. Roberts for a theorba.

L. C. Vol. 738, *p.* 306.

1632, *August* 9.

Warrant to provide livery, at the cost of £16 2s. 6d. to Henry Lawes, appointed musician for the lutes and voices, in the place of Robert Marsh, deceased.

L. C. Vol. 150 ; *L. C. Vol.* 813, *p.* 93.

Accounts ending Michaelmas, 1632.

Accounts for liveries for :—

Daniel Farrant, one of the vialls
Nicholas Lanier, luter

Musicians.

Nicholas Lanier, master of the music

Andrea Lanier	John Lanier
Giles Tompkins	Edward Wormall
Theophilus Lupo	Angelo Notary
Robert Johnson	Alphonso Bales
Thomas Ford	Anthony Roberts
John Lawrence	Stephen Naw
John Kelley	John Woodington
John Coggshall	Henry Bassano
Robert Taylor	Henry Farrabosco
Thomas Day	Jeromino Lanier
John Drew	Clement Lanier

Alphonso Farrabosco, musician violin

John Farrabosco, musician for the windie instruments

Trumpeters.

John Ryleigh	Charles Perkins
Peter Jones	George Porter
Edward Juckes	William Marr
Cuthbert Collins	Humphrey Jenkinson
Josias Broome	William Ramsey
Robert Ramsey	William Smith
Randulph Floyd	Christopher Hopkins
William Allen	John Pendre
Richard Stocke	

Andrew Lanier, musician, for apparel for two boys kept and instructed by him in the science of lez flutes and cornetts.

Account of two sums of £20 per annum paid to Thomas Day quarterly for two boys kept and taught singing by him, for the service of the King.

L. C. Vol. 50.

1632, *December* 5.

Bill for allowance of 2/- per diem unto Robert Ramsey, Randolph Flood and Richard Stock, riding trumpeters.

L. C. Vol. 738, *p.* 312.

1632, *December* 13.

Petition of Thomas Mell, a musician for the wind instruments, that a warrant may be passed " for his entertainment." Answered, viz.—" The petitioner Thomas Mell succeedeth William Nokes as musician for the wind instruments, which is a company of ancient institution and approved attendance in his Majesty's service."

L. C. Vol. 648,

1632-3.

Receipt for the sum of £29 16s. 8d. signed by Andrea Lanier for the apparralling of two singing boyes committed to his custodie. Another receipt for a similar payment to Andrea Lanier is dated 25 June, 1633.

1632-3.

Receipt for two liveries signed by Nicholas Lanier as master of the music, and as lutanist, amounting to £32 5s.

1632-3.

Receipt signed by Andrea Lanier for one livery of £16 2s. 6d., due to him as one of his Majesty's musicians.

1632-3.

Receipt signed by Jerom Lanier for £16 2s. 6d. for a livery due to him as one of his Majesty's musicians.

1632-3.

Receipt for the livery, £16 2s. 6d., of Angelo Notary, musician to his Majesty.

1632-3.

Receipt for two liveries to Henry Ferrabosco, £32 5s., as one of his Majesty's musicians and as musician of the voyces.

1632-3.

Receipts for one livery, *i.e.*, £16 2s. 6d., to each of the following musicians :—

Alfonso Ferrabosco	John Lawrence
Clement Lanier	John Drewe
John Lanier	Robert Taylor
Alphonso Bales	Theophilus Lupo
Anthony Roberts	John Kelly
John Woodington	John Ferribasco
Daniel Farrant	Thomas Day
Edward Wormall	Giles Tomkins
Estienne Nau	Robert Johnson
John Cogshall	Thomas Forde
Henry Bassano	Henry Lawes.

(The receipts are signed as a rule by the recipients, but Thomas Day's receipt is signed by Richard Sandy.)

1632-3, *March* 4.

Warrant for payment of £20. 10. unto Andrea Lanier, for himself and Jerom Lanier, Clement Lanier, Alfonso Ferabosco, Henry Ferabosco, and Robert Baker, junior, for 6 cornets and a sett of bookes; viz. 50/ a piece for 5 treble cornets, £13 for a tenor cornet, and £5 for a sett of bookes.

L. C. Vol. 738, *p.* 324.

1632-3, *March* 16.

Warrant to swear Thomas Flood a trumpeter extraordinary.

L. C. Vol. 738, *p.* 325.

1633, *March* 27.

Warrant to swear John Smith a trumpeter in ordinary in the place of William Allen, deceased.

L. C. Vol. 738, *p.* 325.

1633, *March* 27.

Warrant that the liveries of the eight trumpeters in ordinary appointed to attend his Majesty in his journey into Scotland, be delivered beforehand " that they may go decently and handsomley apparelled " :—

Sergeant Broome	Peter Jones
Robert Ramsey	Richard Stocke
Randolph Floyd	Edward Juxe
George Porter	William Ramsey

L. C. Vol. 813, *p.* 314.

1633, *March* 28.

Warrant for a patent of 1s. 8d. per diem as wages, and £16 2s. 6d. yearly for livery, to Robert Tomkins, a musician for the consort, in the place of Robert Kyndersley, deceased.

L. C. Vol. 738, *p.* 355.

1633, *March* 29.

Warrant for promoting Christopher Hopkins, a trumpeter in ordinary at half pay, to whole wages, upon the decease of William Allen.

L. C. Vol. 738, *p.* 326.

1633, *April*.

Warrant to pay £15 to Mr. Nicholas Lanier for a theorba lute.

L. C. Vol. 738, *p.* 327.

1633, *April*.

Warrant for payment of £15 to Mr. Nau and Davies Mell for two setts of books for the violins.

L. C. Vol. 738, *p.* 330.

1633, April 15.

Receipts signed by the following trumpeters for one livery of £19 : 17 : 8 to each of them :—

Josias Broome	George Porter
Robert Ramsay	Peter Jones
Randoll Floyd	Edward Juckes
Richard Stocke	William Ramsay

L. C. Vol. 179.

1633, May 11.

A Councell's warrant for payment of £18 to Thomas Lupo, one of the musicians for the violin, being an arrear for the attendance of the whole company at an installation in the year 1625.

L. C. Vol. 738, *p.* 334.

1633, May 16.

Receipt signed by Thomas Day for £10 for keeping and apparalling of two singing boyes for one quarter of a year.

L. C. Vol. 179.

1633, May 25.

Memorandum of assignment by John Lanier, one of his Majesty's musicians, to Thomas Dallwenn, £16 2s. 6d.

L. C. Vol. 200, *p.* 7.

1633, May.

List of those appointed to wayte on his Majesty in his Scottish journey, 1633, as it was signed by his Majesty 1632 :—

Trumpeters.

Sergeant Broome	Peter Jones
Robert Ramsey	Richard Stocke
Randolph Floyd	Edward Juxe
George Porter	William Ramsey

The Chappell.

Bases.

Thomas Piers, senior	John Frost, junior
Ezechell Waade	Ralph Amner
Roger Nightingale	Thomas Rayment

Tenors.

George Cooke	John Frost, senior
John Clarke	Walter Porter

Contratenors.

Thomas Day	Richard Sandy
Thomas Pierse	Thomas Laughton
Henry Lawes	Nathaniel Pownell

Organists.

John Tomkins   Giles Tomkins
Eight children of the Chappell.

L. C. Vol. 738 (*at end of Vol.*).

1633, *June* 24.

Receipts signed by the following trumpeters, for liveries of £19 : 17 : 8 to each of them :—

John Ryleigh   William Smyth
Serles Perkins   William Marr
Humphrey Jenkinson   John Pendre
Cuthbert Collins

L. C. Vol. 179.

1633, *August* 30.

Bill signed for allowance of 2/ per diem unto Robert Ramsey, Randolph Flood and Richard Stock, riding trumpeters.

L. C. Vol. 738, *p.* 338.

1633, *September* 27.

Petition of Jane Thorne and Thomas Cooknow, against Angelo Notari, for a debt of £56 and £23.   Answered.

L. C. Vol. 648.

1633, *September* 29.

Warrant for the apprehension of Griffin Jones, upon the complaint of John Heydon, a musition for the violins, for abusive language given him, as "fidling rogue," etc.

L. C. Vol. 738, *p.* 338.

Accounts ending Michaelmas, 1633.

Accounts for liveries for :—

> Daniel Farrant, vn de lez violls
> Nicholas Lanier, luter

Musicians.

Nicholas Lanier, master of the music
Andrea Lanier   John Lanier
Giles Tompkins   Edward Wormall
Theophilus Lupo   Angelo Notarie
Robert Johnson   Alphonso Bales
Thomas Ford   Anthony Roberts
John Lawrence   Stephen Naw
John Kelley   John Wooddington
John Coggshall   Henry Bassano
Robert Taylor   Jeromino Lanier
Thomas Day   Clement Lanier
John Drew

Alphonso Farabosco, musician violin
Henry Farrabosco, vn de lez musicians for the voices
John Farrabosco, musician for the windy instruments
Henry Lawes, musician for the lutes and voices in place
  of Robert Marsh, deceased.

Trumpeters.

John Ryleigh	Charles Perkins
Peter Jones	George Porter
Edward Juckes	William Marr
Cuthbert Collins	Humphrey Jenkinson
Josias Broome	William Ramsey
Robert Ramsey	William Smith
Ranulph Floyd	Christopher Hopkins
Richard Stock	John Pendre

Andrea Lanier, musician, for apparel for two boys, kept
  and instructed by him in the science of lez flutes
  and cornetts.

Account of two sums of £20 per annum paid quarterly to
Thomas Day for two boys kept and taught singing by him, for
the service of the King.

L. C. Vol. 51.

1633, *October.*

Certificate that Mr. Edward Kelley is sworne master of
his Majesty's Chappell royall in Scotland.

L. C. Vol. 738, *p.* 339.

1633, *November* 4.

Warrant to swear John Adson a musician for the flute and
cornet in ordinary, in the place of Henry Lanier, deceased.

L. C. Vol. 738, *p.* 341.

1633, *November* 8.

Bill signed for Robert Ramsey, Randolph Flood and Richard
Stock, riding trumpeters, for 61 days last summer at 2s. per
diem.

L. C. Vol. 738, *p.* 341.

1633, *November* 12.

Assignment by John Lanier, one of his Majesty's musicians
to William Lecrofte of £10.

L. C. Vol. 200, *p.* 9.

1633, *November* 26.

Warrant to swear Mr. Nicholas Duvall a musician for the
lutes and voices in the place of Robert Johnson, deceased ;
followed by a warrant to swear Lewis Evans in another place
held by Mr. Johnson.

L. C. Vol. 738, *p.* 344.

1633, *November* 29.

Warrant for livery for Nicholas Duvall, appointed musician in ordinary in the place of Robert Johnson, deceased.

L. C. Vol. 150 ; *L. C. Vol.* 813, *p.* 97.

1633, *December* 8.

Petition of Elizabeth Pickford against Theophilus Lupo for a debt of £3 10s. " Answered of course."

L. C. Vol. 648.

1633, *December* 10.

Warrant for a patent of £40 per annum as wages, and £20 yearly for lute strings to Mr. Nicholas Duval, musician for the lutes in the place of Robert Johnson, deceased.

L. C. Vol. 738, *p.* 346.

1633, *December* 10.

Warrant for payment of 1ˢ· 8ᵈ· per diem, wages, and £16 : 2 : 6 per annum, livery, unto Lewis Evans, a musician for the lutes in the place of Robert Johnson, deceased.

L. C. Vol. 738, *p.* 346.

1633, *December* 30.

Councells warrant for payment of £34 to Andrea Lanier for books and cornets, etc., upon two several warrants in arrear.

L. C. Vol. 738, *p.* 348.

1633, *December*.

Order to be observed throughout the year by his Majesty's musitions for the wind instruments for waiting in the Chappell and at his Majesty's table :—

Jerom Lanier	These are to wait at
Clement Lanier	the principall feasts
Anthony Bassano	and Collar Days.
	Andrea Lanier
	Henry Bassano
These are to wayte	Alfonso Ferabosco
one week	Henry Ferabosco
	Robert Parker
	Thomas Mell
	Richard Blagrave
	Robert Baker
These are to wayte	John Mason
the other week	Christopher Bell
	William Gregory
	John Adson

It is ordered also that the whole company shall wait on all the solemn feasts and Collar days of the year. If any man be sick or have an excusable cause that detaynes him, he is to procure one of his fellows to wayte for him. If any of the company shall neglect to observe this order the Maister of the Musique is to complain or be liable to the like punishment himself as they by their negligence may incur.

L. C. Vol. 738, *p.* 345.

1633.

Petition of Jone Lanier, widow of Henry Lanier, deceased, desiring to dispose of her child to Andrea Lanier, to be trained in the quality of Musique. Answered that Andrea Lanier should take the child into his care to instruct him in Musique, as soon as he shall be capable thereof.

L. C. Vol. 648.

1633-4, *January* 17.

Warrant for payment of £20 unto Mr. John Coggeshall for lute strings for a year.

L. C. Vol. 738, *pp.* 348 *and* 350.

1633-4, *January* 19.

Warrant for payment of £16 to John Kelly and John Laurence for two treble lutes, against his Majesty's Masque at Shrovetide, 1633.

L. C. Vol. 738, *p.* 350.

1633-4, *January* 29.

Warrant for the apprehension of :—

James Hodgson
Edward Hodgson
Gregory Saunders
George Bosgrave and
Francis Newton, trumpeters

upon complaint of the sergeant, for usurpation of the title of the King's trumpeters.

L. C. Vol. 738, *p.* 351.

1633-4, *February* 22.

Bill for allowance of 2/- per diem unto Robert Ramsey, Randolph Flood and Richard Stock, riding trumpeters.

L. C. Vol. 738. *p.* 353.

1633-4, *March* 24.

Warrant to swear Robert Tomkins, a musician in ordinary for the consort, in the place of Robert Kyndersley, deceased. Followed on March 28 by a warrant for payment of 1ˢ· 8ᵈ· a day wages, and £16 : 2 : 6 a year for livery to him.

L. C. Vol. 738, *pp.* 354 *and* 355·

1634, *April* 20.

Warrant for the payment of £24 to Mr. Estienne Nau for two tenor violins brought out of France.

L. C. Vol. 738, *p.* 356·

1634, *May* 1.

A warrant to swear Thomas Flooyd as trumpeter in ordinary in the place of John Pendre, deceased.

L. C. Vol. 739, *folio* 1d.

1634, *May* 26.

Warrant for livery for Thomas Floid, appointed trumpeter in ordinary in place of John Pendre, deceased.

L. C. Vol. 813, *p.* 98, *and L. C. Vol.* 150.

1634, *May* 30.

Warrant for livery for John Smith, appointed trumpeter in ordinary in place of William Allen, deceased.

L. C. Vol. 150 ; *L. C. Vol.* 813, *p.* 99.

1634, *June* 28.

Warrant to deliver to Mrs. Sarah Spalding certain clothing, named, for the use of her son Richard Spalding, late child of the Chappell whose voice is changed.

L. C. Papers. Bundle 11.

1634, *July* 10.

Warrant to pay £15 to John Lanier, a musician for the lutes and voices, for a new lute bought by him.

L. C. Vol. 739, *p.* 14·

1634, *July* 10.

Warrant to pay Thomas Lupo and Thomas Warren with ten other of their fellowes, his Majesty's musicians for the violins, the sum of £126, being the amount due to them for attendance on his Majesty yearly at Windsor during the time of the installation of the Lords there, for the space of seven years from 1627 to 1633, at the rate of 5s. per diem to each of them amounting to £18 per annum.

L. C. Vol. 739, *p.* 15·

1634, *November* 2.

Warrant for the committal of William Allen, drum-major.

L. C. Vol. 739, *p.* 20.

1634, *November* 5.

Warrant to swear John Strong a musician for the wind instruments in ordinary; to wait in the place and absence of John Snowsman.

L. C. Vol. 739, *p.* 21.

1634, *November* 24.

Warrant for the payment of £22 to Mr. Edward Norgate, for repairing his Majesty's organs at Whitehall, Greenwich and Hampton Court for two years last past.

L. C. Vol. 739, *p.* 24.

1634, *November* 26.

Warrant for the payment of £20 to Mr. John Coggeshall for lute strings, for a year ended at Michaelmas.

L. C. Vol. 739, *p.* 26.

1634, *November* 26.

Two bills signed for Robert Ramsey, Randoll Floyd and Richard Stock, trumpeters, one for service done from February to July, 1634, amounting to 102 days, and the other for 79 days extraordinary attendance in July, August and September, 1634.

L. C. Vol. 739, *p.* 26.

1634, *December* 16.

Assignment by Henry Bassano, one of his Majesty's musicians for the winde instruments, of £16 2s. 6d. to Richard Clotterbooke.

L. C. Vol. 200, *p.* 45.

1634, *December* 26.

Warrant for 12 surplices for his Majesty's musicians for the wind instruments, at times of their service in the Chappell.

L. C. Vol. 739, *p.* 32.

1634-5, *February* 21.

A bill signed for Robert Ramsey, Randol Flood and Richard Stock, 3 of his Majesty's trumpeters, for 47 days attendance in October, November, December, at 2/- per diem to each, for riding and attending abroad.

L. C. Vol. 739, *p.* 44.

1635, *April* 30.

Warrant to swear Mr. William Lawes a musician to his Majesty in ordinary for the lutes and voices in the place of John Laurence, deceased.

L. C. Vol. 739, *p.* 58.

1635, *May* 14.

Warrant for a patent of £40 per annum to William Lawes one of his Majesty's musicians in ordinary in the place of John Laurence, deceased, to be paid quarterly and to begin at Lady day last past.

L. C. Vol. 739, *p.* 60.

1635, *May* 30.

Warrant to furnish and deliver unto John Willson, one of his Majesty's musicians in ordinary in the place of Alfonso Balles, deceased, such liveries yearly during life, and at such times as the said Alfonso Balles had enjoyed.

Also a patent of £20 per annum to the said Wilson to commence from the death of Alphonso Balles to continue during life.

L. C. Vol. 739, *p.* 62.

1635, *May* 30.

Warrant for a livery to William Lawes, musician in ordinary, in the place of John Lawrence, deceased.

L. C. Vol. 739, *p.* 62.

1635, *June* 7.

Warrant to provide livery, at the cost of £16 2s. 6d. to William Lawes, musician in ordinary to the King in the place of John Lawrence, deceased.

L. C. Vol. 150, *and L. C. Vol.* 813, *p.* 125.

1635, *June* 10.

Warrant to swear Mr. Francis de la France a musician in ordinary for the violins, to be admitted to pay upon the next avoydance upon direction from his Majesty.

L. C. Vol. 739, *p.* 63.

1635, *June* 11.

Warrant for payment of £15 to Mons. Nicholas DuVal, for a lute provided by him, to play in the consort of Mons. le Flelle, upon a certificate from Mr. Nicholas Lanier.

L. C. Vol. 739, *p.* 63.

1635, *July.*

Warrant to pay Francis de la France, sworn a violin, £50 per annum out of the privy purse, and to continue during his Majesty's pleasure.

L. C. Vol. 739, *p.* 86.

1635, *November* 18.

Bill signed for Robert Ramsey, Randall Flood, and Richard Stock, three riding trumpeters, for 92 days attendance in July, August and September, at 2s. per diem to each man.

L. C. Vol. 739, *p.* 79.

1635, *November* 18.

Warrant for the payment of £20 to Mr. John Coggeshall for strings for one year ended at Michaelmas, 1635.

L. C. Vol. 739, *p.* 81.

1635, *December.*

Warrant for payment of £26 to Mr. Edward Norgate for mending and repairing his Majesty's organs at his several houses.

L. C. Vol. 739, *p.* 88.

1635.

Petition of Mrs. Emilia Lanier against Clement Lanier. " Answered of course."

L. C. Vol. 648.

1635-6, *January* 2.

Warrant to swear Deitrick Steiffkyn, musician for the consort in ordinary, in the place of Maurice Webster, deceased.

L. C. Vol. 739, *p.* 92.

1635-6, *January* 16.

Assignment by Henry Bassano, one of his Majesty's musicians for the windy instruments, of power of attorney to Richard Clotterbooke.

L. C. Vol. 200, *p.* 39.

1635-6, *January* 18.

Warrant to pay £4 15s. to John Adson for a treble cornet and a treble recorder.

L. C. Vol. 739, *p.* 97.

1635-6, *February* 28.

Bill for Robert Ramsey, Randolph Floyd, and Richard Stock, riding trumpeters, for 52 days in October, November and December last past.

Several other entries with same names and year.

L. C. Vol. 739, *p.* 101.

1635-6, *March* 4.

Warrant for payment of £20 to Henry Lawes and William Lawes, musicians, for 2 lutes at £10 to each man, upon certificate from Mr. Lanier.

L. C. Vol. 739, *p.* 103.

1635-6, *March* 6.

Warrant to pay £9 to Davis Mell, one of his Majesty's musicians for the violins, viz. :—£6 for a violin and £3 for a sett of books.

L. C. Vol. 739, *p.* 104.

1636, *April* 1.

Warrant for the payment of £6 to Andrea Lanier, one of the musicians for the wind instruments, for 2 treble cornets for the two youthes.

L. C. Vol. 739, *p.* 106.

1636, *April* 22.

Warrant to apprehend several persons, named, for arresting Henry Russell, a drummer extraordinary.

L. C. Vol. 739, *p.* 111.

1636, *June* 20.

" Whereas Robert Taylor, one of his Majesty's musicians in ordinary hath an allowance of £40 per annum by virtue of a warrant bearing date July 11th in the second year of his Majesty's reign, wherein he is joyned with diverse other musicians, the which he is willing to resign, and petitions his Majesty to accept thereof, and to cause a new grant of the said place together with the said fee . . . unto himself and his son John Taylor."

Order thereon granting the petition.

L. C. Vol. 739, *p.* 131.

1636, *December* 2.

Warrant for livery for John Wilson, appointed musician in ordinary to the King in the place of Alphonso Bales, deceased.

L. C. Vol. 813, *p.* 134.

1636-7, *January* 6.

Warrant for the transferring of a livery fee of £16 2s. 6d., from Henry Ferrabosco, musician for the wind instruments, to John Ferrabosco.

L. C. Papers. Bundle 11.

1636-7, February 3.

Warrant to the signet, for a privy seal of £140, to be impressed unto Mr. Edward Norgate, to be employed for the altering and reparation of the organ in the Chappell at Hampton Court and for the making of a new chayre organ there conformable to those already made in the Chappells at Whitehall and Greenwich.

L. C. Vol. 739, *p.* 146.

1636-7, February 13.

Bill for Robert Ramsey, Randolph Flood and Richard Stock, riding trumpeters, for 72 days at 2s. per day.

L. C. Vol. 739, *p.* 147.

1636-7, February.

Warrant to swear James Tasker a phife extraordinary.

L. C. Vol. 739, *p.* 151.

1636-7, March 2.

Warrant to swear David Allen one of his Majesty's trumpeters, at half pay, in the place of William Smith, deceased.

Note.—Mr. Smith was murdered in my Lord Marshall's service in Germany.

L. C. Vol. 739, *p.* 152.

1636-7, March 10.

Warrant for the payment of 8d. per diem to David Allen, one of his Majesty's trumpeters in ordinary, in the place of Thomas Flood. The said fee to commence from the death of William Smith, late one of his Majesty's trumpeters.

L. C. Vol. 739, *p.* 156.

1636-7, March 10.

Whereas Thomas Flood, one of his Majesty's trumpeters in ordinary at half pay, is now upon the death of William Smith to be admitted to whole wages, it is ordered that the said whole wages commence from the death of the said William Smith.

L. C. Vol. 739, *p.* 157.

1636-7, March 10.

Warrant for the payment of £5 to Mr. Deitrick Steiffkin, a musician to his Majesty in the place of Maurice Webster, deceased, for strings for a year ended at Michaelmas, 1636.

L. C. Vol. 739, *p.* 157.

1636-7, March 13.

Warrant for the allowance of a yearly livery to David Allen, trumpeter in ordinary, in a place become voyd by the death of William Smith.

L. C. Vol. 739, *p.* 157.

[*1636-7, March* 16.]

Warrant for the payment of £5 to Maurice Webster for strings for one year ended at Michaelmas 1635. Signed 16th March, 1636-7, but dated 3rd December, 1635.

L. C. Vol. 739, *p.* 158.

1636-7, *March* 17.

Warrant for livery for David Allen, appointed trumpeter in ordinary in place of William Smith, deceased.

L. C. Vol. 813, *p.* 137.

1637, *April* 15.

Bill signed for Robert Ramsey, Randolph Flood, and Richard Stock, riding trumpeters, for 90 days attendance abroad in January, February, and March, 1636 and 1637.

L. C. Vol. 739, *p.* 168.

1637, *June* 15.

Warrant to swear Edward Ottley a drummer extraordinary to his Majesty.

L. C. Vol. 739, *p.* 180.

1637, *July.*

Petition of John Riley, sergeant trumpeter, against his fellows. " Answered."

L. C. Vol. 648.

1637, *October.*

Warrant for the payment of 8d. per diem to George Porter, one of his Majesty's trumpeters in ordinary at half pay, in a place become void by the death of John Rileigh, during his life, or until by another vacancy he shall be admitted to whole wages. To commence from the time of the death of John Rileigh, which was 19 September last past.

L. C. Vol. 739, *p.* 199.

1637, *October* 3.

Warrant to swear John Taylor a musician for the violles and voices in the place of his father, Robert Taylor, deceased.

L. C. Vol. 739, *p.* 196.

1637, *October* 15.

Warrant for the payment of 8d. per diem, being the half pay to Robert Ramsey, junior, one of his Majesty's trumpeters in ordinary in the place of David Allen deceased, from the 25th June, 1637, till the 19th September following. Further warrant for the payment of 16d. per diem to the said Robert Ramsey being whole wages from the said 19th September during his life, the same accrewing to him by the death of John Rileigh, another trumpeter, who died on the said 19th September.

L. C. Vol. 739, *p.* 199.

1637, *October* 15.

Warrant for the allowance of a yearly livery to Robert Ramsey, trumpeter in ordinary, in the place of David Allen, deceased.

The like for George Porter in the place of John Rileigh.

L. C. Vol. 739, *p.* 200.

1637, *October* 23.

Warrant to swear Robert Baker a musician for the wind instruments in the place of his father, Robert Baker, deceased.

L. C. Vol. 739, *p.* 200.

1637, *November* 6.

Warrant for livery for George Porter, the younger, appointed trumpeter in ordinary in place of John Rileigh, deceased.

L. C. Vol. 813, *p.* 145.

1637, *November* 6.

Warrant for livery and banner for Robert Ramsey, the younger, appointed trumpeter in ordinary in place of David Allen, deceased.

L. C. Vol. 813, *p.* 148.

1637, *November* 12.

Warrant for the payment of £20 to Mr. John Coggeshall, one of his Majesty's musicians, for strings for the four lutes, for one year ended at Michaelmas last past.

Note :—This is an accustomed yearly allowance.

L. C. Vol. 739, *p.* 208:

1637, *November* 14.

Warrant for payment of £5 to Deitrick Steiffkin, one of the musicians for the violl, for strings for the base violl for a year ended at Michaelmas 1637.

Note :—This hath been an anuell and accustomed allowance.

L. C. Vol. 739, *p.* 209

1637, *November* 27.

Warrant for livery for John Taylor, appointed musician in ordinary in place of his father, Robert Taylor, deceased.

L. C. Vol. 813, *p.* 146.

1637, *December* 10.

Warrant for the payment of £140 to Edward Norgate for guilding and painting the new organ at Hampton Court, and for extraordinary wages paid to joyners, carvers, and others imployed therein, as also for repairing the great organ, and for the charge of several journeys, and attendance for 6 months.

L. C. Vol. 739, *p.* 218.

1637, *December* 22.

Order to be observed throughout the year by his Majesty's musicians for the wind instruments, for waiting in the Chappell and at his Majesty's table.

Names of those to wait at the principall feasts and upon Collar dayes :—

Jerom Lanier, Clement Lanier and Anthony Bassano.

These are to waite one moneth :—

Andrea Lanier, his two boys one to wait on the tenor cornet and the other on other occasions, Henry Bassano, and William Lanier to wait for him for another place he holdeth, Alfonso Ferabosco, Henry Ferabosco, Robert Parker, Thomas Mell, Edward Bassano, not able, Thomas Blagrave is appointed to wait for him.

These are to waite the other moneth :—

Richard Blagrave, Robert Parker, John Mason, Christopher Bell, for whom, because of his infirmity Thomas Mell is appointed to wait, William Gregory, John Adson, and John Strong.

" It is ordered also that the whole company shall wayte on all the solemn feasts and Collar dayes of the year ; and if any man be sick or have an excusable cause that detaynes him, he is to procure one of his fellowes to wayte for him.   And if any of the company shall neglect to observe this order upon information and complaint made by the master of his Majesty's musicke (who is required to see the same punctually and duly observed), order shall be taken for such punishment to be inflicted on them as their negligence and contempt shall deserve."

L. C. Vol. 739, *p.* 221.

1637, *December* 30.

Warrant to swear Edward Johnson a trumpeter in ordinary in the place of Edward Juxe, deceased.   Further warrant granting him an allowance of 8d. per diem (being half wages) as trumpeter in ordinary, in a place become void by the relinquishment of George Porter, and a yearly livery.

L. C. Vol. 739, *pp.* 222 *and* 223.

1637, *December* 30.

Warrant granting an allowance of 16d. per diem to George Porter one of his Majesty's trumpeters, being admitted to full wages, upon the death of Edward Juxe.

L. C. Vol. 739, *p.* 223.

1637, *December* 30.

Warrant for payment of £10 to M. le Flael, a musician for the harp, for strings for his harp, he having had no allowance till now, and this made upon certificate of Mr. Nicholas Lanier without intention to make it a president for every year.

L. C. Vol. 739, *p.* 223.

1637, *December* 31.

Warrant for payment of £10 to Mons. Jacques Gaultier, for a treble lute for him to be used in masques; this was granted upon certificate of Mr. Nicholas Lanier.

L. C. Vol. 739, *p.* 223.

1637.

Warrant to pay £5 to Mr. Deitrick Steiftkin, one of his Majesty's musicians, for strings for the base violls for a year ended at Michaelmas, 1637.

Note :—This is an accustomed yearly allowance.

L C. Vol. 739, *p.* 219.

1637-8.

Account paid to Andrew Lanier, musician, for clothing two boys and for teaching them the science of lez flutes and cornetts.

L. C. Vol. 151.

1637-8.

To Thomas Day, two separate sums of £20 per annum, paid quarterly for keeping two singing boys.

Various accounts for liveries, banners, etc., for :—

Trumpeters.

John Rileigh (this name is crossed out)

Peter Jones	George Porter
Cuthbert Collins	William Marr
Josia Browne	Humphrey Jenkinson
Robert Ramsey	William Ramsey
Ranulph Floid	Christopher Hopkins
Richard Stock	Thomas Flood
Charles Perkins	John Smith

George Porter, junior, trumpeter in place of John Rileigh, deceased.

Robert Ramsey, trumpeter in place of David Allen, deceased.

Edward Johnson, trumpeter in place of Edward Juckes, deceased.

Musicians.

Andrea Lanier	John Lanier
Jeronimo Lanier	Edward Wormall
Clement Lanier	Angelo Notary
Nicholas Lanier	Anthony Roberts
Thomas Ford	Stephen Nawe
John Kelley	John Woodington
John Coggeshall	Henry Bassano
Robert Taylor (this name	Theophilus Lupo
is crossed out)	Giles Tompkins
Thomas Day	Nicholas Duvall
John Drew	William Lawes

Nicholas Lanier, luter
Alphonso Farrabosco, musician violin
John Wilson, musician in place of Alphonso Bales, deceased.
John Taylor, musician in place of Robert Taylor, deceased.
Henry Farabosco and John Farrabosco, musicians for the windy instruments.
Henry Lawes, musician for the lutes and voices.

L. C. Vol. 151.

1637-8, *January* 3.

Warrant for a new year's gift to Francis de la France, such as the musicians have.

L. C. Vol. 739, *p.* 224.

1637-8, *January* 19.

Councelles warrant for payment of £22 15s. to the musicians for the violins, for waiting at St. Georges Feast last, 7 days, being 13 in number, to Thomas Warren.

L. C. Vol. 739, *p.* 226.

1637-8, *January* 20.

Warrant for livery and banner for Edward Johnson, appointed trumpeter in ordinary in place of Edward Juxe, deceased.

L. C. Vol. 813, *p.* 149.

1637-8, *January* 31.

Warrant for the payment of £12 to Mr. John Woodington, for a Cremona violin, to play to the organ, upon the certificate of Mr. Nicholas Lanier.

L. C. Vol. 739, *p.* 228.

1637-8, *February* 1.

Petition of Nicholas Bowman against Henry Bassano, debt of £3 10s. 4d. "Answered of course."

L. C. Vol. 648.

1637-8, *March* 14.

Warrant for the payment of £12 to Mr. Francis de la France, one of his Majesty's musicians for the violins, for a treble violin bought by him for his Majesty's service.

L. C. Vol. 739, *p.* 235.

1638, *April* 3.

Warrant to Mr. Edward Norgate, keeper of his Majesty's organs and other musical instruments, to repayre to Richmond and upon view of the decayed organ there to cause the same to be repayred and made serviceable. In case it be not reparable, another organ is to be made in the same place for the service of his highness the prince with such stops and registers as are necessary. And that he cause the organ at St. James' to be repayred and put in order for service.

L. C. Vol. 739, *p.* 242.

1638, *April* 20.

Bill for Robert Ramsey, Randolph Flood and Richard Stone, riding trumpeters, for an allowance of 2s. per day to each of them, for 60 days attendance from October to March last; which bill is allowed by virtue of a privy seal dormant, dated 21 May, 1625.

L. C. Vol. 739, *p.* 244.

1638, *May* 29.

Warrant (grounded upon the privy seal) for payment of £46 14s. to Mr. Edward Norgate for mending and repairing organs in his Majesty's several houses.

L. C. Vol. 739, *p.* 258.

1638, *June* 7.

Warrant for a sea livery for John Smith, one of his Majesty's trumpeters appointed to go to sea in his Majesty's great ship called the Souveraigne, and for his man.

L. C. Vol. 739, *p.* 260.

1638, *June* 20.

Warrant to swear Robert Strong a musician to his Majesty for the wind instruments, who is to wayte and serve upon the double sackbutt and among the violins, in the room and absence of Robert Parker who through infirmities incident to old age is almost past service.

L. C. Vol. 739, *p.* 265.

1638, *September* 16.

Warrant to swear Simon Nau a musician for the violins in ordinary, in the place of John Heydon, deceased.

L. C. Vol. 739, *p.* 270.

Accounts ending Michaelmas, 1638.

Accounts for liveries for :—

Trumpeters.

Peter Jones	Humphrey Jenkinson
Cuthbert Collins	William Ramsey
Josias Broome	Christopher Hopkins
Robert Ramsey	Thomas Flood
Ranulph Floid	John Smith
Richard Stocke	David Allen
Charles Perkins	George Porter, junior
George Porter	Robert Ramsey
William Marr	Edward Johnson in place
	of Edward Juckes, deceased

Nicholas Lanier, luter

Musicians.

Andrea Lanier	Anthony Roberts
Jeromino Lanier	Stephen Nawe
Clement Lanier	John Woodington
Nicholas Lanier	Henry Bassano
Thomas Ford	Theophilus Lupo
John Kelley	Giles Tompkins
John Coggeshall	Nicholas Duuall
Thomas Day	William Lawes
John Drewe	John Wilson
John Lanier	John Taylor
Edward Wormall	Henry Farrabosco
Angelo Notary	

Alphonso Farrabosco, musician violin.

John Farrabosco, musician for the windy instruments.

Henry Lawes, musician for the lutes and voices in place of Robert Marsh, deceased.

Andrea Lanier, musician, for apparel for two boys kept and instructed by him " in the science of lez flutes and cornetts."

Account of two sums of £20 per annum paid quarterly to Thomas Day, musician, for two boys kept and taught singing by him, for the service of the King.

L. C. Vol. 52.

Michaelmas, 1638, to Michaelmas, 1639.

Certificate of livery to Angelo Notary, musician.

L. C. Papers, Bundle 1.

1638, *October* 17.

Warrant to swear Thomas Blagrave a musician to his Majesty for the sagbutts and hautboyes, who is also to attend as assistant to his father Richard Blagrave, to come in ordinary in the same place upon vacancy thereof.

L. C. Vol. 739, p. 275.

1638, *November* 18.

Warrant to swear Thomas Creswell trumpeter to his Majesty in ordinary, at half pay, until another avoydance and is now admitted in a place become void by the death of Thomas Flood. Order for the allowance of a yearly livery, dated November 21.

L. C. Vol. 739, p. 283.

1638, *November* 19.

Warrant for the swearing of Francis Smith and John Hixon musicians for the wind instruments :—

Whereas upon the death of Edward Bassano late one of his Majesty's musicians for the wind instruments, his Majesty is graciously pleased that Francis Smith and John Hixon, two young men who have hitherto been bred in that quality at his Majesty's charge, shall for their present mayntenance have the benefit of the said place between them until another vacancy, when they shall both be established in whole places.

L. C. Vol. 739, p. 285.

1638, *November* 21.

Warrant to admit Edward Johnson, trumpeter in ordinary at half wages, to whole wages, being 1s. 4d. per diem, upon the decease of Thomas Lloyd.

L. C. Vol. 739, p. 284.

1638, *December* 12.

Warrant to pay Simon Nau 1s. 8d. per diem as wages and £16 2s. 6d. per annum for livery, as one of his Majesty's musicians for the violins in ordinary, in the room of John Haydon, deceased.

L. C. Vol. 739, p. 293.

1638, *December* 14.

Warrant for the payment of £20 to John Cogshall for strings for his Majesty's lutes for a year ended at Michaelmas last.

L. C. Vol. 739, p. 292.

1638-9, *January* 17.

Warrant for the payment of 1s. 8d. per diem as wages and £16 2s. 6d. for livery, to Francis Smith, one of his Majesty's musicians for the wind instruments in ordinary, and John Hixon between them, as musicians in the place of Edward Bassano, deceased, the said half wages to continue till some other vacancy occur and they be admitted to whole places.

L. C. Vol. 739, p. 297.

1638-9, *January* 21.

Warrant for payment of £212 10s. to Mr. Edward Norgate : for a new organ made and set up at Richmond £120, for carved figures about the gallery of that organ £35, for new gilding and painting the organ at Hampton Court £30, for carved work about the organ loft there, and repayring the old organ £7, for repairing the organ at Whitehall £5 10s. For several journeys to Richmond and portage of utensills, attendance, and other expenses for eight months ending in November, 1638, £15.

L. C. Vol. 739, p. 299.

1638-9, *February* 5.

Warrant for livery and banner for Thomas Creswell, appointed trumpeter in ordinary in place of Thomas Lloyd, deceased.

L. C. Vol. 813, p. 165.

1638-9, *February* 28.

Memorandum of assignment by John Taylor, one of his Majesty's musicians, of £6 10s. of lawful english money, to Christopher Mathews.

L. C. Vol. 200, p. 75.

1638-9, *March* 15.

Warrant to Cuthbert Collins to make 20 brass trumpets for his Majesty's service into the northern parts.

L. C. Vol. 739, p. 321.

1639, *June* 20.

Bill signed for Robert Ramsey, Randolph Flood and Richard Stock, riding trumpeters, for 64 days' attendance abroad.

L. C. Vol. 739, p. 332.

1639, *October* 29.

Whereas his Majesty's musicians for the violins, being 15 in number, were commanded to attend his Majesty at Windsor this last St. George's feast, and for that purpose were at extraordinary charges for themselves and their horses, by the space of 7 days, they therefore pray the usual allowance of 5s. a day to each man, amounting to the sum of £26 5s.

Order thereon to pay the above sum to Thomas Warren for himself and his fellow musicians.

L. C. Vol. 739, *p.* 344.

1639-40, *January* 12.

Whereas Andrea Lanier, one of his Majesty's musicians for the wind instruments, hath long since received Order from his Majesty for the trayning and breeding up of two boyes or youthes in the quality of musique, for which his Majesty was pleased to settle upon him a competent intertainment to be had in the exchequer and great Wardrobe. Forasmuch as I understand that some question is made of the payment of what is settled by his Majesty to that purpose, because the two boyes he lately had, named John Hixon and Francis Smith, are, because enabled, preferred to his Majesty's service, these are to certify that in their room I have appointed two others to be bred by him in musique, namely William Lanier and Thomas Lanier.

L. C. Vol. 739, *p.* 364.

1639-40, *January* 28.

Bill signed for Robert Ramsey, Randolphe Flood and Richard Stock, riding trumpeters, for allowance of 2s. a day for waiting abroad 41 days in August and September, 1639.

L. C. Vol. 739, *p.* 366.

1639-40, *February* 11 & 13.

Warrant to swear Ambrose Beeland a musician to his Majesty for the violins in ordinary, in the place of James Johnson, deceased. Also for the payment of 1s. 8d. per diem · as wages and £16 2s. 6d. yearly for a livery allowance.

L. C. Vol. 739, *p.* 373.

1639-40, *February* 13.

Certificate for Ambrose Beeland expressing these privileges, that he may not be arrested and not to be chosen into any Office nor warned to attend at assizes nor be impanelled on juries, not to be charged with any contributions, taxes or payments but in Court only as other of his Majesty's servants. To be free from watching and warding in regard of his nightly and late attendance at Court.

L. C. Vol. 739, *p.* 374.

1639-40, *February* 24.

Warrant for a privy seal of £60 to be paid to Cuthbert Collins, his Majesty's trumpeter, for 20 trumpets made by him for his Majesty's service in the northern expedition.

L. C. Vol. 739, *p.* 375.

1640, *April* 21.

Warrant to swear William Kent a trumpeter to his Majesty, extraordinary, recommended by Sir John Pennington.

L. C. Vol. 739, *p.* 390.

1640, *May* 17 *and* 18.

Warrant to swear Robert Strong a musician for the wind instruments in ordinary in the place of Robert Parker, deceased. Also for 1s. 8d. per diem wages, and for £16 2s. 6d. as a yearly allowance for livery.

L. C. Vol. 739, *p.* 396 *and p.* 397.

1640, *July* 6 *and* 7.

Warrant to swear William Lanier one of his Majesty's musicians for the wind instruments in ordinary in the room of John Adson, deceased. Also a patent to grant him a fee of 1s. 8d. per diem, and £16 2s. 6d. allowance yearly for a livery.

L. C. Vol. 739, *p.* 408.

Accounts ending Michaelmas, 1640.

Accounts for liveries for :—

Trumpeters.

Peter Jones	Humphrey Jenkinson
Cuthbert Collins	William Ramsey
Josias Broome	Christopher Hopkins
Robert Ramsey	John Smith
Ranulph Floid	George Porter
Richard Stocke	Robert Ramsey
Charles Perkins	Edward Johnson
George Porter	Thomas Cresswell
William Marr	
Nicholas Lanier, luter	

Musicians.

Nicholas Lanier, master of the music	Anthony Roberts
	Stephen Naw
Andrea Lanier	John Woodington
Jeromino Lanier	Alphonso Farrabosco
Clement Lanier	Theophilus Lupo
Thomas Ford	John Farrabosco

John Kelley   Henry Lawes
John Coggeshall   William Lawes
Thomas Day   John Wilson
John Drewe   Henry Farrabosco
Edward Wormall

Account for two sums of £20 per annum paid quarterly to Thomas Day, musician, for two boys kept and taught singing by him, for the service of the King.

L. C. Vol. 53.

Michaelmas, 1640, *to Michaelmas,* 1641.

To Andrea Lanier for apparelling two singing boyes and training them up in musique, £59 13s. 4d.

To Thomas Day for teaching and apparelling two singing boyes, £40.

L. C. Papers. Bundle 1.

Michaelmas, 1640, *to Michaelmas,* 1641.

Accounts payable to the following [musicians] :—
Nicholas Lanier, £32 5s.

Andrea Lanier   John Coggeshall
Jerome Lanier   Henry Bassano
Alphonso Ferrabosco   John Drew
Angelo Notary   John Taylor
Henry Ferrabosco   Theophilus Lupo
Clement Lanier   John Kelly
John Lanier   John Ferrabosco
Anthony Roberts   Thomas Day
Nicholas Duval   Giles Tomkins
John Woodington   Thomas Ford
Daniel Farrant   Henry Lawes
Edward Wormall.   William Lawes
Stephen Nawe   John Wilson

£16 2s. 6d. apiece.

L. C. Papers. Bundle 1.

1640, *October* 30.

Warrant for the payment of £20 to John Coggeshall, one of his Majesty's musicians for the lutes, for strings for his Majesty's four lutes in his custody, for a year ended at Michaelmas, 1640, this being an annual allowance.

L. C. Vol. 739, *p.* 421.

1640, *November* 10.

Bill for the riding trumpeters, Robert Ramsey, Randolph Flood and Richard Stock, for 92 days' attendance from July to September, 1640, at 2s. per diem to each man.

L. C. Vol. 739, *p.* 422.

1640-1, *January* 1.

Warrant for the payment of a New Year's gift to William Lanier, one of his Majesty's musicians for the wind instrument in the place of John Adson. A like warrant for Robert Strong in the place of Robert Parker.

L. C. Vol. 739, *p.* 428.

1640-1, *January* 28.

Warrant for the payment of £25 12s. to Mr. Edward Norgate, keeper of his Majesty's organs, for reparacions of his organs at Whitehall, Greenwich and Hampton Court, for one year ended at Christmas, 1640.

L. C. Vol. 739, *p.* 434.

1641, *May* 2.

Assignment by Daniel Farrant of his livery £16 2s. 6d. to Daniel Giles.

Witness—Alphonso Ferrabosco.

L. C. Vol. 200, *p.* 87.

Michaelmas, 1641 [*to* 1642]. *Torn.*

Accounts for liveries of £16 2s. 6d. to each of the following musicians :—

Andrea Lanier	John Coggeshall
Jerome Lanier	Henry Bassano
Alphonso Ferrabasco	John Drew
Angelo Notary	John Taylor
Henry Ferrabasco	Theophilus Lupo
Clement Lanier	John Kelly
John Lanier	John Ferrabasco
Anthony Roberts	Thomas Day
Nicholas Duvall	Giles Tomkins
John Woodington	Thomas Ford
Daniell Farrant	Henry Lawes
Edward Wormall	William Lawes
Stephen Nawe	John Wilson

To Nicholas Lanier, £32 0s. 0d.

L. C. Papers. Bundle 1.

Michaelmas, 1641, *to Lady-Day,* 1642.

[Accounts paid or due to various officers of the King's household.] To each of the following trumpeters, £19 17s. 8d.

Josias Broome	Cuthbert Collins
Robert Ramsey, senior	Serles Perkins
Robert Ramsey, junior	Peter Jones

Randall Lloyd	Humphrey Jenkinson
Richard Stocke	William Marre
George Porter, senior	Edward Johnson
Christopher Hopkins	Thomas Creswell
John Smith	William Ramsey
George Porter, junior	

L. C. Papers. Bundle 1.

1641, *November* 8.

Richard Dorney admitted a musician in his father's place upon the following petition to the Earl of Essex, Lord Chamberlain :—

The humble petition of Margaret Dorney, widow of Richard Dorney, late one of his Majesty's musicians for the violins in ordinary, shewing that her said husband, for the support of the petitioner and six small children, did, in his long time of sickness, procure his Majesty's gracious promise, together with your noble predecessor's, that his sonne, Richard Dorney, should be admitted into his father's place, which all the rest of his fellow servants did well approve of, forasmuch as he was an ancient servant to his Majesty, and was seven months in Spain with his Majesty, he leaving no maintenance for the petitioner and his children but the hopes of his place for their livelyhood.

This petition was signed and approved of by the following violins :—

Estienne Nau	Thomas Warren
John Hopper	Ambrose Biland
Nicholas Picart	Davis Mell
Simon Nau	

Followed by a certificate signed by Essex for the swearing of the said Richard Dorney as musician for the violins as soon as he shall become fit for the place, he being at present in his minority, and not capable of taking the necessary oath. In the meantime his place is to be filled by some able man. Dated November 3, 1641.

L. C. Vol. 740, *p.* 3.

1641, *November* 11.

Warrant for the payment of 1s. 8d. per diem as wages, and £16 2s. 6d. per annum as livery to Richard Dorney, one of his Majesty's musicians for the violins in ordinary, in the place of his father, Richard Dorney, deceased.

L. C. Vol. 740.

1641, *December* 1.

Warrant for the swearing of Mr. John Mercure a musician to his Majesty for the lutes and voices in ordinary, in the place of Robert Dowland, deceased.

L. C. Vol. 740, *p.* 4.

1641, *December* 2.

Warrant for the swearing of Nicholas Cooke a musician for the lutes and voices extraordinary, to come in ordinary and fee upon the first avoydance that shall happen amongst that company.

L. C. Vol. 740, *p.* 4.

1641, *December* 3.

Warrant issued on January 18, 1641-2, for the swearing of George Hudson a musician to his Majesty for the lutes and voices extraordinary, December 3, 1641.

L. C. Vol. 740, *p.* 5.

1641, *December* 10.

Warrant for the payment of 1s. 8d. per diem as wages, and £16 2s. 6d. per annum as livery, to John Mercure, one of his Majesty's musicians for the lutes in ordinary, in the place of Robert Dowland, deceased.

L. C. Vol. 740.

1641, *December* 10.

Warrant for the payment of 1s. 8d. per diem as wages, and £16 2s. 6d. per annum as livery to John Strong, one of his Majesty's musicians for the wind instruments, in the place of John Snowsman, deceased.

L. C. Vol. 740.

1641, *December* 16.

Warrant for swearing William Porter a trumpeter to his Majesty extraordinary, to come in ordinary and fee upon the first avoydance.

L. C. Vol. 740, *p.* 4.

1641. (*Covering date of Volume.*)

List of Trumpettors.

Josias Broome, sergeant trumpeter
Robert Ramsey
Randolph Flood [crossed out and "dead" written against this].
John Smith
Richard Stocke
George Porter

Serles Perkins
Peter Jones
Edward Johnson
Cuthbert Collins
Humphrey Jenkins
William Ramsey
Robert Ramsey, junior.
George Porter, junior.
Christopher Hopkins
William Marre
Thomas Creswell, at half pay
William Hopkins, in Randolph Flood's place, to be
    in half pay.
William Porter, extraordinary, next in reversion
William Kent, extraordinary.

Drummes and Phife.
William Allen, drum major

John Rudd	Peter Puliard
Jeremy Crews	Henry Puliard

Jeoffry Cruise, phife
James Tasker, phife extraordinary
Henry Russell and Edmund Cooper, drummes extra-
    ordinary

L. C. Vol. 476.

1641. (*Covering date of Volume.*)
    List of his Majesty's musicians :—
        Nicholas Lanier, Master of the Musique
            For the wind Instruments.

Jerom Lanier	William Gregory
Clement Lanier	Christopher Bell
Andrea Lanier	John Mason
Alphonso Ferabosco	Robert Strong
Henry Ferabosco	John Strong
Henry Bassano	William Lanier
Anthony Bassano	Thomas Mell
Francis Smith	Peter Guy, alias Piero
John Hixon	Robert Baker

Richard Blagrave [the word " dead " written and " Thomas
his son, in reversion now admitted, February, 1641," inserted]
            For the violins.

Thomas Warren	John Woodington
Thomas Lupo	Ambrose Beeland
Richard Comer	Davies Mell

Simon Nau
John Hopper
Estienne Nau, composer
Nicholas Picart

Richard Dorney
Theophilus Lupo
Nathaniell Hobson,
     (extraordinary)

For Lutes, Violls and Voices.

Thomas Foord
Thomas Day
John Drew
John Coggeshall
John Lanier
John Taylor
Edward Wormall
John Kelly
Anthony Roberts
Nicholas Duvall
Giles Tomkins
William Lawes
Henry Lawes

John Wilson
Phillip Squire
Lewes Evans
John Friend
Timothy Collins
Deitricht Steiffkyn
Daniel Farrant
John Mercure
Robert Tomkins
Nicholas Cook, next
     in reversion, George
     Hudson next to him.

For the Harp.
Mr. Le Flelle.

Organ keeper and tuner.
Edward Norgate.

For the virginall.
Mr. Warwick.

Musical Instrument Maker.
George Gill.

William Allaby, a musician extraordinary and stringer of the lutes.

L. C. Vol. 476.

1641-2, *January* 1.

Warrant to the Jewel house for such New Year's gifts to be paid to John Mercure, John Strong and Richard Dorney, musicians to his Majesty, as had been enjoyed by their predecessors.

L. C. Vol. 740.

1641-2, *January* 3.

Warrant for the payment of £30 yearly to Simon Hopper, musician to his Majesty for the violins, in the room of Richard Dorney, deceased.

L. C. Vol. 740.

1641-2, *January* 17.

Warrant for the payment of 1s. 8d. per diem as wages and £16 2s. 6d. per annum as livery to Thomas Blagrave, one of his Majesty's musicians for the wind instruments in ordinary, in the place of his father Richard Blagrave.

L. C. Vol. 740.

1641-2, *February* 24.

Warrant for swearing Mr. Thomas Lowe a gentleman of his Majesty's Chappell in ordinary, in the place of Richard Boughton, deceased.

L. C. Vol. 740, *p.* 6.

1641-2, *March* 17.

Warrant to swear William Hopkins a trumpeter to his Majesty in ordinary, in the room of Randolph Flood, resigned.

L. C. Vol. 740, *p.* 7.

1642, *April* 1.

Warrant for the allowance of a yearly livery to William Hopkins, one of his Majesty's trumpeters in ordinary, in place of Randolph Flood, deceased.

L. C. Vol. 740.

1642, *April* 1.

Warrant for the payment of 8d. per diem (being half wages) to William Hopkins, one of his Majesty's trumpeters in ordinary, in a place become void by the resignation of Thomas Cresswell, to enjoy the said fee until he shall be admitted to whole wages upon the next vacancy.

L. C. Vol. 740.

1642, *April* 1.

Thomas Cresswell, one of his Majesty's trumpeters in ordinary at half wages, admitted, upon the death of Randolph Flood, to whole wages, being 1s. 4d. per diem.

L. C. Vol. 740.

1642, *April* 19.

Warrant for livery for William Hopkins, appointed trumpeter in the place of Randolph Flood, deceased.

L. C. Vol. 813, *p.* 272.

1643, *November* 25.

Warrant to swear Mr. William Howes a gentleman of his Majesty's Chappell Royall in ordinary, in the place of Mr. West, deceased, and to enjoy all wages, fees, allowances and profits thereto belonging.

L. C. Vol. 740, *p.* 12.

1643-4, *January* 12.

Warrant to swear Mr. Francis Hull a gentleman of his Majesty's Chappell Royall in ordinary, in the place become void by the death of Beck, to enjoy the full entertainment, fees and profitts to the place belonging.

L. C. Vol. 740, *p.* 13.

1660.

Captain Cooke appointed a base in Mons. Du Vall's place.

L. C. Vol. 477.

1660, *June* 9.

Charles Evans appointed harper.

L. C. Vols. 180 *and* 477 ; *see also Vol.* 482, *p.* 54.

1660, *June* 9.

Arthur Norgate, a patent.

Master of the organs and virginalls, a patent to young Norgate. [This entry is crossed out.]

L. C. Vol. 477.

1660, *June* 9.

Giles Tomkins, appointed a virginall player in the place of Richard Deering.

L. C. Vol. 477.

1660, *June* 11.

William Wing appointed musician upon the violl in the private musick in the place of Mr. Timothy Collins, deceased.

L. C. Vol. 180 ; *L. C. Vol.* 477.

1660, *June* 11.

Appointment as trumpeters in ordinary of the four Dutchmen :—

    Benigne le Ragois

    Nicholas Caperon [at pension, and Christmas in his place]

    Melque Goldt [at pension and Thompson in his place]

    Hugh Fitchert

    and of Symon Beale, William Hopkins and Sylvester Whitmeale.

L. C. Vol. 477 *and Vols.* 479, *p.* 105 ; 482, *p.* 61.

1660, *June* 11.

Appointment of Gervace Price as yeoman of the bowes and gunnes and sergeant trumpeter.

L. C. Vol. 477 *and Vols.* 479, *p.* 105 ; *and* 482. *p.* 61.

1660, *June* 16.

Musitians of the private Musick.

Dr. Coleman appointed for the viall, among the lutes and voices in Mr. Thomas Ford's place.

Mr. Henry Lawes composer in the private musick for lutes and voices in Mr. Thomas Ford's place.

Mr. John Smith in the place of John Taylor, a viol.

Davis Mell, a violin, his own place and in Woodington's place, for the broken consort also.

Humphrey Madge a violin in Theophilus Lupo's place.

William Gregory in the place of Daniel Farrant, private, a viol.

Richard Hudson, a violin in Symon Nau's place.

George Hudson, in Mr. Noe's place for violin.

Harding, in Mr. Wormewell's place, a viol.

Thomas Blagrave, in Peter Piers' place, to performe in the violins.

Richard Dorney, in his father's place for a violin.

Henry Comer, in Richard Comer's place for a violin.

Child, in Forobosco's place, Alphonso's, composer of wind musick.

Mr. Jenkins for the lute, in Mr. John Cockshall's place.

Phillip Beckett, in Lupoe's place, Thomas Lupo, for a violin.

John Rogers, lutinist, in the place of Gaultier.

Mathew Lock composer in the private musick in the place of John Coperario.

L. C. Vol. 477 *; see also Vol.* 180.

1660, *June* 18.

Appointment of John Strong, one of the violins in ordinary, in the place of Nicholas Pickard (also " Picard ") and of Robert Strong in the place of Thomas Warren, deceased.

L. C. Vols. 180 *and* 477.

1660, *June* 20.

William Howes, appointed musician upon the violins in the place of Robert Dowland. Edward Strong, one of the violins in ordinary in the place of John Hopper, deceased.

Robert Deering, one of the virginall players in the place of Richard Deering, deceased.

L. C. Vols. 180 *and* 477.

1660, *June* 20. ·
John Mawgridg appointed drum-major.

L. C. Vols. 477 ; 478 *p.* 89; *and* 482, *p.* 65.

1660, *June* 20.
John Barteeske appointed kettledrummer.

L. C. Vol. 477.

1660, *June* 21.
Jeremy Crewes admitted drummer in ordinary to his Majesty, in the place of Robert Tedder, deceased.

L. C. Vol. 180. *See also Vol.* 482, *p.* 65.

1660, *June* 23.
John Hingeston appointed for a viol, in place of Alphonso Forobosco.

L. C. Vol. 477.

1660, *June* 29.
Henry Cooke, appointed master of the boyes in the private musick.

L. C. Vol. 477.

1660, *July* 2.
John Hingeston, tuner and repairer of organs, virginalls, and wind instruments, in the place of Arthur Norgate.
Robert Blagrave, musician in ordinary.

L. C. Vols. 180 *and* 477.

1660, *July* 10.
Appointment of Humphrey Madge as one of the cornetts and flutes in ordinary, in the place of Jerome Lanier, deceased.

L. C. Vols. 180 *and* 477 ; *L. C. Vol.* 479, *p.* 102.

1660, *July* 12.
Appointment of Edward Strong, one of the wind instruments upon the treble hoboy in ordinary, in the place of Francis Smith, deceased.

L. C. Vols. 180 *and* 477 ; *L. C. Vol.* 479, *p.* 102.

1660, *July* 13.
Andrea Lanier appointed musician upon the flute in ordinary, also admitted musician in ordinary for the education of two boys in musick, for the flute and cornett.

L. C. Vols. 180 *and* 477.

1660, *July* 14.
Stephen Nau appointed musician upon the lute, in the place of Monsieur Mercuer (Mercure), deceased.

L. C. Vols. 180 *and* 477.

1660, *July* 20.

Edw. Ottley appointed drummer [with the note added " dead "].

L. C. Vol. 482, *p.* 65.

1660, *July* 20.

Tertullian Lewis appointed drummer.

L. C. Vols. 478, *p.* 89, *and* 482, *p.* 65.

1660, *August* 9.

Stafford Darcy appointed a tenor in his Majesty's private vocal musick.

L. C. Vols. 180 *and* 477.

1660, *August* 13.

William Anlaby appointed musician in ordinary.

L. C. Vols. 180 *and* 477.

1660, *August* 20.

William Hopkins admitted trumpeter in ordinary to his Majesty.

L. C. Vol. 180.

1660, *August* 28.

Nicholas Lanier appointed master of his Majesty's musick.

L. C. Vols. 180 *and* 477.

1660, *September* 12.

Symon Hopper appointed violin to his Majesty for his practise of dancing, in the place of Richard Darney.

L. C. Vols. 180 *and* 477.

1660, *September* 13.

Warrant to admit the following musicians :—John Hingeston in the place of Alphonso Ferabasco, William Wing in the place of Timothy Collins, William Gregory in the place of Daniel Farrant, deceased.

L. C. Vols. 741, *p.* 243, *and* 180.

1660, *September* 20.

Thomas Sculthorpe appointed trumpeter in ordinary.

L. C. Vols. 479, *p.* 105, *and* 482, *p.* 61.

1660, *September* 27.

Warrant to prepare a mace for the sergeant trumpeter.

L. C. Vol. 180.

Michaelmas, 1660 *to Michaelmas,* 1661.

Bill of Henry Cooke, master of the children of the Chapel, for shoes and gloves provided by him for the said children.

L. C. Papers, Bundle 21.

Michaelmas, 1660 to Michaelmas, 1672.

Quarterly payments of £10 each paid to Henry Cooke, musician to the King, for keeping and teaching two singing boys, Michaelmas, 1660 to 1672.

> L. C. Vol. 460, *folios* 19, 26, 31, 35, 35d, 12b, 17bd, 20b, 37b, 8c, 9cd, 17cd, 19cd, 21c, 33cd ; L. C. Vol. 461, *folios* 5, 17, 18, 22, 5b, 16b, 17b, 21b, 5c, 15c, 16c, 20c, 18d, 19d, 23d ; L. C. Vol. 462 (4 *entries not paged*), *folios* 5, 15, 17, 21, 5b, 17b, 19b ; L. C. Vol. 463, *folios* 5, 16, 18, 23 [*receipt signed by Mary Cooke*].

1660 to 1661, Michaelmas.

Allowance paid to Henry Cooke, master of the boys of the King's Chapel for the keep of two boys and for teaching them.

> L. C. Vol. 152.

1660, October 3.

Warrant to provide mourning coats and cloaks for 16 trumpeters.

> L. C. Vol. 817, *p.* 53.

1660, October 3.

Thomas Sculthorpe and Millibert Meurs admitted as two of his Majesty's trumpeters in ordinary. [This entry crossed out.]

> L. C. Vol. 180.

1660, October 16.

Warrant for wages of 1s. 8d. per diem, and £16 2s. 6d. yearly as livery, to Theophilus Fitz, musician for the violin to his Majesty.

> L. C. Vols. 180 *and* 477 ; Vol. 741, *p.* 246.

1660, November 9.

Warrant to admit the following musicians to his Majesty's private musick in ordinary :—

Henry Cooke in the place of Mons. DuVall for a lute and voyce, £60 per annum, and £20 per annum for strings. Also £24 per annum for breeding a boy for vocall musick which Thomas Day lately enjoyed.

John Rogers in the place of James Gwaltier for a lute, £100 per annum.

Henry Hawes in the broken consort, in the place of Robert Tomkins, formerly belonging to Robert Kinnersley, for a violl, 1s. 8d. per diem and £16 2s. 6d. for livery.

John Harding in the place of Edward Wormwell for a voyce.

John Lilly in the place of John Kelly for a theorboe.

Edward Colman in the place of John Lanier for a voyce.

Alphonso Marsh in the place of Thomas Day for a voyce.

Gregory Thorndell in the place of John Drew for a voyce.

Thomas Bates in the place of Henry Ferabasco for a violl.

William Child in the place of Alphonso Ferabasco.

Nathaniel Watkins in the place of John Fox for a voyce.

John Smyth in the place of John Taylor for a violl.

John Clement in the place of William Lawes for a voyce or theorboe.

Mathew Lock composer in the place of John Coperario which place surrendered by Alphonso Ferabasco and late enjoyed by Henry Ferabasco, deceased.

To each of them £40 per annum, which with all payments above mentioned to be paid quarterly.

L. C. Vols. 180 *and* 477 ; *L. C. Vol.* 741, *p.* 244

1660, *November* 12.

Order for a warrant for the allowance of a yearly livery to Henry Lawes, admitted composer of his Majesty's private musick for lutes and voices in ordinary, in the place of Thomas Ford, deceased.

L. C. Vol. 181, *p.* 39 ; *L. C. Vol.* 741, *p.* 244.

[This entry is crossed out and " vacatur " written against it].

See also Vol. 741, *p.* 9. *L. C. Papers, Bundle* 76.

1660, *November* 15.

Warrant to admit Thomas Lanier as musician upon the flutes and cornetts, or some other musicall part amongst the lutes and voyces in ordinary, in the place of Andrea Lanier, deceased, with the allowances of 1s. 8d. per diem, £7 11s. 8d. yearly for board wages, and £29 9s. 2d. yearly for apparrell ; also one other 1s. 8d. per diem and £16 2s. 6d. yearly for his livery, all of which payments are to be paid quarterly.

L. C. Vol. 741, *p.* 245.

1660, *November* 17.

Warrant to admit Christopher Gibbons musician upon the virginalls, in the place of Thomas Warwick, deceased, with the yearly wages of £86 to be paid quarterly.

L. C. Vol. 477 ; *L. C. Vol.* 741, *p.* 245.

1660, *November* 18.

Order for a warrant for the allowance of a yearly livery to William Child, musician in ordinary to his Majesty, in place of Alphonso Ferabosco, deceased.

L. C. Vol. 181, *p.* 3. *L. C. Papers, Bundle* 76.

1660, *November* 20.

Warrant to deliver to William Child, who is appointed musician in place of Alphonso Ferabosco, deceased, the following materials for his livery :—

" Fourteen yards of chamblett for a gowne, 3 yards of black velvet to gare the same gown, one furre of Budge for the same price £4, 8 yards of damask for a jaquet and three yards of velvet for a doublet."

The above to be delivered to him yearly at every Feast of St. Andrew during his life ; the making also to be paid for out of the Great Wardrobe.

L. C. Vol. 814, *p.* 13.

1660, *November* 28.

Warrant to provide a mourning livery for Gervase Price, sergeant trumpeter in ordinary to his Majesty.

L. C. Vol. 817, *p.* 67.

1660, *November* 28.

Bill of £147 4s. for 64 surplices for the gentlemen of the Chappell at £2 6s. each.

L. C. Papers, bundle 15.

1660, *St. Andrew.*

Payment of £59 13s. 4d. to Thomas Lanier, executor to Andrea Lanier, deceased, late musician to the King, for keeping and teaching two boys. Receipt signed by Thomas Lanier.

L. C. Vol. 460, *p.* 15*d.*

1660, *St. Andrew.*

Payment of £16 2s. 6d. to each of the following of the King's musicians for their liveries :—

Henry Lawes	John Hingeston
Davis Mell	Charles Coleman, senr.
Angelo Notary	Stephen Strong
Nicholas Lanier, master	Henry Bassano
of the music	Humphrey Madge
Nicholas Lanier, luter	William Gregory
Giles Tompkins	Thomas Lanier
Edward Coleman	Anthony Roberts
George Thornedell	John Jenkins
Henry Cooke	John Lillie
George Hudson	John Harding
John Willson	Alphonso Marsh
Mathew Locke	John Gamble
John Smith	Thomas Bates
William Child	John Clement

John Bannister [crossed out, with " vacatur" written against his name].

L. C. Vol. 460.

1660, *November* 30.

Millibert Meurs and John Jones appointed trumpeters in ordinary.

L. C. Vols. 479, *p.* 105, *and* 482, *p.* 61.

1660, *December* 3.

Warrant to provide three score and four surplices of fine holland cloth for the Gentlemen of the Chappell and twelve surplices for the musicians and thirty-four surplices of the like fine holland cloth for the children of the Chappell.

L. C. Vol. 802, *p.* 5.

1660, *December* 5.

Warrant to deliver to Gervace Price, sergeant trumpeter, the mace provided for him.

L. C. Vol. 741, *p.* 111.

1660 (?), *December* 14.

Warrant for the allowance of a livery for James Sweet, a child of the Chappel whose voice is changed ; to be delivered to Dr. Blow, master of his Majesty's music.

L. C. Papers, Bundle 12.

1660, *December* 20.

Warrant to pay John Hingston a bill of £116 18s.

L. C. Vol. 741, *p.* 63.

1660, *December* 31.

Warrant to pay Gervace Price, sergeant trumpeter, £40, being the charges for himself and eight trumpeters for their journey to Portsmouth.

L. C. Vol. 741, *p.* 64.

[1660.]

Warrant for scarlet cloth to be provided for the coronation of King Charles the Second.

"Two yards apiece of scarlet cloth for 12 children of the Chapel.

Four yards apiece of scarlet cloth for 8 of the wind music.

For 4 composers of music 5 yards each of scarlet cloth and for 24 violins each 4 yards of the same cloth."

L. C. Papers, bundle 20.

1660.

Mr. Gybbons approved of by the King at Baynards Castle ; and an organ to be made for him. For the virginall in the Presence in Mr. Warwick's place.

L. C. Vol. 477.

1660.

"Thomas Creswell, trumpeter, sworn to come in on the next avoydance."

L. C. Vol. 482, *p.* 61.

[1660.]

A list of the musicians that do service in the Chappell Royall whose salleryes are payable in the Treasury of His Majesty's Chamber.

(Vizt.) Mr. Thos. Purcell   Pelham Humphryes
   Dr. John Wilson   John Hingston
   Dr. Christopher Gibbon   William Gregory
   Dr. Will. Child   Mr. Steffkyn
   Tho. Blagrave   Mr. Bridges

L. C. Vol. 482, *p.* 56.

[1660.]

A particular of the establishment of the Queen's Majesty's household :—

		£ s. d.
Musicians	Master of the music for himself and 2 boys	480 0 0
	12 others at...	120 0 0 = 1,440 0 0
	one other at...	40 0 0
	another at ...	10 0 0

L. C. Vol. 482, *p.* 196.

1660, *with notes added at different times.*

List of Musicians.

Theorboes.—John Jenkyns in the place of John Coggeshall
   John Lylly   "   "   "   John Kelleye
Treble Lutes.—John Rogers "   "   "   James Gwaltier
   William Howes "   "   "   John Mercuer
Lutemaker.—William Allaby—a new place.
Virginalls.—Giles Tomkyns in the place of Richard Deering
   Christopher Gibbons "   "   Thomas Warwick
Harper.— Charles Evans "   "   "   Phillip Squire
Repayrer and keeper of the Organs.—
   John Hingeston in the place of Arthur Norgate
Organ maker.—James Farre "   "   "   Thomas Craddock
Keeper of Lutes and Violls.—
   Henry Brockwell   "   "   Richard Hudson
[Below this name is the date 20 February, 1667-8.]

L. C. 479, *p.* 101 ; *see also Vol.* 482, *p.* 54.

1660, with additions made at different dates.

Appointment of the following to the private Musick.

Henry Cooke in place of Dr. Coleman, composer in the private Musick.

For lutes and voyces, theorboes and virginalls.

Henry Cooke in the place of Nicholas Duvall

John Coleman	Wm. Gregory
Gregory Thorndale	Henry Hawes
Nathaniel Watkins	John Smyth
Alfanso Marsh	John Singleton
John Hardinge	Thomas Lanier
Edward Coleman [crossed out]	Mr. Bridges " a new
Thomas Bates	place"
John Goodgroome	Thomas Pursell
Charles Coleman	Anthony Roberts
John Hingston	
Dr. John Wilson	William Howes
John Jenkyns	Christopher Gibbons
John Lilly	Blore
John Rogers	Henry Brockwell

Thomas Fitz " a new place "

Joseph Fashon [crossed out and the date 19 October, 1668 placed against it.]

Pelham Humphreys   Deitrick Steifken

Musicians for the wind instruments.

Dr. Wm. Child	Phillip Beckett
Robert Blagrave	Humphrey Madg
John Gamble	Theophilus Fittz
Wm. Clayton	Thomas Blagrave.

William Young, for the flute

Isaack Staggins, for the treble hoboy

John Mason [crossed out and the name Mr. Garrard placed against it.]

Edward Hooton [crossed out]

John Strong [crossed out]

Robert Strong [crossed out]

John Singleton	Will. Howes, cornett
William Gregory	Thomas Lanier
William Saunders.	

[1660] *with additions made at different dates.*

Appointment of the following as His Majesty's musitians.

Composers.

George Hudson [This name is crossed out and the words " Dead Pel. Humphreyes and Th. Purcell " written against it.]

Mathew Lock

Violins.

Isaack Staggins	Theophilus Fitz
John Bannister	John Singleton
Ambrose Beeland	Wm. Young
Richard Dorney	Henry Brockwell
John Atkyns	

Henry Smyth. [This name crossed out and the words " Dead. Joseph Fashion June 25 1670 " against it.]

Symon Hopper	Wm. Howes
Wm. Clayton	John Strong
Edmond Tanner	Robert Strong
Jeoffery Bannister	Thomas Fitz
Wm. Saunders	Phillip Beckett
John Comer	

Wm. Youckney [This name crossed out and the word " Dead " written against it.]

L. C. Vol. 482, p. 51.

[1660] *with additions made at different dates.*

List of musicians in ordinary for the wind instruments, violins, voices and lutes :—

Nicholas Lanier, master [crossed out and the name of Louis Grabu inserted].

Mathew Lock in the place of Alphonso Ferabosco, composer for the wind music.

Wind Music.

William Child, for the cornett in the place of Clement Lanier, deceased

John Gamball in the place of William Lanier

Robert Blagrave   //   //   Anthony Bassano

Phillip Beckett   //   //   Mr. Bell, deceased

John Singleton   //   //   William Lanier, sackbutt

Stephen Strong, for a sackbutt in the place of Clement Lanier

Violins (double places.)

John Strong in the place of John Woodington
  [John Woodington crossed out and Nicholas
  Birkhead inserted.]
Robert Strong in the place of Thomas Warren
Edward Strong in the place of John Hopper
  [This entry crossed out, the name of Jeoffrey Bannister
  inserted with the date 24 December, 1663.]
William Howes in the place of Robert Dowland
Thomas Blagrave   ″   ″   Peter Guy
Symon Hopper, a new place
Theophilus Fitz   ″   ″
Humphry Madge in the place of Theophilus Lupo

Violins (single places.)

Richard Hudson in the place of Symon Nau (crossed
  out). [This entry crossed out and Thomas Fitz
  in Richard Hudson's place inserted, and dated
  18 February, 1667-8.]
Phillip Beckett in the place of Thomas Lupo
Henry Comer   ″   ″   Richard Comer
Richard Dorney   ″   ″   Mr. Dorney his father.
John Singleton   a new place
Thomas Fitz, musitian of the violins in ordinary
  (dated 1664)
Theophilus Fitz   a new place
John Atkyns   ″   ″
Henry Smyth   ″   ″
William Saunders   ″   ″
Walter Yowckney   ″   ″
William Young   ″   ″
Henry Brockwell   ″   ″
Isaack Staggins   ″   ″
William Clayton   ″   ″

Composers for the violins.

George Hudson in the place of Estien Nau
Mathew Lock, a new place
Henry Purcel in the place of Angelo Notari
  [This entry crossed out and John Goodgroome in
  place of Henry Purcell written over it, with the
  date 20 August 1664].
Thomas Purcell in the place of Henry Lawes (dated
  16 November, 1662).

Private music for lutes, violls and voices.

Henry Cook in the place of Thomas Day and
                                   Nicholas Duvall
John Clements //   //   William Lawes
Gregory Thorndell   //   John Drew
Nathaniel Watkyns   //   John Fox
Alphonso Marsh //   //   Thomas Daye
John Harding   //   //   Edward Wormwell
Edward Colman //   //   John Lanier
Thomas Bates   //   //   Alph. Ferabasco and
                                   Henry Ferabasco
Thomas Lanier //   //   Andrea Lanier
Anthony Roberts//   //   Jonas Wrench
Thomas Baltzar, a new place
Charles Colman in the place of Thomas Forde
    [Thomas Forde crossed out and " Dr. Colman "
    written in with the date 4 May, 1665.]
John Hingston in the place of Alphonso Ferabasco
William Gregory //   //   Daniel Ferrand
John Smyth   //   //   John Taylor
Henry Hawes   //   //   Robert Tompkins
John Singleton   //   //   Tymothy Collins
Mr. Bridges, a new place.
Edmund Portington, of the private musick (dated
    22 December, 1663.)

Vol. 479, pp. 99—100.

1660 (*November* 9).

Two warrants admitting the following as musicians, the
payments to commence from Midsummer last :—

William Howes in the place of John Hickson, 1s. 8d. per
diem and £16 2s. 6d. for livery.

Davies Mell in the place of John Woodington, £110 per
annum.

Humphrey Madge in the place of Theophilus Lupo, £40
per annum.

Humphrey Madge in the place of Jerom Lanier,
£40 12s. 8d. per annum.

Edward Stronge in the place of Francis Smith, £66 2s. 6d.
per annum.

Thomas Blagrave, in the place of Peter Guy, 1s. 4d. per
diem and £16 2s. 6d. as livery.

Robert Blagrave in the place of Anthony Bassano,
£58 14s. 2d. per annum.

William Howes in the place of Robert Dowland,
£40 12s. 8d. per annum.

George Hudson, composer, in the place of Stephen Nau,
£42 12s. 10d. per annum.

John Stronge in the place of Nicholas Packard, 1s. 8d. per
diem and £16 2s. 6d. for livery.

Edward Stronge in the place of John Hopper, £46 12s. 8d.
per annum.

Robert Stronge in the place of Thomas Warr, £46 12s. 8d.
per annum.

Richard Hudson in the place of Simon Nau, £46 12s. 8d.
per annum.

Phillip Beckett in the place of Thomas Lupo, £46 12s. 8d.
per annum.

Henry Comer, in the place of Richard Comer, £46 12s. 8d.
per annum.

L. C. Vol. 741, *p.* 243 *and Vol.* 180.

1660—1666.

A Lyst of His Majesty's Musitians.

1660. Nicholas Lanier, Master of the Musick, dead.

1666, November 24th. Monsieur Grabu, Master in his place.

	Violins.	
Edmund Flower		John Myer
Richard Dorney		John Bannister
Theophilus Fitz		Thomas Blagrave
John Singleton		William Howes
Nicholas Staggins		John Strong
Henry Brockwell		Robert Strong
Thomas Finell		Thomas Fitz
Joseph Fashion		Philip Beckett
Symon Hopper		Henry Comer
Isaack Staggins		Jeoffrey Bannister
William Clayton		William Saunders
John Twist		Humphrey Madge.
Thomas Purcill		
Pelham Humphreyes	} Composers.	
Mathew Lock		
Dr. William Child		William Saunders,
Robert Blagrave		[crossed out]
John Gamble		John Mason, [crossed
Henry Gregory		out, with " dead "
William Howes		written against it].
Thomas Lanier		Nicholas Staggins

L. C. Vol. 478, *pp.* 221 & 223.

1660, *December* 31.

Appointment of musicians in ordinary to his Majesty :—
John Jenkins in place of John Coggeshall, deceased, £40 per
annum ; John Lilly in place of John Kelly, £40 per annum.

L. C. Vol. 741, *p.* 246.

1660-1, *January* 1.

Appointment of musicians in ordinary to his Majesty :—
James Rogers in the place of James Gualtiar, for the lute,
£100 per annum ; Thomas Bates in the place of Alphonso
Ferabosco, junior, deceased, which his father Alphonso
Ferabosco enjoyed as instructor to his late Majesty when
Prince of Wales, £50 per annum, and in the place of Henry
Ferabosco, deceased £40 more ; Christopher Bell and Philip
Beckett for the flutes and sackbutts, £40 per annum with
£16 2s. 6d. yearly for apparel.

L. C. Vol. 741, *pp.* 246, 247.

1660-1, *January* 14.

Warrant for a new year's gift to be paid to each of the
musicians of his Majesty's consort in ordinary, they having
presented his Majesty with a considerable new year's gift.

A like warrant for the musicians for the voyces, and the
musicians for the violins in ordinary.

L. C. Vol. 741, *p.* 65.

1660-1, *January* 14.

Warrant to pay Charles Evans, harper in ordinary, for a
new year's gift, such a proportion of money as Phillip Squire
formerly had paid unto him.

L. C. Vol. 741, *p.* 64.

1660-1, *January* 17.

Petition of Thomas Arthur against Thomas Lanier for
payment of a debt. Answered.

L. C. 649.

1660-1, *January* 21.

Edward Homerston appointed trumpeter in ordinary.

L. C. Vols. 479, *p.* 105, *and* 482, *p.* 61.

1660-1, *January* 24.

Warrant to pay to the musicians of his Majesty's private
consort, viz., Matthew Lock, composer, John Singleton,
Theophilus Fitz, John Atkins, John Yowckney, William
Young, Henry Brockwell, James Staggins and William
Clayton, a certain sum of money for their new year's gifts.

L. C. Vol. 741, *p.* 66.

1660-1, *January* 24.

Warrant for the allowance of a livery to John Hingeston such as Alphonso Ferrabosco, one of the violls, formerly held and enjoyed.

L. C. Vol. 741, *p.* 14; *L. C. Vol.* 181, *p.* 19.

1660-1, *February* 19.

Richard Mawgridg appointed drummer.

L. C. Vols. 478, *p.* 89, *and* 482, *p.* 65.

1660-1, *March* 2.

Warrant for Coronation liveries for the sergeant trumpeter in ordinary, and a kettledrummer and sixteen trumpeters.

L. C. Vol. 817, *p.* 112.

1660-1, *March* 8.

Order for a warrant for the allowance of a yearly livery to John Wilson, doctor in musicke, admitted one of the musicians in ordinary to his Majesty, in the place of Alphonso Bales, deceased.

L. C. Vol. 181, *p.* 37; *also L. C. Papers, Bundle* 76.

1660-1, *March* 9.

Warrant to pay John Strong, his Majesty's musitian upon the wind instruments, the sum of £30, for two double sackbutts for service in his Majesty's Chappell.

L. C. Vol. 741, *b.* 68.

1660-1, *March* 11.

Petition of John Troutbeck against Anthony Roberts, one of His Majesty's musicians, upon a bill of exchange £500.

L. C. Vol. 649.

1660-1, *March* 15.

Warrant for the payment of a bill signed by the Master of the Musick, of £121 13s. to Thomas Hingston, keeper and repairer of his Majesty's organs and other instruments.

L. C. Vol. 741, *p.* 68.

1660-1, *March* 15.

Warrant for the allowance of yearly liveries to George Hudson and Davies Mell, two of his Majesty's musicians, such as Stephen Nau and George Woodington formerly held and enjoyed.

L. C. Vol. 741, *p.* 20; *also L. C. Papers, Bundle* 76.

1660-1, *March* 15.

Warrant for the allowance of such livery to Henry Cooke, as to Nicholas Duval was formerly given.

L. C. Vol. 741, *p.* 20.

1660-1, *March* 16.

Henry Thewer, appointed trumpeter in ordinary.
[This name crossed out and "in Ireland" written against it.]

L. C. Vol. 479, *p.* 105 ; *L. C. Vol.* 482, *p.* 61.

1660-1, *March* 20.

Order for a warrant for the allowance of a yearly livery to Humphrey Madge, sworn musician upon the violin in ordinary to his Majesty, in the place of Theophilus Lupo, deceased.

L. C. Vol. 181, *p.* 41 ; *L. C. Papers, Bundle* 76 ; *L. C. Vol.* 741, *p.* 21.

1660-1, *March* 24.

Warrant to pay Gervase Price, sergeant trumpeter in ordinary, the sum of £323 by order of his Majesty, to be given to the trumpeters in ordinary and to his Majesty's kettle drummer, to provide them necessaries against his Majesty's coronation.

L. C. Vol. 741, *p.* 70.

1660-1, *March* 24.

Warrant to prepare seventeen silver trumpets like that of the sergeant trumpeter's, for the use of the seventeen trumpeters in ordinary, so that they may be ready to attend with them at solemnizeing his Majesty's coronation, the said trumpets to be held by them as long as they continue in their places, and upon their death or other avoydance, the trumpets to be delivered up to the jewel house, so that the trumpeter or trumpeters succeeding shall have them.

L. C. Vol. 741, *p.* 118.

1661, *March* 25.

Order for a warrant for the allowance of a yearly livery to Thomas Lanier, sworn musician upon the flutes and cornetts in ordinary to his Majesty, in the place of Andrea Lanier, deceased.

L. C. Vol. 181, *p.* 42 ; *L. C. Vol.* 741, *p.* 22 ; *L. C. Papers, Bundle* 76.

1661, *March* 25.

Warrant directing that as Andrea Lanier, deceased, had allowed to him for the education and breeding of two boys in the art of musick for the flutes and cornetts, winter and summer liveries for the said boys, which liveries were due for one year since his decease ; the same liveries for this tyme only, be delivered to Thomas Lanier, executor of the said Andrea Lanier.

L. C. Vol. 741, *p.* 22 ; *L. C. Vol.* 181, *p.* 43.

1661, *March* 30.

Warrant for such livery to Henry Cooke, master of his Majesty's boyes, as Thomas Day, late deceased, enjoyed as master of his Majesty's boyes; also for a livery as musician in ordinary in the place of Nicholas Duvall.

L. C. Vol. 741, *p.* 23 ; *L. C. Vol.* 181, *p.* 56.

1661. [*March.*]

Certificate addressed to all his Majesty's musicians that Nicholas Lanier is sworn master of his Majesty's musick, and hath power to order and convocate the same at fitt time of practize and service as is expressed in his privy seal given him by his late Majesty when he was Prince of Wales, and that if any of them refuse to wayte at such convenient tymes of practize and service as he shall appoint, and for such instruments, voyces and musick, as he in reason shall think them fitted to serve in, upon his just complaint, I shall punish them either in their persons or their wages as I shall think the offence deserves.

L. C. Vol. 741, *p.* 316.

1661, *April* 4.

Warrant for the allowance of certain liveries to Nicholas Lanier, as master of his Majesty's musick.

L. C. Vol. 741, *p.* 23 ; *L. C. Vol.* 181, *p.* 45.

1661, *April* 6.

Warrant to supply 3 trumpeters of his Majesty's Life Guard under the command of Mr. Oneale, with coronation liveries.

L. C. Vol. 741, *p.* 25.

1661, *April* 6.

Order for a warrant for the allowance of a yearly livery to Angelo Notary, one of his Majesty's musicians.

L. C. Vol. 181, *p.* 47 ; *L. C. Vol.* 741, *p* 24.

1661, A*pril* 6.

Warrant for twelve suits of apparel for the twelve children of our Chappell Royall, to be delivered to Captain Henry Cooke, master of the said children.

L. C. Papers, Bundle 8.

1661, *April* 10.

Warrant to deliver to Daniell Oneall (Oneile), Esquire, three silver trumpets made according to the directions you shall receive from him.

L. C. Vol. 601 ; *L. C. Vol.* 741, *p.* 120.

1661, *April* 11.

Warrant for the payment of £40 to Davies Mell, one of his Majesty's musicians in ordinary for musick books for his Majesty's violins, and also for a Cremona treble violin for his Majesty's service.

L. C. *Vol.* 741, *p.* 72.

1661, *April* 12.

Warrant for liveries to the violins that are to attend in the Chappell and Westminster Hall, at his Majesty's coronation :—

Nicholas Lanier, master of all his Majesty's musick.
George Hudson and Mathew Lock, composers
John Hingeston, master of the organs

Edward Strong	John Strong
Davies Mell	Robert Strong
Humphrey Madge	Symon Hopper
Henry Comer	Walter Yowckney
Phillip Beckett	Thomas Bates
John Bannister	William Gregory
William Saunders	Richard Dorney
Richard Hudson	Theophilus Fitz
Ambrose Beeland	John Singleton
William Young	Isaack Staggins
William Clayton	John Atkyns
John Yowckney	Henry Brockwell

L. C. *Vol.* 741, *p.* 159-160 ; L. C. *Vol.* 817, *pp.* 156 *and* 157.

1661, *April* 13.

Warrant for the allowance of liveries to the following musitians for the wind instruments, against his Majesty's Coronation :—

Clement Lanier	John Mason
William Gregory	Thomas Mell
Henry Bassano	Robert Blagrave
Christopher Bell	John Gamble

L. C. *Vol.* 741, *p.* 160 ; L. C. *Vol.* 817, *p.* 158.

1661, *April* 18.

William Yowckney appointed musician in ordinary without fee.

L. C. *Vol.* 479, *p.* 103.

1661, *April* 20.

Order for a warrant for the allowance of a livery to Henry Lawes, sworn and admitted for the lutes and voyces in ordinary, in the place of Robert Marsh, deceased.

L. C. *Vol.* 181, *p.* 49 ; *also* L. C. *Papers, Bundle* 76.

1661, *April* 20.

Order for a warrant for the allowance of a livery to William Gregory, admitted musician upon the viall in ordinary to his Majesty, in the place of Daniell Farrant.

L. C. Vol. 181, *p.* 51 ; *also L. C. Papers, Bundle* 76.

1661, *April* 20.

Order for a warrant for the allowance of a livery to Dr. Coleman, doctor in musick, and also for his son, Charles Coleman, both sworn and admitted in the place of Thomas Ford, deceased.

L. C. Vol. 181, *p.* 50 ; *also L. C. Papers, Bundle* 76.

1661, *May* 9.

Order for a warrant to allow Henry Cooke, master of the children of his Majesty's Chappell Royall, in the place of Thomas Day, deceased, £40 yearly for the education of two children in his Majesty's private musick, to commence from St. John the Baptist, 1660.

L. C. Vol. 181, *p.* 55 ; *L. C. Vol.* 741, *p.* 28 ; *L. C. Papers, Bundle* 76.

1661, *May* 18.

Warrant to deliver to Nicholas Lanier, master of the musick, Henry Lawes, composer of the private musick for lutes and voices in place of Robert Marsh, deceased, Charles Coleman, senior, in place of Thomas Ford, deceased, George Hudson and Davis Mell, musicians in ordinary in the places of Steven Naw and John Woodington, deceased, John Hingeston, musician for the violls in the place of Alphonso Ferabosco, deceased, Humphrey Madge, musician in ordinary for the violls in the place of Theophilus Lupo, deceased, and William Gregory, musician upon the violl in ordinary in place of Daniel Farrant, deceased, to each of them the materials for their liveries and a yearly livery of £16 2s. 6d., at the feast of St. Andrew.

L. C. Vol. 814, *p.* 91 ; *L. C. Papers, Bundle* 23.

1661, *May* 21.

Warrant for the payment of £46 15s. to John Hingston, keeper and repairer of his Majesty's organs, for repairing and erecting organs, and for other necessaries expressed in his bill.

L. C. Vol. 741, *p.* 73.

1661, *May* 30.

Warrant for the payment of £22 10s. to fifteen of his Majesty's musicians for the violins, for their charges in their journey to Windsor for the installation.

Warrant to pay £20 to Davis Mell, one of the musitians, for strings for his Majesty's violins.

L. C. Vol. 741, *p.* 74.

1661, *May* 31.

Whereas his Majesty hath been graciously pleased to entertayne diverse persons in his service for his band of violins, and that there hath been complaint made to me of diverse neglects in their practize and performance to do his Majesty's faithfull service, these are therefore to will and command all persons concerned that are of his Majesty's said band of violins to take notice that I have ordered George Hudson and Davies Mell to give orders and directions from tyme to tyme to every particular person herein concerned for their practize and performance of musick to prevent their former neglects, and if any of the said musick shall refuse to obey this my order, he is to answer his contempt before me upon complaint of the said George Hudson and Davies Mell.

L. C. Vol. 741, *p.* 316.

1661, *June* 2.

Order for the painting of twenty-five drums for a regiment of foot guards in Dunkirke.

L. C. Papers, Bundle 8.

1661, *June* 4.

Warrant to provide and deliver to the earl of Oxford or his assignes, eight cornetts with stands and other necessaries thereunto belonging, seventeen bannerolls for trumpeters with the Jolley Boyes and cordage to them, with tassells, one payre of handerolls for the kettle-drummers, all according to a model hereunto annexed.

L. C. Papers, Bundle 8.

1661, *June* 9.

Warrant to pay to Henry Cooke, master of the children of the Chappell, the sum of £40 per annum for keeping and teaching two singing boys, in place of Thomas Day, musician, deceased.

L. C. Vol. 814, *p.* 94.

24 *June to Michaelmas,* 1661.

Warrant dormant to remain in force during the above time for materials for livery for William Child, musician.

Similar warrants for Nicholas Lanier, Henry Lawes, Charles Coleman, senior, George Hudson, Davis Mell, John Hingeston, Humphrey Madge, William Gregorie, John Willson, Henry Cooke, Angelo Notarie and Thomas Lanier, musicians; and for an allowance to Henry Cooke, master of the boys of the Chappell Royall, for the keeping and teaching of two boys.

L. C. Vol. 153 ; *L. C. Papers, Bundle* 23.

1661, *Pentecost.*

Payment of £19 17s. 8d. to each of the following trumpeters to the late King Charles I. for their pensions :—

Robert Ramsay George Bosgrove
Thomas Cresswell William Porter
Samuel Markland Henry Peacock
George Porter

L. C. Vol. 460.

1661, *July* 4.

Warrant for the payment of £23 16s. 9d. to Henry Cooke, master of the children of the Chappell, for fetching five boys from Newarke and Lincolnie for his Majesty's service.

L. C. Vol. 741, *p.* 75.

1661, *July* 4.

Warrant for the payment of £50 to Nicholas Lanier, master of his Majesty's musique, Dr. Charles Coleman, Capt. Henry Cooke, Mr. George Hudson and Mr. Mathew Lock for themselves and the rest of his Majesty's private musique, for hiring of two large rooms for the practice of musique and for keeping the instruments in, for one year from 24 June, 1660 to 24 June, 1661.

L. C. Vol. 742, *p.* 76.

1661, *July* 4.

Warrant for the payment of £18 to the 12 musicians for the wind instruments, extraordinary charges for six days' attendance upon his Majesty at Windsor, at the rate of 5s. a day to each man, to be paid to Thomas Blagrave, John Strong, Robert Blagrave, William Howes, for themselves and the rest of their fellows.

L. C. Vol. 741, *p.* 75.

1661, *July* 16.

Warrant for the payment of £10 to Theodore Stofkins, one of his Majesty's musicians, to buy and provide one basse violl for his Majesty's service.

Warrant for the payment of £20 to John Jenkins, musician for the flute, for strings for one year, 1660-1661.

L. C. Vol. 741, *p.* 76.

1661, *July* 29.

Warrant for the apprehension of all such trumpeters, drummers and fifes, as do sound with trumpets or use drums or fifes at any plays, dumb shows or models, without licence from the sergeant trumpeter.

L. C. Vol. 649.

1661, *August* 1.

Warrant for yearly liveries for the following musicians :—
John Wilson
Henry Cooke, and
Thomas Lanier

L. C. Papers, Bundle 23.

1661, *August* 3.

Certificate that Davies Mell and Ambrose Beeland, who
were sworn musicians for the violins to his late Majesty, are to
continue in their said places to his present Majesty, as they
have done since his Majesty's happy restoration.

L. C. Vol. 741, *p.* 317.

1661, *August* 3.

Certificate that by vertue of several patents granted by his
late Majesty to Nicholas Lanier, Clement Lanier, William
Gregory, Henry Bassano, Christopher Bell, John Mason,
Thomas Mell, John Strong, Robert Strong, Thomas Blagrave,
William Howes, William Lanier and Thomas Lanier, for
their places of consort, being his majesty's wind musick during
their lives, they and every one of them are continued in their
said places to his now sacred Majesty, and are to have and
enjoy all allowances thereunto belonging.

L. C. Vol. 741, *p.* 318.

1661, *August* 15.

Warrant to the coffer maker to deliver to Davies Mell three
chests for his Majesty's musicall instruments.

L. C. Vol. 741, *p.* 331 ; *L. C. Vol.* 817, *p.* 207.

1661, *August* 27.

Order for a warrant for the allowance of a yearly livery to
Anthony Roberts, admitted one of his Majesty's musicians in
ordinary for the voyces, in the place of Jonas Wrench, deceased.

L. C. Vol. 181, *p.* 64 ; *L. C. Papers, Bundle* 76 ; *L. C. Vol.* 741, *p.* 34.

1661, *August* 31.

Warrant to deliver to the musicians in ordinary, to
John Willson, doctor in musick in the place of Alphonso Bates,
deceased, to Henry Cooke in the place of Nicholas Duvall,
deceased, to Angelo Notary as formerly received in the tyme
of our Royall father, and to Thomas Lanier, musician upon
the flutes and cornetts in the place of Andrea Lanier, his
father, deceased, the materials for their liveries and a yearly
livery to each of £16 2s. 6d. at the Feast of St. Andrew.

L. C. Vol. 814, *p.* 105 ; *L. C. Papers, Bundle* 23.

1661, *September* 2.

Warrant for the payment of £18 to Phillip Beckett, musician, for a violin and cornett bought by him for His Majesty's service.

Warrant for the payment of £20 to Humphrey Madge, musician, for a violin bought for His Majesty's service, and also for strings bought for, and used in, His Majesty's band of violins.

L. C. Vol. 741, *p.* 93.

1661, *September* 2.

Warrant for the payment of £30 to William Saunders, musician in ordinary, for a base violin for the Chamber and a double sackbutt for His Majesty's Chappell Royall.

L. C. Vol. 741, *p.* 88.

1661, *September* 5.

Warrant for the payment of £34 3s. 4d. to Thomas Baltzer, musician, for two violins bought by him for his Majesty's service.

L. C. Vol. 741, *p.* 83.

1661, *September* 5.

Warrant to provide Daniell Oneale with one kettle-drummer, with all things thereunto belonging.

L. C. Vol. 741, *p.* 35.

1661, *September* 16.

Warrant for the following payment to Henry Cooke, master of the children of his Majesty's Chappell Royall; £19 10s. being extraordinary charges for himself and 12 children, commanded to attend upon his Majesty at Windsor for the space of six days, at the rate of 5s. a day to each, and £2 16s. for torches and lights for practising the musick against his Majesty's coronation.

L. C. Vol. 741, *p.* 85.

1661, *September* 17.

Warrant to deliver to Henry Cooke, master of the twelve children of the Chappell Royall, the following materials for their liveries :—

For each of them, one cloak of bastard scarlett cloth lyned with velvett, one suit and coat of the same cloth made up and trimmed with silver and silk lace after the manner of our footmen's liveries, and also to the said suit three shirts, three half shirts, three pair of shoes, three pair of thigh stocking, whereof one pair of silk and two pair of worsted, two hats with bands, six bands and six pairs of cuffs, whereof two laced and four plain, three handkerchers, three pairs of gloves and two pieces and a half of rebon for trimming garters and shoestrings.

And at Easter, for their summer liveries, for each boy one cloak of bastard scarlett lined with sattin and one doublett of sattin with bastard scarlett trunk hose made and trimmed up as aforesaid, with three shirts, three half shirts, three pair of shoes, three pair of thigh stockings, whereof one pair of silk and two pairs of worsted, two hats with bands, etc.

L. C. Vol. 814, *p.* 106.

1661, September 22.

Warrant for the payment of £100 yearly to Gervase Price as sergeant trumpeter of all the trumpeters, drummers and fifes, and £60 yearly to the following trumpeters to commence St. John Baptist, 1660 :—

Thomas Knollys	Edward Sympson
William Hopkins	Richard Deane
Melque Goldt	Thomas Sculthorpe
Symon Beale	William Bounty
John Jones	Edward Homerston
William Peacock	Ragny Benning

L. C. Vol. 741, *p.* 267.

Accounts ending Michaelmas, 1661.

Accounts for liveries for the following musicians to the King :—

William Child	Humphrey Madge
Nicholas Lanier	William Gregorie
Henry Lawes	John Willson
Charles Coleman, senior	Henry Cooke
George Hudson	Angelo Notarie
Davis Mell	Thomas Lanier
John Hingeston	

Allowance to Henry Cooke, master of the boys of the King's Chappell, of £50, for keeping and teaching two boys for one and a quarter years.

L. C. Vol. 55.

Accounts ending Michaelmas, 1661.

Accounts for liveries of £16 2s. 6d., to six of the musicians to the King, by warrant of 18 May, 1661 :—

Nicholas Lanier	John Hingeston
Charles Colman, senior	Humphrey Madge
George Hudson	William Gregorie

Accounts for liveries to four musicians to the King, by warrant of 31 August, 1661 .—

John Willson   Angelo Notarie

Henry Cooke   Thomas Lanier

L. C. Vol. 152.

1661, *September* 30.

Warrant to pay Thomas Blagrave and William Howes the sum of £3, for attending at Windsor in the quality of musicians for the violins.

L. C. Vol. 741, *p.* 82.

1661, *October* 2.

Order for a warrant for the allowance of a yearly livery to Henry Bassano, admitted one of his Majesty's musicians in ordinary for the wind instruments.

L. C. Vol. 181, *p.* 80 ; *L. C. Vol.* 741, *p.* 284.

1661, *October* 4.

Order for a warrant for the allowance of a yearly livery to Clement Lanier, admitted one of his Majesty's musicians in ordinary for the wind instruments.

L. C. Vol. 181, *p.* 66 ; *L. C. Vol.* 741, *p.* 40.

1661, *October* 18.

Appointment of John Volee in the private musick.

L. C. Vol. 479, *p.* 102.

1661, *November* 4.

Warrant to pay to Thomas Lanier, executor to Andrea Lanier, musician, deceased, the sum of £59 13s. 4d. for liveries due to Andrea Lanier for one year ended St. Andrew last past, for two boys committed to his custody to be trayned up in the knowledge of the flutes and cornetts.

L. C. Vol. 814, *p.* 135.

1661, *November* 11.

Warrant to deliver to Gervase Price, sergeant trumpeter, 18 velvett capps for his Majesty's trumpeters and kettle drummer.

L. C. Vol. 741, *p.* 38.

1661, *November* 13.

Sylvester Whitmeale appointed a trumpeter extraordinary.

L. C. Vol. 479, *p.* 106.

1661, *November* 22.

Gervase Price, sergeant trumpeter, authorised to impresse and take up for his Majesty's service, George Chetham, trumpeter, to be employed in the voyage to Tangier.

L. C. Vol. 741, *p.* 319.

1661, *November* 27.

Warrant for the payment of £80 to Gervase Price, serjeant trumpettor, to be paid by him to the six trumpettors appointed by his Majesty for this voyage to Portugal to attend upon the Queen's Majesty.

L. C. Vol. 741, *p.* 83.

1661, *St. Andrew.*

Payment of £16 2s. 6d. to each of the following musicians to the King for their liveries :—

Matthew Locke	John Smith
John Jenkins	John Gamble
John Lillie	Thomas Bates
Edward Coleman	Henry Bassano
John Harding	John Clement
Gregory Thornedell	Giles Tompkins
Alphonso Marsh	Anthony Roberts
Stephen Strong	John Bannister (crossed out, " vacatur ")
William Child,	Charles Coleman, senior
Nicholas Lanier, master	John Hingeston
Henry Lawes	David Mell
Humphrey Madge	William Gregorie
Henry Cooke	Angelo Notary
Thomas Lanier	

George Hudson, John Willson, Anthony Roberts and Nicholas Lanier, luter, liveries for the years 1660 and 1661.

Thomas Lanier, executor to Andrea Lanier, deceased, for two boys for one year.

L. C. Vol. 460.

1661, *December* 2.

To Nicholas Lanier, master of his Majesty's musick, and to the musicians for the violins in ordinary to his Majesty :—

Whereas William Young, John Atkins, Isaack Staggins, John Yowckney, William Clayton and Henry Brockwell, musitians in ordinary for the violins for his Majesty's private Consort, are not admitted or suffered to exercise in the chamber appointed for that purpose with the rest of the musitians, these are therefore to will and require you forthwith to admit the said musitians into your society in the chamber appointed for the violins and to suffer them to exercise according to their oaths and dutyes.

L. C. Vol. 741, *p.* 318.

1661, *December* 19.

John Baker appointed trumpeter in the place of Anthony Franck.

L. C. Vol. 479, *p.* 105.

1661, *December* 19.

Warrant to admit Gervase Price into the office of sergeant of all trumpeters, drummers and fiffes in ordinary to his Majesty in the place of Henry Martin, deceased.

L. C. Vol. 741, *p.* 263.

1661, *December* 19.

Appointment of trumpeters in ordinary :—
John Baker in Anthony Franke's place, William Bounty, Richard Deane and William Peacock.

L. C. Vol. 482, *p.* 61.

1661, *December* 23.

Warrant to admit Thomas Baltzar musician in ordinary to his Majesty for the violin in the private musick, with the wages of £110 yearly.

L. C. Vol. 741, *p.* 287.

1661, *December* 23.

Warrant for the payment of £60 yearly to the following trumpeters :—
Hugh Fisher, John Baker, Milbert Meurs, Nicholas Shaperoone, and to Hans Berneyoski, kettle drummer.

L. C. Vol. 741, *p.* 262.

1661, *December* 24.

Order for a warrant for the allowance of a yearly livery to Stephen Strong, admitted as musician for the double sackbutt in ordinary to his Majesty, in the place of Clement Lanier, deceased, to commence 13 November, last past.

L. C. Vol. 181, *p.* 69; *and Vol.* 741, *p.* 41.

1661, *December* 24.

Bill amounting to £105 for screen banner, and one kettle drum, richly embroidered, for the Duke of Ormonde's going to Ireland.

L. C. Papers, Bundle 22.

1661, *December* 24.

Warrant for liveries for six trumpeters and a kettledrummer to attend upon his Grace the Duke of Ormond, Lord Lieutenant of Ireland.

L. C. Vol. 741, *p.* 41.

1661, *December* 30.

Warrant for the allowance of such liveries to the following musicians in ordinary :—

John Lylly	Gregory Thorndell
Edward Coleman	Thomas Bates
John Harding	Mathew Lock
Alphonso Marsh	

as were formerly allowed to :—

John Coggeshall	John Drew
John Lylly	Alphonso Ferabosco
John Lanier	Henry Ferabosco
Edward Wormwell	Thomas Day

now deceased.

L. C. Vol. 741, *p.* 42

1661-2, *January* 18.

Christopher Aylmer appointed musician of the private musick extraordinary.

L. C. Vol. 478, *p.* 113 ; *and Vol.* 479, *p.* 103.

1661-2, *January* 25.

Warrant to pay Mathew Lock, John Singleton, John Yowckney, John Atkins, William Clayton, Isaack Staggins, Theophilus Fitz and Henry Brockwell, His Majesty's musicians in ordinary for his private consort, so much money to each of them for their new years guifts as hath been usually allowed to any of His Majesty's musicians.

L. C. Vol. 741, *p.* 98.

1661-2, *January* 27.

Joseph Walker appointed trumpeter extraordinary.

L. C. Vol. 479, *p.* 106.

1661-2, *February* 11.

Petition of Bartholomew Audley and Margaret his wife, against Thomas Lanier, debt £20.

L. C. Vol. 649.

1661-2, *February* 17.

Warrant for the delivery of six silver trumpets, after the manner and fashion as the sergeant trumpeter appointed, to his Grace the Duke of Ormond, Lord Lieutenant of Ireland, for six trumpeters that are to attend his Grace for his Majesty's service there.

L. C. Vol. 601.

1661-2, *February* 20.

Warrant to deliver to Gervice Price, Esquire, his Majesty's sergeant trumpeter, two silver hornes after the same manner and fashion as he shall informe you, and also one coller of SS of silver of the quantity of 15 ounces, for the sergeant trumpeter.

L. C. Vol. 601.

1661-2, *February* 22.

Warrant to pay new years gifts to John Yowckney, John Singleton, John Atkins, William Clayton, William Young, Isaack Staggins, Theophilus Fitz and Henry Brockwell, appointed by his Majesty to increase the number of his violins, also as musicians in ordinary for his private consort, and to Mathew Lock to be composer for them.

L. C. Vol. 741, *p.* 101.

1661-2, *February* 28.

Warrant to pay John Singleton, William Young, William Clayton, John Yowckney, Theophilus Fitz, John Atkins, Isaack Staggins and Henry Brockwell, musicians for the violins in ordinary, the sum of £88 for violins and strings bought by them for his Majesty's service.

L. C. Vol. 741, *p.* 102.

1661-2, *February* 28.

Warrant to deliver to the sergeant trumpeter two silver hunting hornes for his Majesty's service.

L. C. Vol. 741, *p.* 126.

1661-2, *March* 6.

Warrant to pay Henry Comer, musician, the sum of £10, for a treble violin bought by him for his Majesty's service.

L. C. Vol. 741, *p.* 105.

1661-2, *March* 13.

Henry Gregory admitted as musician for the wind instruments in ordinary without fee, to be assistant with his father William Gregory, and after the decease of the said William, to come in ordinary with fee.

L. C. Vol. 741, *p.* 316.

1661-2, *March* 14.

Henry Thewer and Peter Lake appointed trumpeters to attend upon the Duke of Ormond, Lord Lieutenant of Ireland.

L. C. Vol. 478, *p.* 87 ; *and Vol.* 479, *p.* 105.

1661-2, *March* 15.

Warrant for the payment of £7 to Richard Darney, musician in ordinary for a tennor violin bought by him for his Majesty's service.

L. C. Vol. 741, *p.* 106.

1661-2, *March* 17.

William Wing, admitted as musician for the private musick in ordinary without fee, to come in ordinary with fee upon the next avoydance.

L. C. Vol. 741, *p.* 316.

1661-2, *March* 24.

Warrant for the payment of £45 to Henry Cooke, Master of the Children of his Majesty's Chappell Royall, by him expended to masters for teaching the said children to write and to learne and speake latine, from Michaelmas, 1660, to Lady Day next. Also the sum of £5 18s. for a book of the services and anthems for his Majesty's use.

L. C. Vol. 741, *p.* 107.

1662, *March* 26.

Warrant for the payment of £17 to Mr. Gregory for a violl and for strings for one whole year, bought by him for his Majesty's service.

L. C. Vol. 741, *p.* 110.

1662, *March* 28.

Letter of assignment from George Porter, trumpeter, of the parish of Stepney, Middlesex, appointing Marie Porter, his wife, as his true and lawful attorney.

L. C. Vol. 181, *p.* 111.

1662, *April* 7.

Devereux Clothier appointed drummer in Ottley's place.

L. C. Vol. 482, *p.* 65.

1662, *April* 7.

Robert Mawgridg appointed drummer.

L. C. Vol. 478, *p.* 89.

1662, *April* 7.

Warrant for a livery for Robert Aggis, drummer, appointed to attend his grace the Duke of Ormond, Lord Lieutenant of Ireland.

L. C. Vol. 741, *p.* 158.

1662, *April* 10.

Appointment of Robert Aggas, drummer, to attend upon the Duke of Ormond in Ireland.

L. C. Vol. 478, *p.* 89.

1662, *April* 18.

Warrant to admit William Yowckney musician upon the violin in ordinary without fee.

L. C. Vol. 741, *p.* 315.

1662, *April* 18.

Warrant that John Bannister should have the ordering of 12 violins of his Majesty's servants in ordinary to attend his Majesty in the journey to Portsmouth or elsewhere for the reception of her Majesty his dearest consort the Queen, viz. :—John Singleton, William Young, William Clayton, Henry Comer, Phillip Beckett, Henry Smyth, Symon Hopper, Richard Hudson, John Strong, Robert Strong, and Theophilus Fitz.

L. C. Vol. 741, *p.* 315.

1662, *April* 19.

Warrant to pay John Hingston, keeper and repayrer of his Majesty's organs and other instruments the sum of £155, for organs and harpsicord for the King's Chappell at Hampton Court, and also an organ for the Queene's private Chappell.

L. C. Vol. 741, *p.* 209.

1662, *May* 20.

Warrant to provide and deliver to John Hingston, keeper of His Majesty's organs, a curtain of crimson taffata, two yards in depth and twelve yeard in breadth, for the organ loft at Hampton Court.

L. C. Vol. 741, *p.* 161 ; *and Vol.* 817, *p.* 308.

1662, *May* 20.

Bill for 24 black napt casters for the singing boyes.

L. C. Papers, Bundle 10.

1662, *Pentecost.*

Payment of £19 17s. 8d. to each of the following trumpeters to the late King Charles I. for their pensions :—

Robert Ramsey.	George Porter.
Thomas Cresswell.	George Bosgrove.
Samuel Markland.	William Porter.
Henry Peacock.	

L. C. Vol. 460.

1662, *May.*

Henry Cooke's receipt for £50 1s., the amount of his bill for clothing and other expenses, connected with the children of the chapel.

L. C. Papers, Bundle 4.

1662, *June* 6.

Trumpeters to attend the Duke of Ormonde in Ireland :—
Thomas Hadwyn.   Robert Burgesse.
William Castle.   Francis Burton.
        Jean Noell Josse, kettledrummer.

L. C. Vol. 478, *p.* 87 ; *and Vol.* 479, *p.* 105.

1662, *June* 6.

Order for a warrant for the allowance of a yearly livery to John Jenkins, John Lillie, Edward Coleman, John Harding, Gregory Thorndell, Thomas Bates, Mathew Locke and Alphonso Marsh, sworn musicians in ordinary to his Majesty, in the places of John Coggshall, John Kellie, John Lanier, Edward Wormeall, John Drewe, Alphonso Ferabosco, Henrie Ferabosco and Thomas Day, deceased.

L. C. Vol. 181, *p.* 70.

1662, *June* 7.

Warrant to apprehend Humphrey Dance and Robert Ostler serjeant at mace for seizing and assaulting Gervase Price, serjeant trumpeter.

L. C. Vol. 649.

1662, *June* 10.

Warrant to admit Richard Dorney musician in ordinary upon the violin, in the place of his father Richard Dorney, deceased, with the yearly wages of £20, paid quarterly.

L. C. Vol. 741, *p.* 274.

1662, *June* 20.

Warrant to grant Richard Hudson, musician in ordinary, the place of keeping of his Majesty's lutes and violls, in the place of John Taylor and Richard Moller, deceased.

L. C. Vol. 741, *p.* 275.

1662, *June* 23.

Richard Vaux appointed fife, in the place of Tasher, deceased.

L. C. Vol. 478, *p.* 89 ; *and Vol.* 482, *p.* 65.

1662, *July* 4.

Warrant for the payment of £50 to Nicholas Lanier, master of his Majesty's musique, Dr. Charles Coleman, Capt. Henry Cooke, Mr. George Hudson and Mr. Mathew Lock, for themselves and the rest of the private musique, for hireing of two large roomes for the practice of the private musique and for keeping the instruments in, for one year from 24 June, 1661 to 24 June, 1662.

L. C. Vol. 742, p. 77.

1662, *July* 5.

Warrant to pay Dr. Coleman, musician, the sum of £10 for a violl, by him sold and delivered for his Majesty's service.

L. C. Vol. 741, p. 214.

1662, *July* 15.

Order for a warrant for the allowance of a yearly livery to John Smith, as musician in ordinary to his Majesty for a violl, in the place of John Taylor, deceased.

L. C. Vol. 181, p. 73; L. C. Vol. 741, p. 163; L. C. Papers, Bundle 76.

1662, *July* 17.

Warrant for the allowance of liveries to Nicholas Lanier, Anthony Roberts, Mathew Locke, John Jenkins, John Lilly, Edward Coleman, John Hardinge, Gregory Thorndell, and Alphonso Marsh, sworn musicians in ordinary to his Majesty in the places of Robert Hales, Jonas Wrench, Henry Ferabasco, John Coggeshall, John Kelly, John Lanier, Edward Wormwell (also Wormeall), John Drew, and Thomas Day, now deceased.   To commence 24 June, 1660.

L. C. Vol. 181, p. 74; and Vol. 741, p. 163.

1662, *July* 23.

Warrant for the enlarging of his Majesty's organ loft at Whitehall, as John Hingston, keeper of his Majesty's organs, shall inform you shall be necessary.

L. C. Vol. 741, p. 348.

1662, *July* 23.

Warrant for the payment of £76 : 5s. to John Hingeston, for mending and repayring his Majesty's organs in the Chappell Royall at Whitehall, for a base violl, and for erecting an organ in the Banquetting house.

L. C. Vol. 741, p. 217.

1662, *July* 30.

Warrant to pay Thomas Blagrave and Ambrose Beeland, two of his Majesty's band of violins, the sum of £14 for two tenor violins.

L. C. Vol. 741, p. 223.

1662, *August* 27.

Warrant to deliver to Symon Beale, one of his Majesty's trumpeters in ordinary, one silver trumpet, his own trumpet being taken from him for his Majesty's service in Ireland.

L. C. Vol. 741, *p.* 130.

1662, *August* 30.

In reference to the petition of seven old trumpeters belonging to his Majesty's royall father of blessed memory, this is to certify that it hath been the antient custom that those aged servants that were not able to perform their duty in their places were then put to pension and had their salaryes allowed them for the same for their lives, which was to each of them six pounds per annum board wages, and sixteen pence by the day out of the treasury of His Majesty's Chamber and also the sum of £19 . 17 . 8 . out of the Great Wardrobe. Therefore humbly leave to his Majesty's gracious consideracion the case of these petitioners.

L. C. Vol. 649.

1662, *August* 30.

Order that Robert Strong and Edward Strong are to attend with their double curtolls * in his Majesty's Chappell Royall at Whitehall, and Thomas Bates and William Gregory with their violls, every Sunday and Holy day, and all the rest to wayte in their turnes.

L. C. Vol. 741, *p.* 352.

1662, *August* 30.

Warrant to admit William Yowckney musician in ordinary for the violin, in the place of Davies Mell, deceased, with the wages of 1s. 8d. per diem and £16-2-6 yearly for livery.

L. C. Vol. 741, *p.* 277.

1662, *August* 30.

Warrant to pay the following musicians for the violins, £287 : 15s. for their expences and horse hire in their attendance at Hampton Court upon his Majesty, from May 29th, 1662 to August 23rd, 1662 at the rate of 5s. by the day to each man.

Humphrey Madge	Thomas Blagrave
William Howes	Richard Dorney
Ambrose Beeland	Walter Yowckney
Edward Strong	William Sanders
John Atkyns	Henry Brockwell
William Yowckney	George Hudson
Mathew Lock.	

L. C. Vol. 741, *p.* 131.

* *Curtoll, curtal or curtail,* an obsolete wood-wind instrument, having a reed and being of the bassoon type. It was played as a bass to the hautboy (Grove's Dictionary).

1662, *August* 30.

Warrant to admit Lewis Evans musician in ordinary for the lute, in the place of Robert Johnson, deceased, with the wages of 1s. 8d. per diem and £16-2-6 yearly for livery.

L. C. Vol. 741, *p.* 277 ; *Vol.* 479, *p.* 102.

1662, *September* 3.

Certificate that the trumpeters to his late Majesty received a yearly livery at the feast of Pentecost, amounting to £19 : 17 : 8 apiece.

L. C. Vol. 183, *p.* 7.

1662, *September* 4.

Petition of Thomas Johnson against Thomas Lanier.

L. C. Vol. 649.

1662, *September* 4.

Warrant to admit Paul Bridges musician in ordinary for a violl de gambo in his Majesty's private musick, with the wages of £40 yearly and £16-2-6 for livery.

L. C. Vol. 741, *p.* 277.

1662, *September* 4.

Warrant to pay John Smyth, musician in his Majesty's private musick, £12 for a basse violl for his Majesty's service.

L. C. Vol. 741, *p.* 228.

1662, *September* 13.

Patent, granting to William Gregory, John Mason, Thomas Mell, and Henry Gregorie, musicians in ordinary, an allowance of £60 per annum during their lives, and the longer liver of them, for the education and teaching of two boys in the art of musique especially on the flutes and cornetts, for our use and service.

L. C. Vol. 814, *p.* 283*d.*

1662, *September* 23.

Warrant for the allowance of a livery to John Gamble, musician in ordinary in the place of Jerome Lanier, deceased.

L. C. Vol. 181, *p.* 75 ; *and Vol.* 741, *p.* 165.

1662, *September* 26.

Warrant for the allowance of a yearly livery to John Bannister and Thomas Bates, sworn musicians in ordinary in the places of Davies Mell and Alphonso Ferabosco, deceased.

L. C. Vol. 181, *p.* 76 ; *and Vol.* 741, *p.* 166.

1662, *September* 29.

Warrant to pay Richard Hudson, musician, the sum of £20 for strings, on the behalfe of himself and the rest of his Majesty's musicians for the violins for one whole year, from June 24, 1661, to June 24, 1662.

L. C. Vol. 741, *p.* 238.

Accounts ending Michaelmas, 1662.

Accounts for liveries for the following musicians to the King :—

William Child	Humphrey Madge
Nicholas Lanier	William Gregory
Henry Lawes	John Willson
Charles Colman	Henry Cook
George Hudson	Angelo Notary
Davis Mell	Thomas Lanier
John Hingston	

Account of four quarterly payments of £10 to Henry Cook, master of the boys of the King's Chappell, for keeping and teaching two boys for a year. Account of £59 : 8 : 4 paid to Thomas Lanier in the place of his father, Andrea Lanier, deceased, for the keeping and teaching of two boys.

L. C. Vol. 56.

Bill for making 12 surplices for the musicians in the Chappell and for making 34 surplices for the children of the Chappell.

Bill for three very large trunkes barrd strong and bound round with iron, the locks, handles and squiers of the best and lined with fine bayes, for the instruments of music.

Bill for swords for his Majesty's trumpeters and the trumpeters to the Duke of Ormond.

Bill for clothing for a Chappell boy extraordinary.

L. C. Papers, Bundle 10.

Bill for clothing for George Maxene, boy of the Chappell.

L. C. Papers, Bundle 13.

Bill amounting to £44 : 2s. for skins of shammy leather, for the trumpeters and kettle drummers.

L. C. Papers, Bundle 22.

1662, *October* 7.

Warrant to provide and deliver to John Hingston, keeper of His Majesty's organs, a curtain of crimson damaske 12 yards in breadth and 2 yards in depth for the organ loft and gallery in his Majesty's Chappell Royall at Whitehall.

L. C. Vol. 817, *pp.* 332, 367.

1662, *October* 9.

Warrant to pay Thomas Baltzar, musician for the violin in the private musick, the sum of £6. 13s. 4d. for strings for one year, bought by him for his Majesty's service.

L. C. Vol. 741, *p.* 392.

1662, *October* 11.

Warrant to pay John Singleton, musician, the sum of £25 for a theorboe lute, and sackbutt, for his Majesty's service.

L. C. Vol. 741, *p.* 238.

1662, *October* 22.

Warrant for the payment of £12 to Thomas Bates, musician, for a basse violl, bought by him for his Majesty's service, also the sum of £5 for strings until June 24, 1661.

L. C. Vol. 741, *p.* 239.

1662, *October* 24.

Warrant to pay John Bannister £40 for two Cremona violins bought by him for his Majesty's service, and also £10 for strings for two years ending June 24th, 1662.

L. C. Vol. 741, *p.* 240.

1662, *October* 27.

Jeoffrey Bannister appointed musician in ordinary for the violin without fee.

L. C. Vol. 479, *p.* 103; *and Vol.* 741, *p.* 358.

1662, *October* 27.

William Aleworth appointed musician for the violin in ordinary, without fee.

L. C. Vol. 478, *p.* 113; *and Vol.* 479, *p.* 103.

1662, *November* 4.

Warrant to admit Henry Roberts musician in ordinary without fee for the lute, voyall and voyce, to come in ordinary with fee after the decease of Anthony Roberts, his father.

L. C. Vol. 741, *p.* 356.

1662, *November* 4.

Warrant to pay £32. 5s. to each of the following musicians in ordinary :—

Nicholas Lanier in place of Robert Hales, deceased, Anthony Roberts in place of Jonas Wrench, deceased, Matthew Locke in place of Henry Ferabosco, deceased, John Jenkins in place of John Coggeshall, deceased, John Lilly in place of John Kelly, deceased, Edward Coleman in place of John Lanier, deceased, John Harding in place of Edward Wormeall, deceased, Stephen Strong in place of Clement Lanier, deceased, Gregory Thorndell in place of John Drewe, deceased, Alphonso Marsh in place of Thomas Day, deceased, John Smyth in place of John Taylor, deceased, Thomas Bates in place of Alphonso Ferabosco, deceased, John Gamble in place of Jerome Lanier, deceased, and John Bannister in place of Davis Mell, deceased, in consideration of their liveries for two years last past since they were admitted into His Majesty's service; and also for the allowance of a yearly livery of £16 : 2 : 6 to each of them at the feast of St. Andrew.

L. C. Vol. 814, *p.* 202; *L. C. Papers, Bundle* 23.

1662, *November* 9.

Dr. Charles Coleman, appointed composer in his Majesty's private musick for voyces in ordinary, in the place of Henry Lawes.

L. C. Vol. 479, *p.* 98.

1662, *November* 10.

Warrant to admit Dr. Charles Coleman composer in his Majesty's private music for the voices in the place of Henry Lawes, deceased, with the wages of £40 per annum.

L. C. Vol. 741, *p.* 182.

1662, *November* 10.

Thomas Purcell appointed to the private musick for lutes, voyall and voyces, in the place of Henry Lawes.

L. C. Vol. 479, *p.* 100.

1662, *November* 14.

John Myer appointed musician in ordinary for the violin without fee; and Henry Purcell musician in ordinary for lute and voyce in the same place with Angelo Notari.

L. C. Vol. 479, *p.* 103; *L. C. Vol.* 741, *p.* 357.

1662, *November* 15.

Warrant to admit Thomas Purcell musician in ordinary in the place of Henry Lawes, deceased, with the yearly wages and livery of £36-2-6.

L. C. Vol. 741, *p.* 283.

1662, *November* 15.

Warrant to admit Angelo Notari and Henry Purcell musicians in ordinary for the lutes and voyces, with the yearly wages of £40, to commence from St. John Baptist, 1660.

L. C. Vol. 741, *p.* 283.

1662, *November* 17.

Warrant to admit John Clement musician in ordinary for lutes, voyall, and voyces in the place of William Lawes, deceased, with the wages of £40 per annum, to commence from St. John Baptist, 1660.

L. C. Vol. 741, *p.* 282.

1662, *November* 18.

Warrant to pay Paul Francis Bridges the sum of £10. for a basse violl bought by him for his Majesty's service.

L. C. Vol. 741, *p.* 393.

1662, *November* 29.

Warrant to admit Theodor Steifken and Frederick William Steifken musicians in ordinary for the violl, with the wages of 1s. 8d. per diem and £16-2-6 yearly for livery, to commence from St. John Baptist, 1660.

L. C. Vol. 741, *p.* 281.

1662, *November* 29.

Warrant to pay Henry Cooke, one of his Majesty's private musick, the sum of £20 for a theorbo and £5 for strings.

L. C. Vol. 741, *p.* 394.

1662, *St. Andrew.*

Payment of £16. 2. 6. to each of the following musicians to the King for their liveries :—

Nicholas Lanier, master of the music.	John Lillie
	John Harding
Henry Cooke	John Bannister
John Willson	Edward Coleman
Charles Coleman	Gregory Thornedell
Anthony Roberts	Mathew Lock
John Hingeston	Angelo Notarie
William Gregorie	Stephen Strong
George Hudson	Thomas Bates
Humphrey Madge	Alphonso Marsh
Nicholas Lanier, luter.	Henry Bassano
Thomas Lanier	John Clement
John Smith	Thomas Pursell
John Gamble	William Child
John Jenkins	Giles Tompkins

Payment of £29 : 16 : 8 to William Gregorie, John Mason, Thomas Mell and Henry Gregorie, for clothing two boys and educating them in the art of music for half a year.

L. C. Vol. 460.

1662, *December* 4.

Bill for 39 pair of perfumed cord gloves at 3s. per pair for the 13 boys of the Chappell Royall, each having 3 pair.

Also for silk hose, grey worsted hose, and perfumed cord gloves for 17 trumpeters and kettledrummers.

L. C. Papers, Bundle 6.

1662, *December* 10.

Order for a warrant for the allowance of a yearly livery to John Clement, musician in ordinary to his Majesty, in the place of William Lawes, deceased, to commence from St. John the Baptist, 1660.

L. C. Vol. 181, *p.* 79.

1662, *December* 15.

Thomas Greeting appointed musician in ordinary without fee in his Majesty's private musick.

L. C. Vol. 478, *p.* 113 ; *and Vol.* 479, *p.* 103.

1662, *December* 24.

In a bill endorsed " Mr. Young his account of money paid by him," an entry of £15 : 14 : 6 to Mr. Harding, musician.

L. C. Papers, Bundle 18.

[1662.]

A list of the officers of his Majesty's household.

Musicians in ordinary.

Nicholas Lanier, master of the music	John Hingston
Dr. Coleman	Symon Hopper
Mr. Henry Lawes	John Strong
Mr. John Smyth	Robert Strong
David Mell	Edward Strong
Humphrey Madge	John Clemont
William Gregory	Gregory Thorndell
Richard Hudson	Henry Hawes
George Hudson	John Lylley
Mr. Harding	Alphonso Marsh
Thomas Blagrave	William Howes
Mr. Dorney	Thomas Bates
Mr. Comer	Robert Deering
Mr. Child	Captain Cooke
Mr. Jenkins	Nathaniel Watkins
Mr. Beckett	Edward Coleman
John Rogers	Theophilus Fitz
	Christopher Gibbons

Matthew Lock	Stephen Nau
Charles Evans	Andrew Lanier
Henry Cooke	Robert Blagrave
Giles Tomkins	Stafford Darcy
William Wing	William Anlaby
John Gamble	Thomas Lanier
Mr. Bannister	

Trumpeters.

Gervace Price, yeoman of the bowes and
    guns and sergeant trumpeter
Benigne Le Ragois
Nicholas Caperon
Melgue Goldt
Hugh Fitchert
Symon Beale
William Hopkins
Thomas Sculthorpe
Milbert Meurs
Anthony Franck
John Jones
Deane
Edward Sympson
Edward Homerston

L. C. Papers, Bundle 20.

1662-3, *January* 15.

Warrant to provide and deliver to Henry Cooke, master of
the children of his Majesty's Chappell, thirteen Common
Prayer books in octavo, for the said children to doe their
service in his Majesty's Chappell.

L. C. Vol. 817, *p.* 401.

1662-3, *January* 15.

Warrant for the payment of a new years guift to Richard
Dorney, one of his Majesty's private musick.

L. C. Vol. 741, *p.* 406.

1662-3, *January* 23.

Warrant to pay to Richard Hudson, keeper of his Majesty's
lutes and violls, such a proportion of money for his new year's
guifts for the years 1660, 1661, 1662, as any of his Majesty's
musicians.

L. C. Vol. 741, *p.* 407.

1662-3, January 23.

Order for a warrant for the allowance of a yearly livery to Thomas Pursill, one of his Majesty's musicians in ordinary for lutes and voices, in the place of Henry Lawes, deceased, to commence from 1 November, last past.

L. C. Vol. 181, *p.* 81 *; L. C. Vol.* 741, *p.* 284.

1662-3, January 29.

Warrant for the annual allowance of £19-17-8d. to each of the following trumpeters in ordinary to his late Majesty of ever glorious memory, to be paid half yearly, and to commence from Midsummer, 1661 :—

Robert Ramsey	George Porter
Thomas Cresswell	George Bosgrove
Samuel Markland	William Porter
Henry Peacock	

L. C. Vol. 741, *p.* 285.

1662-3, February 11.

Peter Ward appointed one of his Majesty's private musick in ordinary.

L. C. Vol. 478, *p.* 113 *; and Vol.* 479, *p.* 103.

1662-3, February 12.

William Yowckney, suspended from his place as musician, for neglecting to perform his service and duty as commanded.

L. C. Vol. 741, *p.* 362.

1662-3, February 16.

Warrant to pay the sum of £48. 7s. 6d. each to Henry Bassano, musician in ordinary for the wind instruments, and to John Clement, musician in the place of William Lawes, deceased, in consideration of their liveries for three years ended at St. Andrew's last past inclusive, since they were admitted into his Majesty's service ; and to Thomas Pursill, musician in place of Henry Lawes, deceased, the materials for his livery due at St. Andrew last past ; and henceforth yearly at St. Andrew a livery of £16 : 2 : 6 each to Henry Bassano, John Clement and Thomas Pursill.

L. C. Vol. 814, *p.* 221 *; L. C. Papers, Bundle* 23.

1662-3, February 24.

Order for a warrant for the allowance of a yearly livery to William Gregorie, John Mason, Thomas Mell and Henry Gregory, admitted as musicians in ordinary to his Majesty, for the education and breeding of two boyes in the art of musicke for the wind instruments, in the place of Andrea Lanier, deceased, to commence Christmas, 1661.

L. C. Vol. 181, *p.* 86 *; L. C. Vol.* 741, *p.* 187.

1662-3, *February* 28.

Edmund Tanner appointed musician in ordinary for the violin, without fee.

L. C. Vol. 479, *p.* 103 ; *Vol.* 741, *p.* 364.

1662-3, *March* 20.

Warrant to admit John Bannister musician in ordinary for the violins for the private musick in the place of Daniel Mell, deceased, with the yearly wages of £110, to commence from the Annunciation last past.

L. C. Vol. 741, *p.* 286.

1662-3, *March* 24.

Warrant to pay John Lylly, musician for the lutes, the sum of £12 for a lute, sold and delivered by him for his Majesty's service.

L. C. Vol. 741, *p.* 421.

1663, *April* 1.

Warrant for the payment of £67. 11s. to John Hingeston, keeper of his Majesty's organs, for removing and setting up an organ in her Majesty's Chappell at St. James', for removing another organ from Whitehall to St. James' for the French musick, and for portage of a larger organ from Mr. Nicoe's to St. James, and setting it up there.

L. C. Vol. 741, *p.* 420.

1663, *April* 15.

Warrant for the payment of £174. 10s. to John Bannister and 13 of his Majesty's band of violins, for their riding charges for 20 days to Portsmouth in May, 1662, and also for their attendance at Hampton Court for 31 days, at the usual rate of 5s. by the day to each man, being there all the month of July past.

L. C. Vol. 741, *p.* 384.

1663, *April* 15.

Order to Richard Hudson, keeper of his Majesty's lutes and violls.

"Whereas divers of his Majesty's musitians have bought both violls, violins and lutes for his Majesty's service for which they have received warrants to be paid considerable sums of money, these are therefore to require you to take the said instruments into your custody and to cause his Majesty's Armes to be cut in mother of pearl and inlayed in the finger boards of the several instruments as hath been usually done heretofore and that you cause them to be secured in his Majesty's house and not removed from thence but when commanded upon his Majesty's service to the end they be not changed or broken."

L. C. Vol. 741, *p.* 370.

1663, *April* 17.

Warrant for the payment of £19. 17. 8. yearly to the following trumpeters, as a pension for their services done to his late Majesty of blessed memory, to begin at Pentecost, 1661.

Robert Ramsey	George Porter
Thomas Creswell	George Bosgrove
Samuel Markland	William Porter
Henry Peacock	

L. C. Vol. 181, *p.* 87 ; *L. C. Vol.* 741, *p.* 193.

1663, *April* 30.

Warrant to pay Henry Cooke, master of the Children of his Majesty's Chappell, the sum of £21 for himself and 13 boys of the Chappell, for their attendance at Windsor last St. George's feast, 6 days, at the rate of 5s. by the day, also £3 for the attendance of Mr. Bates and Mr. Gregory, and £1 10s. for carrying of the instruments that was for performance of the musick and £2 for their lodging.

L. C. Vol. 741, *p.* 386.

1663, *April* 30.

Warrant for payments for strings and tassels for trumpet banners, eight cornets and ensigne strings, for our regiment of foot at Dunkirk.

L. C. Vol. 802, *p.* 62.

1663, *May* 4.

Order for the arrest of Thomas Lanier at the suit of a blind man.

L. C. Vol. 650.

1663, *May* 4.

Warrant to pay Henry Cooke, master of the Children of his Majesty's Chappell, the sum of £30 expended by him for teaching the said children the latin tongue, and for learning of them to write ; also the sum of £30 for the Children's learning of the violins and the organ.

L. C. Vol. 741, *pp.* 385 *and* 386.

1663, *May* 14.

Warrant to pay Theodor Steifken the sum of £12 for a lyra violl bought by him for his Majesty's service.

L. C. Vol. 741, *p.* 380.

1663, *May* 23.

Appointment of the following as trumpeters extraordinary :

John Humphryes	William Milward
Edward Hopkins	John Crowder
John Christmas	Francis Hall

L. C. Vol. 478, *p.* 119 ; *and Vol.* 479, *p.* 106.

1663, *May* 23.

Warrant to pay to Robert Ramsey, Thomas Cressewell, Samuel Markland, George Porter, George Bosgrove, William Porter and Henry Peacocke, trumpeters to our late Royall father, £19 : 17 : 8 yearly, by way of pension in consideration of their services, to begin Pentecost, 1661 ; also the sum of £39 15s. 4d. arrears of their pensions for the years 1661 and 1662.

L. C. Vol. 814, *p.* 226.

1663, *Pentecost*.

Payment of £19. 17. 8. to each of the following trumpeters to the late King Charles I. for their pensions :—

Robert Ramsey	George Porter
Thomas Cresswell	George Bosgrove
Samuel Markland	William Porter
Henry Peacock	

L. C. Vol. 460.

1663, *May* 24.

Warrant to pay to William Gregory, John Mason, Thomas Mell and Henry Gregory, for the apparelling and breeding up of two boys in the art of musick for the wind instruments, in the place of Andrea Lanier, deceased, and for and in consideration of their summer and winter liveries, the sum of £59. 13s. 4d., and to deliver to them twice a year during his Majesty's pleasure the materials for their summer and winter liveries.

L. C. Vol. 814, *p.* 228.

1663, *June* 1.

Thomas Christmas appointed trumpeter extraordinary.

L. C. Vol. 478, *p.* 119 ; *and Vol.* 479, *p.* 106.

1663, *June* 20.

Warrant to pay Edward Strong, musician, the sum of £50, for three good curtalls,* by him bought and delivered for his Majesty's service.

L. C. Vol. 741, *p.* 424.

1663, *June* 22.

Petition of Thomas Lanier against Joseph Alexander, notice of the above to be given to the said Joseph Alexander.

L. C. Vol. 650.

1663, *St. John the Baptist*.

Payment of £29. 16. 8. (collectively) to William Gregorie, John Mason, Thomas Mell and Henry Gregory, musicians to the King, for clothing and educating two boys in the art of music for half a year.

L. C. Vol. 460.

* See note to p. 147.

1663, *July* 4.

Warrant for the payment of £30 to the following musicians for the wind instruments for their attendance at Windsor :—

Dr. William Child	William Howes
William Gregory	Edward Strong
John Mason	Humphrey Madge
Thomas Mell	Robert Blagrave
John Strong	John Gamble
Robert Strong	Phillip Beckett
Thomas Blagrave	Stephen Strong
John Hingston, keeper of the organs	

L. C. Vol. 741, *p.* 375.

1663, *July* 10.

Warrant for the payment of £48 to the following musicians in ordinary for the violins, for their attendance at Windsor :—

Nicholas Lanier, master of his Majesty's musick	John Singleton
	William Young
Matthew Lock, George Hudson and John Bannister, composers	Henry Comer
	William Clayton
	Phillip Beckett
Humphrey Madg	Henry Smyth
William Yowckney	Richard Hudson
Ambrose Beckland	Symon Hopper
Thomas Blagrave	John Strong
William Saunders	Robert Strong
Edward Strong	Theophilus Fitz
John Atkins	Isaack Staggins
Henry Brockwell	

L. C. Vol. 741, *p.* 375.

1663, *July* 16.

Warrant for the payment of £50 to Nicholas Lanier, master of his Majesty's musique, Dr. Charles Coleman, Capt. Henry Cooke, Mr. George Hudson, and Mr. Mathew Lock, for themselves and the rest of the private musique, for hireing of two large roomes for the practice of the private musique and for keeping the instruments in, for one year from 24 June, 1662 to June, 1663.

L. C. Vol. 742, *p.* 77.

1663, *August* 19.

Appointment of John Banister, musitian, to make choyce of twelve of our four and twenty violins to be a select band to wayte on us whensoever there should be occasion for musick ;

and in consideration of their extraordinary service and the smallnesse of their wages already settled, £600 to be paid to John Banister, for himselfe and 12 of our said violins, to commence 25 March, 1662.

L. C. Vol. 742, p. 371.

1663, *August* 20.

Warrant to the surveyor generall to make and erect a large organ loft by his Majesty's Chappell at Whitehall, in the place where formerly the great double organ stood, and to rebuild the rooms over the bellowes roome, two stories high, as it was formerly, the lower story for the subdeane of his Majesty's Chappell, and the upper story with two rooms, one of them for the organist in wayting and the other for the keeper and repayrer of his Majesty's organs, harpsicords, virginalls and other instruments, each room to have a chymney, and boxes and shelves for keeping the materials belonging to the organ, and the organ books.

L. C. Vol. 741, p. 292.

1663, *September* 16.

Warrant to admit Henry Gregory musician in ordinary for the wind instruments, in the place of his father William Gregory, deceased, with the wages of 1s. 8d. per diem, and £16-2-6 yearly for livery.

L. C. Vol. 741, p. 288.

Accounts ending Michaelmas, 1663.

Accounts for liveries for the following musicians to the King :—

Nicholas Lanier	John Jenkins
Charles Colman, senior	John Lillie
George Hudson	Edward Coleman
John Hingeston	John Harding
Humphrey Madge	Stephen Strong
William Gregorie	Gregory Thornedell
John Wilson	Alphonso Marsh
Henry Cooke	John Smith
Angelo Notarie	Thomas Bates
Thomas Lanier	John Gamble
Nicholas Lanier	Henry Bassano
Anthony Roberts	John Clement
Mathew Lock	Thomas Pursill

Accounts of four quarterly payments of £10 to Henry Cooke for the custody and teaching of two boys.

L. C. Vol. 58.

Account for arrears of pensions for seven trumpeters to the late King Charles I., by warrant of 23 May, 1663 :—

Robert Ramsey   George Bosgrove
Thomas Cresswell   William Porter
Samuel Markland   Henry Peacock
George Porter

Account paid to the musicians William Gregorie, John Mason, Thomas Mell and Henry Gregorie for clothing two boys and educating them in the art of music, by warrant of 24 May, 1663.   *L. C. Vols.* 58 *and* 152.

Accounts for liveries of £16 : 2 : 6 to 13 musicians to the King, by warrant of 4 November, 1662 :—

Nicholas Lanier   Stephen Strong
Anthony Roberts   Gregory Thornedell
Mathew Lock   Alphonso Marsh
John Jenkins   John Smith
John Lillie   Thomas Bates
Edward Colman   John Gamble
John Harding   John Bannister

Accounts for liveries to 3 musicians to the King, by warrant of 16 February, 1662-3 :—

Henry Bassano   John Clement
Thomas Pursill
                                       L. C. Vol. 152.

1663, *October* 13.

Warrant to pay Richard Hudson, one of his Majesty's musicians for the violins in ordinary, the sum of £20 for strings for himself and the rest of the violins for one whole year ending 24 June, 1663.
                              L. C. Vol. 742, *p.* 100

1663, *October* 15.

Warrant for the payment of £124 5s. to John Banister and six other of his Majesty's musicians in ordinary for the violins, for rydeing charges when attending his Majesty to Tunbridge and Bath from 23 July, 1663 to 1 October following, being 70 days at 5s. per diem to each man.
                              L. C. Vol. 742, *p.* 90.

1663, *October* 17.

Warrant for the payment of £27 to Gervase Price, sergeant trumpeter, for the use of William Bownty, Edward Homerston, John Baker and Symon Beale, four trumpeters in ordinary, for their riding charges and expenses at Tunbridge while attending his Majesty for the space of 27 days at 5s. per diem for each man, from 10 June to 7 July, 1663.

L. C. Vol. 742, *p.* 91.

1663, *October* 19.

His Majesty's French Musicians in Ordinary.

Ferdinand de Florence   Nicholas Fleuri
Claude de Grange   Guillaume Santre
Elenor Guigant   Jean de la Vollee.

L. C. Vol. 478, *pp.* 76 & 80; *L. C. Vol.* 479, *p.* 98.

1663, *October* 27.

Warrant to deliver unto Henry Cooke, master of the children of his Majesty's Chappell, certain clothing named, for Thomas Price, one of the children, whose voyce is changed and who is to goe from the Chappell.

L. C. Vol. 742, *p.* 3.

1663, *October* 27.

Warrant to pay Henry Cooke, master of the children of his Majesty's Chappell, the sum of £66. 8s. 6d. for teaching the said children latten and to write, also for teaching them on the violin, and for strings, for one year ended at Michaelmas, 1663.

L. C. Vol. 742, *p.* 94.

1663, *November* 6.

Warrant to pay John Hingston, keeper and repairer of his Majesty's organs, the sum of £83. 15s. for taking down the organ in her Majesty's Chappell at St. James's, and remounting the same in the new musique room; for mending the organs and harpsicords; also for mending her Majesty's harpsicord that stands in her own chamber; for mending a claricon; for erecting an organ in the banquetting house at Whitehall against Maundy Thursday, and for diverse other things; from 25 March, 1663, to 29 September following.

L. C. Vol. 742, *pp.* 96 *and* 97.

1663, *November* 12.

Order for the apprehension of all musitians playing at any dumb shows, modells, gamehouses, taverns, or any other places, in the city of London and Westminster without leave or lycence from the Corporation of the Art and Science of Musick.

L. C. Vol. 650.

1663, *November* 12.

Order that the following musitians of the recorders, the flutes, the hoboyes and sackbutts, the violins, the lutes and voyces, the trumpeters, drummers and fife be discharged from paying the four subsidies lately granted in the Parliament begun the 8 May, 1661 :—

Musitians for the Wind musick.

Nicholas Lanier	Henry Bassano
Humphrey Madg	William Howes
John Mason	Thomas Blagrave
Thomas Mell	Phillip Beckett
John Strong	John Singleton
Stephen Strong	Dr. William Chyld
Robert Strong	John Gamble
Edward Strong	Robert Blagrave

[Alterations made in the list at a later date] :—

The names of Mr. Grabu and William Young inserted for those of Nicholas Lanier and Henry Bassano; and William Clayton in place of Edward Strong.

Violins.

George Hudson	Paule Bridges
Mathew Lock	John Banister
William Yockney	Henry Comer
Ambrose Beland	William Young
William Saunders	William Clayton
Henry Gregory	Henry Smyth
John Atkinson	Richard Hudson
Henry Brockwell	Symon Hopper
John Rogers	Theophilus Fittz
Charles Evans	Isaack Staggins
Lewis Evans, alias Williams	Richard Darney
James Farr	Walter Yockney

Edward Tanner (added at a later date).

Lutes and voices.

Henry Cooke	Angelo Notary
Dr. John Wilson	John Hingeston
Dr. Charles Coleman	William Gregory
John Clemens	Thomas Bates
Thomas Lanier	Nathaniel Watkins
John Harding	John Smyth
Edward Coleman	Henry Hawes
Alphonso Marsh	Theodor Steifken

Gregory Thorndell   John Jenkins
Anthony Roberts   John Lylly
Thomas Purcell   Christopher Gibbons
               Giles Tomkins.

Trumpeters.

Gervase Price   Thomas Sculthorpe
Benigne le Ragois   Milibert Meurs
Nicholas Coperon   John Jones
Melque Goldt   Edward Sympson
Hugh Fitchert   Edward Homerston
Symon Beale   Henry Thewer
Sylvester Whitmeale   John Baker
               Hans Bernihoski

Drummers.

John Mawgridge   Richard Mawgridge
Tertullian Lewis   Richard Vaux, fife
Edward Ottley   Deverick Cloathier.
John Hingeston, keeper of the organs.

L. C. Vol. 742, *pp.* 380-381.

1663, *November* 25.

Warrant to pay Charles Evans, musician to his Majesty in ordinary for the Italian harp, the sum of £15 for a harp bought by him for his Majesty's service, and £5 for strings.

L. C. Vol. 742, *p.* 100.

1663, *St. Andrew.*

Payment of £29. 16. 8. (collectively) to John Mason, Thomas Mell and Henry Gregory, musicians to the King, for clothing, and educating two boys in the art of music for half a year.

Payment of £16. 2. 6. to each of the following musicians to the King, for their liveries :—

John Wilson   Gregory Thornedell
Charles Colman (in a later Mathew Locke
  hand is written "mort") Angelo Notary (in a
Anthony Roberts   later hand is written
John Hingeston   "mort")
William Gregorie   Stephen Strong
George Hudson   Thomas Bates
Humphrey Madge   Alphonso Marsh
Nicholas Lanier, luter   Henry Bassano
Nicholas Lanier, master of Henry Cooke
  the music   Giles Tompkins

Thomas Lanier
John Smith
John Gamble
John Jenkins
John Lillie
John Harding
John Bannister
Edward Colman

John Clement
Thomas Purcell
William Child
John Clement [with note
" This Debentur lost
was twice made out
and twice paid for].

L. C. Vol. 460.

1663, *December* 10.

Names of the Gentlemen of his Majesty's Chappell Royall, exempted from payment of subsidies granted to his Majesty by Parliament, 8 May, 1661.

Gentlemen of the Chappell Royall.

Ralph Amner
Thomas Peers
Thomas Hazard
John Harding
Edward Lowe
Dr. William Chyld
William Howes
Christopher Gibbons
Phillip Tinker
John Sayer
Alfonso March
Raphaell Courtwile
Edward Coleman
Thomas Purcell
Henry Frost
John Goodgroome

Henry Cooke
Durant Hunt
Thomas Balgrave.
Gregory Thorndale
Edward Braddock
Henry Purcell
William Tucker
James Cobb
Nathaniel Watkins
John Cave
George Bettenham
Mathew Peniall
Roger Hill
George Yardly
Dr. John Wilson
William Jackson

L. C. Vol. 742, *p.* 385.

1663, *December* 22.

Edmund Portington appointed musician extraordinary for the private musick.

L. C. Vol. 478, *p.* 113 ; *and Vol.* 479, *p.* 100.

1663, *December* 24.

Warrant to admit Jeoffrye Banister musician in ordinary for the violin, in the place of Edward Strong, deceased, with the wages of £46. 12s. 8d. per annum, to commence at Michaelmas last past.

L. C. Vol. 742, *p.* 388.

1663.

Account for surplices for the dean and sub-dean, gentlemen, musicians, and children, of the Chappell.

L. C. Papers, Bundle 18.

Items in a " brief of the account for one year and half from Xmas 1661, to midsummer 1663."

				£.	s.	d.
Trumpeters	-	-	-	840	0	0
Musicians	-	-	-	812	3	2½

L. C. Papers, Bundle 19.

1663-4, *January* 4.

Letter of assignment from John Jenkins, one of the gentlemen of his Majesty's private musicke, appointing John Lillie, of St. Andrews, Holborn, as his true and lawful attorney.

L. C. Vol. 181, *p.* 114.

1663-4, *January* 16.

Order that Thomas Lanier shall give an appearance at the Common Law, at the suit of Thomas Johnson.

L. C. Vol. 650.

1663-4, *February* 1.

Joseph Walker appointed trumpeter in the place of Thomas Knowles.

L. C. Vols. 479, *p.* 105 ; 482, *p.* 61.

1663-4, *February* 23.

William Tollett, appointed bag-piper in ordinary.

L. C. Vol. 482, *p.* 172.

1663-4, *February* 29.

Warrant to pay Henry Cooke, master of the children of his Majesty's Chappell Royall, £30 yearly for the charge and expense of keeping Thomas Price, late one of the children of the Chappell, to beginn from Michaelmas, 1663.

L. C. Vol. 742, *p.* 117.

1663-4, *March* 2.

Warrant to pay Gervase Price, sergeant trumpeter, William Bounty, John Baker, Richard Deane, John Jones and Silvester Whitmell, five of his Majesty's trumpeters in ordinary, the sum of £64 15s. for riding charges and other expenses in their attendance on his Majesty in his jorney to Bath and back again by the space of thirty-seven days, from 20 August, 1663, to 1 October following, at the rate of 10s. a day for the sergeant trumpeter and 5s. a day to each of the others.

L. C. Vol. 742, *p.* 116.

1663-4, *March* 3.

Warrant to pay Henry Cook, master of the children of his Majesty's Chappell Royall, £20 for fire in the musick room at the Chappell, and also for strings for the base voyall and other instruments belonging to the Chappell, for one whole year from Michaelmas, 1662 to Michaelmas, 1663.

L. C. Vol. 742, *p.* 117.

1664, *Lady Day.*

Bill for 12 large shamway skins to make doubletts for Mr. O'Neal's trumpeters at 8s. a piece.

L. C. Papers, Bundle 2.

A few items of livery, allowed to John Crowder, appointed trumpeter.

L. C. Papers, Bundle 22.

Bill for suits for three children of the Chappell.

L. C. Papers, Bundle 3.

Bill for belts for his Majesty's 18 trumpeters and for Mr. O'Neal's 4 trumpeters.

L. C. Papers, Bundle 4.

Bill for four swords silver and gilt, for four trumpeters belonging to his Majesty's own troop, at 45s. apiece.

L. C. Papers, Bundle 5.

Bill for shoes for twelve children of the King's Chappell, for Mr. O'Neal's 3 trumpeters and kettledrummers and for the three children of the Queen's Chappell.

L. C. Papers, Bundle 10.

1664, *March* 31.

Warrant to deliver to Captain Henry Cooke materials for liveries for the children of the King's Chappell, and to Mr. Ferdinando the same for the three children of the Queen's Chappell.

L. C. Papers, Bundle 5.

1664, *April* 18.

Petition of Sarah Roper, spinster, against Milbert Morrice, trumpeter, the latter to have notice of the petition and to appear before me on Thursday morning next by tenn of the clock at Whitehall.

L. C. Vol. 650.

1664, *May* 10.

Warrant to pay James Farr £30 yearly for the maintenance of Michael Wise, late one of the children of his Majesty's Chappell Royall, whose voice is changed ; to commence from the 29 September, last past.

L. C. Vol. 742, *p.* 122.

1664, *May* 16.

John Crowther appointed trumpeter in ordinary in the place of Edward Sympson, deceased.

Hans Berneyhoski, kettledrummer.

L. C. Vols. 479, *p.* 105 ; 482, *p.* 61.

1664, *May* 23.

Petition of Richard Benyon against Captain Bates. All partyes concerned to appear at Whitehall on Tuesday morning next by nyne of the clock.

L. C. Vol. 650.

1664, *Pentecost.*

Payment of £19. 17. 8. to each of the following trumpeters to the late King Charles I. for their pensions :—

Robert Ramsey	George Porter
Thomas Cresswell	George Bosgrave
Samuel Markland	William Porter
Henry Peacock	

L. C. Vol. 460.

1664, *May* 26.

Warrant for the delivery of certain clothing named, such as was formerly delivered for Thomas Price, late one of the children of the Chappell, to James Farr, for the use of Michael Wise, one of the children of his Majesty's Chappell whose voyce is changed, and is to goe from his Majesty's Chappell.

L. C. Vol. 742, *p.* 22; *L. C. Papers, Bundle* 4.

1664, *May* 28.

Certificate that Mr. Henry Frost and Mr. James Cobb, gentlemen of his Majesty's Chappell, are exempt from bearing any public office, and from any mulct or fine for not submitting to the same.

L. C. Vol. 742, *p.* 443.

[1644, *May.*]

Warrant to pay Thomas Baltzar, one of his Majesty's musicians for the violins in the private musick, the sum of £6. 13. 4d. for strings bought by him for his Majesty's service for one whole year ending 5 September, 1663.

L. C. Vol. 742, *p.* 123.

1664, *June* 10.

Payments yearly made by the treasurer of the chamber, they include :—

To 18 trumpeters £1120
To 42 musicians £2017-8s.

L. C. Papers, Bundle 3.

1664, *June* 17.

Warrant to pay Henry Hawes, musician in ordinary, £10 for a base violl bought by him for his Majesty's service, and £4 for strings.

L. C. Vol. 742, *p.* 128.

1664, *St. John the Baptist.*

Payment of £29. 16. 8. to John Mason, Thomas Mell and Henry Gregorie for clothing and educating two boys in the art of music for half a year.

L. C. Vol. 460.

1664 [*June*].

Account paid to Margaret Pothero, for lodging of Mr. Lock, organist, and his servants, at 10s. per week, £8 10s.

To Mr. Perkins, in Hatton Grounds for lodging Mr. Briges, of the musique, at 5s. per week, £4. 5s., and for the lodging of John Harford, blower of the organs at 4s. per week, £3. 8s.

L. C. Vol. 742, *p.* 127.

1664, *July* 8.

Warrant to grant Henry Cooke the office of composer in his Majesty's private musick for voyces in ordinary, in the place of Dr. Charles Coleman, deceased, with the wages of £40 by the year, to commence from St. John the Baptist last past.

L. C. Vol. 479, *p.* 98 ; *L. C. Vol.* 742, *p.* 390.

1664, *July* 11.

Warrant for the allowance of a yearly livery to Dr. William Child, musician in ordinary to his Majesty in the place of Henry Ferabosco, deceased, to commence St. Andrew, 1662.

L. C. Vol. 742, *p.* 24 ; *L. C. Papers, Bundle* 3.

1664, *July* 16.

Warrant for the apprehension of all persons professing the art and science of musick, playing at any playhouses, gamehouses, taverns, victualling houses, or any place in the city of London and Westminster, without the approbation and lycense of the Marshall and Corporation of musique.

L. C. Vol. 650.

1664, *July* 20.

Warrant for the allowance of liveries for the children of the Chappell to be delivered to Capt. Henry Cooke, master of the said children, also for three liveries to be delivered to Mr. Ferdinando for three children of the Queen's Chappell.

L. C. Papers, Bundle 8.

1664, *August* 3.

Petition of Gervase Price, Esquire, against Edward Hayward.

L. C. Vol. 651.

1664, *August* 9.

Warrant to pay Henry Cooke, master of the children of his Majesty's Chappell Royall, £60 for learning of Latin to the children of the Chappell, and also for teaching of them the lute and organ from Michaelmas, 1663, to Lady Day, 1664; and the sum of £10 for fire and strings for half a year in the musick room and Chappell, £7 for strings for the virginalls and lutes, £11 6s. for charges in coach hire and other expenses to Windsor and Canterbury.

L. C. Vol. 742, *p.* 135.

1664, *August* 12.

Warrant to pay Henry Cooke, master of the children of his Majesty's Chappell, £30 yearly for the maintenance of Thomas Edwards, late one of the children of the Chappell, to commence from the Annunciation, last past; and for the delivery of certain clothing named, such as was lately delivered to Michael Wise, late one of the children, for the use of Thomas Edwards, whose voyce is changed and is to goe from his Majesty's Chappell.

L. C. Vol. 742, *pp.* 27 *and* 136; *L. C. Papers, Bundle* 3.

1664, *August* 20.

John Goodgroome appointed to the private musick for the lutes, voyall and voyces, in the place of Henry Purcell.

L. C. Vol. 479, *p.* 100.

1664, *August* 20.

Account of payment of £138 : 7 : 6 to Captain Henry Cooke, one of the gentlemen of his Majesty's Chappell, for 12 liveries ending the 29 September, 1663.

L. C. Vol. 167, *Bk.* 1. *p.* 1.

1664, *August* 27.

William Pagett appointed musician for the violin extraordinary.

L. C. Vol. 478, *p.* 113; *and Vol.* 479, *p.* 103.

1664, *September* 2.

Account for payment of £16 : 2 : 6 to Mr. Stephen Strong, one of his Majesty's musicians, for livery due 30 November, 1660.

L. C. Vol. 167, *Bk.* 1, *p.* 4.

1664, *September* 15.

Alexander Jackson appointed trumpeter in the place of Thomas Hadwyn, deceased.

L. C. Vol. 479, *p.* 106.

1664, *September* 15.

Trumpeters in ordinary to attend the Lord Lieutenant of Ireland :—

Alexander Jackson, Patrick Ray.

L. C. Vol. 478, *p.* 87.

1664, *September* 16.

Account for payment of £16 : 2 : 6 to Mr. Nicholas Lanier, one of his Majesty's musicians, for livery due 30 November, 1660.

L. C. Vol. 167, *Bk.* 1. *p.* 9.

1664, *September* 19.

Command to Jervace Price, Esquire, His Majesty's serjeant trumpeter, to place two trumpeters and one drummer forthwith at the command of Prince Rupert, choyce having been made of William Bounty and John Crowder, two of his Majesty's trumpeters and Devereux Clothier, one of his Majesty's drummers.

L. C. Vol. 651.

1664, *September* 24.

Account for payment of £19 : 17 : 8 to Mr. Samuel Markland, one of his late Majesty's trumpeters, for livery due 23 May, 1663.

L. C. Vol. 167, *Bk.* 1. *p.* 11.

1664, *September* 28.

Account for payment of £16 : 2 : 6 to Mr. Charles Coleman, one of his Majesty's musicians, for livery due 1 November, 1660.

L. C. Vol. 167, *Bk.* 1. *p.* 11.

1664, *Michaelmas.*

Bill for eighteen swords, " hatcht with silver," for his Majesty's trumpeters at 45 shillings apiece.

L. C. Papers, Bundle 3.

Accounts ending Michaelmas, 1664.

Accounts for liveries for the following musicians to the King :—

Nicholas Laneir	John Lillie
Charles Coleman, senior	Edward Coleman
George Hudson	John Harding
John Hingeston	Stephen Strong

Humphrey Madge	Gregory Thornedell
William Gregory	Alphonso Marsh
John Wilson	John Smyth
Henry Cooke	Thomas Bates
Thomas Lanier	John Gamble
Nicholas Lanier	John Bannister
Anthony Roberts	Henry Bassano
Mathew Locke	John Clement
John Jenkins	Thomas Purcell

Account for the pensions of the following trumpeters to the late King Charles I. :—

Robert Ramsay	George Bosgrave
Thomas Cresswell	William Porter
Samuel Markland	Henry Peacock
George Porter	

Account paid to John Mason, Thomas Mell and Henry Gregory, for clothing and educating two boys in the art of music.

Account paid to Henry Cooke of £40 a year for the custody and teaching of two boys.

L. C. Vol. 59.

Items in a brief of account for one year and a quarter, Midsummer 1663, to Michaelmas, 1664 :—

Trumpeters	- - -	£1,680 : 0 : 0
Musicians	- - -	£1,290 : 8 : 6

L. C. Papers, Bundle 19.

1664, *October* 7.

Warrant to deliver to Captain Henry Cook suits of clothing for the children of the Chapel Royal.

L. C. Papers, Bundle 2.

1664, *October* 8.

Warrant for liveries for the three children of the Queen's Chappell, like in every respect as to the children of his Majesty's Chappell.

L. C. Papers, Bundle 3.

1664, *October* 8.

Warrant to pay Henry Cooke master of the children of his Majesty's Chappell, £78 for teaching of the children of the Chappell upon the organ, violin and lute, and for fire in the musique room, and for strings for violins, lutes and virginalls, and also for books and writing paper.

L. C. Vol. 742, *p.* 145.

1664, *October* 25.

William Clayton appointed one of the wind instruments, in the place of Edward Strong.

L. C. Vol. 479, *p.* 102.

1664, *October* 27.

Warrant for payment for seven hundred and fourty-four ells of holland to make a hundred and ten surplices for the gentlemen, musicians and children of our Chappell.

L. C. Vol. 802, *pp.* 131 *and* 182.

1664, *October* 28.

Warrant to swear John Goodgroome musician in ordinary to his Majesty for the lute and voyce, in the place of Henry Purcell, deceased, with the wages of £40 per annum, to commence from Michaelmas, last past.

L. C. Vol. 742, *p.* 391.

1664, *October* 31.

Warrant to pay to Dr. William Child, appointed musician in place of Henry Ferabosco, deceased, for his liveries for two years, due at the Feast of St. Andrew, 1662 and 1663, the sum of £32 5s., and to deliver to him henceforth a yearly livery of £16 : 2 : 6.

L. C. Vol. 814, *p.* 257 ; *L. C. Papers, Bundle* 23.

1664, *November* 2.

Warrant to admit William Clayton musician in ordinary to his Majesty for the treble hoboy, in the place of Edward Strong, deceased, with wages of £66. 2s. 6d. per annum, to commence from Christmas last past.

L. C. Vol. 742, *p.* 392.

1664, *November* 3.

Warrant to pay John Hingeston, keeper and repayrer of his Majesty's organs, pedalls, harpsicords and other instruments, £90. 19s. 8d. for repairing the organs, harpsicords, pedalls, and other instruments from 29 September, 1664 ; bill signed by Mr. Nicholas Lanier.

L. C. Vol. 742, *p.* 149.

1664, *November* 12.

Account for payment of £19 : 17 : 8 to Mr. Thomas Creswell, one of his late Majesty's trumpeters, for livery due 7 June, 1663.

L. C. Vol. 167, *Bk.* 2, *p.* 5.

1664, *November* 15.

Account for payment of £1 to Mrs. Prudence Porter in part of her husband's livery as one of his late Majesty's trumpeters.

L. C. Vol. 167, *Bk.* 2. *p.* 5.

1664, *November* 22.

Order that Benigne Le Ragois, one of His Majesty's trumpeters, be suspended from wayting on account of several abuses committed by him.

L. C. Vol. 651.

1664, *St. Andrew.*

Payment of £29. 16. 8. (collectively) to John Mason, Thomas Mell and Henry Gregory, for clothing and educating two boys in the art of music for half a year.

Payment of £16. 2. 6. to each of the following musicians to the King for their liveries :—

Nicholas Lanier, master of music	John Gamble
Henry Cooke	John Jenkins
John Wilson	John Lillie
Anthony Roberts	John Harding
John Hingeston	John Bannister
William Gregory	Edward Coleman
George Hudson	Gregory Thornedell
Humphrey Madge	Mathew Locke
Nicholas Lanier, luter	Stephen Strong
Thomas Lanier	Thomas Bates
John Smith	Alphonso Marsh

Henry Bassano
(in a later hand is written " mort ")

John Clement	Giles Tompkins
Thomas Purcell	Charles Coleman
William Child	John Goodgroome

L. C. Vol. 461.

1664, *December* 2.

Thomas Fitz appointed musician for the violins in ordinary.

L. C. Vol. 479, *p.* 99.

1664, *December* 5.

Warrant to deliver to Henry Cooke, master of the children of the Chappell, 13 Common Prayer books with the Testament bound together, for the children to do their service in, in the Chappell.

L. C. Papers, Bundle 9.

1664, *December* 8.

Warrant for liveries for the sergeant trumpeter and sixteen trumpeters, and a kettledrummer.

L. C. Papers, Bundle 2 *and Bundle* 9.

1664, *December* 10.

Order for the apprehension of William Bounty, John Crowther and Devereux Clothier, two trumpeters and a drummer, who have deserted His Majesty's service under Prince Rupert, without his Majesty's leave.

L. C. Vol. 651.

1664, *December* 10.

Warrant for the allowance of such livery and at such time to John Goodgroome, admitted musician in ordinary for the lute and voyce in the place of Henry Purcell, deceased, as enjoyed by Angelo Notary and Henry Purcell, deceased, to commence 24 August, 1664.

L. C. Vol. 742, *p.* 40 ; *L. C. Papers, Bundle* 3.

1664, *December* 20.

Order to musicians :—

I do hereby appoint and give leave to John Singleton, William Clayton, William Young, Theophilus Fitz, Richard Hudson, John Strong, Isaack Staggins, Jeoffrey Bannister and Henry Brockwell to attend at his Majesty's theatre whenever Mr. Thomas Killigrew shall desire them.

L. C. Vol. 742, *p.* 429.

1664.

Henry Cooke's receipt for £12 in payment of part of his bill for money laid out by him for Thomas Price and the other children of the Chappell.

Henry Cook's receipt for £24 12s. the amount of his bill for summer liveries for the children of the Chappell.

L. C. Papers, Bundle 4.

1664-5, *January* 23.

Warrant to pay Charles Evans, his Majesty's harper for the Italian harp, £5 for strings by him bought for the harp for a year ending Christmas last past.

L. C. Vol. 742, *p.* 155.

1664-5, *January* 31.

Warrant to pay Henry Brockwell, one of his Majesty's musicians in ordinary, the sum of £16 for a Cremona tenor violin, bought by him for his Majesty's service, and for strings for three years ending 24 June, 1664, at the rate of £2 per annum.

L. C. Vol. 742, *p.* 156.

1664-5, *February* 7.

Warrant to pay the following musicians in ordinary to his Majesty :—

William Gregory, £12 for a base violl; Thomas Bates, £12 for a base viol; Humphrey Madge, £24 for two violins.

All of them bought for his Majesty's service in the Chapell. Also each of them to be paid £20 per annum for their attendance in his Majesty's Chappell from Easter, 1662 to 25 December, 1664.

L. C. Vol. 742, *p.* 157.

1664-5, *February* 14.

Petition of Henry Comer against John Bannister, musitian.

L. C. Vol. 651.

1664-5, *February* 28.

Nicholas Canon admitted one of his Majesty's drummers in ordinary without fee, to come in ordinary with fee upon the next avoydance.

L. C. Vol. 742, *p.* 427.

1664-5, *March* 20.

A warrant to make up habitts of severall coloured silkes for four and twenty violins, twelve of them being for his Majesty's service in the theatre Royall, and the other twelve habitts for his Majesty's service in his Highness the Duke of York's theatre; and also four and twenty Garlands of severall coloured flowers to each of them after the same manner as those that were delivered to Sir H. Herbert, master of his Majesty's Revells. All these habitts and Garlands to be delivered to Mr. Killigrew for his Majesty's extraordinary service.

A like warrant of March 18 for habitts for the 24 violins, like Indian gowns but not so full, with short sleeves to the elboes, trymmed with tinsell about the neck and bottom and at the sleeves.

L. C. Vol. 742, *pp.* 45 & 46; *L. C. Papers, Bundles* 5 *and* 9.

1664-5, *March* 22.

Warrant to pay Hugh Fisher, one of his Majesty's trumpeters in ordinary, £9. 5s. for his rydding charges and other expenses in his attendance on his Majesty on his jorney to Bath and back again by the space of 37 days, from 26 August, 1663 to the 1 October following, at the rate of 5s. a day.

L. C. Vol. 742, *p.* 166.

1665, *March* 25.

George Pinckney's receipt for 40s. received of Mr. Thomas Townsend, deputy to the Earl of Sandwich, master of the great wardrobe, for the use of Henry Peacock one of his Majesty's pensioner trumpeters.

L. C. Papers, Bundle 4.

1665, *March* 31.

Mons. Grabu appointed composer in his Majesty's musique.

L. C. Vol. 479, *p.* 98

1665, *April* 6.

Warrant to admit Theophilus Fitz musician for the double sackbutt in ordinary, in the place of Stephen Strong, deceased, with wages of 1s. 8d. by the day, and £16. 2s. 6d. by the year for his livery, to commence 25 March last past. Also warrant for the allowance of the livery, dated April 8.

L. C. Vol. 742, *pp.* 48 *and* 422. *L. C. Papers, Bundle* 3.

1665, *April* 8.

Thomas Creswell admitted trumpeter in ordinary without fee, to come in ordinary with fee upon the first avoydance.

L. C. Vols. 478, *p.* 119 ; 479, *p.* 104 ; *and Vol.* 742, *p.* 423.

1665, *April* 11.

Warrant to pay Capt. Henry Cooke, master of the children of his Majesty's Chappell Royall, £115. 10s. 6d. for having the children taught Lattin, to write, to play on the viollin, and the organ, and the lute, for stringing and penning their harpsicords, for fire and strings at the musique room at the Chappell, and for his disbursements for cloathes for Michael Wise, late one of the children of the Chappell, and for going into the country looking after boyes for the Chappell for one half year from Michaelmas, 1664 to Lady Day, 1665. And for nursing of three boys that were sick of the small pox.

L. C. Vol. 742, *p.* 163.

1665, *April* 13.

Warrant to admit Devereux Clothier drummer in ordinary to his Majesty in the place of Edward Ottley, deceased, with the wages of 1s. by the day, and £16. 2s. 6d. by the year for his livery, to commence 25 December, 1664.

L. C. Vol. 742, *p.* 398.

1665, *April* 27.

Patent granting to Theophilus Fittz the office of musician in ordinary for the flute in the private music during his life, with the salary of 20d. by the day, and £16. 2s. 6d. a year for his livery.

L. C. Vol. 815, *p.* 165.

1665, *April* 28.

Warrant for the delivery of a crimson taffata curtain to Mr. John Hingston, keeper and repairer of his Majesty's organs, for the great double organ in his Majesty's Chappell Royall at Whitehall.

L. C. Vol. 742, p. 52 ; L. C. Papers, Bundle 3.

1665, *April* 30.

Warrant to admit John Remus as one of his Majesty's trumpeters extraordinary.

L. C. Vol. 742, p. 420.

1665, *May* 4.

Warrant for the allowance of such livery to Charles Coleman, musician in ordinary to his Majesty for the violl, as Dr. Charles Coleman formerly enjoyed, to commence from 29 September last past.

L. C. Vol. 742, p. 52 ; L. C. Papers, Bundle 3.

1665, *May* 7.

John Renny appointed trumpeter extraordinary.

L. C. Vol. 479, p. 106.

1665, *May* 7.

Warrant for the making of a livery for John Remus, one of his Majesty's trumpeters extraordinary.

L. C. Vol. 478, p. 119; L. C. Vol. 742, p. 52.

1665, *May* 13.

Accounts for payment of £1 to Mrs. Mary Peacock for her husband, Henry Peacock. And of £2 to Mr. Robert Ramsey, trumpeters to the late King.

L. C. Vol. 167, Bk. 2, p. 18 ; L. C. Papers, Bundle 4.

1665, *May* 16.

Warrant to deliver to Mr. Ferdinando three summer liveries for the children of her Majesty's Chappell, with all other necessaries in every respect as to other children of his Majesty's Chappell.

L. C. Papers, Bundle 9.

1665, *May* 17.

Warrants to pay Capt. Henry Cooke, master of the Children of his Majesty's Chappell Royall, the sum of £40 yearly for the maintenance of Pelham Humphryes ; £30 yearly for the maintenance of John Blow ; and £30 yearly for the maintenance of John Blundivile ; late children of his Majesty's Chappell, to commence 25 December last past. Also for the delivery of certain clothing named, to him, for the use of the said children, whose voices are changed and are to go from his Majesty's Chappell.

L. C. Vol. 742, pp. 53 and 169; L. C. Papers, Bundles 2 and 9.

1665, *May* 18.

Account for payment of £16. 2. 6. to Mr. Edward Coleman, one of his Majesty's musicians, for livery due 30 November last.

L. C. Vol. 167, Bk. 2, p. 19.

1665, *May* 20.

Thomas Finell appointed musitian for the violin in ordinary, without fee.

L. C. Vol. 478, p. 113; and Vol. 497, p. 103.

1665, *May* 20.

Accounts for payments of £16. 2. 6. to Mr. George Hudson and to John Banister, his Majesty's musicians, for liveries due 30 November last.

L. C. Vol. 167, Bk. 3, pp. 5 and 6.

1665, *May* 22.

Account for payment of £16 2. 6. to Mr. Thomas Lanier, one of his Majesty's musicians, for livery due 30 November last.

L. C. Vol. 167, Bk. 2, p. 20.

1665, *Pentecost.*

Payment of £19. 17. 8. to each of the following trumpeters to the late King Charles I. for their pensions :—

Robert Ramsey	George Porter
Thomas Cresswell	George Bosgrove
Samuel Markland	William Porter
Henry Peacock	

L. C. Vol. 461.

1665, *May* 24.

Account for the livery due 30 November last of Mr. Henry Gregory, being for apparelling and breeding up two boyes in the art of musick. Account paid to Capt. Thomas Bates, one of his Majesty's musicians, of £10 : 2 : 6, which together with £6 lent to him 28 June last, is in full of his livery due 30 November last.

L. C. Vol. 167, Bk. 3, p. 6.

1665, *May* 26.

Account of £303 : 16 : 8 paid to Captain Henry Cooke, one of the gentlemen of his Majesty's Chappell, for buying of necessaries for the children of the Chappell, for their winter liveries for the year 1664, and for their summer liveries for the present year 1665 ; also £30 for teaching two boys for three quarters of a year, due Michaelmas, 1664 to 25 March last. Account of £16 : 2 : 6 paid to Capt. Henry Cooke, one of his Majesty's musicians, for livery due 30 November last.

L. C. Vol. 167, *Bk.* 3, *p.* 7.

1665, *May* 30.

Account for payment of £16 : 2 : 6 to Mr. John Harding, one of his Majesty's musicians, for livery due 30 November last.

Similar payment to Capt. Thomas Bates, one of his Majesty's musicians, due 30 November, 1661.

L. C. Vol. 167, *Bk.* 3, *p.* 8.

1665, *June* 8.

Account for payment of £48 7. 6 to Mr. Gregory Thornedale, one of his Majesty's musicians, for three liveries due 30 November, 1661, 1662 and 1664.

Account for payment of £16 : 2 : 6 to Mr. Alphonso Marsh, one of his Majesty's musicians, for livery due 30 November last.

L. C. Vol. 167, *Bk.* 3, *pp.* 10 & 11.

1665, *June* 9.

Account for payment of £16 : 2 : 6 to Mr. John Lilly, one of his Majesty's musicians, for livery due 30 November last.

L. C. Vol. 167, *Bk.* 3, *p.* 14.

1665, *June* 10.

Account for payment of £16 : 2 : 6 to Mr. Mathew Lock, one of his Majesty's musicians, for livery due 30 November last.

Account for payment of £27 : 5 to Dr. Child, doctor of musick, which together with £25 lent to him 20 March, 1664, was in full for two liveries for the years 1663 and 1664.

L. C. Vol. 167, *Bk.* 3, *pp.* 14 *and* 15.

1665, *June* 13.

To Robert Ramsey and William Porter, trumpeters to the late King : lent, 5/.

L. C. Vol. 167, *Bk.* 3. *p.* 15.

1665, *June* 14.

Account for payment of £6 : 2 : 6 to Mr. John Gamball, one of his Majesty's musicians, which together with £10 paid to him 10 August, 1664, is in full of his livery due 30 November last.

L. C. Vol. 167, *Bk.* 3, *p.* 16.

1665, *June* 16.

Account for payment of £16. 2. 6 to Mr. William Gregory, one of his Majesty's musicians, for livery due 30 November last.

L. C. Vol. 167, *Bk.* 3, *p.* 17.

1665, *June* 24.

Warrant to pay James Farr, his Majesty's organ maker and organ keeper, such a proportion of money for his New Year's guifts for the years 1660, 1661, 1662, 1663 and 1664 as to any of his Majesty's musicians in ordinary hath been allowed or accustomed.

L. C. Vol. 742, *p.* 175.

1665, *St. John the Baptist.*

Payment of £29. 16. 8. (collectively) to John Mason, Thomas Mell and Henry Gregorie for clothing and educating two boys in the art of music for half a year.

L. C. Vol. 461.

1665, *June* 26.

Account of 10/- paid to Mary Porter, for her husband, George Porter, trumpeter to the late King, in part of his livery ; also 10/- to Prudence Porter, for her husband William Porter, trumpeter to the late King.

L. C. Vol. 167, *Bk.* 3, *p.* 21.

1665, *June* 27.

Account for payment of £16 : 2 : 6 to Mr. Humphrey Madge, one of his Majesty's musicians, for livery due 30 November last.

L. C. Vol. 167, *Bk.* 3, *p.* 23.

1665, *June* 27.

Warrant to deliver to Charles Colman, musician in ordinary for the violls in place of Dr. Charles Colman, his father, deceased, the materials for his livery, and to him and to Theophilus Fittz, musician in ordinary in place of Stephen Strong, deceased, the same, yearly during His Majesty's pleasure.

L. C. Vol. 814, *p.* 262 ; *L. C. Papers, Bundle* 23.

1665, *June* 29.

Account of £4 paid to Walter Cawbraest, one of his Majesty's kettle-drummers, for a banner.

L. C. Vol. 167, *Bk.* 3, *p.* 24.

1665, *July* 10.

Appointment of the following musicians in Mr. Bannister's band of violins :—

John Singleton	Richard Hudson
Theophilus Fitz	Robert Strong
Isaack Staggins	Phillip Becket
William Clayton	John Strong
Symon Hopper	John Myer
Henry Smyth	William Young
Mr. Hudson	Mr. Lock
Humphrey Madge	Ambrose Beeland
Richard Dorney	Thomas Blagrave
William Yowckney	Edward Strong
Jeoffrey Bannister	William Saunders
William Howes	John Atkyns
Walter Yowckney	Henry Brockwell.

This band of violins was made choyce of by Mr. Bannister and appoynted by the Lord Chamberlain.

L. C. Vol. 479, *p.* 102.

1665, *July* 18.

Appointment of Edmund Tanner in Mr. Bannister's band of violins in the place of Walter Yowckney, deceased.

L. C. Vol. 479, *p.* 102.

1665, *July* 20.

Warrant to admit Edmund Tanner musician in ordinary upon the violins, in the place of Walter Yockney, deceased, with the wages of 1s. 8d. by the day, and £16. 2s. 6d. for his livery, to commence 24 June last past.

L. C. Vol. 742, *p.* 400.

1665, *August* 10.

Account of £2 lent to George Bosgrave, Samuel Markland, Robert Ramsey and Thomas Creswell, his late Majesty's trumpeters.

L. C. Vol. 167, *Bk.* 3.

1665, *August* 11.

Warrant to pay unto Joseph Walker, one of his Majesty's trumpeters in ordinary in the place of Thomas Knowles, deceased, the wages of £60 yearly, to commence Michaelmas, 1663.

L. C. Vol. 742, *p.* 400

1665, *August* 24.

Robert Mawgridg appointed drummer in Crewe's place.

L. C. Vol. 482, *p.* 65.

1665, *September* 5.

Isaack Staggins appointed musitian in ordinary for the treble hoboy in the place of Henry Bassano, deceased; and William Young for the flute in the place of Henry Bassano, deceased.

L. C. Vol. 479, *p.* 102.

1665, *September* 5.

Warrant to admit Isaack Staggins musician in ordinary to his Majesty for the tenner hoboy, in the place of Henry Bassano, deceased.

L. C. Vol. 742, *p.* 404.

1665, *September* 6.

Warrant for the allowance of such livery to Richard Hudson, musician in ordinary to his Majesty, as Henry Bassano, late musician to his Majesty formerly enjoyed.

L. C. Vol. 742, *p.* 61.

Accounts ending Michaelmas, 1665.

Half-yearly payment of £20 to Henry Cooke, master of the boys of the Chapel Royal, for the keep of two boys and for teaching them singing.

Accounts for liveries for the following musicians to the King :—

Nicholas Lanier	John Harding
George Hudson	Stephen Strong
John Hingeston	Gregory Thornedell
Humphrey Madge	Alphonso Marsh
William Gregory	John Smith
John Willson	Thomas Bates
Henry Cooke	John Gamble
Thomas Lanier	John Bannister
Nicholas Lanier	John Clement
Anthony Roberts	Thomas Purcell
Matthew Lock	William Child
John Jenkins	Charles Coleman
John Lillie	Theophilus Fittz
Edward Colman	

Annual pensions to the following trumpeters to the late King Charles I. :—

Robert Ramsay	George Porter
Thomas Cresswell	George Bosgrove
Samuel Markland	William Porter

Henry Peacock

Account paid to John Mason, Thomas Mell and Henry Gregory, for clothing, and educating two boys in the art of music.

L. C. Vol. 60 *; L. C. Vol.* 154.

Bill for £3 for making 5 large curtains of crimson taffata for the organ loft at Whitehall.

L. C. Papers, Bundle 9.

Bill for embroidering the heads of five drum cases with his Majesty's letters in gold and silver amounting to £3 : 15.

L. C. Papers, Bundle 22.

Bill of Samuel Mearne, his Majesty's book binder. Item for 13 common prayerbooks and new testaments for the children of the Chappell £10 : 8.

L. C. Papers, Bundle 23.

1665, *October* 28.

Edward Wharton appointed drummer extraordinary without fee for the first vacancy.

L. C. Vol. 478, *p.* 121.

1665, *November* 27.

Warrant to pay Robert Mawgridg one of his Majesty's drummers in ordinary, in the place of Jeremiah Crewes, the wages of 1/ by the day, and £16 : 2 : 6 by the year for his livery, to commence 29 September, 1665.

L. C. Vol. 742, *p.* 401.

1665, *St. Andrew.*

Payment of £16. 2. 6d. to each of the following musicians to the King, for their liveries :—

Nicholas Lanier, master of music.

Nicholas Lanier, luter.

Henry Cooke	John Bannister
John Willson	Edward Colman
Anthony Roberts	Gregory Thorndell
John Hingeston	Mathew Locke
William Gregory	Theophilus Fittz

George Hudson	Thomas Bates
Humphrey Madge	Alphonso Marsh
Thomas Lanier	John Clement
John Smyth	Thomas Pursell
John Gamble	William Child
John Jenkins	Charles Colman, junior
John Lillie	John Goodgroome
John Harding	Giles Tompkins

Payment of £29. 16. 8. (collectively) to John Mason, Thomas Mell, and Henry Gregory, for clothing and educating two boys in the art of music for half a year.

L. C. Vol. 461.

1665, *December* 23.

Letter of assignment from Mathew Lock, one of his Majesty's musick, of a livery of £16 : 2 : 6 to Richard Elton.

L. C. Vol. 181, *p.* 123.

1665-6, *January* 7.

Warrant to pay Giles Tomkins, musician, for seven years' arrears of livery.

L. C. Papers, Bundle 23.

1665-6, *February* 26.

Warrant to pay Charles Evans, his Majesty's harper for the Italian harp, £5 for strings bought by him for the saide harp for one year ended at Christmas last past, 1665.

L. C. Vol. 742, *p.* 189.

1665-6, *March* 10.

Pelham Humphreyes appointed musician for the lute in the place of Nicholas Lanier, deceased.

L. C. Vol. 479, *p.* 98.

1665-6, *March* 17.

Warrant to pay Richard Hudson, musician in ordinary, £56. 10s. for keeping of his Majesty's lutes, violls and violins, and for causing his Majesty's armes to be sett on them, and for mending and altering severall of the said instruments being broken upon removes, and for strings, bridges, bows and cases with locks and keys; from June, 1660 to June, 1665. Also for strings and mending of instruments in his Majesty's removes to Salisbury and Oxford in 1665.

L. C. Vol. 742, *p.* 190.

1665-6, *March* 17.

Warrant for such livery to Giles Tomkins, admitted musician in ordinary to his Majesty for the virginalls in the place of Richard Deereing, deceased, as the latter formerly enjoyed, to commence 24 June, 1660.

L. C. Vol. 742, *p.* 66.

1665-6, *March* 17.

Warrant to deliver to Captain Henry Cooke, master of the children of the Chappell, three curtains of crimson damask for the organ loft.

L. C. Papers, Bundle 77.

1665-6, *March* 24.

Probate of the will of Nicholas Lanier, late of Greenwich, granted to Elizabeth his widow, followed by a certificate of Thomas Plume, vicar of Greenwich, to the effect that Mr. Nicholas Lanier was inhabitant of the parish of East Greenwich in Kent, and there dyed, and was carried to his funerall on the 24th February 1665-6.

L. C. Vol. 181, *p.* 123.

1666, *Lady Day.*

Items in an account of the treasurer of the chamber :—

	£.	s.	d.
To 18 trumpeters and 7 pensioners for one year and half - - - - - -	1,290	0	0
To the musicians for four years - - -	2,107	8	0

L. C. Papers, Bundle 19.

1666, *March* 28.

Account of £48 : 7 : 6 paid to Mr. Anthony Roberts, one of his Majesty's musicians, for three liveries due 30 November, 1660, 1661 and 1662.

L. C. Vol. 167, *Bk.* 4, *p.* 10.

1666, *April* 20.

Warrant to pay John Bannister the sum of £464 for himself and seven others of his Majesty's musitians, viz. :—

> Mathew Lock,
> Jeoffery Bannister,
> William Young,
> Symon Hopper,
> Richard Hudson,
> Isaack Staggins, and
> Theophilus Fitz,

for their riding charges and other expenses to Oxford and Hampton Court, by the space of 232 days, from the last of June, 1665 to 18 February following, at the rate of 5s. a day to each of them.

L. C. Vol. 742, p. 199.

1666, *April* 27.

Account of £8 : 10 paid to Mr. Henry Gregory, musician, for himself, John Mason and Thomas Mell, for apparelling and breeding upp two boyes in the art of musick for one year and a half, from 24 June, 1662 to 1663.

L. C. Vol. 167, Bk. 4, p. 11.

1666, *May* 9.

Order that Millibert Meurs, Nicholas Caperon, Thomas Sculthrop and John Crowther, four of his Majesty's trumpeters, doe attend his Highness Prince Rupert and his Grace the Duke of Albemarle at sea.

Also a warrant, dated May 11, for the allowance of sea liveries to them.

L. C. Vol. 742, pp. 67 and 358. L. C. Papers, Bundle 77.

1666, *May* 16.

Warrant to pay William Peacock, Nicholas Caperon, John Crowther, and Thomas Sculthrop, four of his Majesty's trumpeters in ordinary, £40 for their present supply, they being to attend his Highness Prince Rupert and his Grace the Duke of Albemarle at sea.

L. C. Vol. 742, p. 201.

1666, *May* 20.

Warrant to admit Pelham Humphreyes musician in ordinary to his Majesty for the lute, in the place of Nicholas Lanier, deceased, with the wages of £40 yearly, and £16. 2s. 6d. yearly as livery, to commence the Annunciation last past.

L. C. Vol. 742, p. 274.

1666, *Pentecost.*

Payment of £19. 17. 8. to each of the following trumpeters to the late King Charles I. for their pensions :—

Robert Ramsey	George Porter
Thomas Cresswell	George Bosgrove
Samuel Markland	William Porter
Henry Peacock	

L. C. Vol. 461.

1666, *May* 25.

Warrant to admit William Young musician in ordinary to his Majesty for the flute in the place of Henry Bassano, deceased, with the wages of 1s. 8d. by the day, and £16. 2s. 6d. by the year as livery, to commence 24 June, 1665.

Warrant to admit Isaack Staggins musician in ordinary for the tenner hoboy, in the place of Henry Bassano, deceased, with the same wages to commence from the same tyme as Mr. Yonge's doth.

L. C. Vol. 742, p. 273.

1666, *June* 2.

Account for £2. lent to Mr. John Gamball, musician; also £5 lent to him on October 20th, 1666.

L. C. Vol. 167, Bk. 6. p. 1; Bk. 9. p. 4.

1666, *June* 22.

Warrant to pay Walter Vanbright, his Majesty's kettle-drummer, the sum of £10 for his present supply, he being to attend his Highness Prince Rupert and his Grace the Duke of Albemarle at sea.

Also a warrant for a sea livery for him.

L. C. Vol. 742, p. 205 and p. 70.

1666, *St. John the Baptist.*

Payment of £29. 17. 8. to John Mason and Henry Gregorie, musicians, for clothing and educating two boys in the art of music for half a year.

L. C. Vol. 461.

1666, *July* 2.

William Bull appointed trumpeter extraordinary.

L. C. Vol. 478, p. 119; and Vol. 479, p. 104.

1666, *July* 6.

Warrant to pay to :—

John Banister	Richard Hudson
William Young	Theophilus Fitz
Isaack Staggins	Jeoffrey Banister
Simon Hopper	

musicians in ordinary for the violins, the sum of £140 by way of advance to fitt and enable them to attend the Queene to and at Tunbridge.

L. C. Vol. 742, p. 363.

Accounts ending Michaelmas, 1666.

Accounts for liveries to the following musicians to the King:—

George Hudson	John Harding
John Hingeston	Gregory Thornedell
Humphrey Madge	Alphonso Marsh
William Gregorie	John Smyth
John Willson	Thomas Bates
Henry Cooke	John Gamble
Thomas Lanier	John Bannister
Anthony Roberts	John Clement
Mathew Locke	Thomas Purcell
John Jenkins	William Child
John Lillie	Charles Colman
Edward Coleman	Theophilus Fittz

Account of £59 : 13 : 4 paid to John Mason and Henry Gregory for clothing and educating two boys in the art of music.

Account for pensions for one year to each of the following trumpeters to the late King :—

Robert Ramsey	George Bosgrove
Samuel Markland	William Porter
George Porter	Henry Peacock

Account of £40 paid to Henry Cooke master of the boys of the Chappell Royall in allowance for one year, for the keep of two boys and for teaching them to sing.

L. C. Vols. 155 and 461.

Bill amounting to £217 for the liveries of the sergeant trumpeter, trumpeters, kettle-drummers, and drummers.

L. C. Papers, Bundle 2.

1666, *October* 15.

For a lute, Henry Brockwell in the place of Lewis Evans.

L. C. Vol. 479, p. 102.

1666, *October* 31.

The following musicians are to meet and practize with Mr. Becket, his Lessons :—

John Singleton,	Richard Hudson,
William Clayton,	Ambrose Beeland,
William Young,	John Strong,
Theophilus Fitz,	Robert Strong,

Isaack Staggins.

L. C. Vol. 742, p. 366.

1666, *October* 31.

Warrant to admit Henry Brockwell musician in ordinary to his Majesty for the lute, in the place of Lewis Evans, deceased, with the wages of 1s. 8d. by the day, and £16 2s. 6d. by the year for his livery, to commence Michaelmas, 1666.

L. C. Vol. 742, p. 274.

1666, *November* 8.

Lent to Mr. Lilly, musician, £5.

Paid to Mr. Lanier, musitian, £16 : 2 : 6 for his livery due 30 November, 1665.

L. C. Vol. 167, Bk. 9, pp. 8 and 9.

1666, *November* 9.

Account of £16 : 2 : 6 paid to Mr. Mathew Lock, musician, for livery due 30 November last.

L. C. Vol. 167, Bk. 9, p. 10.

1666, *November* 24.

Warrant to swear and admit Louis Grabu master of the English chamber musick in ordinary to his Majesty, in the place of Nicholas Lanier, deceased, to inspect and governe the same, with the accustomed allowances and powers as Mr. Lanier formerly hath done, with all rights and privileges as he formerly enjoyed.

L. C. Vol. 742, p. 367 ; and Vol. 482, p. 51.

1666, *St. Andrew.*

Payment of £16. 2. 6. to each of the following musicians to the King, for their liveries :—

Henry Cooke	Gregory Thornedale
John Willson	Mathew Lock
Anthony Roberts	Thomas Bates
John Hingeston	Alphonso Marsh
William Gregory	John Clement
George Hudson	Thomas Pursell
Humphrey Madge	William Child
Thomas Lanier	John Goodgroome
John Smyth	Theophilus Fittz
John Gamble	Charles Colman
John Jenkins	Richard Hudson
John Lillie	Giles Tompkins
John Harding	Lewis Grabu, master of
John Bannister	the music
Edward Colman	

Payment of £29. 16. 8. to John Mason and Henry Gregory for clothing, and educating two boys in the art of music for half a year.

L. C. Vol. 461.

1666, December 4.

Warrant for the delivery of certain clothing to Capt. Henry Cook, master of the children of his Majesty's Chappell, for the use of William Turner, John Loggins and Nicholas Saunderson, three of the pages of his Majesty's Chappell Royall, theyr voyces being changed and are to go from his Majesty's Chappell.

L. C. Vol. 742, p. 260 ; L. C. Papers, Bundle 77.

1666, December 7.

Edward Hooton appointed musician for the wind instruments, in the place of Thomas Mell, deceased.

L. C. Vol. 479, p. 98.

1666, December 24.

Order that Mr. Bannister and the 24 violins appointed to practice with him and all his Majesty's private musick doe, from tyme to tyme, obey the directions of Louis Grabu, master of the private musick, both for their tyme of meeting to practise, and also for the tyme of playing in consort.

L. C. Vol. 742, p. 367.

1666.

Account of the Earl of Sandwich, master of his Majesty's great wardrobe, for goods by him bought and provided upon the death of her royal highness, the Dutchesse of Saxony :—

Account for mourning liveries for the Sergeant, 18 Trumpettors and a Kettle-Drummer.

Account for mourning liveries for the Drumme Major, fowre drummers and a Phife.

L. C. Vol. 560, pp. 7d. and 9.

[1666.]

Arrears due for liveries to the following musicians :—

> Capt. Henry Cooke, three years ending 1665
> Capt. Henry Cooke, for teaching and apparelling two boys for three years ending 1666
> Dr. John Wilson, 1663 and 1664
> Anthony Roberts, 1663
> John Hingston, 1663
> William Gregory, 1663 and 1664
> George Hudson, 1663 and 1664
> Humphrey Madge, 1663 and 1664

Thomas Laneer, 1663, 1664, 1665
John Smith, 1663
John Gamble, 1663, 1664, 1665
John Jenkins, 1663
John Lilly, 1663, 1664, 1665
John Bannister, 1663, 1664
Gregory Thorndale, 1663 & 1664
Matthew Lock, 1663, 1664, 1665
Thomas Bates, 1663 and 1664
Alphonso Marsh, 1663 and 1664
John Clement, 1663
Dr. William Child, 1663, 1664, 1665
Henry Gregory, for teaching and apparelling two
 boys bred in the art of musick for three half
 years ending St. Andrew 1664
Angelo Notary, 1663
Thomas Purcell, 1663
Humphrey Madge, 1663 and 1664
Dr. Charles Coleman, 1663
Edward Coleman, 1663 and 1664
Henry Bassano, 1663
Nicholas Laneer, as master of music 1663, and as
 musician 1663
Stephen Strong, 1663

L. C. Papers, Bundle 23.

1666-7, *January* 7.

Warrant to allow Giles Tompkins, musician to his Majesty
in ordinary in the place of Richard Deering, deceased, a livery
of £16 : 2 : 6 a year, and by a warrant of his late Majesty of
blessed memory, liveries for the years 1660 to 1666.

L. C. Vol. 742, *p.* 262.

1666-7, *January* 29.

Warrant to deliver to Captain Henry Cook 13 Common
Prayerbooks bound with the new testament for the children of
the Chappell, and also three curtains of black taffata for the
organ loft in Lent.

L. C. Papers, Bundle 77.

1666-7, *February* 20.

Warrant to prepare and deliver to Gervase Price, esquire,
his Majesty's serjeant trumpeter, one guilt trumpet weighing
forty ounces or thereabouts, as a guift from his Majesty.

L. C. Vol. 601, *and Vol.* 742, *p.* 330.

1666-7, *February* 27.

Warrant for a patent to be granted unto Lewis Grabu, master of his Majesty's musique in the place of Nicholas Lanier, deceased, with the wages and fees of £200 by the year, to commence 25 March last past, 1666, together with all profitts, comodityes, allowances and advantages enjoyed by the said Nicholas Lanier.

L. C. Vol. 742, *p.* 277.

1666-7, *March* 14.

Whereas John Bannister appointed to make choyce of 12 of the 24 violins, to be a select band to wayte upon his Majesty, was paid £600 for himselfe and the 12 violins in augmentation of their wages, his Majesty authorises the payment of £600 to Lewis Grabu, master of his Majesty's musick, appointed in the place of John Bannister, for himself and the 12 violins following :—

John Singleton	Isaack Staggins
William Young	Henry Smyth
William Clayton	Richard Hudson
Henry Comer	John Strong
Phillip Beckett	Robert Strong
Symon Hopper	Theophilus Fitz

L. C. Vol. 742, *p.* 278.

1666-7, *March* 20.

Warrant to pay Charles Evans, his Majesty's harper for the Italian harp, the sum of £5 for strings bought by him for the said harp for one year ending at Christmas, 1666.

L. C. Vol. 742, *p.* 228.

1666-7, *March* 23.

Whereas there is owing by William Yowckney, one of his Majesty's musitians, unto Francis Jennings the sum of £4 16s., these are to pray you out of such moneys as are due to the said William Yowckney, to cause to be paid the said Francis Jennings the sum of £4 16s.

L. C. Vol. 742, *p.* 228.

1667, *March* 25.

Letter of assignment from Charles Coleman, of his Majesty's private musicke, of £16 2s. 6d. due 30 November, 1665, to Mr. John Lillie, of his Majesty's private musicke, for attending in his place.

L. C. Vol. 181, *p.* 125.

1667, *March* 25.

Thomas Fittz and John Myer, appointed to wayt in the place of Henry Comer, one of his Majesty's musicians, who hath leave to travell for some years.

L. C. Vol. 742, *p.* 369.

1667, *April* 1.

Petition of Isabell Sympson, wife of Edward Sympson, trumpetter, late deceased, against the serjeant trumpetter and the rest of the trumpetters.

L. C. Vol. 651.

1667, *April* 3.

Warrant to pay Capt. Henry Cooke, master of the children of his Majesty's Chappell, £30 by the year for the keeping of William Turner, one of the children of the Chappell whose voyce is changed, and gone from the Chappell, to commence 29 September, 1666.

A like warrant for the keeping of John Loggins, to commence 25 March, 1666.

L. C. Vol. 742, *p.* 231.

1667, *April* 4.

Theophilus Fitz, Clayton, Humphrey Madg and Myre, appointed to attend at his Majesty's Chappell Royall at Whitehall soe often as they shall be appoynted by Capt. Cooke for his Majesty's service.

L. C. Vol. 742, *p.* 369.

1667, *April* 9.

Warrant for the payment of £60 to William Bounty, John Baker, John Crowther, and Symon Peirson, four of his Majesty's trumpeters appointed to attend upon the Right Honble. the Lord Hollis and the Hon. Henry Coventry, Ambassadors to the States of the United Netherlands, towards their expenses and charges, attending upon the said Ambassadors to Breda, being £15 apiece.

L. C. Vol. 742, *p.* 229.

1667, *April* 17.

Warrant to pay Capt. Henry Cooke, master of the Children of his Majesty's Chappell, £110. 4s. for learning of the said children to play on the lute, theorboe, violin and the organ, and to write, and for fire and strings for the musick roome in the Chappell, for paper and penns, and for tuning the harpsicord, and for strings for the lute and theorboe, for one whole year from Lady Day, 1666.

L. C. Vol. 742, *p.* 230.

1667, *April* 30.

Warrant to provide livery for John Remus, trumpeter in extraordinary.

L. C. Papers, Bundle 77.

1667, *May* 10.

Warrant for making 114 surplices, for the Dean, Sub-Dean, gentlemen, musitians and children of our Chappell Royall.

L. C. Vol. 802, *p.* 302.

1667, *May* 16.

Warrant to pay John Crowther, Thomas Sculthorpe and Nicholas Chaperone, three of his Majesty's trumpeters, £126 for their attendance on his Highness Prince Rupert and his Grace the Duke of Albemarle for 168 days at sea, from 23 April 1666 to the 17 October next following, at the rate of 5s. per diem to each man.

L. C. Vol. 742, *p.* 235.

1667, *May* 20.

A bill to be prepared that the musitians for the recorders, flutes, hoboyes and sackbutts, violins, lutes and voyces, be discharged from paying the poll money granted in the Parliament begun 8 May, 1661.

L. C. Vol. 742, *p.* 280.

1667, *May* 22.

Warrant to deliver to Gervase Price, his Majesty's serjeant trumpeter, a pair of kettle-drummes for his Majesty's service.

L. C. Vol. 742, *p.* 269.

1667, *Pentecost.*

Payment of £19. 17. 8. to each of the following trumpeters to the late King Charles I. for their pensions :—

Robert Ramsay	George Bosgrove
Samuel Markland	William Porter
George Porter	Henry Peacock

Thomas Cresswell ["mort ante diem"]

St. John the Baptist.

Payment of £29 : 16 : 8 to John Mason and Henry Gregory, musicians to the King, for clothing two boys and educating them in the art of music for half a year.

L. C. Vol. 461.

1667, *August* 13.

Warrant to stopp £5. 15s. of Mr. Brockwell's pay, one of his Majesty's musicians; to be paid to Mr. Morris.

L. C. Vol. 742, *p.* 240.

1667, *September* 29.

Warrant to pay Gervase Price, Esquire, serjeant trumpeter to his Majesty, on behalf of himself and six of his Majesty's trumpeters, the sum of £410 for their attendance upon his Majesty in the progress at Hampton Court, Salisbury and Oxford, from 27 July, 1665 to 17 February following; 205 days at 10s. to the sergeant and 5s. to each trumpeter.

L. C. Vol. 742, *p.* 209.

1667, *Michaelmas.*

Account paid to Henry Cooke for the custody and teaching of two singing boys for one year.

L. C. Vol. 461.

1667, *October* 22.

Appointment of Thomas Finall to wayt in the room of Robert Strong, musician in ordinary to his Majesty for the violin.

L. C. Vol. 742, *p.* 343.

1667, *October* 22.

Stephen Gibson appointed drummer extraordinary. Clement Newth appointed fife in ordinary without fee.

L. C. Vol. 478, *p.* 121.

1667, *November* 16.

Thomas Fitz appointed musician for the violins in the private musick in the place of Thomas Baltzar.

L. C. Vol. 479, *p.* 98.

1667, *St. Andrew.*

Payment of £16. 2. 6. to each of the following musicians to the King for their liveries :—

Henry Cooke	Edward Colman
John Wilson	Gregory Thornedell
Anthony Roberts	Mathew Locke
John Hingeston	Thomas Bates
William Gregory	Alphonso Marsh
George Hudson	John Clement
Humphrey Madge	Thomas Pursill
Thomas Lanier	William Child
John Smyth	John Goodgroome
John Gamble	Theophilus Fittz
John Jenkins	Charles Colman
John Lillie	Richard Hudson
John Harding	Giles Tomkins
John Bannister	Lewis Grabu, master of the music

Payment of £29. 16. 8. to John Mason and Henry Gregory, musicians to the King, for clothing and educating two boys in the art of music for half a year.

L. C. Vol. 461.

1667, *December* 12.

Warrant to prepare a bill for the grant to Thomas Fitz, of the office of musician in ordinary for the violin in the private musique, in the place of Thomas Baltzar, deceased, with the fee of £110 a year, to commence from 24 June, 1667.

L. C. Vol. 743, *p.* 289.

1667, *December* 26.

Warrant for the allowance of liveries for the children of the Chappell to be delivered to Captain Henry Cooke, master of the said children.

L. C. Papers, Bundle 12.

1667.

Liveries in arrear from June, 1660 to Michaelmas, 1667 :—

> To Henry Cooke, livery for 1666, and for teaching two boys for 1667.
> Dr. John Wilson, liveries for 1665 and 1666.
> Anthony Roberts, for 1664, 1665, 1666.
> John Hingston, for 1664, 1665, 1666.
> William Gregory, for 1665 and 1666.
> George Hudson, for 1665 and 1666.
> Humphrey Madge, for 1665 and 1666.
> Thomas Lanier, for 1666.
> John Smith, for 1664, 1665, 1666.
> John Gamble, for 1666.
> John Jenkins, for 1661, 1664, 1665, 1666.
> John Lillie, for 1661 and 1666.
> John Harding, for 1661, 1664, 1665, 1666.
> John Bannister, for 1665 and 1666.
> Gregory Thorndell, for 1665 and 1666.
> Matthew Lock, for 1666.
> Thomas Bates, for 1665 and 1666.
> Alphonso Marsh, for 1665 and 1666.
> John Clement, for 1664, 1665, 1666.
> Dr. William Child, for 1666.
> John Mason and Henry Gregory for keeping and teaching two boys for 1664, 1665, 1666, 1667.
> Edward Coleman, for 1665 and 1666.
> Theophilus Fitz, for 1665 and 1666.

Thomas Purcell, for 1662, 1664, 1665, 1666.

To the assignee of Giles Tomkins, for 1660, 1661, 1662, 1663, 1664, 1665, 1666.

John Goodgroome, for 1666.

Angelo Notary, deceased, and his executor Solomon Burbury, for 1661 and 1664.

To the executors of Dr. Charles Coleman for his livery for 1663.

To Charles Coleman, junior, for 1664, 1665, 1666.

To the executors of Henry Bassano, for 1660, 1661, 1662.

To the executors of Henry Lawes, for 1660 and 1661.

To the executors of Davies Mell, for 1661.

To Nicholas Lanier as master of the music, for 1661, 1662, 1664, 1665.

L. C. Papers, Bundle 23.

1667-8.

Payment of £29. 16. 8. to Henry Gregorie and John Mason for teaching and apparrelling two boys for half a year.

Payments of £10 to Henry Cooke, for each quarter of the year, for keeping and teaching two boys.

Payments of £5 each quarter to Jervis Price, yeoman of the bowes and gunns.

To five trumpeters to his late Majesty, £19 : 17 : 8 apiece.

L. C. Vol. 709, *p.* 37 *to* 39.

Liveries &c. yearly payable out of the great wardrobe :—

To the Musicians

Henry Cooke	Gregorie Thorndell
John Willson	Matthew Lock
Anthony Roberts	Thomas Bates
John Hingston	Alphonso Marsh
William Gregory	John Clement
George Huddson	William Child
Humphrey Madge	Edward Coleman
Thomas Lanier	Charles Coleman
John Smith	Theophilus Fitz
John Gamble	Thomas Purcell
John Jenkins	Richard Hudson
John Lillie	Giles Tompkins
John Harding	John Goodgroome
John Bannister	

To Henry Gregory & John Mason for teaching and apparelling two boys.

L. C. Papers, Bundle 3.

1667-8, *January* 7.

Christopher Preston appointed musician in ordinary to his Majesty for the virginalls and private musique without fee in the place of Dr. Christopher Gibbons, to come in ordinary with fee after the decease of the said Dr. Gibbons, and then to enjoy the same place.

L. C. Vol. 478, *p.* 113 ; *and Vol.* 479, 102.

1667-8, *January* 13.

Account for liveries for the singing boyes at the King's Chappell.

L. C. Vol. 201, *p.* 8*d.*

1667-8, *January* 17.

Symon Peirson appointed trumpeter in ordinary to his Majesty, without fee, to come in ordinary with fee upon the next avoydance or vacancy of either of his Majesty's trumpeters.

L. C. Vol. 478, *p.* 119 ; *and Vol.* 479, *p.* 104.

1667-8, *January* 20.

Order for the allowance of liveries for the drum major, four drummers and a fife. Also for red cases, and bages, for the drums.

L. C. Papers, Bundle 12.

1667-8, *January* 20.

Warrant to prepare a bill for the delivery of fees, liveries, etc., to Lewis Grabu, sworn and admitted master of his Majesty's musick, in place of Nicholas Lanier, deceased ; to commence from 25 March, 1666.

L. C. Vol. 743, *p.* 13.

1667-8, *January* 20.

Account for twelve black felts edged with black and lined, for his Majesty's singing boys of the Chapell.

L. C. Vol. 201, *p.* 14.

1667-8, *January* 20.

Warrant to admit Christopher Preston musician in ordinary to his Majesty for the virginalls and private musick, without fee, in the place of Dr. Christopher Gibbons, to come in ordinary with fee after the decease of the said Dr. Gibbons, then to enjoy the same places with the wages and fees of £46 per annum and £40 per annum, the same as Thomas Warwick, deceased, or any other formerly enjoyed.

L. C. Vol. 742, *p.* 282.

1667-8, *January* 27.

Warrant to prepare a bill for the King's signature, granting liveries, fees, etc., to Pelham Humphryes, sworn musician in ordinary for the lute, in the place of Nicholas Lanier, deceased ; to commence from the Annunciation, 1666.

L. C. Vol. 743, *p.* 6.

1667-8, *January* 29.

Warrant to pay to John Hingeston, keeper and repairer of His Majesty's organs, the sum of £111. 4s. 6d. for mending the organs at Hampton Court, St. James' and Whitehall, and for strings for the pedals, harpsicords, and virginalls, and for other services done by him from 29 September, 1664, to 29 September, 1667.

L. C. Vol. 743, *p.* 109.

1667-8, *January* 31.

Warrant to pay a bill of £120. 4s. for clothing for the twelve children of the Chappell.

L. C. Papers, Bundle 2.

Accounts for liveries, etc., for the children of his Majesty's Chappell.

L. C. Vol. 201, *pp.* 8, 13, *and* 16ᵈ.

Bill for twelve pair of shoes for the children of the Chappell at 3s. 6d. a pair.

L. C. Papers, Bundle 5.

1667-8, *February* 10.

Assignment by William Porter of his debenture dated 1663, to Jarvice Price, sergeant trumpeter.

L. C. Vol. 198, *p.* 31.

1667-8, *February* 10.

Assignment by George Bosgrave, of his debenture bearing date 1666, to Jarvice Price, sergeant trumpeter.

L. C. Vol. 198, *p.* 30ᵈ.

1667-8, *February* 12.

Warrant to pay to Nicholas Sanderson, late one of the children of his Majesty's Chappell Royall, the sum of £30 by the year, during his Majesty's pleasure, his voice being now changed ; to commence from Christmas, 1666.

L. C. Vol. 743, *p.* 110.

1667-8, *February* 17.

Assignment by Henry Peacock, trumpeter to his late Majesty, of his debenture bearing date 1665, to Jarvice Price, sergeant trumpeter to his Majesty.

L. C. Vol. 198, *p.* 31.

1667-8, *February* 24.

Assignment by Thomas Creswell, of his debenture bearing date 1665, to Jarvice Price, esquire, sergeant trumpeter.

L. C. Vol. 198, *p.* 31.

1667-8, *March* 16.

Warrant to reduce the number of salaries :—the pay of 17 trumpeters and a kettledrummer amounts unto £1290, whereof eleven being put into the Guard and their salleryes of £60 paid each being taken off, there will be saved £660.

L. C. Vol. 743, *p.* 2.

1667-8, *March* 20.

Warrant to prepare and deliver to Gervase Price, esquire, sergeant trumpeter and yeoman of the bowes and guns, one silver hunting horn of the quantity of 40 ounces or thereabouts, being a guift from his Majesty.

L. C. Vol. 743, *p.* 215.

1667-8, *March* 21.

Assignment by William Youkney, one of the band of violins to his Majesty, of the sum of £46. 12s. 6d., to Jeffery Banister, his fellow servant.

[This entry is crossed out.]

L. C. Vol. 195, *p.* 8.

1668, *March* 27.

Warrant to prepare a bill conveying a grant to Thomas Fitz, one of the musicians in ordinary for the violin, in place of Richard Hudson, deceased, to enjoy the same place for life, with the fee of £46. 12s. 8d. to commence from 25 March, 1668.

L. C. Vol. 743, *p.* 290.

1668, *April* 6.

Warrant to pay to Captain Cooke, master of the children of the Chappell Royall, the sum of £120 3s. for his charges and expenses in teaching the said children to learn on the lute, violin and theorboe, for fire and strings in the musick room in the Chappell, for paper and ink, for strings for the lutes, for one whole year ending at Lady Day, 1668, and likewise for his charges three days going to Windsor, for two boys.

L. C. Vol. 743, *p.* 112.

1668, *April* 7.

Warrant to pay John Myer, one of His Majesty's musitians upon the viollin, the sum of £20 for his attendance on his Majesty in the Chappell Royal from Michaelmas, 1666, to Lady Day, 1668.

L. C. Vol. 743, *p.* 112.

1668, April 7.

Warrant to deliver to Henry Cook, esquire, master of the children of his Majesty's Chappell Royall, two new suits of playne cloath, for Richard Hart, one of the said children, whose voyce is changed, with all other necessaryes thereto belonging.

L. C. Vol. 743, *p.* 13 ; *and Vol.* 836, *p.* 1.

1668, April 17.

Warrant to pay to Lewis Grabu, master of his Majesty's musick, the sum of £165 9s. 6d. for fayre writing severall dances, aires and other musick, and for drawing the said musick into severall parts, for penns, ink and paper, for chamber rent and for the prickers dyett, and for fire and candles and for other necessaryes, from 4 November, 1666 to 25 March, 1668.

L. C. Vol. 743, *p.* 113.

1668, April 27.

Warrant to prepare a Bill to admit Thomas Fitz musician in ordinary to his Majesty for the violin, in the place of Richard Hudson, deceased, with the wages and fees of £46. 12s. 8d. the first payment to commence 25 March, last past.

L. C. Vol. 771, *p.* 171.

1668, April 29.

The names of four and twenty violins as they were appointed to wayte, twelve each month, by order dated 29 April, 1668 :—

Mr. Singleton,	Mr. Clayton,
Mr. John Bannister,	Mr. Jeoffery Bannister,
Mr. Fashen,	Mr. Madge,
Mr. Young,	Mr. Fitz,
Mr. Tanner,	Mr. Greeting,
Mr. Beckett,	Mr. Dorney,
Mr. Smyth,	Mr. Youckney,
Mr. Beeland,	Mr. Blagrave,
Mr. Hopper,	Mr. Finall,
Mr. Strong,	Mr. Atkyns,
Mr. Brockwell,	Mr. Staggins,
Mr. Saunders,	Mr. Fitz.

" I doe hereby order that his Majesty's musitians above-named doe wayt and attend upon his Majesty as they are here sett downe, twelve one month and twelve the other till further order."

L. C. Vols. 478, *p.* 81 ; 482, *p.* 55 ; 743, *p.* 366 *and* 771, *p.* 204.

1668, *May* 1.

Assignment by Henry Smith, of the parish of St. Margaret's, Westminster, to Joseph Fashen, of the parish of St. Andrew's, Holborn, of the yearly sum of £20, for his practise and performance of musique in Henry Smith's place and stead in his Majesty's band of violins. Order thereon from the Lord Chamberlain to Sir Edward Griffin, treasurer of the Chamber.

L. C. Vol. 195, *p.* 7.

1668, *May* 5.

Warrant to prepare and deliver three chaynes and medalls of gold, of the value of £30 a piece, to be presented unto Signier Vencenso Albrigi, Don Bartholomew Albrigi and Leonora Albrigi, three Italian musitians, as guifts from his Majesty.

L. C. Vol. 743, *p.* 215; *Vol.* 771, *p.* 137.

1668, *May* 8.

Warrant to the Signet, for Henry Brockwell, for the keeping of the lutes and violls, during his life, in the place of Richard Hudson, deceased, with the fee of 12d. by the day, to commence from 25 March, 1668.

Whereas Pelham Humphryes is sworn musitian in ordinary to his Majesty for the lute, in place of Nicholas Lanier, deceased, he is to enjoy all fees, liveries thereto belonging.

L. C. Vol. 743, *p.* 291.

1668, *Pentecost.*

Payment of £19 17. 8. to each of the following trumpeters to the late King Charles I. for their pensions :—

Robert Ramsay	George Bosgrove
Samuel Markland	William Porter
Henry Peacock	

L. C. Vol. 461.

1668, *May* 25.

Warrant to stop the sum of £20 yearly out of the salary of Henry Smyth, musician for the violin, and to pay it to Joseph Fashen according to an agreement whereby the said Henry Smyth assigned the said sum yearly to the said Joseph Fashen for his attendance in place of the said Henry Smyth.

L. C. Vols. 743, *p.* 117; *and Vol.* 771, *p.* 106.

1668, *May* 28.

Appointment of John Myer as one of his Majesty's musicians for the violins in place of William Youckney, deceased.

L. C. Vol. 482, *p.* 51.

1668, *June* 3.

Account for the winter and summer liveries for the 12 children of his Majesty's Chappell amounting to £385.

L. C. Vol. 709, *p.* 10d.

1668, *June* 3.

Warrant to pay to Captain Cooke, master of the children of his Majesty's Chappell Royall, the sum of £30 a year during his Majesty's pleasure, for keeping Richard Hart, one of the children of the Chappell, whose voyce is changed and is to go from the Chappell; to be paid quarterly, to commence from the 25 March, 1668.

L. C. Vol. 743, *p.* 117; *and Vol.* 771, *p.* 1.

1668, *June* 15.

Assignment by Mathew Locke, one of the composers in ordinary to his Majesty's band of violins, of the sum of £20 to James Ogleby, of the city of Westminster, in course after the assignments already made to Mr. Edward Darling, Mr. Isaack Walton, and Mr. Richards.

[This entry is crossed out.]

L. C. Vol. 195, *p.* 8.

1668, *St. John the Baptist.*

Payment of £29. 16. 8. to John Mason and Henry Gregory for clothing, and educating two boys in the art of music for half a year.

L. C. Vol. 461.

1668, *June* 27.

Warrant to prepare and deliver two medalls, of the value of £36, unto the two Italian musitians as a guift from his Majesty.

L. C. Vol. 743, *p.* 217; *Vol.* 771, *p.* 138.

1668, *July* 6.

" Whereas William Watson, yeoman of ye great bakehouse, is willing to deliver unto the musitians the roome over the same; these are therefore to require you to deliver it to them accordingly, and unto Sir Winston Churchill the roome adjoyneing to his lodgings over the great buttery now in the possession of the musitians for the violins with the little cole roome at the foot of the stayres leading to ye said lodgings."

L. C. Vols. 743, *p.* 369; *and* 771, p. 205.

1668, *September* 11.

Warrant for payment of £99 : 8 : 4 to Samuel Markland, trumpeter to his late Majesty, for his pension payable at Pentecost, at the rate of £19. 17. 8. per annum, for five years, 1664 to 1668.

Warrant for payment of the same amount to Robert Ramsey, trumpeter to his late Majesty, for five years, 1664 to 1668.

Warrant for payment of £139 : 3 : 8 to George Bosgrave, trumpeter to his late Majesty, for his pension for seven years, 1662 to 1668.

L. C. Vol. 711, *pp.* 39*d. and* 40.

Accounts ending Michaelmas, 1668.

Account paid to porters for bringing his Majesty's trumpeters their cloth out of Hatton Garden to the great Wardrobe.

L. C. Vol. 201, *p.* 67.

Account paid to Henry Cooke for the custody and teaching of two singing boys, for one year.

L. C. Vols. 461, 462.

1668, *November* 20.

Assignment by Theodor Steffken of the sum of £8 out of the next salary due to him, to Mr. John Hingston.

L. C. Vol. 195, *p.* 7.

1668, *St. Andrew.*

Payment of £16. 2. 6. to each of the following musicians to the King for their liveries :—

Henry Cooke	John Banister
John Wilson	Edward Coleman
Anthony Roberts	Gregory Thorndale
John Hingeston	Mathew Lock
William Gregory	Thomas Bates
George Hudson	Alphonso Marsh
Humphrey Madge	John Clement
Thomas Lanier	Thomas Pursill
John Smith	William Child
John Gamble	John Goodgroome
John Jenckins	Theophilus Fittz
John Lillie	Charles Colman
John Harding	

Richard Hudson (" mortuus est " written against his name).

Giles Tomkins (inscribed in a later hand " mortuus ante diem ").

Lewis Grabu, master of the music.

Pelham Humphryes, luter.

Payment of £29. 16. 8. to John Mason and Henry Gregory, musicians to the King, for clothing, and educating two boys in the art of music for half a year.

L. C. Vols. 156 *and* 462 ; *and Vol.* 709, *p.* 36.

1668, *December* 4.

Warrant to the sergeant trumpetter to take his free course
at law against certain persons who do act, play and sett forth
dumb shows and modells and refuse to satisfie his Majesty's
serjeant trumpetter those fees which are due to him according
to his patent, and also divers trumpetters and drummes and
fifes do sound, beat and play at the said plays, dumb shows,
and modells, without the lycence of the said serjeant first
obteyned.

L. C. Vol. 652.

1668, *December* 24.

Account for bits, stirrups, etc., for the sergeant trumpeter's
horse.

L. C. Vol. 201, *p.* 76*d.*

1668.

Account for pensions for one year paid to each of the
following trumpeters to the late King :—

Robert Ramsey	George Bosgrove
Samuel Markland	William Porter

Henry Peacock

Account paid to Henry Cooke, master of the boys of the
Chappell Royall, for his allowance for the keep of two boys
and for teaching them singing.

L. C. Vol. 156.

1668.

A list of the musicians paid in the Treasury of the Chambers
Office, 1668.

Monsr. Grabu, Master, to have the teaching of 2 boys.

Violins.

As they were settled 1668 and 1669. All these are paid
£46 : 10 : 10 apeece per annum :—

Ambrose Beeland	Isaack Staggins
Richard Dorney	William Clayton
Theophilus Fitz	Walter Yowckney (now
John Singleton	Edmund Tanner)
William Young	William Yowckney (now
Henry Brockwell	John Myer)
John Atkinson	John Bannister
Henry Smyth	Thomas Blagrave
Symon Hopper	

These are paid £46 : 12 : 8 apeece per annum :—

Richard Hudson (now	Jeoffrey Bannister
Thomas Fitz)	William Howes
Phillip Beckett	John Strong
Henry Comer	Robert Strong

William Saunders and Humphrey Madge, £58. 14. 2. per annum.

Composers.

George Hudson paid per annum, £42. 10. 10.
Matthew Lock, £46 : 10 : 10.
Mons. Legrange for a Basse.

Wind Musick.

To each £46 : 10 : 10 :—

John Strong	Fr. Child
Henry Gregory	

Thomas Lanier is for the wind and private musick.

Thomas Blagrave plays with the violins but his patent is for the flutes.   Entered before with the violins.

Private Musick.	£	s.	d.
Nicholas Lanier (now Pelham Humphryes) -	56	2	6
John Singleton - - - - - - -	56	2	6
Dr. John Wilson - - - - - -	46	10	10
Dietrick Steifken - - - - - -	46	10	10
Lewis Evans (now Brockwell) - - - -	46	10	10
John Hingeston - - - - - -	50 .0	0	
Thomas Purcell - - - - - -	36	2	6
Paul Bridges - - - - - - -	56	2	6
William Gregory - - - - - -	46	0	0
Dr. Christopher Gibbons - - - - -	40	0	0

Thomas Fitz succeeds one Mr. Baltzar, the Swede.   He plays with the violins, £110.

Virginalls.

Dr. Gibbons, virginall player, £46.

Organ tuner and repayrer.

John Hingeston, tuner and repayrer of the wind instruments and organs by patent under the Broad Seal, £60.

Richard Hudson (now Mr. Brockwell), keeper of the King's instruments, £18 : 5.

L. C. Vols. 478, *pp.* 77, 81, 82 ; *and* 482, *pp.* 56 *to* 58.

Composers.

Thomas Purcell and Pelham Humfrye (in the place of George Hudson, deceased), and Mathew Lock.

Henry Cooke in the place of Dr. Coleman, composer in the private Musique.

Private musick for lutes and voyces, theorboes and virginalls.

Henry Cooke in the place
    of Nicholas Duvall
John Coleman
Gregory Thorndale
Nathaniel Watkins
Alfonso March
John Hardinge
Edward Coleman
Thomas Bates
John Goodgroome
Charles Coleman
John Hingston
William Gregory
Henry Hawes
John Smyth

John Singleton
Thomas Lanier
Bridges
Thomas Purcell
Anthony Roberts
Dr. John Wilson
John Jenkins
John Lylye
John Rogers
William Howes
Christopher Gibbons
Blow
Henry Brockwell
Thomas Fitz
Edward Hooton.

L. C. Vol. 478, *pp.* 77, 78.

1668.

Musicians for the Wind Instruments.

Dr. William Child
Robert Blagrave
John Gamble
William Clayton
Phillip Beckett
Humphrey Madge
Theophilus Fitz
Thomas Blagrave
William Young for ye flute
Isaack Staggins for the treble Hoboy

John Mason
Edward Hooton
John Strong
Robert Strong
John Singleton
William Gregory
William Howes
Thomas Lanier
William Saunders

L. C. Vol. 478, *p.* 79.

John Hingston, organ maker.
Keeper of ye lutes and violls, Henry Brockwell
    Harper, Charles Evans
Repairer and keeper of ye organs, John Hingston
    Organ maker, James Farr
Harpsicall maker, Andrea Testa

L. C. Vol. 478, *p.* 80; *and Vol.* 482, *p.* 53.

Trumpeters in Ordinary.

Gervase Price, Sergeant Trumpeter.

Benigne Le Ragois	Edward Homerston
Nicholas Caperon	Henry Thewer
Melque Goldt	John Baker
Hugh Fitchert	William Bounty
Symon Beale	Richard Deane
Sylvester Whitmeale	William Peacock
Thomas Sculthorpe	Joseph Walker
Millibert Meurs	John Crowther
John Jones	Hans Bernghoski, kettle drummer.

L. C. Vol. 478, *p.* 85 ; *and Vol.* 485, *p.* 75.

1668.

A List of the Musitians that doe service in the Chappell Royall, whose Salleryes are paid in the Treasury of His Majesty's Chamber.

Mr. Thomas Purcell	Pelham Humphryes
Dr. John Wilson	John Hingston
Dr. Christopher Gibbon	William Gregorye
Dr. William Child	Dietrick Steffkyn
Thomas Blagrave	Mr. Bridges.

L. C. Vol. 478, *p.* 81.

1668-9, *January* 2.

Account for painting and guilding in oyle one trumpett banner of his Majesty's Armes and Supporters : £3.

L. C. Vol. 201, *p.* 95.

1668-9, *January* 8.

Warrant to deliver to Captain Henry Cook, master of the children of the Chappell, certain clothing for the use of Henry Montagu, Thomas Tedway and John Farmer three of the pages of the Chappell whose voices are changed and who are gone from the Chappell.

L. C. Papers, Bundle 18.

1668-9, *January* 9.

A list of the names of his Majesty's musitians payable at the Receipt of the Exchequer with their several yearly fees, vizt :—

	£	s.	d.
Lewis Grabu - - - - - - -	200	0	0
George Hudson, composer - - - -	200	0	0
Henry Cook (Capt. Cook has £40 ; composer of the private musick £40 : master of the boys £48 ; for 2 boys in the private musick £40 ; £20 for strings in the private musick)	188	0	0

	£	s.	d.
Charles Coleman, private musick - - -	60	0	0
John Wilson, private musick - - - -	20	0	0
Symon Hopper, private musick - - -	60	0	0
Robert Strong, wind instrument - - -	46	10	10
William Howes, violin and wind instrument -	46	10	10
John Rogers, private musick - - - -	100	0	0
John Gamble, wind instrument - - -	46	10	10
Thomas Bates, £50; £40 private musick -	90	0	0
John Harding, private musick - - - -	40	0	0
Gregory Thorndell, private musick - - -	40	0	0
Thos. Lanier, private musick - - - -	67	9	2
John Jenkyns, private musick - - - -	40	0	0
John Smyth, private musick - - - -	40	0	0
Nathaniel Watkyns, private musick - -	40	0	0
Alphonso Marsh, private musick - - -	40	0	0
Humphrey Madge, violin and wind instrument	86	12	6
Phillip Becket, wind instrument - - -	60	2	6
Thomas Blagrave, violin and wind instrument -	40	9	2
Robert Blagrave, violin and wind instrument -	58	14	2
Charles Evans, private musick - - -	46	10	10
John Mason, wind instrument - - - -	46	10	10
Mathew Lock, composer of musick - - -	40	0	0
Anthony Roberts, private musick - - -	40	0	0
Henry Hawes, private musick - - - -	46	10	10
Edward Coleman, private musick - - -	40	0	0
John Singleton, wind musick - - - -	46	10	10
Richard Dorney, violin - - - - -	20	0	0
John Clement, private musick - - - -	40	0	0
John Lylly, private musick - - - -	40	0	0
John Bannister, private musick - - -	110	0	0
John Mason and Henry Gregory, wind instrument - - - - - - -	66	0	0
William Clayton, wind instrument - - -	66	2	6
John Goodgroome, private musick - - -	40	0	0
James Farr, organ maker - - - -	20	0	0
Theophilus Fitz, wind instrument - - -	46	10	10
Henry Bassano, wind instrument - - -	46	10	10
Thomas Mell, wind instrument - - -	46	10	10

William Young.   Isaac Staggins.   Edward Hooton.
Blow in the place of Giles Tomkyns.

1668-9, January 15.

Appointment of John Blow in place of Giles Tompkins, as one of His Majesty's musicians for the virginalls.

L. C. Vol. 482, p. 52.

1668-9, January 18.

Warrant for habitts of several coloured rich taffatas for twenty-four violins, like Indian gowns, *but not so full*, with short sleeves to the elbow and trymed with tinsell, to be delivered to the master of his Majesty's revels; and also twenty-four garlands of several coloured flowers for each of them.

L. C. Vol. 836, p. 13.

1668-9, January 18.

Warrant to pay to Lewis Grabu, appointed master of the musique in place of Nicholas Lanier, deceased, in consideration of his liveries for three years last past, 1666, 1667 and 1668, the sum of £48. 7s. 6d., and to deliver to him during His Majesty's pleasure a yearly livery of £16 : 2 : 6.

L. C. Vol. 814, p. 279d.

1668-9, January 19.

Warrant to pay to Charles Evans, harper for the Italian harp, the sume of five pounds, for strings by him bought and provided for ye harpe for one whole yeare ending at Christmas, 1668.

L. C. Vol. 771, p. 3.

1668-9, January 20.

Edward Hooten appointed musician in place of Gregory Thorndale.

L. C. Vol. 478, pp. 76, 78; Vol. 482.

1668-9, February 3.

Bryan Quinne appointed trumpeter in ordinary to attend the Duke of Ormond in Ireland in the place which Robert Burgesse and Richard Musson lately enjoyed.

L. C. Vol. 479, p. 105.

1668-9, February 3.

Warrant to prepare a Bill conteyning a grant unto John Myer of the place of musician in ordinary to his Majesty for the violin, in the place of William Youckney, deceased; wages 20d. by the day and £16. 2s. 6d. for his livery yearly, during his Majesty's pleasure. The first payment to commence on St. John the Baptist last past, 1668.

L. C. Vol. 771, p. 172.

1668-9, February 20.

Account for liveries for three children of the Chappell, whose voyces are changed.

L. C. Vol. 201, *p.* 96.

1668-9 February 21.

CHARLES R.

" Whereas in the late retrenchment of payments out of our Treasury of our Chamber, bearing date 16 March, 1667, we did further signifie and declare our pleasure that our foure and twenty violins together with the master of our musick with two boyes, two composers and Monsieur Le Grange for a basse, whose names are mentioned in a list should be continued and theire sallerys paid them as formerly, as also that our musick in our chappell be continued and paid for theire services there as formerly, any order of retrenchment to the contrary notwithstanding, which wee have thought fitt hereby to signifie unto you, to the end you may conforme yourselfe thereunto and governe yourselfe herein accordingly, for which this shalbe your warrant.   Given at our court at Whitehall the 21st day of February in ye 21st yeare of our reigne 1668-9."

Lewis Grabu, master of his Majesty's musick, and to have the teaching of two boyes.

Violins.

Ambrose Beeland	John Myer
Richard Dorney	John Bannister
Theophilus Fitz	Thomas Blagrave
John Singleton	William Howes
William Young	John Strong
Henry Brockwell	Robert Strong
John Atkinson	Thomas Fitz
Henry Smyth	Phillip Beckett
Symon Hopper	Henry Comer
Isaac Staggins	Jeoffery Bannister
William Clayton	William Saunders
Edmund Tanner	Humphrey Madge

Composers.

George Hudson	Mathew Lock

Monsieur Le Grange, for a basse.

L. C. Vol. 771, *pp.* 229, 230.

1668-9, *February* 27.

Payment of one year's livery to John Hingston, Dr. John Wilson, John Banister, Alphonso Marsh, Dr. William Child, Charles Coleman, John Gamble, William Gregory, Humphrey Madge, George Hudson, John Jenkins, John Lillie, John Harding, John Clement, Anthony Roberts, John Smith, and Henry Cooke, musicians, due St. Andrew, 1668.

L. C. Vol. 712.

1668-9, *March* 1.

Warrant to pay to Pelham Humphryes, appointed musician in ordinary for the lute, in place of Nicholas Lanier, deceased, for his liveries for three years, 1666, 1667, and 1668, the sum of £48. 7s. 6d., and to deliver to him yearly during His Majesty's pleasure a livery of £16 : 2 : 6.

L. C. Vol. 814, *p.* 281.

1668-9, *March* 1.

Liveries of £16. 2. 6 each, due St. Andrew, 1668, were paid to Thomas Laneir, Thomas Bates, Edward Coleman and Lewis Grabu, musicians.

L. C. Vol. 712.

1668-9, *March* 3.

Payment of one year's livery to Gregory Thorndell, musician, and to Pelham Humphryes, musician, due St. Andrew, 1668.

L. C. Vol. 712.

1668-9, *March* 17.

The sum of £30 by the year to be paid to Captain Henry Cook, master of the children of his Majesty's Chappell Royall, from Michaelmas, 1668, quarterly every year during the King's pleasure, for keeping of Thomas Tedway, one of the children of his Majesty's Chappell, whose voyce is changed and is to goe from the Chappell.

L. C. Vol. 771, *p.* 6.

1668-9, *March* 18.

Payment of £16. 2. 6. to Henry Cooke, for livery due to Mathew Lock, musician, for the year 1668.

L. C. Vol. 712, *p.* 72.

1668-9, *March* 23.

Payment of £16. 2. 6. to Theophilus Fitz, musician, livery due St. Andrew, 1668.

L. C. Vol. 712, *p.* 56.

1669, *March* 27.

Account for the liveries and banners of kettle-drummers and trumpeters.

L. C. Vol. 201, *p.* 106.

1669, *March* 31.

William Aleworth, having given his attendance upon his Majesty in the place of Henry Comer, one of his Majesty's violins, from 25 March, 1668 to 27 March, 1669, the sum of £23 to be stopped out of Comer's salary and paid unto the said William Aleworth.

L. C. Vol. 771, *p.* 117,

1669, *April* 5.

Warrant to the Treasurer of the Chamber to pay to Sarah Montagu, mother of Henry Montagu, one of the children of his Majesty's Chappell Royall, whose voyce is changed and is to go from the Chappell, the sum of £30 by the year, quarterly, for his keeping, during his Majesty's pleasure, from 25 March, 1669.

L. C. Vol. 771, *p.* 15.

1669, *April* 9.

Warrant to pay unto John Hingston, keeper and repayrer of his Majesty's organs, pedalls and other instruments, the summe of £53. 3s. for stringing, penning and repayring harpsicords, for preparing an organ in the banquetting house, for mending the organ at Whitehall and for other necessaryes by him performed for one yeare and a halfe from the 29th of September, 1667 to the 25th of March, 1669.

L. C. Vol. 771, *p.* 15.

1669, *April* 9.

Order to repair the lodgings of Captain Henry Cook, master of the children of His Majesty's Chappell Royall, at the further end of the Old Bowleing Alley at Hampton Court, and that you erect chymneyes there necessary and convenient for the said lodgings.

L. C. Vol. 771, *p.* 233.

1669, *April* 10—*April* 20.

Account for trumpets and kettledrums :—

    17 trumpett strings at 16s. a pair.

    2 pairs of strings for 2 kettle-drummes, 15s. a pair.

    2 spanner strings for the said kettle-drummes at 8s. a pair.

    2 pairs of drumm-stick strings at 2s. 6d. a pair.

    32 buttons and loops for the 2 kettle-drummes at 6s.

Account for 4 trumpeters and a kettledrummer, appointed to attend the Lord Howard ; 2 pairs of drumme sticks, and string of silk and silver with tassels : £1.

L. C. Vol. 201, *pp.* 112*d*, 125*d*, 131*d*.

1669, *April* 14.

Warrant to pay to John Goodgroome, appointed musician in ordinary for the lute and voyce, in place of Henry Purcell, deceased, for his livery for five years past, 1664, 1665, 1666, 1667 and 1668, the sum of £80. 12s. 6d., and to deliver to him yearly during His Majesty's pleasure a livery of £16 : 2 : 6.

L. C. Vol. 814, *p.* 284*d*.

1669, *April* 26.

Warrant for payment of £32. 5s. to the executrix of Richard Hudson, late one of his Majesty's musique, by vertue of an assignment from George Hudson, one other of his Majesty's musique, being two years' liveries due for the years 1665 and 1666.

This entry crossed out and " vacatur " written against it.

L. C. Vol. 711, *p.* 51*d*.

[1669, *May*.]

Warrant to pay Captain Henry Cooke, master of the children of his Majesty's Chappell Royall, £30 by the year, quarterly from 25 March, 1669, during his Majesty's pleasure, for the keeping of John Farmer, whose voice is changed and who is to go from the chapel.

L. C. Vol. 771, *p.* 16.

1669, *May* 3.

Warrant to pay John Crowther, John Jones, George Monroe and William Peacock, four of his Majesty's trumpeters, and Walter Vanbright, kettle-drummer, the sum of £20 each for their charges and expenses in attending upon the Rt. Hon. the Lord Henry Howard, ambassador from his Majesty to the Emperor of Morocco.

L. C. Vol. 771, *p.* 16.

1669, *May* 6.

Payment of £16. 2. 6 to John Goodgroome, musician, for livery due St. Andrew, 1668.

L. C. Vol. 712.

1669, *May* 10.

George Munroe appointed a trumpeter extraordinary.

L. C. Vol. 478, *p.* 119 ; *and Vol.* 479, *p.* 105.

1669, *May* 10.

Warrant to pay to Capt. Henry Cooke, master of the children of his Majesty's Chappell Royall, £192 12s., for learning the children on the violin, lute, theorbo and organ, for paper, penns and inke, and for strings for tuneing the virginalls, for fire and strings in the musick roome in the Chappell, and for his charges in fetching and bringing up boys from severall places for one whole year, from Lady Day, 1668 to Lady Day, 1669.

L. C. Vol. 771, *p.* 16.

1669, *May* 14.

Warrant for payment of £79 : 10 : 8 to George Porter, trumpeter to his late Majesty, for his pension at the rate of £19. 17. 8. per annum, for four years, 1664 to 1667.

L. C. Vol. 711, *p.* 41d.

1669, *Pentecost.*

Payment of £19. 17. 8. to each of the following trumpeters to the late King Charles I. for their pensions :—

Robert Ramsay	George Bosgrave
Samuel Markland	William Porter
Henry Peacock.	

L. C. Vol. 462.

1669, *May* 26.

Bill for 8 black casters at 12s. apiece for trumpeters.

L. C. Papers, Bundle 4.

1669, *June* 1.

Bill amounting to £144 6s., for liveries for trumpeters and drummers, &c.

L. C. Papers, Bundle 6.

1669, *June* 18.

"These are to certifie that by an order of his Majesty concerning the retrenchment of his Majesty's musick, dated February 21, 1668-9, his Majesty was pleased to exempt out of the said retrenchment his musick of the Chappell, whose names are :—

Thomas Purcell	Pelham Humphreyes
Dr. Christopher Gibbons	John Hingston
Dr. William Child	William Gregory
Dr. John Wilson	Theodore Steftkin
Thomas Blagrave	Paul Bridges

and which are his Majesty's private musick likewise, and these are the persons his Majesty intends to be continued and paid in their respective places in the Treasury Chamber as formerly.

L. C. Vol. 771, *p.* 239. *A copy of this same certificate, dated* 31 *March*, 1669, *is entered on p.* 231.

1669, *June* 18.

Warrant to apprehend Anthony Devant, Benjamin Dobson, William Cradock, John Parsons, Arthur Pickering, George Chaundler and Richard Betts, for keeping playhouses and sounding trumpets, drums and fifes at dumb shows and modells without paying the fee due to his Majesty's serjeant trumpeter by Letters Patent dated 24 January 13 Charles II. whereby the said serjeant trumpeter ought to receive twelve pence from every playhouse for every day they act, his Majesty's players excepted.

No trumpets, drums or fifes being allowed to be sounded without his lycence.

L. C. Vol. 652.

1669, *St. John the Baptist.*

Payment of £29. 16. 8. to John Mason and Henry Gregory for clothing, and educating two boys in the art of music for half a year.

L. C. Vol. 462.

1669, *June* 25.

Warrant to pay Captain Henry Cooke, Master of the children of his Majesty's Chappell, the sum of £86. 2s. upon a bill for provisions for the said children.

L. C. Vol. 618, *p.* 15*d.*

1669, *June* 28.

Warrant to apprehend George Smyth, Francis Pendleton, Mosse, Cæsar Duffill and Josiah Priest, for teaching, practising and executing music in companies or otherwise, without the approbation or lycence of the Marshall and Corporation of musick, in contempt of his Majesty's authority and the power granted to the Marshal and Corporation.

L. C. Vol. 652.

1669, *July* 1.

Account for Francis Braban, kettledrummer to Sir Phillip Howard, for guilding and painting 2 kettledrumme banners, £7.

L. C. Vol. 201, 130*d*, 131*d.*

1669, *July* 3 *to July* 31.

Account of Jarvis Curtis to Francis Braban, kettle-drummer to Sir Phillip Howard; 2 pairs of strings at 15s. 8d. a pair; for 1 spanner string, 8s.; for 18 buttons and loops with olive heads, 3s.; 2 pairs of drum stick strings at 2s. 6d. a pair.

L. C. Vol. 201, *pp.* 128*d.* *to* 139 ; 149*d. ; L. C. Papers, Bundle* 7.

1669, *July* 12.

Several items and accounts for the liveries of the drum-major, four drummers, one fife and fourteen trumpeters : and for trimming the banners of the kettledrummers and phifes belonging to Sir Philip Howard.

L. C. Vol. 201, *pp.* 129, 130*d.*

1669, *July* 16.

Warrant for the delivery to Thomas Haynes, esquire, of 64 surplices for the gentlemen of the Chappell Royall, 12 surplices for the musicians, and 36 surplices for the children.

L. C. Papers, Bundle 7.

1669, *July* 19.

Assignment by Mathew Lock, of St. Martin's in the Fields, of the sum of £20, to Venables Stanton, of the same parish, to be paid out of wages due from the Treasury Chamber after the assignments already made.

[This entry is crossed out.]

L. C. Vol. 195, *p.* 10.

1669, *July* 20—*August* 3.

Accounts for the summer liveries for the children of the Chappell.

L. C. Vol. 201, *pp.* 125, 127*d.*

1669, *July* 21.

Warrant to swear and admit William Clayton musician in ordinary to his Majesty in the private musick without fee, to come in ordinary with fee upon the next avoydance of any of the private musick.

L. C. Vol. 771, *p.* 251.

1669, *July* 22.

Petition of Alexander Clerke, Chyrurgion, against William Ayleworth, musitian. William Ayleworth to appear.

L. C. Vol. 652.

1669, *July* 31.

Warrant to prepare a Bill conteyning a grant appointing William Young musician in ordinary for the flute, and Isaac Staggins musician for the tenner hoboy in ordinary to his Majesty, in the place of Henry Bassano, deceased, who enjoyed both the said places ; with the wages of 20d. by the day and £16. 2s. 6d. yearly for livery unto each of them. To commence from St. John the Baptist, 1665.

L. C. Vol. 771, *p.* 183.

1669, *August* 8.

Accounts for velvett belts for four trumpeters and a kettle-drummer attending the Lord Howard to Morocco; also for a drum-major, 4 drummers and a phife.

L. C. Vol. 201, *pp.* 132, 146.

1669, *August* 13.

Assignment by Richard Darney, a musician, of the sum of £10. 7s. 9d., to Sir William Boreman, of Whitehall.
[Entry crossed out.]

L. C. Vol. 195, *p.* 13.

1669, *August* 13.

Whereas Henry Brockwell, one of his Majesty's musitians, is appoynted keeper of all his Majesty's musicall instruments; these are therefore to require all his Majesty's musitians that they presume not to carry any of his Majesty's said instruments out of his Majesty's palace, but after service ended from tyme to tyme that they deliver them unto ye custody of the said Henry to be by him safely kept for his Majesty's service.

L. C. Vol. 771, *p.* 242.

1669, *September* 3.

Trumpeters to attend His Majesty's state, and also the Lord Lieutenant, Lord Deputy, Lords Justices, or any other chief governor for the tyme being in the kingdom of Ireland.

Henry Thewer   Patrick Ray
       Peter Lake.

L. C. Vols. 482, *p.* 62 ; 483, *p.* 78.

1669, *September* 3.

Warrant to prepare a Bill conteyning a grant to William Clayton of the office of musician in ordinary for the lute and voyce, in the place of Edward Coleman, deceased; wages £40 per annum, to commence Michaelmas, 1669.

L. C. Vol. 482, *p.* 52 ; *and Vol.* 771, *p.* 184.

1669, *September* 14.

Account for the mourning livery of Gervice Price, sergeant trumpeter to his Majesty, on the death of the Queen mother of England.

L. C. Vol. 201, *p.* 260; *L. C. Papers, Bundles* 2 *and* 18.

Accounts ending Michaelmas, 1669.

Account of 4s. for gilding a new carved cornett for a coach for the master of the horse.

L. C. Vol. 201, *p.* 220.

Account paid to Henry Cooke, for keeping and teaching two singing boys, for one year.

                                        L. C. Vol. 462.

" A breviat of Sir Edward Griffin's account " includes

Trumpeters -   -   -   -   -   -   - 1350 : 00 : 0
Violins   -   -   -   -   -   -   - 1733 : 16 : 0
Wind Musique -   -   -   -   -   - 0255 : 19 : 7
Private Musique - -   -   -   -   - 0889 : 15 : 7
Tuner & Repairer of the wind musique   - 0240 : 00 : 0
Virginalls   -   -   -   -   -   -   - 0086 : 00 : 0

                                  L. C. Papers, Bundle 21.

1669, *October* 25.

Warrant to pay to Thomas Fittz, one of his Majesty's musicians in ordinary, £21. 10s. for his ryding charges and other expenses in attending upon his Majesty at Newmarkett, May 1668 ; 21 days at Bagshott and Portsmouth in June ; 11 days at Newmarkett ; and Audley End 33 days ; and again at Newmarkett in March following 15 days ; and in April, 1669,. 6 days ; being in all 86 days, at the rate of 5s. by the day.

                          L. C. Vols. 771, *p.* 21 ; 772, *p.* 29.

1669, *November* 19.

Warrant to deliver to William Clayton, appointed musician in ordinary for the lute and voyce, in place of Edward Coleman, deceased, the materials for his livery yearly at the Feast of St. Andrew during His Majesty's pleasure.

                                 L. C. Vol. 814, *p.* 293.

1669, *November* 30.

Warrant to pay the sum of £52 to Robert Strong, one of his Majesty's musicians in ordinary, for two double curtolls, bought and delivered for their Majesties' service, and given to Segnior Francisco for the service of the Queenes Majesty.

                          L. C. Vols. 771, *p.* 21 ; 772, *p.* 30.

1669, *St. Andrew.*

Payment of £16. 2. 6. to each of the following musicians to the King, for their liveries :—

Henry Cooke	Gregory Thorndell
John Willson	Mathew Locke
Anthony Roberts	Thomas Bates
John Hingeston	Alphonso Marsh
William Gregory	John Clement
George Hudson	Thomas Purcell
Humphrey Madge	William Child

Thomas Lanier
John Smith
John Gamble
John Jenckins
John Lillie
John Harding
John Bannister
Edward Colman (" mort
ante diem " written
against his name)

John Goodgroome
Theophilus Fittz
Charles Colman
Lewis Grabu, master of
the music
Pelham Humphries
William Clayton

Payment of £29. 16. 8. to John Mason and Henry Gregory for clothing two boys and educating them in the art of music, for half a year.

L. C. Vol. 462.

1669, *December* 15.

Patent granted to Robert Mawgridge to be one of his Majesty's drummers, in the place of Jeremy Crewes, deceased; wages 12d. by the day and £16. 2s. 6d. yearly for livery, to commence 29 September, 1665.

L. C. Vol. 771, *p.* 186.

1669, *December* 17.

Warrant to prepare and deliver unto Thomas Sculthorpe, Richard Deame and William Bounty, three silver trumpetts, of the same value and proportion as they formerly received, they first returning in their old trumpets.

L. C. Vol. 771, *p.* 153.

1669, *December* 17.

Warrant to apprehend Roger Arthur, Nicholas Elliott, Edward Wynson, Arthur Cooke, and Anthony Marrant, for practising and exercising musick or otherwise playing in public in several places, without the approbation or lycence of the Marshall and Corporation of musick and in contempt of his Majesty's authority.

L. C. Vol. 652.

1669, *December* 18.

Warrant for a livery for Symon Peirson, trumpeter to the Duke of Monmouth, for the present year, 1669.

L. C. Vol. 836, *p.* 47.

1669, *December* 31.

Warrant to pay £73. to Dr. Walter Jones, sub-deane of his Majesty's Chappell Royall, for paper books, pricking services and anthems for his Majesty's service, and for other things, from May, 1662 to 10 December, 1668.

L. C. Vols. 771, *p.* 57; 772, *p.* 31.

1669-70, *January* 4.

Warrant to prepare and deliver unto Symon Beale and William Bounty, two of his Majesty's trumpeters, two silver trumpetts of the same quality, value and proportion as they have formerly received, they first returning in their old trumpetts.

L. C. Vol. 601; *and Vol.* 771, *p.* 154.

1669-70, *January* 22.

Concerning the retrenchment of his Majesty's musick, this is to certify that Mr. John Strong is one of the musitians that doth service in his Majesty's Chappell Royall and is to be continued and paid in his respective places in the Treasury Chamber as formerly.

L. C. Vol. 771, *p.* 257.

1669-70, *January* 22.

Warrant to pay Charles Evans, harper for the Italian harp, the sum of £5 for strings provided by him for the said harp for one whole year ending at Christmas, 1669.

L. C. Vols. 771, *p.* 22 ; 772, *p.* 32.

1669-70, *February* 19.

Concerning the retrenchment of his Majesty's musick, this is to certify that Mr. John Singleton is one of the musitians that doth service in his Majesty's Chappell Royall and is to be continued in his respective places in the Treasury Chamber as formerly.

L. C. Vol. 771, *p.* 259.

1669-70, *March* 15.

Italian musitians :—

Giovanni Sebenico, Pietro Cefalo, Mr. Killigrew.

L. C. Vol. 482, *p.* 55.

1670, *March* 26.

Patent granted to Devereux Clothier of the office and place of drummer in ordinary to his Majesty in the place of Edward Ottley, deceased ; wages 12d. by the day and £16. 2s. 6d. yearly for livery, during his Majesty's pleasure, to commence 25 December, 1664.

L. C. Vol. 771, *p.* 191.

1670, *May* 4.

Petition of Dr. Child, musician for the wind instruments, against the rest of his fellows, for deteyning six years and a half of board wages upon the pretence of his not attending the service.

L. C. Vol. 653.

1670, *May* 6.

Musitians to attend in the Chappell.

Mr. Madge	Mr. Brockwell
Mr. John Banister	Mr. Finall
Mr. Greeteing	
Mr. Hopper	Mr. Singleton
Mr. John Strong	Mr. Clayton
	Mr. Beckett
Mr. Young	Mr. Gamble
Mr. Thomas Fitz	Mr. Staggins
Mr. Theophilus Fittz	

I doe hereby order that his Majesty's musitians above-named doe wayte and attend in his Majesty's Chappell Royall as they are here sett downe, five in one moneth and five in another. Soe that each person attend every third moneth as they will answere the contrary.

L. C. Vol. 771, *p.* 275.

1670, *Pentecost.*

Payment of £19. 17. 8. to each of the following trumpeters to the late King Charles I. for their pensions :—

Robert Ramsay	George Bosgrave
Samuel Markland	William Porter
Henry Peacock	

L. C. Vol. 462 ; *and Vol.* 545, *p.* 38d.

1670, *May* 29.

Warrant to pay John Hingston, keeper and repairer of his Majesty's organs, the sum of £56. 16s., for stringing and repairing the harpsicords, and for mending and tueneing the great organ, for strings for the virginalls, and for diverse other things from 29 March, 1669 to 29 March, 1670.

L. C. Vol. 772, *p.* 36.

1670, *May.*

Bill of William Edwards, pike maker, for gilting the head of a cornet staffe and swivell, £1. 5s.

L. C. Vol. 202, 55d.

1670, *St. John the Baptist.*

Payment of £29. 16. 8. to John Mason and Henry Gregory, musicians to the King, for clothing 2 boys and educating them in the art of music for half a year.

L. C. Vol. 462.

1670, *June* 25.

Warrant to pay Capt. Cooke, master of the children of his Majesty's Chappell Royall, the sum of £145. 6s., for fetching of boyes from Rochester, Lyncolne, Peterborough, Worcester, and other places, and for learning the boyes on the organ and theorbo, also for fire and strings for the musique room in the Chappell, and for other services by him performed in the year 25 March, 1669 to 25 March, 1670.

L. C. Vol. 772, *p.* 37.

1670, *June* 25.

Joseph Fashion appointed one of the musicians for the violins to the King, in place of Henry Smyth, deceased.

L. C. Vol. 482, *p.* 51.

1670, *June* 30.

Warrant to swear and admit Edmund Flower one of his Majesty's musicians in ordinary in the private musique for the theorboe or lute, without fee.

L. C. Vol. 771, *p.* 282.

1670, *July* 8.

A warrant to prepare and deliver unto Matteo Bataglio, Italian musician to his Majesty, a chayne and medall of gold of the value of £40, to be presented unto him as a guift from his Majesty.

L. C. Vol. 771, *p.* 160.

1670, *July* 9.

Giovanni Sebenico and Symon Cottereau appointed Italian musicians in ordinary for the private musique.

L. C. Vol. 479, *p.* 103.

1670, *July* 15.

Warrant to prepare a Bill conteyning a grant to Joseph Fashion of the office of musician in ordinary to his Majesty for the violin, in the room of Henry Smyth, deceased; wages 20d. by the day and £16. 2s. 6d. yearly for livery, to commence St. John the Baptist last past, 1670.

L. C. Vol. 771, *p.* 192.

1670, *July* 20.

Estimate for two suits apiece with all compleate furniture for Richard Hart and Richard Symcoll, two children of the Chappell whose voyces are changed and are going off from the said Chappell : £30. 0. 9.

L. C. Vol. 545, *p.* 7.

1670, *July* 23.

Bill for 141 ells of holland for 36 surplices for 12 boys of his Majesty's Chappell, £28 : 4s.

L. C. Vol. 202, *p.* 22.

1670, *July* 27.

Warrant for payment for twenty-seven ells, three quarters of black taffaty for curtaines for the organ loft at Whitehall.

Warrant for payment for thirty-nine ells and a half of crimson taffaty to make curtaines for the great double organ at Whitehall; and for crimson damask to make banners for the 17 trumpettors and a kettledrummer.

L. C. Vol. 803, *pp.* 54, 107.

1670, *July* 30.

" Whereas diverse persons do sett forth and authorise playes, dumb showes and modells, and there are several drummers, trumpetts and fifes that do sound, beate and play at them, without lycence from his Majesty's sergeant trumpeter according to a patent granted to him, this is to order that all such persons shall be apprehended, and brought before me to answer such things as shall be objected against them."

L. C. Vol. 653.

1670, *August* 6.

Petition signed by Robert Ramsay, George Bosgrave, William Porter, Henry Peacock and Samuel Markland, to the Master of the Great Wardrobe, for their allowances as pentionary trumpeters, due at Pentecost, 1670.

L. C. Papers, Bundle 2.

1670, *August.*

Bill for liveries for Richard Symcoll and Richard Hart, two boys of his Majesty's Chappell whose voices are changed.

L. C. Vol. 202, *pp.* 26, 29*d*, 31*d* ; *L. C. Papers, Bundles* 12 *and* 19.

1670, *Michaelmas.*

Accounts for £3 : 7s. paid to Henry Cooke, disbursed by him for the children of the Chappell.

L. C. Papers, Bundle 19.

Account paid to Henry Cooke, for the custody and teaching of two singing boys for one year.

L. C. Vol. 462.

1670, *St. Andrew.*

Payment of £16. 2. 6. to each of the following musicians to the King, for their liveries :—

Henry Cooke	Gregory Thornedell
John Willson	Matthew Locke
Anthony Roberts	Thomas Bates

John Hingeston	Alphonso Marsh
William Gregory	John Clement
George Hudson	Thomas Purcell
Humphrey Madge	William Child
Thomas Lanier	John Goodgroome
John Smith	Theophilus Fittz
John Gamble	Charles Colman
John Jenkins	Lewis Grabu, master of
John Lillie	the music
John Harding	Pelham Humfries
John Bannister	William Clayton

Payment of £29. 16. 8. to John Mason and Henry Gregory for clothing two boys and educating them in the art of music for half a year.

L. C. Vol. 462 *; and Vol.* 545, *pp.* 37 *to* 39.

1670, *December* 5.

Warrant to swear and admit Richard Browne musician in ordinary for the violin, without fee, to his Majesty, to attend in the absence of Henry Comer.

L. C. Vol. 771, *p.* 292.

1670, *December* 19.

Warrant to swear and admit John Spicer musician for the violin in extraordinary to his Majesty.

L. C. Vol. 478, *p.* 113 *; and Vol.* 771, *p.* 294.

1670.

Warrant to pay the sum of £120 to Henry Brockwell, on behalf of himselfe and his Majesty's four and twenty violins in ordinary :—

Ambrose Beeland	John Banister
Richard Dorney	Robert Strong
Theophilus Fitz	Thomas Blagrave
John Singleton	William Howes
William Young	John Strong
John Attkinson	Thomas Fitz
Henry Smyth	Phillip Beckett
Simon Hopper	Henry Comer
Isaack Staggins	Jeoffery Banister
William Clayton	William Saunders
Edmund Tanner	Humphrey Madg
John Myer	

for their ryding charges and other expenses in their attendance upon his Majesty to Dover for 20 days, from 16 May to 4 June, 1670, at the rate of 5s. by the day to each man.

L. C. Vol. 772, *p.* 46.

1670.

Order to Thomas Lanyer and the rest of the wind musick, to appear at Whitehall on Thursday next by nine o'clock.

L. C. Vol. 653.

1670.

Petition from the underwritten musicians to his Majesty, to the Earl of Sandwich, master of his Majesty's great Wardrobe, praying that their liveries due to them for the year 1669 may be assigned to them :—

John Wilson, John Hingston, William Gregory, John Bannister, William Clayton, Theophilus Fittz, Charles Coleman, Thomas Bates, and Thomas Lanier.

L. C. Vol. 198, *p.* 32.

1670.

Accounts of liveries of £16 : 2 : 6, due for four years, 1667 to 1670 inclusive, to the following musicians :—

John Hingston	John Jenkins
Dr. John Willson	John Lillie
Thomas Laneir	John Harding
Theophilus Fitz	John Clement
John Gamble	Anthony Roberts
Charles Coleman	Gregory Thorndell
William Gregory	John Smith
Thomas Bates	Henry Cook
John Banister	John Goodgroome, 1664
Alphonso Marsh	to 1670
Dr. William Child	Pelham Humphries, 1666
Lewis Grabu, Master of	to 1670
the musick	Edward Coleman, 1667
Humphrey Madge	and 1668
George Hudson	William Clayton, 1669
Mathew Lock	and 1670

L. C. Vol. 712, *folios* 55—81.

1670-1, *January* 9 & 10.

Payment of one year's livery to Dr. William Child, Thomas Laneir and Alphonso Marsh, musicians, due St. Andrew, 1670.

L. C. Vol. 712.

1670-1, *January* 12.

Thomas Fitz, musician for the violin in the place of Richard Hudson, deceased. There being some money in arrears due for the service of Hudson which ought to be paid unto his widdow, half of the first year's salary due to Fitz shall be given to Elizabeth, relict of Richard Hudson, who is very poor and much in necessity. Thomas Fitz to receive the like sum out of the arrears of Hudson's salary.

L. C. Vol. 771, p. 124.

1670-1, *January* 14.

Payment of one year's livery to Dr. John Wilson, musician, due St. Andrew, 1670.

L. C. Vol. 712, p. 56.

1670-1, *January* 17.

Mr. Gregory Thorndall departed this life, the 17 January, 1670-1.

L. C. Vol. 198, p. 72.

1670-1, *January* 26.

Payment of one year's livery to Mathew Lock, musician, due St. Andrew, 1670.

L. C. Vol. 712.

1670-1, *January* 28.

Warrant to prepare a Bill conteyning a grant unto Edward Hooton of the place of musician in ordinary to his Majesty for the lutes and voices in the place of Gregory Thorndell, deceased ; with yearly livery of £40, to commence from the Annunciation next ensuing.

L. C. Vol. 771, p. 196.

1670-1, *February* 1.

Order for the appearance of Thomas Sculthorpe, trumpeter, upon the petition of Francis Parsons, widdow, executrix of John Parsons, deceased, concerning a debt of £40 by bond due from his wife's late husband.

L. C. Vol. 653.

1670-1, *February* 4.

Payment of one year's livery to Lewis Grabu, musician, due St. Andrew, 1670.

L. C. Vol. 712.

1670-1, *February* 7.

Payment of livery of £16. 2. 6. each to Henry Cook, John Lillie and John Harding, musicians, due St. Andrew, 1670.

L. C. Vol. 712.

1670-1, *February* 8.

Warrant to cause the musique room in his Majesty's Chappell Royall to be enlarged 3½ feet in length towards his Majesty's closet.

L. C. Vol. 771, p. 297.

1670-1, *February* 11.

Mr. Bannister's receipt for the sum of £16-2-6 from the Earl of Sandwich, for his livery as musician.

L. C. Papers, Bundle 4.

1670-1, *February* 11.

Payment of one year's livery to John Clement, musician, due St. Andrew, 1670.

L. C. Vol. 712.

1670-1, *February* 11.

Bill of Thos. Haynes, sergeant of His Majesty's vestry for making 38 surplices for the children of the King's Chappell; and 76 surplices for the Gentlemen and musitians.

L. C. Vol. 202, *p.* 96.

1670-1, *February* 15.

Warrant to prepare a Bill conteyning a grant to Thomas Fynell of the office of one of his Majesty's musicians in ordinary for the violin, in the place of John Atkins, deceased; wages 20d. by the day and £16. 2s. 6d. by the year for his livery during his Majesty's pleasure, to commence from the Annunciation next ensueing, 1671.

L. C. Vol. 771, *p.* 195.

1670-1, *February* 17.

Robert Ramsey, trumpeter to his Majesty is indebted to Robert Young in eleven pounds. Stopped out of his salary in two payments of £5. 10s. each, to be paid to Robert Young.

L. C. Vol. 771, *p.* 125.

1670-1, *February* 25.

Receipt signed by Henry Cooke for the following materials out of the great wardrobe for liveries for the twelve children of the Chappell; 12 tunicks, vests and breeches of scarlet cloth lyned with sky shalloone and laced with silk and silver lace,

15 pieces of scarlet, sky and white 6d. tafita ribon,

3 dozen of whole shirts, 64 ells;

3 dozen of half shirts, 62 ells;

4 dozen of plain bands and cuffs and

2 dozen of laced bands and cuffs, 16½ ells;

3 dozen of handkerchers, 7½ ells;

1 dozen of silk hose,

2 dozen of worsted hose,

3 dozen of gloves,

2 dozen of hatts,

3 dozen of shoes,

1 dozen sashes.

L. C. Papers, Bundle 23.

1670-1, *February* 27.

Payment of one year's livery to Pelham Humphryes, musician, due St. Andrew, 1670.

L. C. Vol. 712.

1670-1, *March* 7.

Jervice Price, serjeant trumpeter, craves allowance for liveries for himself and 16 trumpeters and one kettle drummer for the year 1668.

John Mawgridge, drum major, craves allowance for liveries for himself, 4 drummers and a phife for the year 1668.

L. C. Vol. 202, *pp.* 50*d to* 54 ; *L. C. Papers, Bundle* 15.

1670-1, *March* 13.

Estimate for black taffata curtaines for the musique room in the King's Chappell : £30.

L. C. Vol. 545, *p.* 11.

1670-1, *March* 14.

Warrant to pay Theodore Stefkin, musician for the private music, the sum of £12 for a Lyra violl bought by him for his Majesty's service.

L. C. Vol. 772, *p.* 34.

1670-1, *March* 15.

Order that Humphrey Madge, one of his Majesty's musicians, should within one week refer the matter in difference between him and George Reason to arbitration.

L. C. Vol. 653.

1670-1, *March* 21.

Warrant to deliver to Captain Cooke, master of the children of his Majesty's Chappel Royall, three crimson dammaske curtaynes for the musicke room in the Chappell, the musick room being enlarged.

L. C. Vol. 836, *p.* 238.

1670-1, *March* 23.

Warrant to pay Charles Evans, harper for the Italian Harp, £5 for strings for the said harp for one whole year ending at Christmas, 1670.

L. C. Vol. 772, *p.* 53.

1671, *March* 28.

Bill for 22 yards of black taffata at 9s. per yard for curtains for the organ loft at Whitehall.

L. C. Vol. 202, *p.* 100*d.*

1671, *March* 29.

Order that Sarah Glascock, widdow, doe take her course at law against Paul Bridges, musitian, unless he satisfy her in a debt of £10 within one month.

L. C. Vol. 653.

1671, *March* 31.

Order for the apprehension of John Beardwell, junior, Thomas Stone, Robert Perry and Symon Burr, for that they do take upon themselves to teach, practise, and exercise musick in companyes, or otherwise to play at publique meetings, without the approbation or lycence of the Marshall and Corporation of musick.

L. C. Vol. 653.

1671, *April* 15.

Warrant to deliver unto Henry Thewer, Peter Lake, Alexander Jackson, William Castle and Francis Burton, five of his Majesty's trumpeters attending upon the Lord Lieutenant of Ireland, one silver trumpet each, of the same manner and fashion as they formerly received, they first returning in the old trumpets.

L. C. Vol. 771, *p.* 168.

1671, *April* 27.

Warrant to pay John Hingston, keeper and repairer of his Majesty's organs, the sum of £37. 5s. od. for strings for the base violl, pedals and harpsicords; and for bellows and blower.

L. C. Vol. 772, *p.* 35.

1671, *May* 16.

Order to his Majesty's tailors to make liveries for a trumpeter attending upon his Majesty's troop of Guards commanded by the Duke of Monmouth, one kettle-drummer attending upon her Majesty's troop of Horseguards, commanded by Sir Philip Howard, and one kettle-drummer attending upon his Majesty's troop commanded by the Rt. Hon. Lord Hawley; unto each of them a velvet coat trymmed with silk and silver lace, after the same manner and fashion as his Majesty's trumpeters and kettle-drummer according to a pattern shewed and approved by his Majesty.

L. C. Vol. 773, *p.* 4.

1671, *May* 23.

The sum of £167. 17s. 4d. to be paid to Capt. Cook, master of the children of his Majesty's Chappell Royall, for learneing the children on the organ, on the lute and theorbo, for fire and strings in the musique room in the Chappell, for doctors, nurses, and for looking to severall of the children when they were sick; for going to Westchester, Litchfield, Canterbury and Rochester to look for boyes, and for other service for one year from Lady Day, 1670, to Lady Day, 1671.

L. C. Vol. 773, *p.* 10

1671, *Pentecost.*

Payment of £19. 17. 8. to each of the following trumpeters to the late King Charles I. for their pensions,

Robert Ramsay George Bosgrave
Samuel Markland William Porter
Henry Peacock

L. C. Vol. 462.

1671, *May 27.*

Bill for 20 yards of red Manchester bayes at 2s. 6d. a yard for drumme cases. £2. 10.

L. C. Vol. 202, *p.* 111*d.*

1671, *May 29.*

A lyst of His Majesty's servants appoynted to attend His Majesty at St. George's Feast the 29 day of May, 1671.

It includes :—

Gentlemen of the Chappell.
Musitians.
16 Trumpeters.
Capt. Cook and the children of the Chappell.
Serjeant trumpeter.
Drumme major, 4 drums and a fife.

L. C. Vol. 547, *p.* 17.

1671, *June 24.*

" Whereas diverse of his Majesty's servants and others doe act, play and sett forth dumb showes and modells and refuse to satisfie his Majesty's sergeant trumpetter those fees which are due to him according to his patent, and also diverse trumpetters, drumers and fifes doe sound beate and play at ye said playes, dumbe showes and modells without lycence of ye said sergeant first obteyned, I doe therefore give leave to ye sergeant trumpetter to take his free course at law against all such persons as shall refuse to pay him his fees according to his patent, or sound or beate or play without his lycence as in his patent is specified."

" Whereas divers persons doe sett forth and authorize playes, dumb showes and modells, and there are severall drums, trumpetts and fyfes that doe sound, beate and play at many dumb showes and modells without lycence of his Majesty's sergeant trumpetter or his deputy according to a patent granted unto him under the Greate Seale of England beareing date ye 24th day of January in ye 13th yeare of his Majesty's reigne, these are therefore to require you to apprehend and take into your custody the bodyes of all such persons as shall sett forth and authorize any playes, dumb showes or modells and that sound or beate and play at any of them without lycence from the sergeant trumpetter or his deputy, according to his patent. And that you bring them before me to answere unto such things as shalbe objected against them. And all mayors, sheriffes, justices of ye peace, baylyffes, constables, head boroughs, and other his Majesty's offices, civill and military, are required to be ayding and assisting in ye execution of this my warrant."

St. Alban.

L. C. Vol. 773, *p.* 29*b.*

1671, *St. John the Baptist.*

Payment of £29. 16. 8. to John Mason and Henry Gregorie for clothing 2 boys and educating them in the art of music for half a year.

L. C. Vol. 462.

1671, *July* 23.

John Billon Lamarre admitted one of his Majesty's gentlemen of the Chapel Royal.

L. C. Vol. 483, *p.* 117.

1671, *August* 4.

"Apprehension for exercising musique without lycence from the Corporation."

Whereas John Beardnell, junior, Thomas Stone, Robert Perrey, Jonathan Jenkes, Rutland, Francis Pendleton, Francis Cooper, Thomas Mathewes, Kingston, doe take upon them to teach, practice and exercise musick in companyes or otherwise, to play at publique meetings without the approbation or lycence of the Marshall and Corporation of musick and in contempt of his Majesty's authority and the power granted to the said Marshall and Corporation under the Greate Seale of England. These are therefore to require you to apprehend and take into your custody the bodyes of the said John Beardnell and others abovenamed, and bring them before me to answer unto such things as shall be objected against them, and all mayors, sheriffs, justices of the peace, bayliffs, constables, headboroughs, and all other his Majesty's officers, civil and military, are required to bee ayding and assisting in the execution of this warrant."

L. C. Vol. 773, *p.* 49*b.*

1671, *August* 8.

Warrant to deliver to Capt. Cook, master of the children of his Majesty's Chappell, £30 by the year, during his Majesty's pleasure, for the keeping of Peter Isaack, late one of the children of his Majesty's Chappell, whose voice is changed and is gon from the Chappell. To commence 25 December last past, 1670.

L. C. Vol. 773, *p.* 28. *L. C. Papers, Bundle* 6.

1671, *August* 24.

Sea liveries ordered for two of his Majesty's trumpeters to attend upon his Excellency Henry Coventry, his Majesty's ambassador extraordinary to the King of Sweden.

L. C. Vol. 773, *p.* 32.

1671, *August* 25.

Warrant for the payment of £20 each to Benigne Ragois and John Christmas, trumpeters attending upon Right Honble. Henry Coventry, his Majesty's ambassador to the King of Sweden, for their charges and expenses. Also for each of them one crimson taffata scarfe with silver fringe.

L. C. Vol. 773, *p.* 33.

1671, *August* 30.

John Mawgridge appointed drummer in ordinary to the King, without fee, to come in ordinary with fee upon the next avoydance.

L. C. Vol. 478, *p.* 121; *and Vol.* 773, *p.* 51.

1671, *September* 18.

Claude de Grange appointed one of his Majesty's French musicians in ordinary, being established among the violins for singing the basse, with the wages of £100 by the year, during his Majesty's pleasure, to commence the Annunciation, 1668.

L. C. Vol. 773, *p.* 44.

1671, *September* 27.

Assignment by Henry Peacock, trumpeter to his late Majesty, of all his right, and title interest in his debenture due to him out of his Majesty's great Wardrobe for the year 1671, to Robert Ramsay, trumpeter to his late Majesty.

L. C. Vol. 198, *p.* 30d.

1671, *Michaelmas.*

Account paid to Henry Cooke, for the custody and teaching of two singing boys for one year.

L. C. Vols. 462, 463.

[1671, *October.*]

Petition from John Clement, Thomas Purcell, and William Child, musicians of his Majesty's private musick, that the arrears due to them from his Majesty's great Wardrobe for the years 1669, 1670, and 1671, may be assigned to their fellow musician, Humphrey Madge.

L. C. Vol. 198, *p.* 31*d.*

1671, *October* 9.

Payment of one year's livery to John Hingston, Dr. John Wilson, Thomas Laneir, Theophilus Fitz, William Clayton, Thomas Bates, Charles Coleman, John Gamble and William Gregory, musicians, due St. Andrew, 1669.

L. C. Vol. 712.

1671, *October* 25.

Payment of two liveries to John Smith, musician, due St. Andrew 1669 and 1670.

L. C. Vol. 712.

1671, *October* 28.

William Kydwell appointed musician in ordinary to the King, without fee, to come in ordinary with fee, upon the first avoydance.

L. C. Vol. 483, *p.* 127 ; *and Vol.* 773, *p.* 53.

1671, *October.*

Letter from the undermentioned musicians to Thomas Townsend, esquire :—

We whose names are underwritten, musitians to his Majesty, desire you will be pleased to deliver our talleys, and order on the fee farmes for one year's liverie due at St. Andrews, 1669, unto our fellow John Hingeston, and his acquittance in the behalf of us shall be a sufficient discharge. John Willson, Thomas Bates, William Gregorie, Thomas Lanier, Theophilus Fittz, John Gamble, William Clayton, Charles Colman.

L. C. Vol. 198. *p.* 7.

1671, *November* 4.

Order to pay to Capt. Thomas Cook £431. 12s. for the gentlemen of his Majesty's Chappell, an organist and two base violls, for their attendance on his Majesty at Windsor in May, June and July, 1671 ; vizt., 24 gentlemen and 2 base violls and 4 violins, attendance 6 days, from 24 to 30 May, 1671, and for 12 gentlemen and 2 base violls and 4 violins, 47 days, from 30 May to 15 July, 1671, and for the organist's attendance 53 days, from 24 May to 15 July, 1671, at the rate of 8s. by the day unto each of them.

The names of the gentlemen that attended at Windsor :—

Mr. John Harding	Thomas Purcell
Capt. Henry Cooke	Henry Frost
Thomas Blagrave	George Bettenhave
William Tucker	Roger Hill
Alphonso Marsh	George Yardley
James Cobb	Blase White
Nathaniel Watkins	Charles Husband
Raphaell Courtevile	Henry Smith
Pellham Humphryes	William Howes
William Turner	Dr. Child
James Hart	Edward Bradock
Richard Hart	John Goodgroome

Violls.

Captain Bates   William Gregory

Organist.
John Blow

4 *Violins.*

William Clayton	Theophilus Fittz
Thomas Farmer	Thomas Fittz

These attended 6 days.

Gentlemen.

Pellham Humphryes	Capt. Cooke
William Turner	Thomas Blagrave
Richard Hart	William Tucker
Edward Bradock	Nathaniel Watkins
Mr. Tinker	Thomas Purcell
John Goodgroome	Blase White

4 *Violins.*

William Clayton	Theophilus Fittz
Thomas Farmer	Thomas Fittz

Violls.

Capt. Bates   William Gregory

Organist.
John Blow

These attended 47 days.

1671, *November* 4.

Musitians to wayte in the Chappell.

October.

Mr. Madg	Mr. Brockwell
Mr. John Bannister	Mr. John Strong
Mr. Jeoffery Bannister	

November.

Mr. Singleton	Mr. Hopper
Mr. Staggins, junior	Mr. Staggins, senior
Mr. Hall	

December.

Mr. Clayton	Mr. Gamble
Mr. Thomas Fittz	Mr. Finall
Mr. Theophilus Fitz	

" I doe hereby order that his Majesty's musitians above-named doe wayte and attend in his Majesty's Chappell Royall as they are here sett down, five in one month and five in another. Soe that each person attend every third month, or they will answere the contrary."

L. C. Vol. 773, *p.* 62.

1671, *November* 4.

Order to deliver to Capt. Henry Cooke, master of the children of his Majesty's Chappell, winter liveries for the twelve children of the Chappell for the year 1671.

L. C. Vol. 773, *p.* 58.

1671, *November* 4.

£112. 14s. paid to Capt. Henry Cook, master of the twelve children of his Majesty's Chappell Royall, for himself and the twelve boyes wayting at Windsor 14 days, and for himself and six boys waiting there 7 weeks and 3 days, from 25 May to 15 July, 1671, at the rate of 10s. per diem for himself, and 4s. per diem for each of his boyes, and for other services by him done.

L. C. Vol. 773, *p.* 59.

1671, *November* 6.

John Twist admitted musician for the violin, in the place of Edmund Tanner.

L. C. Vol. 483, *p.* 127.

1671, *November* 11.

Payment of one year's livery to Humphrey Madge, Lewis Grabu, George Hudson, John Jenkins, John Goodgroome, Pelham Humphryes, Mathew Lock, John Lillie and John Harding, musicians, due St. Andrew, 1669.

L. C. Vol. 712.

1671, *November* 16.

Payment of one year's livery to John Banister, musician, due St. Andrew, 1669.

L. C. Vol. 712.

1671, *November* 21.

Bill of William Barber for a cornet staff gilt being 15 foot long for the King's troop under the command of the Duke of Monmouth. £3.

For gilding painting and making it longer £1. 5.

L. C. Vol. 203, *entry* 53.

1671, *November* 23.

Payment of two years' liveries to Anthony Roberts, musician, due St. Andrew, 1669 and 1670.

L. C. Vol. 712, *p.* 78.

1671, *St. Andrew.*

Payment of £16. 2. 6. to each of the following musicians to the King for their liveries :—

Henry Cooke	Mathew Locke
John Willson	Thomas Bates
Anthony Roberts	Alphonso Marsh
John Hingeston	John Clement
William Gregory	Thomas Purcell
George Hudson	William Child
Humphrey Madge	John Goodgroome
Thomas Lanier	Theophilus Fittz
John Smith	Charles Colman
John Gamble	Lewis Grabu
John Jenkins	Pelham Humphryes
John Lillie	William Clayton
John Harding	Edward Hooton.
John Bannister	

Payment of £29. 16. 8. to John Mason and Henry Gregory for clothing two boys and educating them in the art of music for half a year.

L. C. Vol. 463.

1671, *December* 13.

John Twist appointed musician in ordinary to his Majesty for the violin, in the place of Edmund Tanner, deceased. With wages of 20d. by the day and £16. 2s. 6d. yearly for livery, to commence from Michaelmas last past, 1671.

L. C. Vol. 773, *p.* 80.

1671, *December* 14.

Payment of one year's livery to Henry Cooke, musician, due St. Andrew, 1669.

L. C. Vol. 712.

1671, *December* 20.

Order to pay £40. 10s. to Jervase Price, esquire, his Majesty's sergeant trumpeter, for himself and four of his Majesty's trumpeters, for ryding charges and other expenses in their attendance upon his Majesty to Norwich, Yarmouth, Newmarkett, Cambridg and elsewhere, for 27 days, from 25 September to 21 October, 1671, at the rate of 10s. by the day to the sergeant, and 5s. by the day to each trumpeter.

L. C. Vol. 773, *p.* 92.

1671, *December* 21.

Nicholas Staggins appointed musician in ordinary to his Majesty for the violin in the place of William Young, deceased, with wages of 20d. by the day and £16. 2s. 6d. a year for livery, to commence Michaelmas, 1670.

L. C. Vol. 773, *p.* 93.

1671.

Account due to Henry Cooke, musician, for keeping two boys from 1667 to 1671.

Account for £238 due to Henry Gregory and John Mason, for keeping, and teaching two boys in the art of musick from 1667 to 1671.

Account due to the following trumpeters for four years' pensions, from 1668 to 1671, amounting to £79. 10. 8 :—

William Porter	George Bosgrave
Robert Ramsey	Samuel Markland
Henry Peacock.	

L. C. Vol. 712, *pp.* 81 *to* 89.

1671 *and* 1672.

List of musicians :—

Violins :—

Lewis Grabu, master of the music.

Ambrose Beeland	John Twist
Richard Dorney	John Myer
Theophilus Fitz	John Bannister
John Singleton	Thomas Blagrave
William Young	William Howes
Henry Brockwell	John Strong
John Atkinson	Robert Strong
Joseph Fashion	Thomas Fitz
Symon Hopper	Phillip Beckett
Isaack Staggins	Henry Comer
William Clayton	Jeoffery Bannister
William Saunders	Humphrey Madge.

Composers.

George Hudson (since deceased) and Mathew Lock; Thomas Purcell and Pelham Humphreys, appointed in George Hudson's place, and Monsieur le Grange for a basse.

L. C. Vol. 483, p. 71.

1671-2, *January* 10.

Thomas Purcell and Pelham Humphreys, gent., appointed composers in ordinary to his Majesty for the violin without fee, and assistant to George Hudson, and upon the death or other avoydance, to come in ordinary with fee.

L. C. Vol. 773, p. 107.

1671-2, *January* 25.

Order to provide rich liveries for four of his Majesty's sixteen trumpeters in ordinary; those four to attend the Duke of Richmond, ambassador extraordinary to the King of Denmark.

Another order, dated 16 February, to provide sea liveries for them.

L. C. Vol. 773, pp. 114, 129.

Warrant for liveries for sixteen trumpeters.

L. C. Papers, Bundle 2.

1671-2, *January* 27.

Order to pay £5 to Charles Evans, his Majesty's harper for the Italian harp, for strings for the said harp for one year ending at Christmas last past, 1671.

L. C. Vol. 773, p. 115.

1671-2, *February* 19.

Payment of one year's livery to Dr. William Child, and to John Clement, musicians, due St. Andrew, 1669.

L. C. Vol. 712.

1671-2, *February* 21.

Order that half the yearly salary of Henry Comer be stopped and paid to Richard Browne, musician in ordinary for the violin, who doth wayte and attend on his Majesty, in the absence of Henry Comer.

L. C. Vol. 195, *p.* 18 ; *and Vol.* 773, *p.* 131.

1671-2, *February* 27.

Whereas Richard Hudson, late keeper of his Majesty's lutes and violls, did assign unto Alphonso Maley all his wages and salary due for the said place during his life and at his death, amounting to the sum of £71 4s., £18. 5s. to be paid annually, Henry Brockwell since coming into the said place, these are to pray you, to make stop of half the said wages payable to the said Henry Brockwell, and pay the same to Mr. Maley until the said sum be fully paid.

L. C. Vol. 195, *p.* 18.

1671-2, *February* 27.

Assignment by Richard Hudson, late keeper of his Majesty's lutes and viols, to Alphers Maley, of the sum of £71. 4s. at £18. 5s. per annum during his life and at his death. Henry Brockwell became keeper of the instruments, half his salary being stopped to pay the said Maley.

L. C. Vol. 773, *p.* 138.

1671-2, *February* 27.

Order for liveries for his Majesty's sergeant trumpeter, twelve trumpeters and a kettle drummer, for the year 1672.

L. C. Vol. 773, *p.* 139.

1671-2, *February* 29.

" A warrant to apprehend those that practice musick."

"Whereas Robert Reade, Robert Leighborne, Richard Dyble and Richard Jones, doe take upon them to teach, practice and exercise musick in companyes or otherwise, to play at publique meetings without ye approbacion or lycence of ye marshall and corporacion of musique, and in contempt of his Majesty's authority and the power granted to ye said marshall and corporacion under the Greate Seale of England, These are therefore to require you to apprehend and take into your custody the bodyes of ye said Robert Reade, and others abovenamed, and bring them before me to answer unto such things as shall be objected against them."

L. C. Vol. 773, *p.* 175b.

1671-2, *March* 6.

Will of John Mason, musician, of Wokeing, in the county of Surrey, bequeathing legacies of £10 each to his sister Ann Blagrave, his cousin Anthony Blagrave, his cousin Allan Blagrave, his cousin John Burton, £20 to his cousin Magdalen Blagrave, £10 to his cousin Bridgett Johnson, and £5 each to his godson John Goodwyn, his cousin Ann Searle, his cousin Ann Ealmes, his cousin Cheney Blagrave's son Thomas Blagrave, his goddaughter Mary Blagrave the daughter of his cousin Allan Blagrave, making his kinsman Thomas Blagrave his executor.

L. C. Vol. 198, *p.* 29.

1671-2, *March* 7.

Letter of assignment from John Gamble, one of his Majesty's musick, to Joseph Parrott, of the sum of £16 : 2 : 6 due out of his Majesty's great Wardrobe, St. Andrew, 1670.

L. C. Vol. 198, *p.* 9.

1671-2, *March* 11.

Warrant to pay to Lewis Grabu, master of his Majesty's musick, the sum of £117. 4s. 6d. for fayre writeing and pricking severall sorts of musick, and for the prickers' and writers dyes, and chamber rent, in the months of April, July, October, December, 1668, and February 1668-9, and for other services done by him.

L. C. Vol. 744, *p.* 8.

1671-2, *March* 11.

Warrant to pay to Mr. Lewis Grabu, master of his Majesty's musick, the sum of £20 for his rydeing charges and expenses in attending upon His Majesty to Dover, 20 days, from 16 May to 4 June, 1670, at the rate of 20s. per diem.

L. C. Vol. 744, *p.* 17.

1671-2, *March* 19.

Warrant to admit Edmund Flower one of his Majesty's musicians in ordinary for the violin, in place of Ambrose Beeland, surrendered.

L. C Vol. 744, *p.* 14.

1671-2, *March* 23.

Warrant to pay John Myer, musician in ordinary to his Majesty, the sum of £12, for the like sum by him disbursed for a violin by him bought, for His Majesty's service.

L. C. Vol. 744, *p.* 22.

1672, *March* 25.

List of musicians to attend in the Chappell :—

March.

Mr. Clayton	Mr. Theophilus Fittz
Mr. Thomas Fittz	Mr. Gamble
Mr. Hooton	Mr. Finall

April.

Mr. Madge	Mr. Hopper
Mr. Singleton	Mr. Jo. Strong
Mr. Twist	Mr. Hall

May.

Mr. John Bannister	Mr. Greeting
Mr. Staggins, junior	Mr. Brockwell
Mr. Mire	Mr. Staggins, senior

Order that his Majesty's musicians abovenamed do wayte and attend in the Chappell Royall as they are here sett down, six in one month and six in another, so that each person attend every third month.

L. C. Vol. 744, *p.* 24.

1672, *March* 26.

Bill for two plain liveries for Peter Isaac, a Chappell boy gone off. On April 4 another account for Peter Isaac, a page of the Chappell going off.

L. C. Vol. 203, *entries* 70, 81, 95, 96, *and* 97.

1672, *March* 30.

" Whereas Nicholas Staggins is admitted as musician in ordinary to his Majesty for the violin, in place of William Young, deceased, and there is arrears of salary due to William Young, these are to order that stop be made of half the wages due to the said place, and as it shall become payable, the same to be paid to the said Nicholas Staggins, and the other half to the executor or administrators of William Young, until the arrears are fully paid."

L. C. Vol. 159, *p.* 19 ; *L. C. Vol.* 744, *p.* 25.

1672, *March* 30.

Warrant to pay to Joseph Fashion, musician in ordinary to his Majesty for the violin, the sum of £12, for a violin by him bought for His Majesty's service.

L. C. Vol. 744, *p.* 26.

1672, *April* 2.

To John Lilley and John Jenkins, musicians, £16. 2. 6 each, for liveries due St. Andrew, 1671.

L. C. Vol. 715, *p.* 10.

1672, *April* 3.

Warrant to pay Edmund Flower, one of his Majesty's musicians, the sum of £12 for a tenner violin by him bought and provided for His Majesty's service.

L. C. *Vol.* 744, *p.* 31.

1672, *April* 15.

Assignment by John Crowder, trumpeter to his Majesty, of the sum of £23. 16s. to William Collins.

L. C. *Vol.* 195, *p.* 19.

1672, *April* 15.

Warrant to pay to Captain Henry Cooke, master of the children of his Majesty's Chappell Royall, the sum of £117. 18s. for learneing the children on the lute, violin and theorbo, for fire and strings for the musique room in the Chappell, for ruled paper, penns and ink, and for strings for the lutes and theorboes, and for other services by him done, for one whole year ending Lady Day, 1672."

L. C. *Vol.* 744, *p.* 310.

1672, *April* 19.

Symon Darrant admitted musician, to play in the sickness or absence of any of the private musick.

L. C. *Vol.* 483, *p.* 127.

1672, *May* 15.

" It is his Majesty's pleasure that if any of his Majesty's musicians that are appoynted to attend in the Chappell Royall shall refuse or neglect their attendance there, or meeting to exercise for that service, that then such person for offending, upon complaint made thereof, shall forthwith be suspended his place."

L. C. *Vol.* 744, *p.* 56.

1672, *May* 21.

Petition of Anne Yockney, widow, for the moyety of the sallary of John Myer, who came in the place of William Yockney, deceased, her son, he being in her debt £8 by bond.

L. C. *Vol.* 654.

1672, *Pentecost.*

Payment of £19. 17. 8. to each of the following trumpeters to the late King Charles I. for their pensions :—

Robert Ramsay	George Bosgrave
Samuel Markland	William Porter
Henry Peacock	

L. C. *Vol.* 463.

1672, *June* 2.

Order for liveries for 1672 for Symon Person, trumpetter to his Majesty's Troop of Guards, under the command of his Grace the Duke of Monmouth ; for the kettledrummer attending the Queen's Majesty's Troop of Guards under the command of Sir Philip Howard ; and for the kettledrummer attending the Troop of Horse under the command of Lord Hawley.

L. C. Vol. 744, *p.* 72.

1672, *June* 20.

John Dallam appointed one of his Majesty's organ tuners in ordinary.

L. C. Vol. 483, *p.* 127.

1672, *St. John the Baptist.*

Payment of £29. 16. 8. to John Mason and Henry Gregory, musicians to the King, for clothing two boys and educating them in the art of music for half a year.

L. C. Vol. 463.

1672, *June* 28.

Assignment by Mr. Thomas Finell, musician, of the parish of St. Margaret's, Westminster, of the sum of £10, with the usual interest of £6 per cent., within a year to Mr. Jeoffrey Bannester, of the parish of St. Clement Danes.

L. C. Vol. 195, *p.* 24.

1672, *July* 1.

Warrant unto Dr. Gibbons and Mr. Pickering to provide mourning for the sergeant trumpettor, twelve trumpettors and one kettledrummer, the drumme-major, four drums and a fife, for the funeral of the Earl of Sandwich.

L. C. Vol. 744, *p.* 521.

1672, *July* 2.

Whereas his Majesty is displeased that the violins neglect their duty in attending in his Chappell Royall, it is ordered that if any of the violins shall neglect to attend, either to practice or to wayte in the Chappell, whensoever they have received notice from Mr. Purcell or Mr. Humphryes, that for such fault they shall be suspended their places.

L. C. Vol. 744, *p.* 70.

1672, *July* 6.

Will, dated as above, of Henry Cooke, of Hampton, county Middlesex :—Desires to be buried in the cloisters in Westminster near his daughter Mary Cooke, a grave to be left between for the interment of his wife. Deals with his land at Pluckly (Kent), leaving it to his wife, and at her death to be divided between his daughters. States that there is owing to him from the King's exchequer five hundred pounds in orders, and last midsummer one salary of one hundred and eighty-eight pounds, and two hundred and thirty pounds due as being executor to Mr. Thornell, upon bill in the treasury chamber; one hundred and twelve pounds for travelling wages to Windsor in 1671; and the remainder of a bill of about fifty pounds there. The testator continues, "and I am owed a bill, though not yet in the office, for teaching the boys the lute and the virginalls, there stringing and penning, and five pounds for strings for their lutes, with twenty pound allowance for fire and for the musick room in the Chappell, this being due at Lady Day, 1672." Deals with six liveries due upon Mr. Thornell's account, being ninety-six pounds, fifteen shillings; and "at least two hundred pounds without they have set their hand to the book for me. In the coffery there is due to him at Michaelmas two hundred and fifteen pounds." He is indebted to Mr. Boughy two hundred pounds, for which the said Mr. Boughy has a mortgage upon the houses in Longditch. He gives to his daughter Katherine Cooke, £300 of the first £500 mentioned, and to his daughter Amy £200; also to his daughter Katherine one hundred and twenty broad pieces of gold now in the house, provided his debts and funeral expenses be discharged, and "the small legacies, which will be a ring of ten shillings price" to those of the gentlemen of the Chappell who are at his burial. List of debts, etc., follows:— Owes to John Harding, £10; "I am owed to Ned Hooten, £4; I am owed from Dr. Cunstable of Dertford, £5; Mr. Marsh owes me, 20/-."

L. C. Vol. 198, *p.* 83.

1672, *July* 13.

Capt. Henry Cooke departed this life the 13 July, 1672.

L. C. Vol. 198, *p.* 72.

1672, *July* 15.

Warrant to apprehend Gates, Salmon, Bodenham, Southen, and Ruben Golden for taking upon them to teach, practise and exercise musique in companies, or otherwise to play at publique meetings without the lycence of the Marshall and Corporation of musique.

L. C. Vol. 654.

1672, *July* 15.

Warrant to swear and admit William Turner in the place and quality of musician in ordinary in his Majesty's private musick for lute and voyce, in the place of Henry Cooke, deceased.

Warrant to swear and admit Pelham Humphryes in the place and quality of Master of the children of his Majesty's Chappell Royall, and composer in his Majesty's private musick for voyces in ordinary, in the place of Henry Cooke, deceased.

L. C. Vol. 744, *p.* 76.

1672, *July* 15.

Whereas John Myer is sworn and admitted musician in ordinary to his Majesty for the violin in the place of William Yockney, deceased, and there being arrears of sallary due for his service, it is ordered that stop be made of half the yearly sallary that shall grow due to the said John Myer, and the same paid to Anne Yockney, widow, mother of the said William Yockney, to whom he was indebted by bond, until the arrears due to the said William Yockney be fully paid.

L. C. Vol. 195, *p.* 20 ; *L. C. Vol.* 744, *p.* 78.

1672, *August* 14.

Order that if any of his Majesty's musicians shall neglect to attend or to practise when thereunto required by the master of his Majesty's musick, that they shall be suspended their places upon complaint made by the master.

L. C. Vol. 744, *p.* 87.

1672, *August* 14.

Warrant to pay to Benigne Le Ragois and John Christmas, two of his Majesty's trumpetters, the sum of £155 for their charges in attendance upon the Hon. Henry Coventry, esquire, His Majesty's Ambassador in Sweden, for the space of 310 days, from 26 August, 1671 to 1 July, 1672, at the rate of 5s. by the day each.

L. C. Vol. 744, *p.* 88.

1672, *September* 4.

Warrant to pay to Joseph Fashion, musician in ordinary to his Majesty for the violin, the sum of £12, for a violin bought by him for His Majesty's service.

L. C. Vol. 744, *p.* 98.

1672, *September* 10.

Edward Dyer admitted musician in ordinary.

L. C. Vol. 483, *p.* 125.

1672, September 25.

Mr. Charles Coleman admitted musician in ordinary for the violl in his Majesty's private musick.

L. C. Vol. 483, *p.* 125.

1672, September 25.

Warrant to pay to William Peacock, John Jones, John Crowder, George Monrowe and Walter Vanbright, four of His Majesty's trumpeters and kettledrummer, the sum of £551. 5s. for their charges in attending upon Lord Henry Howard, Ambassador to Morrocco, by the space of 441 days, from 10 June, 1669 to 25 August, 1670, at the rate of 5s. by the day each.

L. C. Vol. 744, *p.* 105.

Accounts ending Michaelmas, 1672.

For three quarters of a year, 1671-1672, £30 to Henry Cooke, master of the boys of the Chappell Royall, for the keep of two boys and for teaching them singing.

Accounts for liveries of £16 : 2 : 6 each, to the following musicians to the King :—

George Hudson	John Smith
John Hingeston	Thomas Bates
Humphrey Madge	John Gamble
William Gregorie	John Bannister
John Willson	John Clement
Henry Cook	Thomas Purcell
Thomas Lanier	William Child
Anthony Roberts	Charles Coleman
Matthew Lock	Theophilus Fittz
John Jenkins	Pelham Humphries
John Lillie	John Goodgroome
John Harding	William Clayton
Alphonso Marsh	

Lewis Grabu, master of music to the King.

Annual pensions of £19 : 17 : 8 to each of the following trumpeters to the late King Charles I. :—

Robert Ramsay	George Bosgrave
Samuel Markland	William Porter

Henry Peacock

Account of £59 : 13 : 4 paid to John Mason and Henry Gregorie for clothing and educating two boys in the art of music.

L. C. Vol. 61; *L. C. Vol.* 157.

1672, *October* 1.

Warrant for the allowance of summer liveries for the 12 children of the Chappell, to be delivered to Pelham Humphryes, master of the children of the Chappell Royal.

L. C. Papers, Bundle 15.

1672, *October* 2.

Warrant for the apprehension of William Hill, John Collis, Thomas Edes, William Eames, Robert Leighbourne, Richard Jones, Henry Grove, William Ashley, John Pyball, Robert Reade, Henry Evens, Edward Mills, Benjamin Foster, John Everett, Robert Nash, Thomas Mills, and Mitchell, who do teach, practise and exercise music without lycence of the Marshall and Corporation of Musick.

L. C. Vol. 654.

1672, *October* 15.

Letter of assignment from William Child, doctor of musick, appointing Thomas Haines, esquire, as his true and lawful attorney.

L. C. Vol. 195, *p.* 56.

1672, *November* 4.

Estimate for 64 surplices of fine holland cloth for the gentlemen, 12 for the musicians and 36 for the children of his Majesty's Chappell Royall.

L. C. Vol. 545, *p.* 28.

1672, *November* 6.

John Christmas admitted trumpeter in ordinary without fee, to come in ordinary with fee upon the next avoydance.

L. C. Vol. 483, *p.* 124 ; *and Vol.* 744, *p.* 125.

1672, *November* 12.

Warrant to admit Edmund Flower to the office of musician in ordinary to his Majesty for the violin, in the place of Ambrose Beeland, surrendered, with the fee of 20 pence by the day and £16. 2. 6. yearly for his livery. To commence from 19 January last past, 1671-2.

L. C. Vol. 744, *p.* 130.

1672, *November* 18.

Warrant to provide liveries for Albion Thompson, trumpeter attending upon his Majesty's Troop of Guards, commanded by his Grace the Duke of Monmouth ; and John Christmas, trumpeter to the Queen's Majesty's Troop, commanded by Sir Philip Howard.

L. C. Vol. 744, *p.* 136.

1672, *November* 25.

Appointment of Clement Newth as a fife.

L. C. Vol. 478, *p.* 89.

1672, *November* 30.

Warrant to pay to Pelham Humphryes, master of the children of his Majesty's Chappell Royall, the sum of £58. 18s., for learneing the children on the lute, for learneing them on the violin and theorbo, for fire and strings for the musick room in the Chappell, for ruled paper, penns and inke, and for strings for the lutes and theorboes, and further service by him done from Lady Day to Michaelmas, 1672.

L. C. Vol. 744, *p.* 141.

1672, *St. Andrew.*

Payment of £16. 2. 6. to each of the following musicians to the King for their liveries :—

John Willson	Thomas Bates
Anthony Roberts	Alphonso Marsh
John Hingeston	John Clement
William Gregory	Thomas Purcell
George Hudson	William Child
Humphrey Madge	John Goodgroome
Thomas Lanier	Theophilus Fittz
John Smith	Charles Coleman
John Gamble	Lewis Grabu
John Jenkins	Pellham Humphrys
John Lillie	William Clayton
John Harding	Edward Hootten
John Bannister	William Turner.
Mathew Lock	

Payment of £29. 16. 8. to John Mason and Henry Gregory for clothing two boys and educating them in the art of music for half a year.

L. C. Vol. 463.

1672, *December* 10.

Nuncupative will of George Hudson, of the parish of St. Martin's in the Feilds, composer of musick to his Majesty, deceased, made at the house of Mr. John Warrells, at East Greenwich, county Kent, bequeathing to Humphrey and Elizabeth Warrells one hundred pounds each.

L. C. Vol. 198, *p.* 29d.

1672, *December.*

Letter of assignment from John Lillie of St. Andrews, Holborne, one of his Majesty's private musick, to John Turner, merchant, of the city and university of Cambridge, of two years' liveries, amounting to the sum of £32 : 5.

L. C. Vol. 198, *p.* 16*d.*

1672-3, *January* 17.

Warrant to provide and deliver to Pelham Humphryes, master of the children of his Majesty's Chappell Royall, for the use of Henry Hall, late child of the Chappell, whose voyce is changed and is gon from the Chappell, two suites of playne cloth, two hatts and hatt bands, four whole shirts, four half shirts, six bands, six pair of cuffs, six handkerchiefs, four pair of stockings, four pair of shoes, and four pair of gloves.

L. C. Vol. 744, *p.* 174.

1672-3, *January* 17.

Warrant to pay to Pelham Humphryes, master of the children of his Majesty's Chappell Royall, the sum of £30 by the year during His Majesty's pleasure, for keeping of Henry Hall, late child of the Chappell, whose voyce is changed, and is gone from the Chappell. To commence from 25 December last past.

L. C. Vol. 744, *b.* 175.

1672-3, *January* 22.

Bill for pensions due to Robert Ramsey, George Bosgrave, Samuel Markland, William Porter and Henry Peacock, pensionary trumpeters.

L C. Papers, Bundle 20.

1672-3, *January* 23.

Warrant to admit Nicholas Staggins to the place of musician in ordinary to his Majesty for the flute in the place of William Young, deceased.

L. C. Vol. 744, *p.* 181.

1672-3, *January* 24.

Assignment by John Wilson, doctor of musick, of the sum of £40. to Mr. Richard Stockton, citizen and freholder of London.

L. C. Vol. 195, *p.* 22.

1672-3, *January* 28.

Warrant to pay John Myer his full year's salary, notwithstanding an order made to stop half of it and pay the same to Anne Yockney.

L. C. Vol. 744, *p.* 183.

1672-3, January 28.

Warrant to pay to Charles Evans, his Majesty's harper for the Italian harp, the sum of £5 for strings for the harp for one year ending at Christmas, 1672.

L. C. Vol. 744, *p.* 201.

1672-3, January 30.

Bill for embroidering fower drummers' and six trumpeters' coats with crowns, letters and knotts on the back and brest.

Bill for 7 swords with neat silvergilt handles for six trumpeters and kettledrummer, to attend the Lord Duras into France.

L. C. Vol. 203, *entries* 18 *and* 19*b.*

1672-3, February 1.

Order to pay to Milbert Morris, one of his Majesty's trumpeters, for himself and three other trumpeters and a kettledrummer, who are to attend Lord Duras in his Majesty's service beyond the seas, the sum of £100 for their present expenses, £20 being allowed unto each of them.

L. C. Vol. 744, *p.* 186.

1672-3, February 21.

Account payable to Thomas Purcell as Groom of the Robes, and also as one of the Private Music.

L. C. Papers, Bundle 2.

1672-3, February 21.

Payment of one year's livery to John Gamble, musician, due St. Andrew, 1670.

L. C. Vol. 712.

1672-3, February 22.

Warrant to pay to Peter Anthony, late one of His Majesty's trumpeters, a pension of sixteen pence a day for his life, as hath been allowed unto Thomas Creswell, one of his Majesty's pentionary trumpeters.

L. C. Vol. 744, *p.* 198.

1672-3, March 13.

Warrant to pay to Peter Anthony, trumpeter, late servant to Her Majesty the Queen Mother, deceased, the sum of £50 for his extraordinary charges in attending and also in fitting to go to sea this summer in His Majesty's service with his Highness Prince Rupert.

L. C. Vol. 744, *p.* 209.

1673, *April* 12.

Warrant to provide and deliver to Pelham Humphryes, master of the children of his Majesty's Chappell Royall, for the use of Thomas Heywood, late child of the Chappell, whose voyce is changed, and is to goe from the Chappell, two suits of plain cloth, two hatts and hattbands, four whole shirts, four half shirts, six bands, six pair of cuffs, six handkerchiefs, four pair of stockings, four pair of shoes and four pair of gloves.

Warrant to pay to Pelham Humfryes, master of the children of his Majesty's Chappel Royall, the sum of £30 by the year during His Majesty's pleasure for keeping of Thomas Heywood, late child of the Chappell, whose voyce is changed and is gon from the Chappell. To commence 25 December, 1672.

L. C. Vol. 744, *p.* 223.

1673, *April* 19.

Assignment by Richard Dorney, of the parish of St. Margaret's, Westminster, one of his Majesty's musicians in ordinary, to Mr. Roger Sizer, of the parish of St. Martin's in the Fields, of the sum of £244. 6s. 10d. due to the said Richard Dorney out of the Treasury of his Majesty's Chamber for five years and a quarter's wages, from Christmas 1667 to Lady Day 1673, at £46 : 10 : 10 per annum.

L. C. Vol. 195, *p.* 25.

1673, *April* 19.

Warrant to pay to Edmund Flower, one of his Majesty's musicians, the sum of £15 for a theorbo, bought by him for his Majesty's service in his Chappell Royall.

L. C. Vol. 744, *p.* 230.

1673, *April* 25.

Warrant to pay to John Hingston, keeper and repairer of his Majesty's organs, the sum of £45. 3. 6. for keeping, repairing and amending his Majesty's organs, harpsicords and pedalls, for the rent of a room to keep them in, and for strings for the base violls, and for a base violl by him bought, and for other services for the space of two years, from 25 March, 1671 to 25 March, 1673.

L. C. Vol. 744, *p.* 236.

1673, *April* 25.

Warrant to pay to Benigne Le Ragois and John Christmas, trumpeters, the sum of £155 for their charges in attendance upon the Hon. Henry Coventry, esquire, late his Majesty's Ambassador in Sweden, from 26 August, 1671 to 1 July, 1672, at the rate of 5s. by the day to each of them.

L. C. Vol. 744, *p.* 235.

1673, April 25.

Warrant to provide and deliver sea liveries to Benigne Ragois and John Christmas, two of his Majesty's trumpeters, to attend upon Sir Leoline Jenkins and Sir Joseph Williamson, Ambassadors to the Netherlands. Also the sum of £20 each for their charges in their attendance.

L. C. Vol. 744, *pp.* 236, 239.

1673, May 2.

Warrant to pay to Pelham Humfryes, master of the children of his Majesty's Chappell Royall, the sum of £58. 19., for the children's learneing on the lute, violin and theorbo, for fire and strings for the musick room in the Chappell, for ruled paper and penns and ink, and for strings for the lutes, theorboes, and for other service by him done for half a year, from Michaelmas, 1672 to Lady Day, 1673.

Laid out by Pelham Humfryes for teaching the said children for half a year from Michaelmas, 1672 to Lady Day, 1673 :—

	£	s.	d.
For the children's learneing on the lute	15	0	0
For their learneing on the violin	15	0	0
For their learneing on the theorbo	15	0	0
For fire and strings for the musick room in the Chappell	10	0	0
For ruled paper, penns and inke	1	3	6
For strings for the lutes and theorboes	2	15	6

Signed :—Pell. Humfryes.

" In this warrant was nothing for fetching children from several cathedrals, as is sometymes."

L. C. Vol. 744, *p.* 243.

1673, May 13.

Warrant to pay to Henry Brockwell, keeper of his Majesty's musicall instruments, the sum of £42 for two base violls by him bought, for mending the instruments, and for strings, and for removing and carriage of instruments severall times in the space of five years, from Lady Day, 1668 to Lady Day, 1673.

L. C. Vol. 744, *p.* 247.

1673, May 23.

Assignment by Lewis Grabu, to Walter Lapp, citizen and mercer of London, of the sum of £137. 4s. 6d. due to the said Lewis Grabu as master of his Majesty's musick, for faire writing and pricking several sorts of musick and for the prickers and writers dyes and chamber rent, in the months of April,

July, October, December and February, 1668-9, and for other services the sum of £117. 4s. 6d. And the sum of £20 for rideing charges and other expenses in his attendance upon his Majesty with his man at Dover by the space of twenty days, from 16 May to 4 June, 1670.

L. C. Vol. 195, p. 28.

1673, *May 23.*

Warrant to admit John Young musician in ordinary for a violl de Gambo in his Majesty's private musick, in the place and upon the surrender of Paul Bridges.

L. C. Vol. 744, p. 255.

1673, *Pentecost.*

Payment of £19 . 17 . 8 . to each of the following trumpeters to the late King Charles I. for their pensions :—

Robert Ramsay	George Bosgrove
Samuel Markland	William Porter
Henry Peacock.	

L. C. Vol. 463.

1673, *May 30.*

Order for a bill conteyning a grant to John Young of the office and place of musician in ordinary for a violl de Gambo in His Majesty's private musick, in the place and on the surrender of Paul Bridges, with the fee of £40 a year and £16 . 2 . 6 . for his livery. To commence 24 June, 1673.

L. C. Vol. 744, p. 267.

1673, *June 2.*

Warrant to pay Henry Brockwell in behalf of himself and six other of His Majesty's musicians, the sum of £36 15 . 0 . for their rydeing charges and other expenses in their attendance upon His Majesty at Newmarkett for 21 days, from 1 to 21 October, 1672, at the rate of 5s. by the day.

L. C. Vol. 744, p. 263.

1673, *June 10.*

Warrant to admit Henry Purcell in the place of keeper, maker, mender, repayrer and tuner of the regalls, organs, virginalls, flutes and recorders and all other kind of wind instruments whatsoever, in ordinary, without fee, to his Majesty, and assistant to John Hingston, and upon the death or other avoydance of the latter, to come in ordinary with fee.

L. C. Vol. 744, p. 309.

1673, *June 20.*

Mr. Robert Smyth admitted a musician in ordinary.

L. C. Vol. 483, p. 127.

1673, June 23.

Order that whereas Thomas Finell is admitted musician in ordinary to his Majesty, in the place of John Atkins, and arrears being due to the said John Atkins, of which his executors have received one whole year's wages since his death, stop shall be made of the arrears now due, and the first year's salary that shall become due shall be paid to Thomas Finell, and afterwards half the year's salary only shall be paid him, the other half to go to the executors of the said John Atkins until the arrears be fully paid.

L. C. Vol. 744, *p.* 273.

1673, St. John the Baptist.

Payment of £29 . 16 . 8 . to Henry Gregory, musician to the King, for clothing two boys and educating them in the art of music for half a year.

L. C. Vol. 463.

1673, June 30.

Order to prepare a bill, conteyning a grant to Nicholas Staggins of the office and place of musician in ordinary to his Majesty for the flute, in the place of William Young, deceased, with the fee of 20 pence by the day and £16 . 2 . 6 . by the year for his livery, during his naturall life.

L. C. Vol. 744, *p.* 282.

1673, June 30.

Warrant to pay to Nicholas Staggins, one of his Majesty's musicians, the sum of £12 for a violin by him bought for His Majesty's service.

L. C. Vol. 744, *p.* 282.

1673, July 1.

Whereas an order that John Myer, for one tyme only should receive a whole year's wages was made, these are to require you according to a former order, to pay to Anne Yockney half the yearly salary due to John Myer, until the arrears due to William Yockney be fully paid.

L. C. Vol. 744, *p.* 283.

1673, July 1.

Warrant to prepare and deliver a chayne and medall of gold, of the value of £70 or thereabouts, to be given to Johanni Le Benico, master of the Italian musick, as a guift from His Majesty to him.

L. C. Vol. 744, *p.* 283.

1673, *July* 10.

Warrant to admit William Clayton musician in ordinary for the sackbutt to his Majesty, in the place of Thomas Mell, deceased.

L. C. Vol. 744, *p.* 290.

1673, *July* 12.

Order to prepare a bill conteyning a grant of the office of musician in ordinary upon the sackbutt to William Clayton, in the place of Thomas Mell, deceased, with the fee of 20d. by the day and £16 . 2 . 6 . by the year for his livery.

L. C. Vol. 744, *p.* 294.

1673, *July* 15.

Order to prepare a bill, containing a grant of the office and place of composer in ordinary to his Majesty for the violins, to Thomas Purcell and Pelham Humfryes, Gent, in the place of George Hudson, deceased, with the wages and fee of £42. 15s. 10d. per annum during their lives, and the longest liver of them.

Order to prepare a bill, for a patent to be granted to Thomas Purcell and Pelham Humfryes, Gent, of the office and place of composer in ordinary to His Majesty for the violins, in the place of George Hudson, deceased, with the wages and fee of £200 by the year during their naturall lives, and the longest liver of them.

L. C. Vol. 744, *pp.* 296, 297.

1673, *July* 17.

Warrant for the apprehension of John and William Staples, Gideon Taylor, Humphrey Rand, Ralph Watkins, Thomas Leicester, and William Day that they teach, practise and exercise musick at publique meetings without the approbation of the Marshall and Corporation of Musick.

L. C. Vol. 655.

1673, *July* 17.

Warrant to pay to Pelham Humfryes, master of the children of his Majesty's Chappell Royall, the sum of £22 for two basse violls of the value of £5 apeece, and two theorboes of the value of £6 apeece by him provided for his Majesty's service, for teaching the children of the Chappell on the said instruments.

L. C. Vol. 744, *p.* 299.

1673, *July* 24.

Order to prepare a bill for a patent to be granted to
Pelham Humfryes for keeping and instructing two boys for his
Majesty's private musique for voyces, and to have the sum of
£24 yearly for every of them which Henry Cooke lately had,
and also as one of the private musick in ordinary for the lute
and voyce in the place of the said Henry Cooke, deceased, with
the yearly fee of £40 and £20 for strings, in all the sum of
£108 yearly during his naturall life.

L. C. Vol. 744, *p.* 305.

1673, *July* 24.

Order to prepare a bill for a patent to be granted to Pelham
Humfryes, one of the gentlemen of his Majesty's Chappell
Royall, of the office of master of the children of the Chapell
Royall, with the fee of £40 by the year for life, for the teaching
of twelve children of the Chappell.

Order to prepare a bill, for a patent, to be granted to
Pelham Humfryes of the office of composer in the private
musique for voyces, in ordinary to his Majesty, in the place of
Henry Cooke, deceased, with the fee of £40 by the year, to
commence Michaelmas, 1672.

L. C. Vol. 744, *pp.* 304, 305.

1673, *July.*

Bill of Thomas Heanes, serjeant of the vestry, for making
36 surplices for the gentlemen and musicians of the Chappell
at 5s. apiece : £19.

For making 38 surplices for the children of the Chappell at
2/6d. apiece : £4. 15.

L. C. Vol. 203, *Entry* 170.

1673, *August* 15.

Payment of £80. 12. 6. to John Clement, one of his
Majesty's musique, for arrears of liveries due to him for the
years 1664 to 1667, and 1671, at the rate of £16. 2. 6. per
annum.

L. C. Vol. 711, *p.* 47.

1673, *August* 19.

Warrant for payment of £188. 7. 6. to the executors of
Henry Cooke, late master of the children of his Majesty's
Chappel, for teaching and apparelling two children for 3½ years
ended at Lady Day, 1672, at the rate of £10 per quarter, also
for liveries for three years ended at the feast of St. Andrew,
1671.

Warrant for the payment of £80 : 12 : 6 to Gregory Thorndell, late of the private musick to his Majesty, arrears of five years' liveries ended at St. Andrew, 1670.

Warrant for payment of £16. 2. 6. to Pelham Humphries, of the private musick to his Majesty, for livery due at St. Andrew, 1671.

L. C. Vol. 711, *p.* 47d.

1673, *August* 23.

Warrant for payment of £32. 5s. to William Clayton, one of the private musick to his Majesty, arrears of two years' liveries due to him for the years 1670 and 1671.

L. C. Vol. 711, *p.* 48.

1673, *August* 28.

Warrant for payment of £48. 7. 6. to Thomas Lanier, one of his Majesty's private musique, arrears of three years' liveries due to him for the years 1666, 1667 and 1671, at the rate of £16. 2. 6. per annum.

Warrant for payment of £80. 12. 6. to William Gregory, one of his Majesty's private musick, arrears of liveries due to him for 5 years, 1665 to 1667, 1670 and 1671.

Warrant for payment of £48. 7. 6. to Mathew Lock, one of his Majesty's private musick, for arrears of liveries due to him for the years 1666, 1667 and 1671.

L. C. Vol. 711, *pp.* 48 *and* 48d.

1673, *September* 1.

Warrant to prepare and deliver liveries to Simon Peirson and Albion Thompson, trumpeters, to attend the Duke of Monmouth at sea.

L. C. Vol. 744, *p.* 322.

1673, *September* 2.

Warrant to provide liveries for Gervase Price, his Majesty's sergeant trumpettor, sixteen trumpettors and a kettledrummer.

L. C. Vol. 744, *p.* 323.

1673, *September* 5.

To Thomas Purcill, musician, a livery of £16. 2. 6., due St. Andrew, 1672.

L. C. Vol. 715, *p.* 1.

1673, *September* 7.

Bill for gloves for Thomas Haywood and Henry Hall, two Chappell boys, whose voices are changed.

Other accounts, for Spanish cloth, shoes and hats for the same boys.

L. C. Vol. 203, *Entries* 144, 154, 161, 164, 180 *and* 219.

1673, *September* 16.

Warrant to admit Francis Cruys musician in ordinary to his Majesty in the private musick, in the place and on the surrender of John Smyth.

L. C. Vol. 744, *p.* 332.

1673, *September* 18.

Warrant to provide a second livery for Nicholas Caperone, one of his Majesty's trumpeters, for the year 1672, his livery for that year being delivered to the trumpeter that did attend Lord Duras to France.

L. C. Vol. 744, *p.* 334.

1673, *September* 29.

Articles of agreement between Pelham Humfreys, of Westminster, master of the children of his Majesty's Chappell Royall, and John Lilly, of the parish of St. Andrew's, Holborne, one of his Majesty's musicians in ordinary :—

The said John Lilly shall from time to time and at all times after the date of the agreement teach and instruct four of the said children (to be appointed by the said Humfreys) on the violl and theorbo, in place of the said Pelham Humfreys. In consideration whereof Humfreys shall pay to him the sum of £30 yearly out of such salary as shall be paid to the said Humfreys, or a proportionally greater or lesser sum according to the salary received.

L. C. Vol. 195, *p.* 30.

1673, *September* 29.

Warrant to pay to Pelham Humfryes, master of the twelve children of his Majesty's Chappell Royall, the sum of £68. 5s. 4d., for the children's learning on the lute, violin and theorbo, for fire and strings for the musick room in the Chappell, for ruled paper, penns and ink, for strings for the lutes and theorboes, and for nursing one of the children being sick of the small pox, in the half year ending at Michaelmas, 1673, and for other services.

L. C. Vol. 744, *p.* 336.

Accounts ending Michaelmas, 1673.

Account of £15. 11s. 6d. paid to Pelham Humphries, master of the children of the Chappell Royall, for his winter livery, etc.

Accounts for liveries for Jervis Price, the King's chief trumpeter ; and John Mawgridge, the King's drum-major.

Accounts for liveries of £16 : 2 : 6 each, to the following musicians to the King :—

George Hudson	John Smith
John Hingeston	Thomas Bates
Humphrey Madge	John Gamble
William Gregory	John Bannister
John Willson	John Clement
Thomas Lanier	Thomas Purcill
Anthony Roberts	William Child
Matthew Lock	Charles Coleman
John Jenkins	Theophilus Fittz
John Lilly	John Goodgroome
John Harding	Pelham Humphries
Alphonso Marsh	William Clayton

Lewis Grabu, master of music to the King

Account for annual pensions of £19 : 17 : 8 to each of the following trumpeters to the late King Charles I. :—

Robert Ramsay	William Porter
Samuel Markland	Henry Peacock
George Bosgrave	

Account of £59 : 13 : 4 paid to Henry Gregorye for clothing and educating two boys in the art of music.

L. C. Vol. 62 ; *L. C. Vol.* 157.

1673, *September* 30.

Order to prepare a bill containing a grant of the office of musician in ordinary to his Majesty for the violin, to Francis Cruys, in the place and on the surrender of John Smyth, with the fee of £40 by the year for his life. To commence St. John Baptist, 1673, last past.

L. C. Vol. 744, *p.* 338.

1673, *September.*

Bill for embroidering 16 coats on back and breast with the letters C.R. and crown for 13 trumpeters and 3 kettle drummers at 50 shillings a coat. The sergeant and drum-major by themselves.

L. C. Vol. 203, *Entry* 203.

1673, *October* 4.

Bill for 4 yards of red bayes for a drumm case at 2s. per yard, part of the bill of John Mawgridge, drum major.

L. C. Vol. 203, *Entry* 188.

1673, *October* 7.

Warrant to pay to Thomas Greeting, one of his Majesty's musicians, the sum of £12 for a violin by him bought for His Majesty's service.

Bill signed by Monsieur Grabu ; and delivery certified by Mr. Brockwell, instrument keeper.

L. C. Vol. 744, *p.* 345.

1673, *October* 13.

Warrant to deliver to Mr. Pelham Humphryes, liveries for the children of the Chappell.

L. C. Papers, Bundle 76.

1673, *October* 20.

Estimate for furnishing the organ lofts with silk curtaines at the Chapple at Whitehall and Hampton Court.

Estimate for furnishing each boy of the Chappell (as they change their voyces) with two suites and cloaks and with all double proportion of lynnen and other necessaries.

L. C. Vol. 545, *p.* 35.

1673, *November* 13.

Certificate that Francis Garrard is sworn and admitted one of His Majesty's violins in ordinary without fee, to come in ordinary with fee upon the first avoydance of any of His Majesty's violins.

L. C. Vol. 483, *p.* 127 ; *and Vol.* 744, *p.* 365.

1673, *November* 17.

Warrant for payment of £80 . 12 . 6 . to John Smith, one of his Majesty's musick, for arrears of liveries due to him for 5 years, 1664 to 1667 and 1671.

L. C. Vol. 711, *p.* 50.

1673, *November* 18.

Warrant to pay to John Twist, musician in ordinary to his Majesty, the sum of £12 for a violin by him bought for His Majesty's service.

L. C. Vol. 744, *p.* 369.

1673, *St. Andrew.*

Payment of £16 . 2 . 6 . to each of the following musicians to the King for their liveries:—

John Willson ("mortuus post diem" added after his name)	Thomas Bates
	Alphonso Marsh
Anthony Roberts	John Clement
John Hingeston	Thomas Purcell
William Gregory	William Child

George Hudson (" mortuus ante diem ")	John Goodgroome
Humphrey Madge	Theophilus Fittz
Thomas Lanier	Charles Colman
John Smith	Lewis Grabu
John Gamble	Pelham Humphryes
John Jenkins	("mortuus" added
John Lillie	after his name)
John Harding	William Clayton
John Bannister	Thomas Purcell
Mathew Lock	Edward Hootten
	William Turner

Payment of £29 . 16 . 8 . to Henry Gregory for clothing two boys and educating them in the art of music for half a year.

L. C. Vol. 463.

1673, *December* 1.

Warrant to pay Peter Anthony, trumpeter, £36. 5s. for his attending his Highness Prince Rupert at sea, from 23 April, 1672 to 14 September, 1673, at the usual rate of 5s. by the day.

L. C. Vol. 744, *p.* 376.

1673, *December* 9.

Bill for habitts for 24 violins.

L. C. Vol. 204, *Entry* 15.

1673, *December* 14.

Bill for 24 garlands at 5s. each, for His Majesty's musick at the theatre in Whitehall.

L. C. Vol. 204, *Entry* 16.

1673, *December* 17.

Warrant to provide outfit of clothing for Henry Purcell, late child of his Majesty's Chappell Royall, whose voice is changed, and gon from the Chappell.

Warrant to pay to Henry Purcell, late one of the children of his Majesty's Chappell Royall, whose voyce is changed and is gon from the Chappell, the sum of £30 by the year, to commence Michaelmas, 1673, last past.

L. C. Vol. 744, *p.* 384 ; *L. C. Papers, Bundle* 76.

1673, *December* 24.

To Robert Ramsey, pentionary trumpeter, £19 : 17 : 8, pension due Pentecost, 1672.

L. C. Vol. 715, *p.* 2.

1673, *Christmas.*

Payment of £60 to Pelham Humphries for keeping and teaching two singing boys for 1½ years.

L. C. Vol. 463.

[1673.]

Mr. Edmund Flower for the next place of the musick that shall be voyd either private or wind musick.

L. C. Vol. 655.

1673-4, *January* 8.

Bill for fine holland for Henry Purcell, child of the Chappell, going off.

L. C. Vol. 204, *Entry* 23.

1673-4, *January* 15.

Bill for 181 yards of tinsell at 12d. per yard for habitts for 24 violins and for the 24 shashes about 5½ yards to each habitt, and 2 yards to each shash.

L. C. Vol. 204, *Entry* 30.

1673-4, *January* 19.

To John Gamble, musician, livery of £16 . 2 . 6, due St. Andrew, 1672.

L. C. Vol. 715, *p.* 2.

1673-4, *January* 23.

Order for a bill enabling the Master of the Great Wardrobe to pay to Pelham Humfryes, master of the children of his Majesty's Chappell Royall in place of Captain Henry Cooke, deceased, the sum of £40 by the year, for the education of two children for His Majesty's private musick, to commence 24 June, 1672.

L. C. Vol. 744, *p.* 408.

To John Gamble, musician, the sum of £16 . 2 . 6, livery due St. Andrew, 1671.

L. C. Vol. 715, *p.* 3.

1673-4, *January* 26.

Warrant to provide liveries for the present year, 1673, for Simon Pearson and Albion Thompson, trumpeters to His Majesty's troop of Guards commanded by the Duke of Monmouth, and for John Cristmas, trumpeter, and for the kettledrummer attending the Queen's Troop commanded by Sir Philip Howard and to the kettledrummer to the Troop of Horse under Lord Hawley.

L. C. Vol. 744, *p.* 419; *L. C. Papers, Bundle* 76.

1673-4, *January* 26.

Warrant to pay to William Turner, late child of his Majesty's Chappell Royall, whose voice being changed, went from the Chappell, the sum of £30 by the year, by the space of four years, from Michaelmas, 1666, to Michaelmas, 1670, in all £120.

L. C. Vol. 744, *p.* 411.

1673-4, *January* 26.

Warrant to provide liveries for Gervase Price, esquire. his Majesty's sergeant trumpeter, for sixteen trumpeters and a kettledrummer.

L. C. Vol. 744, *p.* 410.

1673-4, *January* 26.

Order to prepare a bill enabling the Master of the Great Wardrobe to furnish such liveries for Pelham Humfryes and Thomas Purcell, composers for his Majesty's violins in ordinary in place of George Hudson, deceased, and to the longest liver of them, as were allowed to the said George Hudson, to commence Michaelmas, 1672.

L. C. Vol. 744, *p.* 420.

1673-4, *February* 2 *and* 20.

Bill for handkerchiefs for Pursell a boy gone off from the chapel.

Account for fine cloth for 2 suites for a Chappell boy, whose voice is changed.

L. C. Vol. 204, *Entries* 41, 42.

1673-4, *February* 2.

Warrant to pay to Charles Evans, harper for the Italian harp, the sum of £5 for strings for one year ending at Christmas, 1673.

L. C. Vol. 744, *p.* 420.

1673-4, *February* 6.

To John Clement, musician, the sum of £16 . 2 . 6, livery due St. Andrew, 1671.

L. C. Vol. 715, *p.* 3.

1673-4, *February* 7.

Warrant to admit Thomas Greeting in the place of musician in ordinary to his Majesty for the violin without fee, to come in ordinary with fee, on the death or other avoydance of William Saunders.

L. C. Vol. 744, *p.* 423.

1673-4, *February* 7.

To John Allen for making of habitts for the King's musicke, £12.

L. C. Vol. 407, *Entry* 21.

1673-4, *February* 16.

To Pelham Humphryes, musician, the sum of £16 . 2 . 6, livery due St. Andrew, 1671.

L. C. Vol. 715, *p.* 3.

1673-4, February 17.

Warrant to make up habitts of severall coloured rich taffatas for four and twenty violins, like Indian gowns, with short sleeves to the elbow and trymed with tinsell about the neck and bottom and at the sleeves, and girdles of tinsell after the same manner and fashion as formerly, and two armed chayres two foot two inches broad, of crymson velvett for the King and Queene, two high stooles of crymson velvett for the Duke and Duchess, a crymson velvett cloth to lay before them and two long cushions of crymson velvett and four and twenty garlands of severall coloured flowers for each of the violins, and also a curtain of blue, red, and white in breadths, of stuffe of what kind you think fitt, to fall down before the stage, and two cases to put all these things in.

L. C. Vol. 744, *p.* 436; *L. C. Papers, Bundle* 76.

1673-4, February 25.

Warrant to suspend from his place and wayting until further order Hugh Fisher, one of his Majesty's trumpeters, for misdemeanour and neglect of His Majesty's service.

L. C. Vol. 744, *p.* 441.

1673-4, February 25.

To Thomas Purcell, as groom of the robes and as musician, liveries due 1671, £56 . 2 . 6.

L. C. Vol. 715, *p.* 4.

1673-4, February 26.

Letter of assignment from William Child, doctor in musick, appointing Mr. Richard Cole, of Dotton Park, Bucks, his true and lawful attorney.

L. C. Vol. 198, *p.* 30*d.*

1673-4, February 27.

To William Child, musician, the sum of £16 . 2 . 6, livery due St. Andrew, 1671.

To George Hudson, musician, the sum of £32 . 5, for liveries due St. Andrew, 1671 and 1672.

To Thomas Bates, musician, the sum of £48 . 7 . 6, for liveries due St. Andrew, 1671, 1672 and 1673.

L. C. Vol. 715, *p.* 4.

1673-4, February 27.

Certificate of the burial of Dr. Wilson, doctor in musick, in the cloyster belonging to the Collegiate Church of St. Peter's, Westminster, on the 27 February, 1673. Signed, Steph. Crespion, chanter.

L. C. Vol. 198, *p.* 78.

1673-4, February 27.

Order to prepare a bill enabling the master of the Great Wardrobe to provide liveries for Edward Hooton, admitted musician in ordinary in his Majesty's private musick, in place of Gregory Thorndell, deceased, to commence 25 December, 1670.

L. C. Vol. 744, p. 443.

1673-4, February 27.

Order to prepare a bill enabling the master of the Great Wardrobe to provide liveries for John Blow, admitted musician in ordinary to his Majesty for the virginalls, in place of Giles Tompkins, deceased, to commence Christmas, 1668.

L. C. Vol. 744, p. 443.

1673-4, February 27.

Warrant to Gervase Price, sergeant trumpeter, to be in readynesse with one of His Majesty's trumpettors at the gate of the Palace of Whitehall, by tenn of the clock tomorrow morning, being the last of February, in the usuall manner to attend the proclayming of peace between His Majesty and the States General of the United Provinces.

L. C. Vol. 744, p. 442.

1673-4, February 27.

Warrant to pay to William Clayton, musician in ordinary to his Majesty, the sum of £12 for a violin by him bought for his Majesty's service in the Chappell Royall.

L. C. Vol. 744, p. 444.

1673-4, February.

Warrant for payment of £58. 7. 6. to John Bannister, one of his Majesty's musicians, arrears of liveries due to him for 4 years, 1665 to 1667 at the rate of £16 : 2 : 6 per annum, and also £10 due at St. Andrew, 1670.

L. C. Vol. 711, p. 51.

1673-4, March 4.

To John Harding, musician, the sum of £16. 2. 6, livery due St. Andrew, 1671.

L. C. Vol. 715, p. 4.

1673-4, March 6.

Order to prepare a bill conteyning a grant unto Thomas Greeting of the office of musician in ordinary to his Majesty for the violin and also for the sackbutt in ordinary in his Majesty's Chappell Royall, in place of William Saunders, deceased, with the fee of 2s. 4d. a day, and £16. 2s. 6d. a year for his livery, to commence the Annunciation now next coming, 1673.

L. C. Vol. 744, p. 446.

1673-4, *March* 7.

To John Sharpe for habitts for 24 violins, £9 1s.

L. C. Vol. 407, *entry* 30.

1673-4, *March* 9.

Warrant to admit Thomas Purcell musician in ordinary to his Majesty in the private muisck in the place of John Wilson, deceased.

L. C. Vol. 744, *p.* 447.

1673-4, *March* 9.

Warrant to provide liveries for two trumpettors and a kettledrummer to attend Lord Duras into France.

L. C. Vol. 744, *p.* 448.

1673-4, *March* 10.

Warrant to pay to Pelham Humphries, appointed master of the children of the Chappell, in place of Henry Cook, deceased, the sum of £60 due to him for keeping and teaching two singing boys for one year and a half last past, from St. John Baptist, 1672 to Christmas, 1673, at the rate of £40 per annum; and henceforth to pay him £10 quarterly for the same.

L. C. Vol. 815, *p.* 62.

1673-4, *March* 16.

Warrant dormant to pay to Thomas Purcell and Pelham Humphries, appointed composers for the violins, in place of George Hudson, deceased, for their liveries for two years past, 1672 and 1673, the sum of £32. 5s., and to deliver to them yearly at the Feast of St. Andrew the materials for their liveries during his Majesty's pleasure.

L. C. Vol. 815, *p.* 49d.

1673-4, *March* 17.

Warrant to provide and deliver to Mr. Pelham Humfryes master of the children of his Majesty's Chappell Royall, 13 Bibles bound with the Common Prayer in quarto for the use of the children of the Chappell.

L. C. Vol. 744, *p.* 450 ; *L. C. Papers, Bundle* 76.

1673-4, *March* 17.

Warrant by the Earl of St. Albans, Lord Chamberlain, to the clerk of the Signet and Privy Seal, signifying what offices are in his gift; the list of offices includes musicians, sergeant trumpett and trumpettors, drum major and drummers.

L. C. Vol. 744, *p.* 451.

1673-4, *March* 20.

To John Bannister, musician, the sum of £16. 2. 6, livery due St. Andrew, 1671.

L. C. Vol. 715, *p.* 5.

1674, *March* 25.

Warrant to provide habitts of several coloured rich taffetas for four and twenty violins like Indian gowns, &c., after the same manner and fashion as formerly.

L. C. Papers, Bundle 76.

1674, *March* 25.

Payment of £10 to Pelham Humphries for keeping and teaching two singing boys for quarter of a year.

L. C. Vol. 463.

1674, *March* 27.

Warrant to deliver to Monsieur Grabu, or to such as he shall appoynt, such of the scenes remayning in the theatre at Whitehall as shall be useful for the French opera at the theatre in Bridges Street, and the said Monsieur Grabu to return them again safely after 14 days' tyme, to the theatre at Whitehall.

L. C. Vol. 744, *p.* 456.

1674, *April* 1.

To John Mason and Henry Gregory, the sum of £89 : 10, due St. Andrew, 1671 and 1672.

To Henry Gregory, musician, for teaching two boys, the sum of £59 : 13 : 4, due St. John Baptist, and St. Andrew, 1673.

L. C. Vol. 715, *pp.* 5, 11.

1674, *April* 14.

A list of the gentlemen of the Chappell that are to wayte and constantly attend his Majesty's service at Windsor during his residence there :—

Bases.

For Decani side.	For Cantoris side.
Mr. White	Mr. Tucker
Mr. James Hart	Mr. Yardley
Mr. Richard Hart	Mr. Howes, junior

Counter Tenners.

Mr. Turner	Mr. Blagrave
Mr. Richard Jones	Mr. Gadbury
Mr. Goodgroome	Mr. Watkins

Tenners.

Mr. Howes, senior	Mr. Braddock
Mr. Purcell	Mr. Frost
Mr. Humfryes	Mr. Cobb
Dr. Child, organist	

The six gentlemen of the Chappell were at Windsor for six days at St. George's Feast, 1674: —

Mr. John Hardinge	Mr. Husbands
Mr. Marsh	Mr. Irebeck
Mr. Courtevile	Mr. Bettenham

L. C. Vol. 745, *p.* 53.

1674, *April* 16.

Warrant for payment of £112 . 17 . 6 . to John Hingeston, one of his Majesty's musicke, for arrears of liveries due to him for the years 1664 to 1668, 1670 and 1671.

L. C. Vol. 711, *p.* 52d.

1674, *April* 18.

To John Allen for the twelve pages of the Chappell, £22. 10s.

L. C. Vol. 407, *entry* 85.

1674, *April* 22.

Assignment by Ambrose Sanders, of the parish of St. Bride's, alias Bridgetts, son and administrator of William Sanders, late one of his Majesty's musicians in ordinary, to William Parkes, of the parish of St. Margaret's, Westminster, of the sum of £352. 5s., which are wages due out of the Treasury Chamber for six years' salary and livery for the services of the said William Sanders until Christmas last past, at the rate of £58. 14s. 2d. per annum.

L. C. Vol. 195, *p.* 27.

1674, *April* 23.

Warrant to admit Thomas Heywood musician in ordinary to his Majesty without fee, to come in ordinary with fee on the death, surrender, or other avoydance of John Rogers, now musician in ordinary to his Majesty for the French lute.

L. C. Vol. 744, *p.* 468.

1674, *April* 27.

Warrant to deliver to Sir Christopher Wren, His Majesty's surveyor generall of the works, the scenes belonging to His Majesty's Theatre at Whitehall, which were formerly delivered to Mr. Grabu for the use of the French opera in Bridges Street.

L. C. Vol. 744, *p.* 471.

1674, *May* 6.

Warrant to admit Albion Thompson trumpeter in ordinary to his Majesty in place and upon the surrender of Melque Goldt.

L. C. Vol. 478, *p.* 85 ; *L. C Vol.* 744, *p.* 480.

1674, *May* 7.

These are to certify that Thomas Heywood is sworne and admitted musician in ordinary without fee, to come in ordinary with fee on the death, surrender or other avoidance of John Rogers, now musician in ordinary for the French lute.

L. C. Vol. 744, *p.* 485.

1674, *May* 13.

Warrant for payment of £48 . 7 . 6 . to the relect and administratrix of Dr. John Wilson, late one of his Majesty's musitians, arrears of liveries due to him for the years 1665 to 1667.

L. C. Vol. 711, *p.* 53*d.*

1674, *May* 13.

Payment to John Mawgridge, drum major, his livery the yeare 1674, £52. 17s. 8d.

L. C. Vol. 407, *entry* 93.

1674, *May* 13.

Warrant to admit John Young musician in ordinary to his Majesty for the violl de Gambo, in the place and upon the surrender of Paul Bridges.

L. C. Vol. 744, *p.* 490.

1674, *May* 16.

Chappellmen for ye theatre.

It is his Majesty's pleasure that Mr. Turner and Mr. Hart or any other men or boys belonging to his Majesty's Chappell Royall that sing in ye Tempest at His Royal Highnesse Theatre doe remaine in towne all the weeke (dureing his Majesty's absence from Whitehall) to performe that service, only Saturdayes to repaire to Windsor and to returne to London on Mundayes if there be occasion for them. And that [they] also performe ye like service in ye opera in ye said theatre or any other thing in ye like nature where their helpe may be desired upon notice given them thereof.

L. C. Vol. 774, *p.* 3.

1674, *May* 18.

Warrant to admit John Christmas trumpeter in ordinary to his Majesty in the place and on the surrender of Nicholas Shaperoone.

L. C. Vol. 483, *p.* 124; *and Vol.* 744, *p.* 495.

1674, *May* 20.

Assignment by John Banister, of St. Dunstan's in the West, one of his Majesty's musicians in ordinary, to William Parkes, of the parish of St. Margaret's, Westminster, of the sum of

£116. 7s. 1d., wages due out of the Treasury Chamber to the said John Banister for two and a half years, at £46. 10s. 10d. per annum.

L. C. Vol. 195, folio 28d.

1674, *Pentecost.*

Payment of £19 . 17 . 8 . to each of the following trumpeters to the late King Charles I. for their pensions :—

Robert Ramsay   George Bosgrove
Samuel Markland   William Porter
              Henry Peacock.

L. C. Vol. 463.

1674, *May 26.*

To Isaac Boddington for scarfes for 4 trumpetters and a kettle-drummer attending the Lord Duras into France, £26. 18s. 5d.

L. C. Vol. 407, entry 57.

1674, *May 29.*

A lyst of his Majesty's servants appointed to attend his Majesty at St. George's Feast, the 29 day of May, 1671 :—

Gentlemen of the Chappell.
Musicians.
16 Trumpeters.
Mr. Humphryes and the children of the Chappell.
Sergeant trumpeter.
Drumme major, 4 drums and a fife.

L. C. Vol. 547, p. 41.

1674, *June 1.*

Assignment by Jeffrey Banester, of St. Dunstan's in the West, one of his Majesty's musicians in ordinary, of the sum of £267. 16s. 6d., to William Parkes, of the parish of St. Margaret's, Westminster.

L. C. Vol. 195, p. 29.

1674, *June 16.*

Warrant for the payment of £183 to John Christmas and Benigne Le Ragois, two of his Majesty's trumpeters, for their attendance upon their Excellencies Sir Leoline Jenkins and Sir Joseph Williamson, his Majesty's plenipotentiaries for treating of peace with the states of the United Netherlands at Coloigne, from 8 May, 1673 to 8 May, 1674, at the rate of 5s. by the day to each man.

L. C. Vol. 774, p. 9 ; L. C. Vol. 482.

1674, *June* 16.

Thomas Cresswell appointed trumpeter in ordinary to his Majesty in the place and upon the surrender of John Jones.

L. C. Vol. 482; *L. C. Vol.* 774, *p.* 10.

1674, *June* 16.

A Bill to be prepared for his Majesty's signature, granting unto Thomas Cresswell, trumpeter, £60 by the year, to be paid quarterly, the first payment on 24 June, 1674.

L. C. Vol. 774, *p.* 10.

1674, *St. John the Baptist.*

Payment of £29. 16. 8. to Henry Gregory for clothing two boys and educating them in the art of music for half a year.

L. C. Vol. 463.

1674, *St. John Baptist.*

Payment of £10 to Pelham Humphries for keeping and teaching two singing boys for quarter of a year.

L. C. Vol. 463.

1674, *June* 24.

Order to admit James Castle trumpeter in ordinary to his Majesty, in place of John Crowther, deceased.

L. C. Vol. 482; *Vol.* 483, *p.* 75; *and Vol.* 774, *p.* 15.

1674, *July* 4.

Order that the twelve violins following doe meet in his Majesty's theatre within the palace of Whitehall on Wednesday morning next by seven of the clock, to practice after such manner as Monsr. Combert shall enforme them, which things are hereafter to be presented before his Majesty at Windsor upon Saturday next :—

John Strong	Jeoffery Elworth
Richard Dorney	John Bannister
Thomas Finell	Phillip Beckett
Thomas Greeteing	Edward Hooton
John Gamble	John Myer
Richard Browne	Morgan Harris

L. C. Vol. 774, *p.* 16.

1674, *July* 14.

Mr. Pelham Humphries departed this life 14 July, 1674.

L. C. Vol. 198, *p.* 72.

1674, *July* 23.

Warrant to swear and admit John Blow master of the children of his Majesty's Chappell Royall and composer in his Majesty's private musick for voyces in ordinary, in the place of Pelham Humfryes, deceased.

L. C. Vol. 744, *p.* 510.

1674, *July* 28.

To John Hingeston, musician, the sum of £16 : 2 : 6, for livery due St. Andrew, 1671.

L. C. Vol. 715, *p.* 5.

1674, *August* 3.

Warrant to swear and admit Robert Smyth musician in ordinary to his Majesty in place of Pelham Humphryes, deceased.

L. C. Vol. 482 ; *L. C. Vol.* 774, *p.* 28.

1674, *August* 15.

Warrant to swear and admit Nicholas Staggins, gentleman, master of his Majesty's violins in ordinary.

L. C. Vol. 744, *p.* 518.

1674, *August* 24.

Letter of assignment by John Smith, late one of his Majesty's private musick, appointing Mr. Jeffery Banister his true and lawful attorney.

L. C. Vol. 198, *p.* 91.

1674, *August* 27.

Henry Dove appointed musician in ordinary to his Majesty for the violin, in the place and upon the surrender of Phillip Beckett.

L. C. Vol. 774, *p.* 31.

1674, *August* 27.

To Thomas Lanyer, musician, the sum of £32 : 5 for liveries due St. Andrew, 1671 and 1672.

L. C. Vol. 715, *p.* 5.

1674, *August* 28.

Order to prepare a bill for his Majesty's Royal signature for the appointment of Henry Dove to the place of musician in in ordinary to his Majesty for the violin, in the place and upon the surrender of Philip Beckett, with the wages of £46. 12. 8. yearly, payment to commence Michaelmas next ensueing.

L. C. Vol. 482 ; *Vol.* 774, *p.* 33.

1674, *September* 3.

Order to pay to Theophilus Fittz and Thomas Fittz, musicians to his Majesty, £24 for two violins bought by them for his Majesty's service in the Chappell Royall. As may appear by the bill signed by Mr. Purcell.

L. C. Vol. 774, *p.* 52.

1674, September 4.

Order to pay £163 to Jervas Price, esquire, his Majesty's sergeant trumpeter, for John Baker, William Bounty, John Crowther and Symon Person, four of his Majesty's trumpeters, for their attendance on the Rt. Hon. Lord Hollis and Henry Coventry, esquire, ambassadors at Breda, by the space of 103 days, from 15 April to 25 September, 1667, at the rate of 5s. by the day unto each man.

L. C. Vol. 774, *p.* 48.

1674, September 6 *and* 7.

Order to deliver two suits of clothes, etc., to James Greene, late child of his Majesty's Chappell Royall, whose voyce is changed and is gon from the chappell. Further order to pay him £30 a year during his Majesty's pleasure, to commence 24 June, 1674.

L. C. Vol. 774, *pp.* 39, 40 ; *L. C. Papers, Bundle* 76.

Accounts ending Michaelmas, 1674.

Walter Lapp, for twenty-four wreathes for the King's musicians in the theatre at Whitehall.

Account for a felt hat for Henry Purcell, a boy leaving the Chappell Royall.

Account paid to Henry Cook late master of the children of the Chappell Royall.

Accounts for liveries for Jervis Price, sergeant trumpeter to the King, and John Mawgridge, the King's drum-major.

Accounts of liveries of £16 : 2 : 6 each, to the following musicians to the King :—

John Hingston	John Banister
Humphrey Madge	John Clements
William Gregory	Thomas Purcell (2 liveries)
Thomas Laneir	William Child
Anthony Roberts	John Goodgroome
Mathew Lock	William Clayton
John Jenkins	Pelham Humphryes (2 liveries)
John Lillie	Charles Coleman
John Harding	Theophilus Fitz
Alphonso Marsh	Lewis Grabu, master of music
Thomas Bates	to the King.
John Gamble	

Account for pensions of £19 : 17 : 8 paid to each of the following trumpeters to the late King :—

Robert Ramsay	George Bosgrave
Samuel Markland	William Porter
Henry Peacock	

Account of £59 : 13 : 4 paid to Henry Gregory for clothing and educating two boys in the art of music.

Account paid to Pelham Humphryes for the keep of two boys and for teaching them singing for two years ending 1674 : £80.

L. C. Vol. 63 ; *L. C. Vol.* 157.

1674, *October* 7.

Petition of Ambrose Henbrough against Charles Evans, harper, for £200, by bond. Evans to appear.

L. C. Vol. 655.

1674, *October* 24.

To John Clement, musician, the sum of £16 : 2 : 6 for livery due St. Andrew, 1672.

L. C. Vol. 715, *p.* 5.

1674, *October* 28.

Warrant for livery for Edward Hooton admitted musician in ordinary to his Majesty, in the place of Gregory Thorndell, deceased. To commence 25 September, 1670.

L. C. Vol. 745, *p.* 22.

1674, *October* 30.

Warrant dormant to pay to John Blow, appointed musician in ordinary in place of Giles Tompkins, deceased, in consideration of his liveries for the years 1669, 1670, 1671, 1672 and 1673, the sum of £80. 12s., and to deliver to him yearly at the Feast of St. Andrew during His Majesty's pleasure the materials for his livery of £16 : 2 : 6.

L. C. Vol. 815, *p.* 47.

1674, *October* 31.

Warrant for the payment of £159 to Nicholas Staggins, master of his Majesty's violins, for himself and the following musicians, for riding charges and other expenses while attending upon his Majesty at Windsor for 53 days, from 11 July to 1 September, 1674, at the rate of 5s. by the day, to each of them :—

John Strong	John Gamble
John Bannister	Edward Hooton
Richard Dorney	Richard Browne
Thomas Finell	Jeoffrey Alworth
Thomas Greeting	John Myer.
Morgan Harris	

Certified by Mr. Staggins, master of the musick.

L. C. Vol. 745, *p.* 23.

1674, *November* 6.

Warrant for the payment of £54 to :—

John Singleton,	Isaack Staggins,
William Clayton,	Henry Brockwell,
Theophilus Fitz	Joseph Fashion,

Six of his Majesty's musicians in ordinary for the violin, for rydeing charges and other expenses in their attendance upon the Queenes Majesty at Hampton Court for 36 days, from 17 September to 24 October, 1674, at the rate of 5s. by the day to each of them.

L. C. Vol. 745, *p.* 44.

1674, *November* 7.

Order to pay Mr. John Blow, master of the children of his Majesty's Chappell Royall, the sum of £163. 10s., for himself and eight boys, for their attendance upon his Majesty at Windsor for 109 days, from 18 May to 3 September, 1674, at the usuall rate of 6s. by the day for the master and 3s. by the day for each child :—

William Holder	Augustine Benford
William Sarell	Francis Smyth
John Waters	William Goodgroome
Gilbert Conisby	Bartholomew Isaack

L. C. Vol. 745, *p.* 54.

1674, *November* 9.

Warrant for a patent to grant unto John Blow the place of musician in ordinary to his Majesty, in the place of Giles Tompkins, deceased, with the wages of £40 per annum. To commence 25 March, 1669.

L. C. Vol. 745, *p.* 56.

1674, *November* 9.

Warrant for the payment of £36. 15s. to Nicholas Staggins, master of his Majesty's violins, for himself and Thomas Fittz, Thomas Farmer, John Twist, Edmund Flower, Richard Tomlinson, and Cesar Duffill, musicians, for ryding charges and other expenses in their attendance upon his Majesty at Newmarket, for 21 days from 22 September to the 12 October, 1674, at the rate of 5s. by the day.

L. C. Vol. 745, *p.* 63.

1674, *November* 9.

Warrant for the allowance of winter liveries for the twelve children of the Chappell Royall, to be delivered to John Blow, master of the said children.

L. C. Papers, Bundle 7.

1674, *November* 9.

Warrant for a patent to grant unto William Turner the place of one of his Majesty's private Musick in ordinary for the lute and voyce, in the place of Henry Cooke, deceased, with the wages of £40 per annum and an allowance of £20 yearly for strings. To commence 29 September, 1672.

L. C. Vol. 745, *p.* 68.

1674, *November* 11.

Warrant dormant to deliver to Thomas Purcell, appointed musician in ordinary, in the place of Dr. John Wilson, deceased, the materials for his livery of £16 : 2 : 6 from henceforth yearly at the Feast of St. Andrew during his Majesty's pleasure.

L. C. Vol. 815, *p.* 48.

1674, *November* 20 *and* 21.

To John Bannister, musician, two sums of £16 : 2 : 6 for liveries due St. Andrew, 1672 and 1673.

L. C. Vol. 715, *pp.* 6, 11.

1674, *November* 24.

To John Hingeston, musician, the sum of £16 : 2 : 6 for livery due St. Andrew, 1672.

L. C. Vol. 715, *p.* 6.

1674, *November* 25.

To John Clement, musician, the sum of £16 : 2 : 6 for livery due St. Andrew, 1673.

L. C. Vol. 715, *p.* 11.

1674, *November* 26.

Warrant to pay to Edward Hooten, appointed one of the private musick in ordinary, in the place of Gregory Thorndell deceased, the sum of £48. 7s. 6d. for liveries for three years past, 1671, 1672 and 1673, and to deliver to him yearly at the Feast of St. Andrew the materials for his livery of £16 : 2 : 6, during his Majesty's pleasure.

L. C. Vol. 815, *p.* 48*d.*

1674, *November* 27.

To Henry Peacock, pentionary trumpeter, the sum of £19 : 17 : 8 for pension due Pentecost, 1672.

L. C. Vol. 715, *p.* 6.

1674, *November* 30.

Appointment by John Banester, of the parish of Whitefriars, one of his Majesty's musicians for the violin in ordinary, of Lewis Pere, haberdasher, of the city of Westminster, as his true and lawful attorney.

L. C. Vol. 195, *p.* 33.

1674, *St. Andrew.*

Payment of £16. 2. 6. to each of the following musicians to the King, for their liveries :—

Anthony Roberts	John Lillie
John Hingeston	John Harding
William Gregorie	John Bannister
Humphrey Madge	Matthew Lock
Thomas Lanier	Thomas Bates
John Smith	Alphonso Marsh
John Gamble	John Clement
John Jenkins	William Child

Thomas Purcell in the place of Henry Lawes
John Goodgroome (" memorandum—a book lent ")

Theophilus Fittz	Charles Colman

Lewis Grabu [" vacatur.   Mr. Staggins in his place "]

William Clayton	John Blow

Thomas Purcell (in the place of Dr. John Wilson)
Thomas Purcell (in the place of George Hudson)

Edward Hootten	William Turner

Payment of £29. 16. 8. to Henry Gregory for clothing two boys and educating them in the art of music for half a year.

Payment of £80. 12. 6. to John Blow, musician to the King, for his liveries for the years 1669 to 1673.

L. C. Vol. 463.

1674, *December 22 and 23.*

To William Gregory and Theophilus Fitz, musicians, £16 : 2 : 6 each, for liveries due St. Andrew, 1671.

L. C. Vol. 715, *p.* 6.

1674, *December 24.*

To Samuel Markland, pentionary trumpeter, the sum of £19 : 17 : 8 for pension due Pentecost, 1672.

To the musicians, Edward Hooton, for livery due St. Andrew, 1671, John Gamble, for livery due St. Andrew, 1673, and Thomas Lanyer for liveries due St. Andrew, 1673 and 1674, four payments of £16 : 2 : 6.

L. C. Vol. 715, *pp.* 6, 12.

1674, *December 26 and 27.*

To John Goodgroome, Mathew Lock, Humphrey Madge, John Wilson and Charles Coleman, musicians, £16. 2. 6. each, for liveries due St. Andrew, 1671.

L. C. Vol. 715, *p.* 6.

1674, *December* 29.

To Lewis Grabu, musician, the sum of £32 : 5 for liveries due St. Andrew, 1671 and 1672.

To John Blow, musician, £16 : 2 : 6 for livery due St. Andrew, 1674.

L. C. Vol. 715, *pp.* 6, 12.

1674, *December* 30.

To Alphonso Marsh and William Clayton, musicians, £16 : 2 : 6 each for liveries due St. Andrew, 1671.

L. C. Vol. 715, *p.* 6.

[1674].

	£	s.	d.
Mr. Humphryes for teaching children ...	68	8	6
Musicians for ryding charges at Windsor ...	159	0	0
Musicians ryding charges for attending the Queen at Hampton Court	54	0	0
Chappell-men for Windsor	715	17	0
Master and children of the Chappell	163	10	0
Musicians, Newmarket	36	15	0

L. C. Vol. 774 *(at end)*

1674.

Order that John Strong, Richard Dorney, Thomas Finel, Thomas Greeting, John Gamble, Richard Browne, Jeoffrey Elworth, John Bannister, Philip Becket, Edward Hooton, John Myer, Morgan Harry, twelve violins, shall meet in his Majesty's theatre at Whitehall on Wednesday morning next by seven of the clock to practice after such manner as Monsr. Combert shall inform them, which things are hereafter to be presented before his Majesty at Windsor on Saturday next 4 July, 1674.

L. C. Vol. 482.

[1674.]

Musicians in the Mask, 1674 :—

Singers.

Mrs. Davies,	Mrs. Peirce,
Mrs. Knight,	Mrs. Shepheard,
Mrs. Butler,	Mrs. Dorcase,
Mrs. Blunt,	Mrs. Benson.
Mrs. Masters,	
Mr. Hart,	Mr. Ford,
Mr. Turner,	Mr. Robert,
Mr. Richardson,	Mr. Preston,
Mr. Degrang,	Mr. Letelier,

Mr. Shepheard,
Mr. Maxfield,
Mr. Marsh,

Mr. Bopius,
Mr. Bury.

Boys.

Jack,
Waters,

Coningsby,
Smyth.

Harpsicalls. 2.

Mr. Corneville.

Mr. Bartleme.

Bass Violls. 3.

Mr. Coleman,

Mr. Stephkins,

Mr. Bates.

Theorboes. 2.

Mr. Marshe,

Mr. Lylly.

Recorders. 4.

Mr. Paisible,
Mr. Bootell,

Mr. De Breame,
Mr. Giton.

Gittars. 4.

Mr. Frasico Corbett,
Mr. Cutom,

Mr. Deloney,
Mr. Delloney.

Trumpetters. 4.

Mr. Bounty,
Mr. Thompson,

Mr. Ragway,
Mr. Christmas.

Kettle-drummer.

Mr. Vanbright.

Violins.

Mr. Nicholas Staggins,
Mr. Singleton,
Mr. Clayton,
Mr. Thomas Fitz,
Mr. Hewson,
Mr. Myres,
Mr. Thomas Farmer,
Mr. Aleworth,
Mr. John Bannister,
Mr. Ledgier,
Mr. Harris,
Mr. Theophilus Fitz,
Mr. Price,
Mr. Pagitt,
Mr. Duffill,
Mr. Kidwell,

Mr. Greetinge,
Mr. Ashton,
Mr. Gamble,
Mr. Fashions,
Mr. Flower,
Mr. Dorney,
Mr. Isaack Staggins,
Mr. John Strong,
Mr. Finell,
Mr. Browne,
Mr. Brockwell,
Mr. Spicer,
Mr. John Farmer,
Mr. Basrier,
Mr. Viblett,
Mr. Hall,

Mr. Eagles.

1674.

Livery fees of £16 : 2 : 6, payable out of His Majesty's Great Wardrobe at the Feast of St. Andrew, to each of the following musicians to the King :—

Lewis Grabu, Master of the musick	John Bannister, junior
	Edward Hooton
Thomas Purcell	Matthew Lock
Anthony Roberts	Thomas Bates
John Hingston	Alphonso Marsh
William Gregory	William Child
Thomas Purcell	William Clayton
Humphrey Madge	Charles Coleman
Thomas Lanier	Theophilus Fittz
John Smyth	Thomas Purcell
John Gamble	John Clement
John Jenkins	William Turner
John Lilley	John Goodgroome
John Harding	John Blow

[The following alterations in the list of musicians were made at a later date]:—

The name of Dr. Staggins inserted for that of Grabu, John Goodwyn for Thomas Purcell, Robert Carr for Hingston, Nathaniel French for Thomas Purcell, Jeoffery Aleworth for Humphrey Madge, Francis Cruyur for John Smyth, John Mosse for Jenkins, Edmund Flower for Lilley, John Bowman for Harding, Henry Purcell for Matthew Lock, William Gregory for Thomas Bates, John Abell for Alphonso Marsh.

To Henry Gregory for keeping and teaching two boys in the art of musick, payments of £29 . 16 . 8 at St. Andrew and at St. John Baptist.

Pensions of £19 : 17 : 8 payable at the Feast of Pentecost, to each of the pentionary trumpeters :—

Robert Ramsey	George Bosgrove
Samuel Markland	William Porter
Henry Peacock	

To John Blow for keeping and teaching two boys, four quarterly payments of £10, at Christmas, at the Annunciation, at St. John the Baptist and at Michaelmas.

1674-5.

Warrant to pay Thomas Haynes, sergeant of the vestry for making surplices for the gentlemen, musicians and children of the Chappell.

L. C. Vol. 804, p. 2.

1674-5, *January* 4.

Warrant for the payment of £30 yearly to Thomas Heywood, late child of his Majesty's Chappell, whose voyce is changed and is gon from the Chappell, for his keep and maintenance. To commence 25 December last past, 1673, notwithstanding a former warrant in April, 1673.

L. C. Vol. 745, p. 96.

1674-5, *January* 9.

Warrant for the payment of £381. 10s. to the following musicians for their wayting and attending upon His Majesty at Windsor in the Chapell for the space of 109 days, from 18 May to 3 September, 1674, at the rate of 5s. by the day to each man:—

William Clayton	John Mire
William Farmer	Edmund Flower
Isaack Staggins	Richard Thomlinson
Theophilus Fittz	William Gregory
John Twist	Nicholas Staggins
Edward Hooton	John Lylly
Thomas Fitz	Richard Browne.

L. C. Vol. 745, p. 124.

1674-5, *January* 11.

To John Clement, musician, £16. 2. 6 for livery due St. Andrew, 1674.

L. C. Vol. 715, p. 12.

1674-5, *January* 15.

To Anthony Roberts, musician, £16. 2. 6 for livery due St. Andrew, 1671.

L. C. Vol. 715, p. 6.

1674-5, *January* 19.

Warrant for the payment of £5 to Charles Evans, harper for the Italian harp, for strings for one year ending at Christmas, 1674.

L. C. Vol. 745, p. 108.

1674-5, *January* 23.

Payment of two years' liveries to John Banister, musician, due St. Andrew, 1667 and 1670.

L. C. Vol. 712.

1674-5, January 29.

Warrant to admit Nicholas Staggins master of the English chamber musick in ordinary to his Majesty, in the place of Lewis Grabu, to inspect and govern the same with the accustomed allowances and power of Mr. Grabu, and to enjoy all privileges belonging thereto as Mr. Grabu or Mr. Lanier or any other formerly enjoyed.

Warrant for a bill to be prepared to grant him the wages of £200 by the year for the said place, to commence 29 September, 1674.

L. C. Vol. 480, *p.* 103 ; *and Vol.* 745, *p.* 120.

1674-5, January 29.

Warrant to pay the executors of George Hudson, deceased, late one of his Majesty's private musick, the sum of £64. 10s. arrears of liveries due to him for four years, 1665 to 1667 and 1670.

L. C. Vol. 711, *p.* 56.

1674-5, February 5.

To Thomas Purcell, as groom of the robes, £40 due at All Saints, 1673 ; and as musician, £80 : 12 : 6, being five liveries, two due at St. Andrew, 1673, and three at St. Andrew, 1674.

L. C. Vol. 715, *p.* 12.

1674-5, February 8.

Warrant for payment of £64. 10s. to Thomas Bates, one of his Majesty's private musick, arrears of liveries due to him for 4 years, 1665 to 1667, and 1670.

L. C. Vol. 711, *p.* 56d.

1674-5, February 9.

Warrant for the payment of £21 to Jervas Price, sergeant trumpetter, for four brasse trumpetts and a pair of new kettle-drumes, provided by him for his Majesty's service.

L. C. Vol. 745, *p.* 123.

1674-5, February 13.

Assignment by William Gregory, of London, gentleman, one of the private musick to his Majesty, to William Parkes, of St. Margaret's, Westminster, of all arrears due to him for the years 1665, 1666, 1667 and 1670, as one of the private musick, amounting to £64. 10s., also appointing him, the said William Parkes, his true and lawful attorney. Witnessed by Henry Gregory and William Hill.

L. C. Vol. 198, *p.* 60d.

1674-5, *February* 15.

Payment of one year's livery to John Gamble, musician, due St. Andrew, 1667 ; and of two years' liveries to William Gregory, musiciam, due St. Andrew, 1667 and 1670.

L. C. Vol. 712.

1674-5, *February* 16.

Bill of Nicholas Fownes for material supplied for the masque at Whitehall :—

For 20 *viollyns.*

31½ ells of cherry coloured taffata at 13s. ...	20	9	6
For 31½ ells of sky rich taffata at 11s. ...	17	6	6
27 ells of yellow taffata at 11s.	14	17	0
150 yards of narrow silver gawes at 1s. ...	7	10	0

For four gytarrhs.

18 ells of white rich taffata at 11s.	9	18	0
16 yards of broad gold gawes at 2s.	1	12	0
2 yards of broad gold gawes at 2s.		4	0
	£71	17	0

For two hoaboyes.

18 yards of green avinnion printed with silver at 6s. 6d.	5	17	0
4 yards of narrow silver gawes		4	0
	£6	1	0

For four trumpetts and a kettle drummer.

140 yards of silver gawes at 1s.	7	0	0
9 yards of broad silver gawes at 2s.		18	0
2½ yards of broad gold gawes at 2s.		5	0
2½ yards of flase silver tabby at 7s.		17	6
	£9	0	6

L. C. Vol. 204, *entry* 45*b*.

1674-5, *February* 24.

Bill of William Goslin for materials supplied for the maske at Whitehall. For 57 yards of gold and silver lace for shepherds of the chorus. £8 11.

L. C. Vol. 204, *entry* 41*b*.

1674-5, *March* 1 *and* 5.

To Jervace Price for livery and all complete furniture for himself and 16 trumpettors and one kettledrummer for the year 1673, £1,362 : 17 : 3.

To John Mawgridge for livery for himself, four drummers, and a fife, for the said year (1673), £317 6s.

L. C. Vol. 407, *entries* 230, 231.

1674-5, *March* 2.

To John Lylly, musician, the sum of £16 : 2 : 6 for livery due at St. Andrew, 1672.

L. C. Vol. 715, *p.* 7.

1674-5, *March* 11.

Daniel Deives' bill for materials supplied for the maske at Whitehall, for 20 garlands at 5s. apiece, for the 20 violins.

L. C. Vol. 204, *entry* 48b.

1674-5, [*March* 11].

Bill of John Allen and William Watts, his Majesty's tailors :—

For the six shepherds of the chorus.

For making a gold tinsell waistcoat and a green taffaty breeches the waistcoat lined with callico and coloured sleeves faced with green taffaty and laced with a broad silver tinsell lace and one in every seam, the breeches lined with callico and laced with two laces of gold and silver down each mid thigh and two round each knee, the bag and strings of green taffaty laced with gold fringe and a pair of drawers...	1	5	0
For canvas buckerome and whalebone ...		4	0
For silk and thread		4	0
For three dozen breast buttons		1	0
For callico to line the waistcoat and breeches		7	0
For one is	2	1	0
For six in all is... ...	12	6	0

For 20 violins.

For making a taffaty gown laced with gawes downe before round the bottom round the neck and the sleeves with all small furniture		10	0
For 20 in all	10	0	0

For four kittars.

For making a taffaty gowne laced with gawes down before round the sleeves and neck and bottom with all small furniture ...	10	0
For making a cap of gilt leather stiffened lined and adorned with feathers ...	4	0
For gilt leather...	4	0
For one is	18	0

For four in all is... ...	3	12	0

For two Hoa Boyes.

For making a gown of green avinnion printed with silver with all small furniture ...	8	0
For making a gilt leather cap lined and stiffened	4	0
For gilt leather...	4	0
For one is	16	0

For two is	1	12	0

Trumpeter and four drummers.

For making a vest with hanging sleeves of cherry coloured taffaty lined with callico sleeves faced with taffaty laced with silver gawes in every seam and round the hanging sleeves bottom of the vest and a banner of red taffaty laced round with silver gawes...	18	0
For canvas stiffening silk and thread ...	4	0
For callico to line it	6	0
For hooks, eyes and buttons	1	6
For making a cap of gold gawes lined and stiffened	5	0

For one is	1	14	6
For five in all is ...	8	12	6

L. C. Vol. 204, *entry* 50b.

1675, *March.*

Order for eighty large rings for the organ curtains in the Chappell at Whitehall.

L. C. Vol. 205, *entry* 31.

1675, *April* 1.

Warrant for the payment of £30 by the year to Mr. Blow, master of the children of his Majesty's Chappell Royall, for the maintenance of William Holder, late one of the children of the Chappell, whose voyce is changed and is gon from the Chappell. To commence 29 September, 1674.

L. C. Vol. 745, *p.* 149.

1675, *April* 3.

To George Bosgrove, pentionary trumpeter, the sum of £19 . 17 . 8 for pension due Pentecost, 1674.

L. C. Vol. 715, *p.* 12.

1675, *April* 3.

Agreement between John Bannister of the parish of St. Martin's in the Feilds, one of his Majesty's musicians, and John Hill, gentleman, of the same parish. In consideration of the sum of £40 paid by the said John Hill, Bannister assigns his yearly livery of £16. 2s. 6d. payable from the great Wardrobe every feast of St. Andrew. Should the said livery be passed in the account, and there be no present money to satisfy the same, the said Hill shall sustaine the damage and loss, but if the same be made void or discontinued by any act, forfeiture, or surrender, then the loss and damages shall be to the said John Bannister.

L. C. Vol. 198, *p.* 68.

1675, *April* 20.

To Theophilus Fitz, musician, the sum of £16 : 2 : 6 for livery due St. Andrew, 1672.

L. C. Vol. 715, *p.* 7.

1675, *April* 22.

To John Banister, musician, the sum of £16 : 2 : 6 for livery due St. Andrew, 1674.

L. C. Vol. 715, *p.* 13.

1675, *April* 26.

Bill for two black castors for James Greene, Chappell boy, £1 . 4 .

L. C. Vol. 204, *entry* 99b.

1675, *April* 27.

Warrant to prepare a Bill to grant unto John Blow the office of composer in the private musick for voyces in ordinary to his Majesty, in the place of Henry Cooke deceased, with the wages of £40 by the year. To commence 24 June, 1672.

Warrant to prepare a Bill to grant unto John Blow, one of the Gentlemen of his Majesty's Chappell Royall, the office of Master of the Children of the Chappell Royall, in the place of Henry Cooke, deceased, with wages of £40 by the year for the teaching of 12 children, to commence 24 June, 1672.

L. C. Vol. 745, pp. 168, 169.

1675, *April* 27.

A Bill to be prepared to grant unto John Blow, master of the children of his Majesty's Chappell, for keeping and instructing two boys for his Majesty's private musick for the voyces, the sum of £24 yearly for each of them, which Henry Cooke lately had. To commence 24 June, 1672.

L. C. Vol. 745, p. 168.

1675, *April* 27.

Warrant for the payment of £12 to John Twist, musician in ordinary to his Majesty, for a violin bought by him for his Majesty's service in the Chappell Royall.

L. C. Vol. 745, p. 174.

1675, *April* 28.

Warrant for the payment of £42. 15s. to the following musicians for their attending upon his Majesty at Newmarket, for 19 days from 9 March to 27 March, 1675 at the rate of 5s. by the day to each of them :—

Nicholas Staggins, master of his Majesty's musick	Richard Thomlinson
	Thomas Farmer
Isaack Staggins	Jeoffery Aleworth
Thomas Fitz	Edmund Flower
Joseph Fashion	John Twist.

L. C. Vol. 745, p. 177.

1675, *May* 16.

To Thomas Purcell, the sum of £40 as groom of the robes ; and on May 23, three liveries due St. Andrew, 1675, £48 . 7 . 6.

L. C. Vol. 715, p. 25.

1675, *Pentecost*.

Payment of £19 . 17 . 8 to each of the following trumpeters to the late King Charles I. for their pensions :—

Robert Ramsay	George Bosgrove
Samuel Markland	William Porter
Henry Peacock.	

L. C. Vol. 463.

1675, *May* 27.

Warrant for the payment of £221 unto Nicholas Staggins, master of his Majesty's Musick, for himself and the persons named in the list hereunto annexed for their service and attendance in the Maske at Whitehall :—

Vocall musick.

Mr. Turner, extraordinary attendance.
Mr. Hart, extraordinary attendance.
Mr. Marsh, junior.
Mr. Ford.
Mr. Maxsine.

Frenchmen.

Bury	Le Fillier
Beaupuis	Robert
Panine	

French violins and hoboyes.

Paisable		
de Bresmes	}	hoboyes
Guiton		
Boutet		
Begard		Cornelius
	Violett	

Harpsicalls, and lute, extraordinary attendance.

Mr. Marsh, senior   Mr. Bartholomew

Violins.

Hall	Duffill
Eagles	Ridwell
Ledger	John Farmer
Ashton	Price
Pagett	

For writing and pricking the tunes in the Maske, and for paper, pens, and inke, etc. : £10.

L. C. *Vol.* 745, *p.* 197.

1675, *June* 3.

Warrant for payment of £93 7s. 6d. to John Blow, master of the children of his Majesty's Chappell Royall, for the children learning on the lute, violin and theorbo, fire in the musicke roome in the Chappell and for strings; also his charges in going to Cambridge for a boy for the Chappell.

L. C. *Vol.* 745, *p.* 205.

Warrant to deliver to John Blow, liveries for the year 1675 for the twelve children of the Chappell.

L. C. Papers, Bundle 7.

1675, *June* 3.

Warrant for the payment of £11 4s. 4d. to Thomas Ward, assigned to him by Sarah Stephkins, administratrix of Fredrick Stephkins, deceased, late one of his Majesty's musicians.

L. C. Vol. 745, *p.* 207.

1675, *St. John the Baptist.*

Payment of £29. 16. 8. to Henry Gregory, musician to the King, for clothing, and educating two boys in the art of music for half a year.

L. C. Vol. 463.

1675, *June* 24.

Warrant for surplices for the musicians and the children of the Chappell.

L. C. Papers, Bundle 11.

1675, *July* 7.

Assignment by Thomas Bates, of the parish of St. Margaret's, Westminster, one of his Majesty's private musick, of his livery of £16. 2s. 6d. due to him from his Majesty's great Wardrobe the St. Andrew ensuing, to Robert Gale, citizen and habber-dasher, of London, and appointing him his true and lawful attorney.

L. C. Vol. 198, *p.* 82

1675, *July* 8.

Appointment by Elizabeth Hudson, widow of Richard Hudson, late one of his Majesty's musicians for the violin in ordinary, of Lewis Peare, haberdasher, of Westminster, as her true and lawful attorney.

L. C. Vol. 195, *folio* 37d.

1675, *September* 4.

Warrant to admit Thomas Farmer musician in ordinary to his Majesty for the violin, in the place of John Strong, deceased.

Warrant to admit Jeoffery (also Joseph) Aleworth musician in ordinary to his Majesty for the wind instruments, in the place of John Strong, deceased.

L. C. Vol. 480, *p.* 103 ; *and Vol.* 745, *p.* 243.

1675, September 20.

Warrant to pay Nicholas Staggins, master of his Majesty's musick, £28, for a new violin bought by him for his Majesty's service, for paper books for the twenty-four violins, and for his ryding charges and other expenses while attending his Majesty at Windsor for 16 days, from 15 August to 1 September, 1674, at the rate of 10s. by the day.

L. C. Vol. 745, *p.* 248.

1675, September 23.

Assignment by Rebecka Smith, widow and administratrix of Henry Smith, late one of his Majesty's musicians in ordinary, (in consideration of the sum of £52 paid to her by Joseph Fashion, one of his Majesty's musicians in ordinary), of all such arrears of wages as are due from the Treasury of the Chamber for the services of the late Henry Smith, to the said Joseph Fashion.

L. C. Vol. 195, *p.* 38.

1675, September 28.

Warrant for the payment of £198 to the following musicians in ordinary to his Majesty, for their attendance and rydeing charges at Windsor for 66 days, from 7 July to 11 September, 1675, at the rate of 5s. by the day to each of them :—

William Clayton	John Myer
Isaack Staggins	Joseph Fashion
Henry Brockwell	Thomas Greetinge
Theophilus Fitz	Edmund Flower
Thomas Fitz	Richard Tomlinson
Thomas Farmer	William Hall.

L. C. Vol. 745, *p.* 252.

1675, September 28.

Warrant for the payment of £55 to John Bannister, musician in ordinary to his Majesty, for strings bought by him for the space of eleven years, viz. from 1664 to 1674.

L. C. Vol. 745, *p.* 252.

1675, September 28.

Warrant for the allowance of liveries for Symon Peirson, trumpeter attending upon the Troop of Guards, commanded by the Duke of Monmouth.

L. C. Papers, Bundle 7.

Accounts ending Michaelmas, 1675.

Account for two black beaver hats for James Greene, a boy leaving the Chapell Royall.

Accounts for liveries for :—

Jervis Price, chief trumpeter.
John Mawgridge, the king's drum-major.

Accounts for liveries of £16 . 2 . 6 each, for the following musicians to the King :—

John Hingestone	John Clement
Humphrey Madge	Thomas Purcell (3 liveries)
William Gregorie	William Child
Thomas Lanier	Charles Coleman
Anthony Roberts	Theophilus Fitz
Mathew Lock	John Goodgroome
John Jenkins	William Clayton
John Lillie	Dr. John Wilson, for the year
John Harding	1673
Alphonso Marsh	John Blow, 1669 to 1673,
Thomas Bates	5 years
John Gamble	Edward Hootten, 1671 to 1673,
John Bannister	3 years

Account for annual pensions for the following trumpeters to the late King Charles I. :—

Robert Ramsey	George Bosgrave
Samuel Markland	William Porter

Henry Peacock

Account of £59 : 13 : 4 paid to Henry Gregorie for clothing and educating two boys in the art of music.

L. C. Vol. 64 *; L. C. Vol.* 157.

1675, *October* 14.

Fee paid for one debenter for William Porter, pentionary trumpeter, due at Pentecost, 1675.

L. C. Vol. 458.

1675, *October* 17.

To Charles Coleman and Mathew Lock, musicians, £16 : 2 : 6 each, for liveries due St. Andrew, 1672.

On October 18 : To William Gregory and John Goodgroome, like payments.

L. C. Vol. 715, *p.* 8.

1675, *October* 18.

Fees of 5s. each, paid by the following musicians for debenters due at St. Andrew, 1672 :—

Mr. Coleman	Mr. John Goodgroome
Mr. Lock	Mr. Clayton
Mr. Gregory	Mr. Marsh

Mr. Madge

Mr. Lilly for Mr. Jenkins' debenter.

L. C. Vol. 458.

1675, *October* 19.

To William Porter, pentionary trumpeter, £19 . 17 . 8, for pension due Pentecost, 1672.

To Humphrey Madge, Alphonso Marsh, John Jenkins and William Clayton, musicians, £16 . 2 . 6 each for liveries due St. Andrew, 1672.

L. C. Vol. 715, *p.* 8.

1675, *October* 20.

Fee of 5s. received for Mr. Bosgrave's debenter ; fee of 5s. received of Mr. Willson for a debenter of 1672.

L. C. Vol. 458.

1675, *October* 21.

To George Bosgrove, pentionary trumpeter, £19 . 17 . 8 for pension due at Pentecost, 1672.

On October 23 : To John Harding, musician, £16 . 2 . 6 for livery due St. Andrew, 1672.

L. C. Vol. 715, *p.* 8.

1675, *October* 26.

Warrant for the payment of £410. 8s. to Mr. Thomas Purcell for the eighteen gentlemen of his Majesty's Chappell Royall and an organist, for their attendance on his Majesty at Windsor for 72 days, from 1 July to 11 September, 1675, at the rate of 6s. by the day unto each of them :—

Mr. Thomas Purcell	Mr. Hopwood
Mr. Blagrave	Mr. Watkins
Mr. Braddock	Mr. Blow
Mr. James Hart	Mr. Goodgroome
Mr. Turner	Mr. Richardson
Mr. Richard Hart	Mr. Frost
Mr. Tucker	Mr. Cobb
Mr. Howes, junior	Mr. Gadbury
Mr. Crispin	Mr. Harding

Mr. John Blow, organist.

L. C. Vol. 745, *p.* 276.

1675, *October* 27.

Payment to Jervis Price, sergeant trumpeter for his livery.

L. C. Vol. 407, *entry* 174b.

1675, *November* 3.

Warrant for a patent to grant Nicholas Staggins, admitted master of his Majesty's musick in the place of Lewis Grabu, and also musician in ordinary to his Majesty for the wind instruments in the place of Richard Hudson, deceased, such liveries as were delivered to the said Lewis Grabu or Nicholas Lanier, or any other of the masters of his Majesty's musick, and at such times as formerly, to commence from 29 September, 1874; and such liveries as Richard Hudson or Henry Bassano or any other in his place formerly had, to commence 29 September, 1672.

L. C. Vol. 745, *p.* 286.

1675, *November* 8.

Letter from William Child, written from Windsor Castle, asking that the rest of his livery, of which he has received £10, may be paid to the bearer, sergeant Haynes.

L. C. Vol. 198, *p.* 80.

1675, *November* 10.

Warrant to pay to Nicholas Staggins, appointed master of the musick, in place of Lewis Grabu, for his livery due St. Andrew, 1674, the sum of £16. 2s. 6d., and to deliver to him yearly at the Feast of St. Andrew the materials for his livery.

Warrant also to pay to the said Nicholas Staggins appointed musician in ordinary for the wind instruments, in place of Robert Hudson, deceased, the sum of £48 7s. 6d., being the arrears for liveries due for three years ending St. Andrew, 1674, also to deliver to him yearly the materials for his livery for the said place.

L. C. Vol. 815, *p.* 66.

1675, *November* 19.

Fees received of Mr. John Gamble, musician, for his debenter 1674; of Mrs. Humphryes for 2 debenters for her late husband as musician, viz., 1672 and 1673, 12s. 6d.; of Mr. Purcell for 4 debenters, one as groome of the roabes and three as musician, £1 : 5.

L. C. Vol. 458.

1675, *November* 22.

Warrant to admit Richard Hart musician in ordinary to his Majesty for the lute, in the place of Robert Smyth, deceased.

L. C. Vol. 480, *p.* 103; *and Vol.* 745, *p.* 290.

1675, *St. Andrew.*

Payment of £16. 2. 6. to each of the following musicians to the King for their yearly liveries :—

Anthony Roberts	John Clement
John Hingeston	Thomas Purcell, three
William Gregory	liveries in the places
Humphrey Madge	of Henry Lawes, Dr.
Thomas Lanier	John Wilson and
John Smith	George Hudson

John Gamble	William Child
John Jenkins	John Goodgroome
John Lillie	Theophilus Fittz
John Harding	Charles Coleman
John Banister	William Clayton
Mathew Lock	John Blow
Thomas Bates	Edward Hooton
Alphonso Marsh	William Turner

Nicholas Staggins, master of music in the place of Lewis Grabu; and musician in the place of Richard Hudson, liveries for the years 1672 to 1675.

Payment of £29. 16. 8. to Henry Gregory, musician to the King, for clothing two boys, and educating them in the art of music for half a year.

L. C. Vol. 464.

1675, *December* 7.

Letter of assignment from William Porter, one of the pentioner trumpeters of his Majesty, now bound out to sea to the East Indies in the good ship called the Loyall Eagle, appointing his daughter, Prudence Porter, his true and lawful attorney.

L. C. Vol. 198, *p.* 118d.

1675, *December* 10.

Certificate of the burial of Captain Henry Cooke, master of the children of his Majesty's Chappell Royall in the cloyster belonging to the Collegiate Church of St. Peter's, Westminster, on the 17 July, 1672. Signed S. Crespion, Chanter.

L. C. Vol. 198, *p.* 82d.

1675, *December* 20.

Warrant to admit Jacob Langley drummer in ordinary to his Majesty without fee.

L. C. Vol. 480, *p.* 190; *and Vol.* 745, *p.* 314.

1675, *December* 24.

To John Bannister, musician, the sum of £16 . 2 . 6 for livery due St. Andrew, 1675.

L. C. Vol. 715, *p.* 25.

1675.

To Pelham Humphries for teaching and keeping 2 boys, four quarterly payments of £10, at Christmas, the Annunciation St. John the Baptist, and Michaelmas.

L. C. Vol. 545, *pp.* 37d to 39.

1675.

Bill of John Mawgridge, drum major, for his livery for the year 1675.

L. C. Vol. 204, *entry* 174*b.*

1675-6, *January* 24.

Warrant for the delivery of one silver trumpet to Symon Beale, as one of the silver trumpets in his custody was lately lost and stolen from off the Horse Guard and cannot be heard of.

L. C. Vol. 745, *p.* 343.

1675-6, *January* 27.

Warrant to pay Nicholas Staggins, master of his Majesty's musick, £93. 2s., for faire writing and pricking severall sorts of musick, and for paper, penns and inke, and for the writers and prickers' dyes, and chamber rent as follows :—

1675, *May, at Windsor.*

For the fayre writing of severall airs of musick for the selected band of violins at Windsor from the fowle originall in score, the foure parts together, and prickers' dyes	£9	12
For drawing the said musick into 24 severall parts for the 24 violins, dyes included	8	10

July.

For penns, inke, ruled paper and chamber rent ...	£1	10
For the fair writing of a chaccon with severall others that was played at Scaramoucha from the fowle original in score, the foure parts together and the prickers' dyes	6	5
For drawing the said musick into their severall parts for the band of violins, every man a part to himselfe, and dyes	5	12
For chamber rent, pens, inke and ruled paper ...	2	5

October.

For the faire writing of an anthem, composed for the voyces of the Chappell and lutes and violls and other instruments in score, from the fowle draft, the prickers' dyes included	£5	9
For drawing the said Anthem for the voyces and instruments into severall parts, one for every man, the prickers, chamber rent, fire, candle, ruled paper, ink and pens	4	2

November.

For the faire writing of the Aires composed for the
Maske from the fowle original, on score, dyes
included £13 10

For fire, candle, chamber rent, ruled paper, ink
and penns 3 5

For drawing the said musick for the voyces, with
the instrumentall musick composed at the
same time... ... ... 10 0

December.

For the faire writing of severall Aires that was
performed at the King's dinner from the fowle
original in score, the foure parts together, and
prickers' dyes £8 12

For drawing the said musick into 24 parts for the
24 violins... ... ... 7 5

For penns, inke, ruled paper and chamber rent ... 1 10

January.

For the fayre writing of a song for New Yeare's day
and other Aires performed at the same tyme
from the fowle original in score, all the parts
together for the violins, with prickers' dyes ... £3 5

For drawing the said musick into severall parts
from the score, one for every man, penns and
inke, ruled paper and chamber rent 2 10

£93 2

1675-6, *January* 29.

Warrant for payment of £12 to Henry Dove, one of his
Majesty's musicians, for a violin bought by him for his Majesty's
service.

1675-6, *February* 7.

Warrant for the payment of £133. 5s. 6d. to Mr. John
Hingston, keeper and repairer of all his Majesty's organs, in his
Chappells and Privy Lodgings, all harpsicords, pedalls and all
other instruments, for the following items :—

1673.

For two new locks for 2 of his Majesty's harpsicords and for a new lock for the organ in the
privy lodgings... ... ... £0 10 0

For repairing and mending two harpsicords for
the practise of the private musick in the
Great Hall £1 10 0
For repairing and amending two harpsicords and
carrying them to the playhouse 0 10 0
For portage for his Majesty's chamber organ,
and to Bernard Smyth for his charge to
Windsor 2 10 0
For repareing and setting up an organ in the
banquetting house for Maundy Thursday ...   1 10 0
To George Wyatt for blowing the organs at
Whitehall for one year 8 0 0
For the rent of a large roome to keepe his
Majesty's instruments in for one whole year   8 0 0

1674.

For my charges to Windsor in giving order to
make a new loft for the new organ there and
seeing it placed, being there at severall
tymes, 14 dayes 5 0 0
For three new locks and six keyes for the organ
loft at Whitehall 0 12 0
To Bernard Smyth, the organ maker, for
cleanseing the organ at Whitehall 5 10 6
To Bernard Smyth, the organ maker, for the
loane of an organ for the banquetting house
and for three days tyme 2 0 0
For the setting it up in the banquetting house...   2 0 0
For 4 of his porters for carrying it thither   ...   0 18 0
For portage for instruments for two whole years   2 10 0
To Mr. Charles Haward for mending the harpsi-
cords and pedalls in the Great Hall in the
Privy Lodgings and for the private musick,
for 2 whole years 6 10 0
To George Wyat for blowing the organ at
Whitehall, and for his journey to and time
att Windsor, 15 weekes 12 10 0
For the rent of a large roome to keepe his
Majesty's instruments in for one whole year   8 0 0

1675.

To Mr. Humphrey Madg for a cornett for the
private musick 6 10 0
To Mr. Fittz for a sagbutt for the wind musick   12 10 0

June.

For my charges to and at Windsor 4 days to
putt his Majesty's organ in the Chappell in
order against his coming thither £1 10   0
To Mr. Smyth, organ maker, for his charges and
his worke there 2 10   0

September.

For my charges to Windsor, and for 20 yards of
sail cloth to cover and secure the organ
there from the weather and dust 1 10   0
For the rent of a large room to keep his
Majesty's instruments in for half a year   ...   4   0   0
To one to blow the organ, his Majesty being at
Windsor 1 10   0
For strings for the harpsicords and pedalls for
half a year 0 10   0
For portage for instruments for half a year   ...   0 15   0
To Mr. Haward, the virginall maker, for mending
the harpsicords   2   0   0
To Mr. Beale for mending and altering two
recorders   2   0   0
For a greate harpsichord with 3 ranks of strings
for his Majesty's musick in the hall and in
the privy lodgings   30   0   0
Signed by N. Staggins, master of the musick.

L. C. Vol. 745, *pp.* 354-355.

1675-6, *February* 12.

Warrant to pay Mr. John Blow, master of the children of
his Majesty's Chappell Royall the sum of £63 19s. for the
children's learneing on the lute, violin and theorbo, for fire and
strings for the musick roome in the Chappell, for paper, penns
and inke, for strings for the lute, and theorboes for half a year
ending 29 September, 1675 ; and also for the transport of the
children with their necessaryes to Windsor and back to London.

L. C. Vol. 745, *p.* 368.

1675-6, *February* 14.

Warrant to pay Charles Evans, harper for the Italian harp,
the sum of £5 for strings for one year ending at Christmas,
1675.

L. C. Vol. 745, *p.* 358.

1675-6, *February* 17.

Warrant to pay William Addis the sum of £6. 1s. 6d. for repairing and amending of severall of his Majesty's musicall instruments, since the 30 June, 1673.

L. C. Vol. 745, *p.* 361.

1675-6, *February* 28.

Payment of two yeares' liveries to George Hudson, musician, due St. Andrew, 1667 and 1670.

L. C. Vol. 712.

1675-6, *March* 9.

Letter of assignment by John Gamble, one of his Majesty's musicians, to Joseph Talcott, apothecary, of Westminster, of one debenture for a livery of £16 : 2 : 6, due 30 November, 1674.

L. C. Vol. 198, *p.* 100.

1675-6, *March* 20.

Bill for making various articles of clothing for Mr. Greene, page of the Chappell, £1. 12. 0.

L. C. Vol. 204, *entry* 138*b*.

1675-6, *March* 20.

Fee received of Mr. Parkes for 4 debenters for George Hudson, musician.

L. C. Vol. 458.

1675-6, *March* 20.

Receipt of Brook Bridges, esquire, Auditor, for warrants dormant for liveries for Lewis Grabu, master of the music, Pelham Humphreys, John Goodgroome and William Clayton, musicians.

L. C. Papers, Bundle 18.

1676, *March* 27.

Letter of assignment by Nicholas Staggins, master of his Majesty's musick, appointing his father, Isaac Staggins, one of his Majesty's musicians in ordinary, his true and lawful attorney.

[The assignment witnessed by Charles Colman, Thomas Staggins, and John Staggings.]

L. C. Vol. 195, *p.* 42 ; *L. C. Vol.* 198, *folio* 97*d*.

1676, *March* 28.

Warrant to admit Richard Thomlinson musician in ordinary to his Majesty without fee, to come in ordinary with fee upon the death or other avoydance of John Jenkins or

William Howes, and then to enjoy either of the places of musician for the violin, wind instruments, or private musick, which shall first become voyd.

L. C. Vol. 745, *p.* 377.

1676, *April* 6.

Fee received of Mr. Gamble, musician, for his debenter, 1675.

L. C. Vol. 458.

1676, *April* 16.

Fee of 5s. received of Mr. Bates, musician, for a debenter, 1674.

L. C. Vol. 458.

1676, *April* 16.

To Thomas Bates, musician, the sum of £16 : 2 : 6 for livery due at St. Andrew, 1674.

L. C. Vol. 715, *p.* 14.

1676, *April* 24.

To Pelham Humphryes, musician, two liveries of £16 : 2 : 6 each, due at St. Andrew, 1672 and 1673.

L. C. Vol. 715, *pp.* 9, 14.

1676, *April* 26.

Order for rich crimson velvet, for two trumpeters to attend Mr. Hyde.

Order for three yards of black material for James Greene, a Chappell boy gone off.

L. C. Vol. 205, *entry* 64.

1676, *April* 29.

Assignment by Jeoffrey Banester one of the musicians in ordinary for the violin, of all the wages due to him, to William Parkes, of the parish of St. Margaret's, Westminster, in consideration of the sum of £150 paid by the said Parkes.

L. C. Vol. 195, *p.* 52*d.*

1676, *May* 3.

Warrant to admit Richard Tomlinson musician in ordinary to his Majesty for the violin, in the place of William Howes, deceased.

Warrant to admit Edmund Flower musician in ordinary to his Majesty for the wind instruments, in the place of William Howes, deceased.

L. C. Vol. 480, *p.* 103; *L. C. Vol.* 745, *p.* 384.

1676, *May* 6.

To John Smyth, musician, the sum of £32 : 5, for liveries due St. Andrew, 1671 and 1672.

L. C. Vol. 715, *p.* 9.

1676, *May* 8.

Warrant to admit James Bannister musician in ordinary to his Majesty for the violin, in the place and upon the surrender of Henry Comer, with all rights and profitts.

L. C. Vol. 480, *p.* 103 ; *L. C. Vol.* 745, *p.* 385.

1676, *May* 12.

To Anthony Robert, musician, the sum of £16 : 2 : 6 for livery due St. Andrew, 1672.

L. C. Vol. 715, *p.* 9.

1676, *May* 15.

Warrant to prepare a Bill granting Richard Tomlynson the office of musician in ordinary to his Majesty for the violin in the place of William Howes, deceased, with wages of £46 12s. 8d. yearly, to commence 25 March, 1676.

L. C. Vol. 745, *p.* 389.

1676, *Pentecost.*

Payment to each of the following trumpeters to the late King Charles I. for their pensions, the sum of £19. 17. 8. :—

Robert Ramsay	George Bosgrave
Samuel Markland	William Porter
Henry Peacock	

L. C. Vol. 464.

1676, *May* 24.

Warrant for the payment of £20 to Jervase Price, Esq., his Majesty's sergeant trumpeter, for the present supply of James Castles, one of his Majesty's trumpeters who is going upon his Majesty's service to Dantrick.

L. C. Vol. 745, *p.* 392.

1676, *May* 24.

Warrant to prepare a Bill granting Thomas Farmer the office of musician in ordinary to his Majesty for the violin, in the place of John Strong, deceased, with the wages and fees of £46. 12s. 8d. yearly, to commence 29 September, 1675.

L. C. Vol. 745, *p.* 392.

1676, *May* 26.

Warrant for payment of £44 to :—

Isaack Staggins	Edmund Flower
Thomas Fitz	Richard Tomlynson
Henry Brockwell	John Twist
Jeoffery Aleworth	Joseph Fashion

Musicians in ordinary to his Majesty for attendance at Newmarket for 22 days, from 27 March to 17 April, 1676, at the rate of 5s. by the day to each of them.

L. C. Vol. 745, *p.* 401.

1676, June 9.

Warrant for the payment of £40 to Jervas Price his Majesty's sergeant trumpeter, for liveries for the present supply of John Christmas and Albion Thompson, two of his Majesty's trumpeters that are to attend the Hon. Lawrence Hyde, master of his Majesty's Roabes, to Poland.

L. C. Vol. 745, p. 406 ; L. C. Papers, Bundle 13.

1676, June 15.

Whereas Bernard Symth hath petitioned for leave to take his course at law against John Hingston for debt due, order that John Hingston give an appearance at the common law.

L. C. Vol. 655.

1676, St. John the Baptist.

Payment of £29 : 16 : 8 to Henry Gregory for clothing two boys and educating them in the art of music for half a year.

L. C. Vol. 464.

1676, St. John the Baptist.

Payment of £80 to John Blow, master of the children of the King's Chappell, for keeping and teaching two singing boys for the space of two years.

L. C. Vol. 464.

1676, June.

Material, and two swords with silver handles for two trumpeters for Poland.

L. C. Vol. 205, entries 67 and 68.

1676, July 4.

Assignment by Jeffery Banester, of the parish of St. Dunstan's in the West, one of the band of violins in ordinary to his Majesty, in consideration of the sum of £150 paid by Thomas Bates, of the parish of St. Margaret's Westminster, of all the wages of £46. 12s. 8d. per annum due to him, to the said Thomas Bates.

L. C. Vol. 195, p. 47d.

1676, July 10.

Warrant to pay John Blow, master of the children of his Majesty's Chappell Royall, £30 yearly, for the maintenance of Austin Benford, late child of the Chappell, whose voice is changed and is gon from the Chappell ; also for William Searle, late child of the Chappell, the same amount, with the customary outfit of clothing for each of them.

L. C. Vol. 745, p. 423 ; L. C. Papers, Bundle 13.

1676, *July* 10.

Warrant to prepare a Bill granting Richard Hart the office of musician in ordinary for the lute, in the place of Robert Smyth, deceased, with the wages of £40 by the year, and an allowance of £16. 2s. 6d. yearly for livery, to commence 29 September, 1675.

L. C. Vol. 745, *p.* 425.

1676, *July* 18.

Warrant for payment of £212. 5s. to Jervas Price, his Majesty's sergeant trumpeter, for John Crowther, Milbert Morris and Thomas Cresswell, three of his Majesty's trumpeters, for their charges and expenses while attending his Grace the Duke of Richmond, his Majesty's ambassador to Denmark, in the year 1672, for the space of 283 days, from 29 March to the 6 January following, at the rate of 5s. by the day to each of them. Some of them have since been imployed in his Majesty's service beyond the seas, so that they could not bring in their bills for their service at that tyme.

L. C. Vol. 745, *p.* 424.

1676, *July* 24.

Assignment by Mathew Locke, of the parish of the Blessed Mary, alias Savoy, in the County of Middlesex, composer in ordinary for his Majesty's violins, of the sum of £174. 10s. 7½d. due to him out of the Treasury Chamber, for three years and three-quarters' salary, to Thomas Whitfield, of the parish of St. Martins in the Fields.

L. C. Vol. 195, *p.* 45.

1676, *August* 1.

A catalogue of severall Services and Anthems that have been transcribed into the books of his Majesty's Chappell Royall since anno 1670 to Midsummer, 1676:—

> Farrant's High Service.
> Mr. Humphryes' service.
> Mr. Blowe's service in A.
> Mr. Blowe's service in G.
> Mr. Blowe's Benedicite.
> His Te Deum to the Benedicite.
> Mr. Tucker's Benedicite service.
> Dr. Child's Benedicite service.
> Dr. Child's evening service in G.
> Mr. Ferrabosco's evening service.

Dr. Rogers' service in E.
Dr. Rogers' sharpe service in D.
Dr. Child's Te Deum to his Benedicite.
Dr. Rogers' service in G.
Dr. Rogers' evening service in A.
Mr. Wise's service.
Mr. Henry Alldridg's service.
Dr. Child's service in E flatt.
Dr. Child's service in A re.

Anthems.

Turn thou us O good Lord - - -	John Blow.
In Thee O Lord - - - -	Jefferies.
O God, the proud - - - -	Bird.
I will magnifie Thee - - -	Hooper.
O prayse God in his holynesse - -	White.
O give thanks - - - - -	Mr. Tucker.
Hear my prayer, O God - - -	Battens.
Teach mee, O Lord - - -	Dr. Rogers.
O prayse the Lord - - - -	Dr. Child.
O prayse God in his Holynesse -	Gregory.
Behold how good, etc. - - -	Blow.
Blessed is he that considereth the poor -	Wise.
Prepare ye the way - - - -	Wise.
Awake - - - - - -	Wise.
How long - - - - -	Dr. Gibbons.
Thou O God - - - - -	Dr. Holder.
Have pitty - - - - -	Wise.
O prayse our God - - - -	Dr. Holder.
By the waters of Babylon - -	Ferrabosco.
The Lord said unto my Lord - -	Wise.
I beheld and lo a great - - -	Dr. Rogers.
O clap your hands - - - -	Dr. Rogers.
O pray for the peace of Jerusalem -	Dr. Child.
O clap your hands - - - -	Mr. Tucker.
I was glad - - - - -	Mr. Tucker.
Praise the Lord ye servants - -	Mr. Tucker.
O Lord I have sinned - - -	Mr. Blow.
Lord how are they increased - -	Mr. Blow.
Lord how long - - - -	Mr. Tucker.
Wherewithall - - - - -	Mr. Tucker.
This is the day - - - -	Mr. Tucker.

My heart is fixed - - - - - Mr. Tucker.
Unto thee O Lord - - - - - Mr. Tucker.
Comfort ye my people - - - - Mr. Tucker.
Have mercy upon mee O God - - - Mr. Humfryes.
How are the mighty fallen - - - Mr. Wise.
I will magnifie thee, O God my King - Mr. Tucker.
O praise God in his holinesse - - - Mr. Wise.
By the waters of Babilon - - - Mr. Wise.
The earth is the Lords - - - - Dr. Child.
O be joyfull - - - - - - Mr. Humfryes.
Not unto us O Lord - - - - Mr. Lock.
The Lord is my shepherd - - - Mr. Wise.
Thou art my king O God - - - Dr. Child.
The prodigall - - - - - - Mr. Wise.
O lett my mouth be filled - - - Dr. Child.
Behold how good and joyfull - - - Dr. Child.
Lett God arise - - . - - Dr. Child.
O sing unto the Lord - - - - Dr. Child.
O Lord our Governor - - - Mr. Isaac Blockwell.
Christ riseing - - - - - - Mr. Wise.
Lord what is man - - - - Mr. William Turner.
O Lord God of hosts - - - - Mr. Turner.
If the Lord himselfe - - - - Mr. Henry Alldridg.
O how amiable - . - - - Mr. Blow.
God is our hope and strength - - - Mr. Blow.
O God wherefore art thou absent - - Mr. Blow.
Save mee O God - - - - - Mr. Blow.
Lord teach us to number our dayes - - Mr. Humfryes.
Heare O heavens - - - - - Mr. Humphryes.
O Lord thou has searched mee out - - Mr. Blow.
Lord thou has been our refuge - - Mr. Turner.
Like as the hart - - - - - Mr. Humphryes.
O Lord my God - - - - - Mr. Humphryes.
O Lord rebuke me not - - - - Dr. Child.

L. C. Vol. 745, *pp.* 431-433.

1676, *August* 7.

Warrant to prepare a Bill granting Jeoffery Ayleworth the office of musician in ordinary to his Majesty for the sagbutts, in the place of John Strong, deceased, with the wages of 1s. 8d. by the day and £16. 2s. 6d. yearly for livery, to commence 29 September, 1675.

L. C. Vol. 745, *p.* 440.

1676, *August* 8.

Fee of 5s. received of Mr. Markland, pentionary trumpeter, for his debenter, 1676; fee of 30s. received of Mr. Henry Gregory for 5 debenters, St. John the Baptist, 1674, St. Andrew, 1674; St. John the Baptist, 1675, St. Andrew, 1675; St. John the Baptist, 1676.

L. C. Vol. 458.

1676, *August* 12.

Warrant to admit Giles Stevens musician in ordinary to his Majesty for the violin, in the place of Henry Dove.

L. C. Vol. 745, *p.* 442.

1676, *August* 21.

Warrant to pay eight of his Majesty's musicians £132 for their rydeing charges and other expenses in their attendance upon his Majesty in his Chappell at Windsor by the space of 66 days, from 7 July to 11 September, 1675, at the rate of 5s. by the day:—

Edward Hooton,	William Gregory,
John Twist,	Thomas Bates,
Charles Coleman,	Thomas Finell,
John Lilley,	John Gamble.

L. C. Vol. 745, *p.* 448.

1676, *August* 31.

Fee of £3 : 19 received of Mr. Staggins for entring of a double warrant and a letter of attourney, and for two debenters as master of the musick, vizt. 1674 : 1675 : and one debenter in the place of Richard Hudson, vizt. for 1672 : 1673 : 1674 : and another for 1675.

L. C. Vol. 458.

1676, *September* 8.

Warrant to admit James Castle trumpeter in ordinary to his Majesty to attend the Lord Lieutenant of Ireland for the tyme being, in the place of William Castle, deceased.

L. C. Vol. 480, *p.* 189 ; *L. C. Vol.* 745, *p.* 453.

1676, *September* 9.

Warrant to prepare a Bill for a patent granting Thomas Purcell the office of one of his Majesty's musicians in ordinary for the private musick, in the place of Dr. John Wilson, deceased, with wages of £20 by the year to commence 25 March, 1674.

L. C. Vol. 745, *p.* 458.

1676, *September* 19.

Warrant dormant to pay to John Blow, appointed master of the children of the Chappell Royall, in place of Pelham Humphries, deceased, the sum of £80, for keeping and teaching two singing boys, to be educated in the private musick, for two years ended St. John Baptist last past, and henceforth to pay him £40 per annum.

L. C. Vol. 815, *p.* 67.

1676, *Michaelmas.*

Payment of £40 to Dr. John Blow, master of the children of the King's Chappell, for the custody and teaching of two singing boys for a year. In quarterly payments of £10 at Christmas, the Annunciation, St. John the Baptist and Michaelmas.

L. C. Vols. 157 *and* 464.

Accounts ending Michaelmas, 1676.

Accounts for liveries of £16 : 2 : 6 each, for the following musicians to the King :—

John Hingston	John Gamble
Humphrey Madge	John Banister
William Gregory	John Clement
Thomas Laneir	Thomas Purcell (3 liveries)
Anthony Roberts	William Child
Mathew Lock	Charles Coleman
John Jenkins	Theophilus Fitz
John Lilly	John Goodgroome
John Harding	William Clayton
Alphonso Marsh	John Blow
Thomas Bates	Edward Hooten

Account paid to Nicholas Staggins master of the King's music in the place of Lewis Grabu for the years 1674 and 1675 ; £32 : 5.

To the same in the place of Richard Hudson for the years 1672, 1673, 1674 and 1675 ; £64 : 10.

Account for annual pensions for the following trumpeters to the late King Charles I. :—

Robert Ramsay	George Bosgrave
Samuel Markland	William Porter
	Henry Peacock

Account of £59 : 13 : 4 paid to Henry Gregory for clothing and educating two boys in the art of music.

Account paid to John Blow, master of the boys of the Chappell Royall, for the keep of two boys and for teaching them singing for two years and one quarter; £90.

L. C. Vol. 65; *and Vol.* 157. *L. C. Papers, Bundle* 18.

1676, *October* 20.

To Anthony Robert, William Gregory, John Jenkins, John Lilly, musicians, £16 : 2 : 6 each for liveries due St. Andrew, 1673.

To Robert Ramsey, pentionary trumpeter, £19 : 17 : 8 for pension due Pentecost, 1674.

L. C. Vol. 715, *p.* 15.

1676, *October* 20.

Fees of 5s. each paid for their debentures of 1673 by Mr. Lilley, Mr. Robert and William Gregory.

L. C. Vol. 458.

1676, *October* 21.

To Charles Colman, musician, £16 : 2 : 6 for livery due St. Andrew, 1673.

L. C. Vol. 715, *p.* 15.

1676, *October* 21.

Fees of 5s. paid by Mr. Lilley for Mr. Jenkins' debenter, 1675; by Mr. Lanier for his own debenter, 1675; and by Mr. Colman for his debenter, 1673.

L. C. Vol. 458.

1676, *October* 23.

Warrant to prepare a Bill for a patent to grant to Thomas Heywood the office of musician in ordinary to his Majesty for the lute, in the place of John Rogers, deceased, with wages of £100 by the year, the first payment to commence Michaelmas, 1676.

L. C. Vol. 745, *p.* 466; *Vol.* 480, *p.* 103.

1676, *October* 23.

To Edward Hooton and Nicholas Staggins, musicians, £16 : 2 : 6 each for liveries due St. Andrew, 1672.

To John Hingeston, Edward Hooton, John Harding, John Wilson, Lewis Grabu, Humphrey Madge, William Clayton and Nicholas Staggins, musicians, £16 : 2 : 6 each for liveries due St. Andrew, 1673.

L. C. Vol. 715, *pp.* 9, 15, 25.

1676, *October* 23.

Fees of 5s. each, paid for their debenters of 1673, by Mr. Madge, Mr. Clayton and Mr. Fitz.

1676, *October* 24.

Fees of 5s. each, paid by Mr. Blow for his debenter, 1675, and by Mr. Goodgroome for his debenter, 1673.

L. C. Vol. 458.

1676, *October* 25.

To Theophilus Fitz, musician, £16 : 2 : 6 for livery due St. Andrew, 1673.

L. C. Vol. 715, *p.* 15.

1676, *October* 25.

Warrant to admit Christopher Preston one of his Majesty's private musick to play upon the virginalls in the place of Dr. Gibbons, deceased.

L. C. Vol. 480, *p.* 103 ; *and Vol.* 745, *p.* 473.

1676, *October* 26.

To John Goodgroome, musician, £16 : 2 : 6 for livery due St. Andrew, 1673 ; to John Gamble, musician, £16 : 2 : 6 for livery due St. Andrew, 1674 ; to John Blow, musician, £16 : 2 : 6 for livery due St. Andrew, 1675.

L. C. Vol. 715, *pp.* 15, 25.

1676, *October* 27.

To Mathew Lock, musician, £16 : 2 : 6 for livery due St. Andrew, 1673.

To George Bosgrove, pentionary trumpeter, £19 : 17 : 8 for pension due Pentecost, 1675.

L. C. Vol. 715, *pp.* 15, 16

1676, *October* 31.

To William Child, musician, two liveries of £16 : 2 : 6 each, due St. Andrew, 1672 and 1673.

L. C. Vol. 715, *pp.* 10, 16.

1676, *November* 2.

Account for making seventy-six surplices for the gentlemen and musicians of the Chappell Royall, at 5s. each ; and thirty-eight surplices for the Children of the Chappell Royall at 2s. 6d. each.

L. C. Vol. 205, *entry* 111.

1676, *November* 2.

To Alphonso Marsh, musician, £16 : 2 : 6 for livery due St. Andrew, 1673.

L. C. Vol. 715, *p.* 16

1676, *November* 8.

Warrant to pay Mr. John Blow, master of the children of the Chappell the sum of £143 for the children learneing on the lute, violin and theorbo, and for strings and other expenses ;

and for his charges and expenses in his going to Windsor, Oxford, Gloucester, Hereford and Worcester to fetch boyes from these Quires for his Majesty's Chappell Royall in 1676; and for a nurse, chamber rent and firing for keeping of John Cherrington, one of the children of the Chappell, being sick of spotted fever.

L. C. Vol. 745, *p.* 478.

1676, *November* 17.

Henry Gregory for teaching two boys, his allowance at Midsummer 1674, St. Andrew, 1674, and Midsummer, 1675, £89. 10. 0. Also his allowance at St. Andrew, 1675 and Midsummer, 1676, £59 : 13 : 4.

L. C. Vol. 715, *pp.* 16 *and* 25.

1676, *St. Andrew.*

Payment of £16. 2. 6. to each of the following musicians to the King, for their yearly liveries : —

Anthony Roberts	Alphonso Marsh
John Hingeston	John Clements
William Gregory	Thomas Purcell (three
Humphrey Madge	liveries)
Thomas Lanier	William Child
John Smith (" vacatur ")	John Goodgroome
John Gamble	Theophilus Fittz
John Jenkins	Charles Coleman
John Lillie	William Clayton
John Harding	John Blow
John Banister	Edward Hooton
Mathew Lock	William Turner
Thomas Bates	

Nicholas Staggins (in the place of Lewis Grabu and in the place of Richard Hudson).

Francis Cruys, liveries for the years 1673 to 1676.

Payment of £29. 16. 8. to Henry Gregory for clothing two boys, and educating them in the art of music for half a year.

L. C. Vol. 464.

1676, *December* 4.

Fee of £1 received of Mrs. Cook for her husband's debenter, 1671, as Musitian, and for 3 quarters for keeping Boys, due at Midsomer, 1672.

L. C. Vol. 458.

1676, *December* 5.

Bill for shoes for Searle and Benford, two Chappell boys dismist.

L. C. Papers, Bundle 12.

1676, *December* 6.

Henry Cooke, musician, his livery at St. Andrew, 1671, and for keeping and teaching two boys for three quarters of a year ending Midsummer, 1672 inclusive, £46 . 2 . 6.

Pelham Humphryes for teaching two boys a year and a half, at Christmas, 1673, £60.

L. C. Vol. 715, *pp.* 10 *and* 16.

1676, *December* 9.

To Robert Ramsey, Henry Peacock, Samuel Markland, William Porter and George Bosgrove, pentionary trumpeters, £99 . 8 . 4 for pensions due Pentecost, 1673.

L. C. Vol. 715, *p.* 10.

1676, *December* 12.

Warrant for the payment of the following items to Henry Brockwell, keeper of his Majesty's instruments :—

For a new base violin, £10.

Bow and standing case, £10.

For mending his Majesty's instruments and for strings since 1675, £4.

For removing his Majesty's instruments from London to Windsor and to Newmarkett and delivering backwards and forwards for 3 years, £5.

For strings for himself for 3 years, £6.

L. C. Vol. 745, *p.* 490.

1676, *December* 13.

Letter of assignment from John Gamble, of the parish of St. Gyles in the Feilds, one of his Majesty's musicians, appointing John Spicer, of the parish of St. Martin's in the Feilds, his true and lawful attorney.

L. C. Vol. 198, *p.* 112d.

1676, *December* 15.

Warrant for the liveries of William Turner, sworn one of his Majesty's private musick in ordinary for the lute and voyce, in the place of Capt. Cook, deceased, and for Francis Cruys, musician in ordinary to his Majesty for the violin, in the place and upon the surrender of John Smyth. To commence St. John Baptist, 1673.

L. C. Vol. 745, *p.* 493.

1676, *December* 18.

Thomas Purcell as groom of the King's robes, at All Saints, 1676, £40; and 3 liveries as musician at St. Andrew, 1676, £48 . 7 . 6.

L. C. Vol. 715, *p.* 35.

1676, *December* 18.

Fee of 15s. received of Mr. Thomas Purcell for 3 debenters as musician.

L. C. Vol. 458.

1676, *December* 19.

To Samuel Markland, pentionary trumpeter, £19 . 17 . 8 for pension due Pentecost, 1674.

L. C. Vol. 715, *p.* 17.

1676, *December* 22.

John Blow for keeping and teaching two boys for 2 years ending Midsummer, 1676, £80 . 0 . 0 .

L. C. Vol. 715, *p.* 35.

1676, *December* 23.

To Henry Peacock, pentionary trumpeter, £19 . 17 . 8 for pension due Pentecost, 1674.

To John Clements, musician, £16 . 2 . 6 for livery due St. Andrew, 1675.

L. C. Vol. 715, *pp.* 17, 26.

1676, *December* 28.

To John Bannister, musician, £16 . 2 . 6 for livery due St. Andrew, 1676.

L. C. Vol. 715, *p.* 35.

1676, *December* 29.

Edward Dyer appointed musician in ordinary without fee, for the first vacancy of violins or private musick.

L. C. Vol. 480, *p.* 103.

1676.

Account due to John Mawgridge, his Majesty's drum-major, for liveries for himself, four other drummers and a phife for the year 1676.

Account due to Symon Peirson, trumpeter, and two kettle-drummers, attending his Majesty's Troop of Guards, commanded by his Grace the Duke of Monmouth.

L. C. Vol. 205, *entries* 202*b*, 203*b*.

1676-7, *January* 2.

Warrant for the payment of £5 to Charles Evans, harper for the Italian harp, for strings for one year ending at Christmas, 1676.

L. C. Vol. 745, *p.* 511.

1676-7, *January* 17.

Appointment of the following violins to attend to practise Mons. Grabu's musick :—

Mr. Twist
  ,, Clayton
  ,, Farmer
  ,, Fitz, the elder
  ,, Fitz, the younger
  ,, Meyer

Mr. Greetinge
  ,, James Bannister
  ,, Fashion
  ,, Gamble
  ,, Flower
  ,, Ayleworth

L. C. Vol. 745, *p.* 521.

1676-7, *January* 22.

Warrant dormant to pay to William Turner, appointed one of the private musick in ordinary for the lute and voyce, in the place of Henry Cook, deceased, for his livery for five years, ending St. Andrew last past, the sum of £80. 12s. 6d., and to Francis Cruys, appointed one of the musicians in ordinary for the violin, in place and upon the surrender of John Smith, for his livery for four years ending St. Andrew last past, the sum of £64. 10s., and to deliver to them yearly henceforth the materials for their liveries.

L. C. Vol. 815, *p.* 90.

1676-7, *January* 24.

A sum of £29 : 16 : 8 paid to Henry Gregory, musician, for teaching and keeping two boys ; due S. Andrew, 1676.

L. C. Vol. 715, *p.* 37.

1676-7, *January* 26.

To Gregory Bosgrove, pentionary trumpeter, £19 . 17 . 8 for pension due Pentecost, 1676.

L. C. Vol. 715, *p.* 26.

1676-7, *February* 13.

Warrant for payment for one and twenty ells, three quarters of holland, for four whole shirts, four half shirts and for bands and cuffs for Henry Purcell, a child gone off from the Chappell.

L. C. Vol. 804, *p.* 41.

1676-7, *February* 26.

Warrant to pay Mr. John Blow £30 for the maintenance of John Waters, late child of the Chappell, whose voyce is changed and is gon from the Chappell; and to provide the usual outfit of clothing.

L. C. Vol. 745, *p.* 541 ; *L. C. Vol.* 205, *entry* 78b.

1676-7, *March* 12.

To William Porter, pentionary trumpeter, £19 . 17 . 8 for pension due Pentecost, 1674.

L. C. Vol. 715, *p.* 17.

1676-7, *March* 19.

Edward Wharton appointed drummer in the place of Richard Mawgridge.

L. C. Vol. 480, *p.* 190.

1677, *March* 25.

Payment of £10 on each of the Feast Days, the Annunciation, St. John Baptist, Michaelmas and Christmas, to John Blow, master of the children of the King's Chappell, for keeping and teaching two singing boys.

L. C. Vol. 464.

1677, *March* 26.

To Edward Hooton, musician £16 . 2 : 6 for livery due St. Andrew, 1674.

1677, *March* 27.

To Robert Ramsey, pentionary trumpeter, £19 . 17 . 8 for pension due Pentecost, 1675.

L. C. Vol. 715, *p.* 17.

1677, *March* 30.

Edward Hooton appointed musician in ordinary without fee, to come in ordinary with fee, for the violin in the private musick, upon the death of Thomas Fittz.

L. C. Vol. 480, *p.* 103.

1677, *April* 4.

To John Goodgroome, musician, £16 . 2 . 6 for livery due St. Andrew, 1674.

L. C. Vol. 715, *p.* 17.

1677, *April* 10.

John Twist appointed musician in ordinary without fee, to come in ordinary with fee upon the death or other avoydance of Thomas Fittz, violin, deceased.

L. C. Vol. 480, *pp.* 103, 191.

1677, *April* 12.

Warrant for payment of £80 . 12 . 6 to Thomas Purcell, musician to his Majesty, arrears of liveries due to him for the years 1662 to 1667.

Warrant for payment of £140 to him as groom of the robes, for the years 1665 to 1667, and 1669, at £40 a year.

L. C. Vol. 711, *p.* 60.

1677, *April* 13.

Letter of assignment from William Child, doctor in musique and one of the gentlemen of his Majesty's Chappell Royall, and of the consorte of wind instruments, appointing Thomas Haynes, sergeant of his Majesty's vestry, his true and lawful attorney.

L. C. Vol. 198, p. 113.

1677, *April* 14.

To Theophilus Fitz, musician, £16 . 2 . 6 for livery due St. Andrew, 1674.

L. C. Vol. 715, p. 18.

1677, *April* 23.

Account for two pair of shoes each, at 4s. 6d. a pair, to Searle, Benford, and Bartholomew Isaac, boys dismist from the Chapell Royall.

L. C. Vol. 205, entry 52b.

1677, *May* 5.

Petition of Lewis Grabu :—

Showing that the petitioner has lately fallen under very grievous misfortune, the greatest of which hath been His Majesty's willingness to receive another person into his place during pleasure. "Your Majesty was nevertheless graciously pleased a few days since to declare that the petitioner should receive the growing benefitt thereof until the arrears due to the petitioner should be paid to him, which he accordingly humbly presents in the paper annexed, which arrears being paid to the petitioner for the keeping him from arrests and the providing some subsistence for his distressed family, your petitioner shall, though with much greife, retire from being a meniall servant to Your Majesty. The petitioner therefore humbly prays Your Majesty according to your Royal compassion to a poor servant, guilty of no crime but misfortune, that you will give effectuall order for the speedy payment of the said arrears, and that in the meanwhile he may be maintained and supported as others are under all circumstances in the like case with him, and that all his salary may run on till the said arrears be paid."

Reference :—

His Majesty refers the consideration of this petition to the Lord Chamberlain, to cause the arrears due to be stated, and then report the same together with his Lordship's opinion thereon.

L. C. Vol. 746, p. 56.

1677, *May* 7.

To John Lilley, musician, £16 . 2 . 6 for livery due St. Andrew, 1674.

L. C. Vol. 715, p. 18.

1677, May 8.

Petition of John Singleton, Theophilus Fitz, Henry Brockwell, Edmund Flower and Joseph Fashion, part of His Majesty's band of violins, against Mr. Charles Killigrew, Master of the Revels, for dismissing them their attendance at the playhouse.

L. C. Vol. 655.

1677, May 8.

John Skyrme appointed drummer in ordinary for the first avoydance.

L. C. Vol. 480, *p.* 190.

1677, May 9.

To Samuel Markland, William Porter, and Henry Peacock, pentionary trumpeters, £59 . 13 for pensions due Pentecost, 1675.

1677, May 10 and 11.

To William Child, Anthony Robert, and John Harding, musicians, £16 . 2 . 6 each for liveries due St. Andrew, 1674.

L. C. Vol. 715, *p.* 18.

1677, May 14.

Letter referring to a petition of Lewis Grabu, late Master of His Majesty's musick concerning arrears of salary due to him until 29 September, 1674, at which time his place was disposed of to Mr. Staggins.

L. C. Vol. 618, *p.* 19.

1677, May 21.

Pelham Humphreys, for teaching two boys half a year, at Midsummer, 1674, £20.

John Blow, musician, for livery at St. Andrew, 1676, £16 : 2 : 6; and for teaching two boys one quarter ending Michaelmas, 1676, £10.

L. C. Vol. 715, *pp.* 18 *and* 35.

1677, May 22.

Order to Mr. Staggins, master of his Majesty's musick, and in his absence to Mr. Lock who officiates for him :—

That all His Majesty's musitians doe attend to practise in the theatre at Whitehall at such tymes as Madame Le Roch and Mr. Paisible shall appoint for the practising of such musick as is to be in the French comedy to be acted before His Majesty on the 29 May instant.

L. C. Vol. 746, *p.* 38.

1677, *Pentecost.*

Payment of £19 . 17 . 8 to each of the following trumpeters to the late King Charles I. for their pensions :

Robert Ramsay   William Porter
Samuel Markland   Henry Peacock

L. C. Vol. 464.

1677, *May 24.*

Account for velvet for drum-cases, 18s.
For 4 yards of bayse for a drum-case, 8s.

L. C. Vol. 205, *entry* 73*b.*

1677, *May 28.*

Payment to John Mawgridge, drum major, his livery from Michaelmas, 1676 to Michaelmas, 1677.

L. C. Vol. 407, *entry* 73*c.*

1677, *June* 1.

Order to supply particulars for liveries for Symon Pearson, trumpeter attending the Troop of Guards under the Duke of Monmouth, and for the kettledrummer attending the Queenes Majesty's Troop of Guards commanded by Sir Philip Howard, and for the kettledrummer to the Troop of Horse under the command of Capt. Legg.

L. C. Vol. 746, *p.* 54.

1677, *June* 5.

Report :—

" In observance of Your Majesty's reference upon the petition of Lewis Grabu by the Hon. Sir Joseph Williamson, one of Your Majesty's Secretaries of State, I do humbly certifie that there is due in arrears to Lewis Grabu, late Master of Your Majesty's music, the sums following in these several offices, vizt. :—

Out of Your Majesty's Exchequer, the sum of £450; out of the office of the Treasury Chamber, £145. 4s. 6d. ; and out of the Great Wardrobe, £32. 5s. And I find his condition to be very poor and miserable, all which I humbly submit to Your Majesty's wisdom."

(Signed)   ARLINGTON.

L. C. Vol. 746, *p.* 56.

1677, *June* 5.

Thomas Barwell appointed trumpeter in ordinary in the place of James Castle.

L. C. Vol. 480, *p.* 188.

1677, June 9.

To John Jenkins and William Gregory, musicians, £16 . 2 . 6 each for liveries due St. Andrew, 1674.

Vol. 715, *p.* 18.

1677, June 12.

To Robert Ramsey, pentionary trumpeter, £19 . 17 . 8 for pension due Pentecost, 1676.

L. C. Vol. 715, *p.* 26.

1677, June 12.

Account for boots for fifteen trumpeters, one kettle-drummer in ordinary, four drummers and a phife.

Also for a trumpeter and two kettle-drummers to the King's Guards.

Shoes for twelve children of the Chapel.

L. C. Vol. 205, *entry* 82b.

1677, June 14.

Account for liveries for sixteen trumpeters, one kettle-drummer, four drummers and one phife, in attendance upon the Duke of Monmouth, Lord Hawley and Sir Philip Howard.

L. C. Vol. 205, *entries* 79b *and* 96b.

1677, June 14.

To Alphonso Marsh, musician, £16 . 2 . 6 for livery due St. Andrew, 1674.

L. C. Vol. 715, *p.* 18.

1677, June 19.

To Charles Coleman, musician, £16 . 2 . 6 for livery due St. Andrew, 1674.

L. C. Vol. 715, *p.* 19.

1677, June 19.

Account for worsted hose for Isaac and Waters, two Chappell boys gone off.

Also two suites for Isaac, a Chappell boy dismist.

Also coloured Suites with all small furniture, for the Chappell boys Isaac, Waters, Benford and Searle.

Also cloth for John Walter, a Chappell boy gone off.

L. C. Vol. 205, *entries* 98b, 99b, 129b.

1677, June 22.

To Nicholas Staggins, musician, £16 . 2 . 6 for livery due St. Andrew, 1674; and on June 23, as musician in another quality, £16 . 2 . 6 for livery due St. Andrew, 1674.

L. C. Vol. 715, *p.* 26.

1677, *St. John the Baptist.*

Payment of £29 . 16 . 8 to Henry Gregory for clothing two boys and educating them in the art of music for half a year.

L. C. Vol. 464.

1677, *June* 24.

Will (dated as above) translated out of the French, and letters of administration of Anthony Robert, musick master dwelling in the city of London :

He desires that he may be buried in Somerset Chappell, in which he served the deceased Queen Mother, Henrietta Maria of France, mother of the now King of England, as musick master for the space of forty years. " If this cannot be done, that at least it may be according to the ordinary rites of the catholiques in this country, charging and commanding my beloved wife, Anne Basile, whome I name executrix of this my last will, to cause a hundred masses to be said for the rest of my soul as soon as she can, according to the pious use of all those who dye in the faith of the Roman Catholique Church, from the which I will not be separated neither in life or death."

He leaves his entire estate to his wife Anne Basile, and " seeing God hath given me authority over my children which shall remain alive, I command unto all of them to honour their mother after my death and to give her more respect than during my life, and to help her in all her necessities as children well educated ought to do." Also that they shall live in perfect union and intelligence one amongst another, and forbidding them upon any pretext to dispute this his last will and testament.

L. C. Vol. 196, *pp.* 9, 10.

1677, *June* 27.

To Thomas Lanier, musician, £16 . 2 . 6 for livery due St. Andrew, 1675.

L. C. Vol. 715, *p.* 26.

1677, *June.*

Account for holland for William Holder, William Searle, Austin Bendford and John Waters, foure Chappell boyes gone off.

L. C. Vol. 205, *entry* 161b ; *L. C. Papers, Bundle* 22.

1677, *July* 19.

John Christmas, one of his Majesty's trumpeters appointed to attend the Honble. Lawrence Hyde, his Majesty's Ambassador to the King of Poland, being killed there and his Majesty's silver trumpet lost, warrant to make and deliver to Jervas Price His Majesty's serjeant trumpeter, a silver trumpet in place of the one lost.

L. C. Vol. 602, *p.* 6.

1677, *July* 20 *and* 21.

To William Clayton and John Hingeston, musicians, £16 . 2 . 6 each for liveries due St. Andrew, 1674.

L. C. Vol. 715, *p.* 19.

1677, *July* 25 *and* 26.

To Francis Cruys, musician, for livery due St. Andrew, 1673 and William Turner, musician, for livery due St. Andrew, 1674, £16 . 2 . 6 each.

L. C. Vol. 715, *p.* 36.

1677, *July* 30.

Warrant to admit Robert Bishop trumpeter in ordinary to his Majesty, to attend upon the Lord Lieutenant of Ireland for the time being, in the place of Patrick Ray.

L. C. Vol. 480, *p.* 188 ; *and Vol.* 746, *p.* 100.

1677, *July* 31.

To Mathew Lock, musician, £16 . 2 . 6 for livery due St. Andrew, 1674.

L. C. Vol. 715, *p.* 19.

1677, *August* 8.

To Francis Cruys, musician, £32 . 5 for liveries due St. Andrew, 1675 and 1676.

L. C. Vol. 715, *p.* 36.

1677, *August* 18.

To Humphrey Madge, musician, £16 . 2 . 6 for livery due St. Andrew, 1674.

L. C. Vol. 715, *p.* 19.

1677, *August* 22.

To John Gamble, musician, £16 . 2 . 6 for livery due St. Andrew, 1675.

L. C. Vol. 715, *p.* 26.

1677, *September* 7.

To Francis Cruys, musician, £16 . 2 . 6 for livery due St. Andrew, 1674.

L. C. Vol. 715, *p.* 36.

1677, *September* 10.

Henry Pursell appointed composer in ordinary with fee for the violin to his Majesty, in the place of Mathew Lock, deceased.

Edward Hooton appointed musician in ordinary with fee for the violin in the private musick, in the place of Thomas Fittz, deceased.

L. C. Vol. 480, *p.* 103.

1677, *September* 16.

Francis Garrard appointed musician in ordinary with fee for the wind instruments, in the place of Edward Hooton, surrendered.

L. C. Vol. 480, *p.* 103.

1677, *September* 17.

Certificate dated " Ratclif, the 17th of 7ber 1677." " That Mr. William Porter, late trumpeter of the Loyall Eagle, being very sick, was left at the Island of St. Helena behind the shipp, in order for the recovery of his health, the 5th of June last past."

Signed by James Bounell, commander, and John Bonne, purser.

L. C. Vol. 198, *p.* 119.

1677, *September* 18 *and* 19.

To John Lilly and Edward Hootton, musicians, £16 . 2 . 6 each, for liveries due St. Andrew, 1675.

L. C. Vol. 715, *p.* 27.

1677, *September* 20.

Account for clothing for William Holder, William Searl, Austin Benford and Bartholomew Isack, four Chappell boyes gone off.

L. C. Vol. 205, *entry* 139*b.*

1677, *September* 22.

Warrant to pay to Gervas Price, his Majesty's serjeant trumpeter, the sum of £60 for himself with four of his Majesty's trumpeters, for their expenses in attending upon the Prince of Orange on his voyage from Holland to England.

L. C. Vol. 746, *p.* 122.

1677, *September* 26 *and* 27.

To John Clement and Thomas Lanier, musicians, £16 . 2 . 6 each for liveries due St. Andrew, 1676.

L. C. Vol. 715, *p.* 36.

1677, *September* 29.

Letter of assignment from Captain Thomas Bates, of Westminster, one of the musicians in ordinary to his Majesty, to John Broadhurst of all sums of £16 : 2 : 6 yearly, from his Majesty's great Wardrobe, from the time of his Majesty's happy Restauration until S. Andrew, 1671.

L. C. Vol. 198, *p.* 133.

1677, Michaelmas.

Payment of £40 to John Blow, master of the children of the King's Chappell, for the custody and teaching of two singing boys for a year. In quarterly payments of £10 at Christmas, the Annunciation, St. John the Baptist and Michaelmas.

L. C. Vols. **157** *and* **464** *and Vol.* **715**, *p.* **37.**

Accounts ending Michaelmas, 1677.

Account paid for cloth for William Holder, William Searle, Augustine Benford, John Waters and Bartholomew Isaack, boys discharged from the Chappell Royall.

Accounts for liveries for :—

John Jervis Price, the king's chief trumpeter.

Simon Peirson, trumpeter.

John Mawgridge, chief drummer.

Accounts for liveries of £16 : 2 : 6 each, for the following musicians to the King :—

John Hingestone	John Gamble
Humphrey Madge	John Banister
William Gregory	John Clement
Thomas Lanier	Thomas Purcell (3 liveries)
Anthony Roberts	William Child
Mathew Lock	Charles Coleman
John Jenkins	Theophilus Fittz
John Lilly	John Goodgroome
John Harding	William Clayton
Alphonso Marsh	John Blow
Thomas Bates	Edward Hooten.

Nicholas Staggins, master of musick in place of Lewis Grabu, and musician in ordinary in place of Robert Hudson, deceased.

William Turner, for the years 1672 to 1676.

Francis Cruys, for the years 1673 to 1676.

Account for pensions of £19 : 17 : 8 to each of the following trumpeters to the late King Charles I. :—

Robert Ramsey	William Porter
Samuel Markland	Henry Peacock

Account of £59 : 13 : 4 paid to Henry Gregory for clothing and educating two boys in the art of music.

Account of £40 paid to John Blow, master of the boys of his Majesty's Chappell Royall, for his allowance for the keep of two boys and for teaching them singing.

L. C. Vol. **66** *; L. C. Vol.* **157.**

1677, *October* 8.

Appointment of Edward Dyer to be composer of musick in the place of Mathew Lock, deceased.

L. C. Vol. 480, *p.* 104.

1677, *October* 10.

Order for a bill containing a grant to Edward Hooton of the office of musician in ordinary to his Majesty for the violin in the private musick, in the place of Thomas Fittz, deceased, with the wages of £110 by the year, during his life. To commence from 29 September last past, 1677.

L. C. Vol. 746, *p.* 128.

1677, *October* 20.

Account for cloth for John Waters and Austin Benford, chapel boys gone off.

L. C. Vol. 205, *entry* 82c.

1677, *October* 20.

Warrant to admit John Scarlett trumpetter in ordinary to his Majesty, to attend upon the Lord Lieutenant of Ireland for the tyme being, in the place of Henry Thewer.

L. C. Vol. 746, *p.* 129.

1677, *October* 20.

Warrant to swear and admit John Twist musician in ordinary to his Majesty with fee for the violin, in the place of Thomas Fittz, deceased.

L. C. Vol. 746, *p.* 132.

1677, *October* 20.

Warrant to pay to Gervas Price, sergeant trumpeter, the sum of £200, to be by him paid to Mrs. Sarah Christmas, widow of John Christmas, one of His Majesty's trumpeters who was killed in Poland, which His Majesty hath been graciously pleased to give unto his widdow and child in regard of the loss of her husband.

L. C. Vol. 746, *p.* 132.

1677, *October* 29.

Petition of Sir Richard Beach against Humphrey Madge. Debt of £500.

L. C. Vol. 655.

1677, *November* 13.

Warrant to pay to John Farmer, heretofore a child of his Majesty's Chappell Royall, his voyce being changed and he being gon from the Chappell, the sum of £90, due for his maintenance for three years, from 25 March, 1672, by warrant from the Earl of Manchester, allowing him £30 yearly during His Majesty's pleasure, which allowance hath not been paid.

L. C. Vol. 746, p. 152.

1677, *November* 17.

To Theophilus Fitz, musician, £16 . 2 . 6 for livery due St. Andrew, 1675.

L. C. Vol. 715, p. 27.

1677, *November* 19.

Warrant to pay to Edward Hooton, Isaack Staggins, Jeoffery Aylyffe, Edward Flower, Joseph Fashion, John Twist, Thomas Farmer and Richard Tomlynson, eight of His Majesty's musicians, the sum of £30 for their rydeing charges and other expenses in their attendance on His Majesty at Newmarket for the space of fifteen days, from 16 April to 30 of the same month, 1677, at the rate of 5s. by the day each.

L. C. Vol. 746, p. 153.

1677, *November* 19.

Warrant to pay John Twist, Thomas Farmer, Jeoffery Aleworth, Richard Tomlynson, Isaack Staggins, Henry Brockwell and Edmund Flower, nine of His Majesty's musicians, the sum of £45 for their rydeing charges and other expenses in their attendance upon His Majesty at Newmarket for the space of 20 days, from 24 September to 13 October, 1677, at the rate of 5s. a day each.

L. C. Vol. 746, p. 153.

1677, *November* 20.

To Edward Hootton, musician, £16 . 2 . 6 for livery due St. Andrew, 1676.

L. C. Vol. 715, p. 36.

1677, *St. Andrew.*

Payment of £16 . 2 . 6 to each of the following musicians to the King for their liveries :—

Anthony Roberts	John Clements
John Hingston	Thomas Purcell
William Gregory	(three liveries)
Humphrey Madge	William Child
Thomas Lanier	John Goodgroome
John Gamble	Theophilus Fittz
John Jenkins	Charles Coleman
("ob. Oct. 1678")	William Clayton
John Lillie	John Blow
("ob. 25 Oct. 1678")	Edward Hooton

John Harding	William Turner
John Banister	Francis Cruys
Thomas Bates	Edward Dyer
Alphonso Marsh	

Nicholas Staggins (master of music in place of Lewis Grabu)
Nicholas Staggins (in the place of Richard Hudson)

Payment of £29 . 16 . 8 to Henry Gregory for clothing, and educating two boys in the art of music for half a year.

L. C. Vol. 464.

1677, *December* 5.

Order to prepare a bill for the Royal signature granting to John Twist the office of musician in ordinary to his Majesty for the violin, in the place of Thomas Fittz, deceased, with the wages of £46. 12s. 8d. yearly during his life. To commence 29 September, 1677.

L. C. Vol. 746, *p.* 165.

1677, *December* 5.

To Thomas Bates, musician, £16 . 2 . 6 for livery due St. Andrew, 1676.

L. C. Vol. 715, *p.* 37.

1677, *December* 5.

Warrant to pay to John Blow, master of the children of his Majesty's Chappell Royall, the sum of £120. 3s. for the children's learning on the lute, violin and theorbo, for fire and strings for the musick room in the Chappell, for ruled paper, pens and ink, for strings for the lutes and theorboes for one year ending at Michaelmas, 1677, and for the cure of a broaken legg of one of the children.

L. C. Vol. 746, *p.* 162.

1677, *December* 7.

Letter of authorisation from Thomas Lanier to Mr. Townsend, requesting that his debenture for his livery due St. Andrew, 1677, may be delivered to his mother, Mrs. Joyce Lanier.

L. C. Vol. 198, *p.* 124d.

1677, *December* 8.

To Theophilus Fitz, musician, £16 . 2 . 6 for livery due St. Andrew, 1676.

L. C. Vol. 715, *p.* 37.

1677, *December* 10.

Fees of 5s. each, for their debenters of 1675 paid by Mr. Coleman, Mr. Robert, Mr. Marsh, Mr. Harding and Mr. Madge, by Mr. Lilly for Mr. Jenkins; by Mr. Lillye for his debenter of 1676; by Mr. Goodgroome for debenters, 1675, 1676, 1677; by William Gregory for his debenters, 1676, 1677; by Mr. Purcell for his debenters, 3 at St. Andrew, 1677, as musician, and 1 at All Saints, 1677, as groom of the Robes; and by Mrs. Lanier for her sonne's debenter, 1677.

L. C. Vol. 458.

1677, *December* 10.

Order to prepare a bill for the Royal signature granting a patent to Edward Dyer of the office of composer of musick in ordinary to his Majesty, in place of Matthew Lock, deceased, with the fee of £40 yearly during his life. To commence 29 September, 1677.

L. C. Vol. 746, *p.* 167.

1677, *December* 11.

Liveries of £16. 2. 6. each, due at St. Andrew, 1675, were paid to the following musicians :—

December 11, to William Turner; December 13, to Thomas Bates; December 14, to Charles Coleman; December 15, to Nicholas Staggins, master of the King's musick; December 17, to William Gregory and John Goodgroome; December 18, to John Jenkins, Anthony Robert and William Child; December 19, to John Harding and William Clayton; December 20, to Alphonso Marsh; December 22, to Humphrey Madge.

L. C. Vol. 715, *pp.* 37, 27.

1677, *December* 23.

Symon Pearson appointed trumpeter in the place of Thomas Cresswell.

L. C. Vol. 480, *p.* 188.

1677, *December* 24.

Warrant for a patent to be granted to Francis Garrard, of the office of musician in ordinary to his Majesty, in the place of John Mason, deceased, with wages of 1s. 8d. by the day, and yearly livery of £16 : 2 : 6.

L. C. Vol. 747, *p.* 2.

1677, *December* 24.

To John Lilly, musician, £16 : 2 : 6 for livery due St. Andrew, 1676.

L. C. Vol. 715, *p.* 37.

1677, *December* 29.

Warrant to admit Edward Homerston trumpeter in ordinary to his Majesty, with fee in the place and upon the surrender of his father Edward Homerston, and to enjoy all fees, etc., thereunto belonging.

L. C. Vol. 480, *p.* 188; *and Vol.* 747, *p.* 7.

1677, *December* 29.

Fee of 10s. paid by Mr. Henry Gregory for his debenter for Michaelmas, 1677.

L. C. Vol. 458.

1677-8, *January* 16.

To John Hingston, musician, £16 : 2 : 6 for livery due St. Andrew, 1675. To Samuel Markland, pentionary trumpeter, £19 : 17 : 8 for pension due Pentecost, 1676.

January 18. To Mathew Lock, musician, £16 : 2 : 6 for livery due St. Andrew, 1675.

January 22. To William Porter and Henry Peacock, pentionary trumpeters, £19 : 17 : 8 each for pensions due Pentecost, 1676.

L. C. Vol. 715, *p.* 27.

1677-8, *January* 24 *and* 25.

To Henry Gregory, musician, £29 : 16 : 8 for keeping and teaching two boys, due St. Andrew, 1676.

To John Blow, musician, £40 for keeping and teaching two boys for one year ending at Michaelmas, 1677.

L. C. Vol. 715, *p.* 37.

1677-8, *January* 26.

Warrant to admit William Bull as trumpeter in ordinary to his Majesty, in the place of John Christmas, deceased.

L. C. Vol. 747, *p.* 21, *and L. C. Vol.* 480, *p.* 188.

1677-8, *January* 31.

To Nicholas Staggins, musician, £16. 2. 6, livery due St. Andrew, 1675.

L. C. Vol. 715, *p.* 28.

1678, *January to May.*

Frequent accounts for liveries and banners for drummers, trumpeters, kettledrummers, and for two hautboys, for the war against France.

L. C. Vol. 168. *L. C. Vol.* 205, *entries* 1-17c.

1677-8, *March* 5.

Order for the payment of £12 to Thomas Farmer, one of his Majesty's musicians, for a new treble violin bought by him for his Majesty's service.

The bill is signed by Mr. Mathew Locke in the absence of the master of the music, and also certified by Mr. Brockwell, keeper of his Majesty's instruments, that the violin is in his custody.

L. C. Vol. 747, *p.* 43.

1677-8, *March* 5.

Order to pay Edmund Flower, musician in ordinary to his Majesty, the sum of £15 for a double sagbutt bought by him for his Majesty's service, and of that value as shown by the bill annexed.

L. C. Vol. 747, *p.* 43.

1678, *March* 25.

Payment to John Blow, master of the children of the King's Chappell for keeping and teaching two singing boys, of £10 on each of the four Feast days, the Annunciation, St. John Baptist, Michaelmas and Christmas.

L. C. Vols. 464 *and* 465.

1678, *March* 27.

To William Turner, musician, £16. 2. 6 livery due St. Andrew, 1676.

L. C. Vol. 715, *p.* 37.

1678, *April* 15.

Order for the payment of £30 yearly to Mr. James Hart, one of the gentlemen of his Majesty's Chappell Royall, for the keeping of Edward Buttler, late child of the Chappell, whose voyce is changed and is gon from the Chappell. Order for the providing of certain clothes for the use of Edward Buttler.

Order for payment of £30 yearly to Dr. John Blow, master of the children of his Majesty's Chappell Royall, for the keeping of Francis Smyth, late child of the Chappell, whose voice is changed and is gon from the Chappell. With an Order for clothes for the use of Francis Smyth.

L. C. Vol. 747, *pp.* 61 *and* 62.

1678, *April* 15.

Order for the summer liveries of the 12 children of the Chappell to be delivered to Dr. John Blow, master of the children of his Majesty's Chappell Royall.

L. C. Vol. 747, *p.* 62.

1678, *April* 19.

Warrant to admit John Moss as musician in ordinary to his Majesty for the private musick, with fee, in the place and upon the surrender of John Jenkins, and to enjoy all rights belonging thereto.

L. C. Vol. 747, *p.* 68, *and L. C. Vol.* 480, *p.* 103, *also p.* 191.

1678, *April* 20.

Order to pay Charles Evans, harper for the Italian harp, the sum of £5 for strings for one year ending at Christmas, 1677.

L. C. Vol. 747, *p.* 71.

1678, *April* 23.

Receipt of Brook Bridges, esquire, auditor, for a book containing a warrant for two liveries for Nicholas Staggins master of the music, and another warrant for an allowance to John Blow for keeping and teaching two boys.

L. C. Papers, Bundle 18.

1678, *April* 29.

To William Turner, musician, £32. 5 for liveries due St. Andrew, 1672 and 1673.

L. C. Vol. 715, *p.* 37.

1678, *May* 3.

Warrant for the payment of £22 14s. to Henry Brockwell, keeper of his Majesty's musical instruments, for following items :—

	£	s.	d.
For a theorbo lute and standing case -	10	4	0
For mending instruments for a year and half - - - - -	5	0	0
For removing his Majesty's instruments three times to Newmarket and back again - - - -	3	10	0
For two years' strings for the instruments - - - - - -	4	0	0
	£22	14	0

L. C. Vol. 747, *p.* 82.

1678, *May* 4.

Warrant for the allowance of liveries to Jervas Price, his Majesty's sergeant trumpeter, to sixteen trumpeters and one kettledrummer.

L. C. Vol. 747, *p.* 83.

1678, *May* 4.

Warrant for the allowance of a livery to Symon Person, trumpeter attending his Majesty's troop of Guards commanded by his Grace the Duke of Monmouth, and to the kettle-drummers.

L. C. Vol. 747, *p.* 84.

1678, *May* 17.

Warrant to admit Richard Robinson as musician in ordinary to his Majesty, with fee, in the consort of wind musick, in the place and upon the surrender of Phillip Beckett.

L. C. Vol. 747, *p.* 87, *and L. C. Vol.* 480, *p.* 103, *also p.* 191.

1678, *May* 17.

Warrant to swear William Gregory as musician in ordinary without fee for the violl in the private musick, to come in ordinary with fee upon the death, surrender or other avoydance of Thomas Bates.

L. C. Vol. 747, *p.* 87, *and L. C. Vol.* 480, *p.* 103, *also p.* 191.

1678, *May* 17.

Warrant for the payment of £30 yearly to Michael Wise, late child of the Chappell, whose voyce was changed and was gon from the Chappell, which payment is to continue during his Majesty's pleasure.

L. C. Vol. 747, *p.* 88.

1678, *May* 19.

Payment of £19 17s. 8d. each to the following trumpeters for their pensions :—

Robert Ramsey	Henry Peacock
Samuel Markland	William Porter

L. C. Vol. 464.

1678, *May* 27.

Patent containing a grant to William Gregory during his natural life, as musician in ordinary for the private musick, in reversion after Thomas Bates, now one of his Majesty's private musick, of the sum of £50 as wages and fees yearly and £40 yearly payable out of the receipt of his Majesty's exchequer, at the four usual feasts of the year.

L. C. Vol. 747, *p.* 91.

1678, *May* 27.

A like patent granted to Richard Robinson of the place of musician in ordinary to his Majesty in the consort of wind musick upon the surrender of Philip Beckett, of £44 per annum and £16. 2s. 6d. yearly for livery.

L. C. Vol. 747, *p.* 97.

1678, *June* 8.

Warrant to admit Edmund Flower as musician in ordinary for the private musick without fee, to come in ordinary with fee upon the first vacancy.

L. C. Vol. 747, *p.* 106, *and L. C. Vol.* 480, *p.* 103.

1678, *June* 8.

Certificate that the following Frenchmen serve his Majesty as musicians in the Chappell Royall :—

> Maxent de Bresmes,
> Cir Felix alias La Montagn Cir.
> Peter Guiton.

L. C. Vol. 747, *p.* 106.

1678, *June* 19.

To Charles Coleman, musician, £16. 2. 6. for livery due St. Andrew, 1676.

L. C. Vol. 715, *p.* 37.

1678, *June* 22.

Account for boots and shoes for 13 trumpeters, 2 kettledrummers, 4 drummers, one phife, and for 12 children of the Chappell.

L. C Vol. 205, *entry* 73c.

1678, *St. John Baptist.*

Payment of £29. 16. 8. to Henry Gregory for clothing, and educating two boys in the art of music for half a year. *L. C. Vol.* 464.

1678, *July* 3.

Account for clothing for Edward Butler, a Chappell boy gone off.

L. C. Vol. 205, *entry* 66c.

1678, *July* 3.

Account for shoes for Francis Smith and James, Chappell boys dismist, and for clothing for the former, a Chappell boy gone off.

L. C. Vol. 205, *entries* 67c *and* 85c.

1678, *July* 3.

Accounts due to John Maugridge, his Majesty's drum major and to Jervice Price, his Majesty's sergeant trumpeter for liveries.

L. C. Vol. 205, *entries* 74c *and* 76c.

1678, *July.*

Accounts for crimson taffata for four drum scarfes ; and for silver hilted swords for 12 trumpeters, 4 drummers, one phife and 2 kettledrummers.

L. C. Vol. 205, *entries* 84c *and* 109c.

1678, *July* 8 *and* 9.

To William Clayton, John Harding, and John Jenkins, musicians, £16. 2. 6 each, and to Nicholas Staggins, musician and master of musick, £32. 5. for liveries due St. Andrew, 1676.

L. C. Vol. 715, *pp.* 37, 38.

1678, *July* 10.

Account for liveries for two hautboys for the troop of Granadeers under his Grace the Duke of Monmouth for the war against the French King.

L. C. Vol. 205, *entry* 17c ; *L. C. Vol.* 168.

1678, *July* 22.

To William Gregory, musician, £16. 2. 6. for livery due St. Andrew, 1676.

L. C. Vol. 715, *p.* 38.

1678, *July* 22.

Account for black felts and black castors for John Water, Austin Benford, Francis Smyth and Edward Butler, boys of the Chappell Royall gone off.

L. C. Vol. 205, *entry* 115*c*.

1678, *July* 29.

Received of Mr. Edward Dyer, musician, for entering his warrant.   [Sum not mentioned.]

L. C. Vol. 458.

1678, *August* 5 *and* 6.

To Samuel Markland, Robert Ramsay and William Porter, pentionary trumpeters, pensions of £19. 17. 8. each, due Pentecost, 1677.

L. C. Vol. 715, *p.* 38.

1678, *August* 9.

Account for red suits for Edward Buckler and Francis Smith, two Chappell boyes dismist.   Also for worsted hose and coats.

L. C. Vol. 205, *entries* 104*d*, 117*c*, *and* 120*c*.

1678, *August* 10.

To Humphrey Madge, musician, £16. 2. 6. for livery due St. Andrew, 1676.

August 13 : to Henry Peacock, pentionary trumpeter, £19. 17. 8. for pension due Pentecost, 1677.

L. C. Vol. 715, *p.* 38.

1678, *August* 19.

Order for the payment of £62. 16s. 6d. to Mr. John Hingston, keeper and repairer of his Majesty's organs, amounts set out as follows :—

	£	s.	d.
" For repairing several harpsicords for the practise of the private musick in the Hall and Privy Lodgings - -	5	15	0
For preparing and setting up an organ in the banquetting house at Whitehall, 1676, against Maundy Thursday	2	5	0
For setting up another 1677 - - -	2	5	0
For setting up another 1678 - - -	2	5	0

	£	s.	d.
For strings for the harpsicords and pedall for three years and a quarter	1	10	6
For portage of instruments for 3¼ years	2	15	0
To George Wyatt for blowing the organ at Whitehall for 2¼ years - -	17	0	0
For the rent of a large room to keep his Majesty's instruments in for 3¼ years	18	0	0
For mending and tuning the great organ in the Chappell at Whitehall at several times - - - -	3	10	6
For my charges to Windsor with an organ maker and two men to mend and tune the organ there in his Majesty's Chappell at several tymes	7	10	6 "

L. C. Vol. 747, *p.* 160.

1678, *September* 27.

Order for the allowance of a yearly livery to John Mosse in the place of John Jenkins, and Edmund Flower in the place of John Lylly, deceased, sworn musicians to his Majesty for the private musick.

L. C. Vol. 747, *p.* 198.

Accounts ending Michaelmas, 1678.

Accounts for liveries for the following musicians :—

John Hingston	Thomas Purcell
Humphrey Madge	(three liveries)
William Gregory	William Child
Thomas Lanier	Charles Colman
Anthony Roberts	Theophilus Fitz
John Jenkins	John Goodgroome
John Lilley	William Clayton
John Harding	John Blow
Alphonso Marsh	Edward Hooten
Thomas Bates	William Turner
John Gamble	Francis Cruys
John Banister	Edward Dyer
John Clement	

Nicholas Staggins, master of the King's musick in the place of Lewis Grabu.

Nicholas Staggins in the place of Robert Hudson.

Account for annual pensions for the trumpeters :—

Robert Ramsay	William Porter
Samuel Markland	Henry Peacock

Account paid to Henry Gregory for clothing, and educating two boys in the art of music.

Account paid to John Blow, master of the children of the King's Chappell, for the keeping and teaching of two singing boys.

L. C. Vol. 67 ; and Vol. 157.

1678, *November* 8.

Certificate that the place of John Lylly, one of his Majesty's musicians for the private musick, is disposed of to Isaack Staggins and Edmund Flower jointly, Edmund Flower only being sworn into the said place, but he to return half the profitts of the same to the said Isaack Staggins ; the latter, should he survive the said Flower, to be admitted to whole wages.

L. C. Vol. 480, p. 103, and L. C. Vol. 747, p. 185.

1678, *St. Andrew.*

Payment of £29. 16. 8. to Henry Gregory for clothing two boys and educating them in the art of music for half a year.

L. C. Vol. 465.

1678, *St. Andrew.*

Payment of £16. 2. 6. each to the following musicians of the King for their liveries :—

> Anthony Roberts (a note is added : " mortuus 9 May, 1679 ").
> John Hingston.
> William Gregory.
> Humphrey Madge (" obiit 29 November, 1679 ").
> Thomas Lanier.
> John Gamble.
> John Harding.
> John Bannister (" Obiit 3 Oct. 1679 ").
> Thomas Bates (" Obiit August, 1679 ").
> John Clements.
> Alphonso Marsh.
> Thomas Purcell* in the place of Henry Lawes.
> Thomas Purcell* in the place of Dr. John Wilson.
> Thomas Purcell* in the place of George Hudson.

[* Entered " by order of Mr. Purcell as by assignment."

Signed, J. Smithsby.]

> William Child.
> John Goodgroome.
> Theophilus Fittz.
> Charles Colman.

William Clayton.
John Blow.
Edward Hooton.
Nicholas Staggins, master of music in the place of Lewis Grabu.
Nicholas Staggins, in the place of Richard Hudson.
William Turner.
Francis Cruys.
Edward Dyer.
John Mosse.
Edmund Flower.

L. C. Vol. 465.

1678, *December* 3.

Order for the liveries for the twelve children of the Chappell Royall to be delivered to Dr. John Blow, master of the children of his Majesty's Chappell Royall.

L. C. Vol. 747, *p.* 201.

1678, *December* 14.

Warrant dormant to pay to John Moss, musician in ordinary in place of John Jenkins, surrendered, and to Edmund Flower, musician in ordinary in place of John Lilly. deceased, for their liveries, the sum of £16. 2s. 6d., and to deliver to them henceforth, yearly, the materials for their liveries.

L. C. Vol. 815, *p.* 111.

1678, *December* 16.

Order for the delivery of yearly liveries to Jervas Price, his Majesty's sergeant trumpeter, to sixteen trumpeters and one kettledrummer.

L. C. Vol. 747, *p.* 227.

1678-9, *January* 22.

Warrant to admit Robert Aggas as drummer in ordinary to his Majesty without fee, to come in ordinary with fee upon the first avoydance.

L. C. Vol. 480, *p.* 190 ; *Vol.* 747, *p.* 256.

1678-9, *February* 18.

Order directed to Mr. Nicholas Staggins, master of his Majesty's music, that his Majesty's four and twenty violins should attend his Majesty every night that a play is acted at Court. Notice to be given them to this effect.

L. C. Vol. 747, *p.* 272.

1678-9, *February* 28.

Order for the payment of £5 to Charles Evans, harper for the Italian harp, for strings for one year ending at Christmas, 1678.

1678-9, *March* 8.

Order for the payment of £124 to Dr. John Blow, master of the children of his Majesty's Chappell Royall, for the following items :—

	£	s.	d.
" For the children learning on the lute -	30	0	0
For those learning on the violin. - -	30	0	0
For those learning on the theorbo - -	30	0	0
For fire and strings in the musick room in the Chappell - - - -	20	0	0
For ruled paper penns and inke - -	2	10	0
For strings for the lutes and theorboes -	5	10	0
	£118	0	0
For 8 days going to Salisbury and bringing a boy from thence - -	6	0	0
Signed : Jo. Blow -	£124	0	0

1679, *March* 25.

Payments of £10 were made on this and the three following Feast days, St. John Baptist, Michaelmas and Christmas to John Blow, master of the children of the King's Chappell for keeping and teaching two singing boys.

1679, *April* 7.

Estimates for liveries and banners for the sergeant trumpeter, 17 trumpeters, 3 kettledrummers, the drum major, 4 drummers and a phife.

1679, *April* 8.

Order for the summer liveries of the children of the Chappell to be sent to Dr. John Blow, master of the children of his Majesty's Chappell Royall.

1679, *April* 8.

Order to pay Mr. Thomas Blagrave the sum of £224 8s. od. due to sixteen gentlemen and one organist of his Majesty's Chappell Royall for their riding charges and other expenses in their attendance on his Majesty at Windsor for 44 days, from 14 August to 26 September, 1678, at 6s. per diem to each of them :—

Mr. John Harding	Mr. Henry Frost
Mr. Stephen Crespion	Mr. James Cobb
Mr. Thomas Purcell	Mr. Alphonso Marsh, senior
Mr. James Hart	Mr. Richard Hart
Mr. Thomas Blagrave	Mr. Alphonso Marsh, junior
Mr. William Hopwood	Mr. Thomas Heywood
Mr. Edward Bradock	Mr. Thomas Richardson
Mr. William Turner	Mr. Henry Smith

Dr. John Blow, organist.

Also the following children of the chapel for the like at 3s. per diem amounting to £52. 16. :—

Gilbert Cunisbo	John Thatcher
Richard Carrington	Hugh Bradock
Francis Piggett	Vaughan Richardson
William Goodgroome	Daniel Purcell

And to Dr. John Blow, master of the children of the Chappell for the same at 6s. per diem:—£13. 4.

1679, *May* 7.

Order to pay Nicholas Staggins, master of his Majesty's musick, the sum of £22 for riding charges and other expenses while attending his Majesty at Windsor for 44 days, from 14 August to 26 September, 1678, at 10s. per diem.

Order to pay the following musicians in ordinary to his Majesty :—

Isaack Staggins	Thomas Greeting
William Clayton	John Myer
Jeoffery Aleworth	Joseph Fashion
Richard Tomlynson	Henry Brockwell
Thomas Farmer	Edmund Flower
Theophilus Fittz	Robert Ashton

the sum of £132 for their riding charges and other expenses while attending his Majesty at Windsor for the space of 44 days from 14 August to 26 September, 1678, at the rate of 5s. per diem to each of them.

1679, *May* 7.

Order to pay nine of his Majesty's musicians in ordinary :—

William Clayton	Edmund Flower
Jeoffery Aleworth	Isaack Staggins
Richard Thomlynson	Henry Brockwell
Francys Cruys	Joseph Fashion
Theophilus Fittz	

the sum of £38. 5s. for their riding charges and other expenses when attending his Majesty at Newmarket for the space of seventeen days, from the 1st to the 17th of October, 1678, at the rate of 5s. per diem to each of them.

L. C. Vol. 747, *p.* 322.

1679, *May* 21.

Order to pay Dr. John Blow, master of the children of his Majesty's Chappell Royall, the sum of £30 yearly, for the maintenance of Richard Elmes, late child of the Chappell, whose voice is changed and is gon from the Chappell. Also certain clothes to be delivered to him for the said Richard Elmes.

L. C. Vol. 747, *p.* 332, *and L. C. Papers, Bundle* 76.

1679, *May* 21.

Petition of Melker Gold, setting forth that he served as a trumpet in his Majesty's troop of Guards ever since his Majesty's happy Restauration till last November, when he was dismist for being a Roman Catholique and having had no allowance since November, is become so very poor, he cannot go into Suabia, his native country, without some releife; there is £75 due to him out of the fee-farm and rents, £60 upon the law bill, and half a year's sallary out of the treasury chamber, being £30, and he prays his Majesty to allow him wherewith to carry him home. The petition is referred to the Duke of Monmouth, his just demands to be satisfied.

L. C. Vol. 183, *p.* 31d.

1679, *May* 23.

" I do hereby give leave unto Mr. John Bannister, one of his Majesty's musicians, to travel beyond the seas, and to be absent from his attendance by the space of 6 months, or longer if his occasions shall require."

L. C. Vol. 747, *p.* 334.

1679, *May* 31.

Warrant to swear John Abell as musician for the private music to his Majesty in ordinary, with fee, in the place of Anthony Roberts, deceased. Patent for a grant of £40 yearly as wages, dated 5 June, 1679.

L. C. Vol. 747, *p.* 337, *and L. C. Vol.* 480, *p.* 103.

1679. *Pentecost. June* 7.

Payment of £19. 17. 8. to each of the following trumpeters to the late King Charles I. for their pensions :—
Robert Ramsay. Samuel Markeland. Henry Peacock.

L. C. Vol. 465 ; *see also L. C. Vol.* 545.

1679, *June* 12.

Bill of Jervice Price, trumpeters and kettledrummers, £367. 2s. 3d. Bill of John Mawgridge, drummers and phife, £321. 16. Bill of Symon Peirson and 2 kettledrummers, £235. 12. 10½.

L. C. Vol. 407, *entries* 201, 202 *and* 203.

1679, *St. John Baptist.*

Payment of £29. 16. 8. to Henry Gregory, musician to the King, for clothing and educating two boys in the art of music for half a year.

L. C. Vol. 465, *and Vol.* 545.

1679, *June* 27.

Warrant to admit William Shore as trumpeter in ordinary to his Majesty, with fee, in the place of John Baker, deceased.

L. C. Vol. 747, *p.* 362, *and L. C. Vol.* 480, *p.* 188.

1679, *July* 28.

Warrant to admit Francis Burton as trumpeter in ordinary to his Majesty, to attend the Lord Lieutenant for the kingdom of Ireland for the time being, in the place of John Scarlett, deceased.

L. C. Vol. 747, *p.* 368, *and L. C. Vol.* 480, *p.* 189.

1679, *July* 28.

Nicholas Castles admitted as trumpeter in ordinary without fee, to attend the Lord Lieutenant for Ireland for the time being, to come in ordinary with fee upon the first vacancy.

L. C. Vol. 747, *p.* 368.

Shorter entry dated 14 *July,* 1679.
Trumpeters for Ireland. Nicholas Castles next January.

L. C. Vol. 480, *p.* 189.

1679, *September* 15.

Assignment by Dr. William Child, one of his Majesty's musicians in ordinary in the place of Henry Ferabosco, deceased, to Mr. William Gregory, of a livery due to the said Dr. Child out of the great wardrobe.

L. C. Vol. 196, *p.* 1d.

Accounts ending Michaelmas, 1679.

Accounts for liveries for :—

Dr. John Blow, Master of the boys of the Chappell Royall.

Musicians.

John Hingston	William Child
Humphrey Madge	Charles Colman
William Gregory	Theophilus Fitz
Thomas Laneir	John Goodgroome
Anthony Robert	William Clayton
John Harding	John Blow
Alphonso Marsh	Edward Hooton
Thomas Bates	William Turner
John Gamble	Francis Cruys
John Banister	Edward Dyer
John Clement	John Mosse
Thomas Purcell (3 liveries)	Edmund Flower

Nicholas Staggins, master of music, in the place of Lewis Grabu.

Nicholas Staggins in the place of Robert Hudson.

Account for annual pensions for :—

Robert Ramsay   -   -
Samuel Markeland   -   } Trumpeters to the late
Henry Peacock   -   -   King Charles I.

Account paid to Henry Gregory for clothing, and educating two boys in the art of music.

Account paid to John Blow, master of the boys of the Chappell Royall, for the keeping and teaching of two singing boys.

L. C. Vol. 68, *and L. C. Vol.* 157.

1679, *November* 6.

Warrant to admit Thomas Farmer as musician in ordinary to his Majesty with fee, for the private musick, in the place of John Bannister, deceased. Followed by a patent of the same date, granting him the yearly fee and allowance of £110, [this is crossed out.]

L. C. Vol. 747, *p.* 401, *and L. C. Vol.* 480, *p.* 103.

1679, *November* 6.

Warrant to admit John Bannister as musician in ordinary for the violin, with fee, in the place of his father John Bannister, deceased.

L. C. Vol. 747, *p.* 402, *and L. C. Vol.* 480, *p.* 103.

1679, *November* 10.

Account for worsted hose for Searl and Benford, 2 Chappell boys gone off.

L. C. Vol. 205, *entry* 76c.

1679, *November* 22.

Warrant for the payment of £14 to Edward Flower, musician in ordinary for the private musick, for a theorboe lute, bought by him for his Majesty's service.

L. C. Vol. 747, *p.* 410.

1679, *St. Andrew.*

Payment of £29. 16. 8. to Henry Gregory for clòthing two boys and educating them in the art of music for half a year.

L. C. Vol. 465.

1679, *St. Andrew.*

Payment of £16. 2. 6. to each of the following musicians to the King for their livery :—

> John Hingston.
> William Gregory.
> Thomas Lanier.
> John Gamble.
> John Harding.
> Alphonso Marsh.
> John Clements.
> Thomas Purcell (in the place of Henry Lawes).
> Thomas Purcell (in the place of Dr. John Wilson).
> Thomas Purcell (in the place of George Hudson).
> William Child (" resignat. William Gregory ").
> John Goodgroome.
> Theophilus Fittz.
> Charles Colman.
> William Clayton.
> John Blow.
> Edward Hooton.
> William Turner.
> Nicholas Staggins (master of the musick in the place of Lewis Grabu).
> Nicholas Staggins (in the place of Richard Hudson).
> Francis Cruys.
> Edward Dyer.
> John Moss.
> Edmund Flower.

L. C. Vol. 465.

1679, *St. Andrew.*

Livery of £16. 2. 6., payable out of his Majesty's Great Wardrobe to each of the following musicians :—

Nicholas Staggins, Master of Musick.

Thomas Purcell	John Harding
William Turner	John Bannister
Anthony Roberts	Edward Hooten
John Hingston	Edward Dyer
William Gregory	Thomas Bates
Thomas Purcell "more"	Alphonso Marsh
Humphrey Madge	William Child
Thomas Laneir	William Clayton
Francis Cruys	Charles Coleman
John Gamble	Theophilus Fitz
John Mosse	Thomas Purcell
Edmund Flower	John Goodgroome

John Clements, in the place of Pellham Humphryes.

Henry Gregory for keeping and teaching two boys, £29. 16. 8.

L. C. Vol. 545.

1679, *December* 11.

Order to pay Dr. John Blow, master of the children of his Majesty's Chappell Royall, the sum of £118 for teaching the twelve children of the Chappell to play the lute, violin and theorboe, and for strings, etc., for the music room ; for one year ending Michaelmas, 1679.

L. C. Vol. 747, *p.* 418.

1679, *December* 13.

Warrant to admit Richard Marsh as trumpeter in ordinary to his Majesty, with fee, in the place of Thomas Calthrope, deceased.

L. C. Vol. 747, *p.* 419, *and L. C. Vol.* 480, *p.* 188.

1679, *December* 13.

The following musicians' names occur in a list of the King's servants paid by the treasurer of the great wardrobe, with the amounts of their wages per annum.

Trumpeters.

Silvester Whitmeal	
Joseph Walker	Each to receive
Jervace Price	£60 per
Thomas Creswell	annum.
Edward Humarston	

Violins (24 in number).

Edmund Flower
Richard Dorney
Theophilus Fitz
John Singleton
Nicholas Staggins
Henry Brockwell
Thomas Pursell   Each to receive
Joseph Fashion   £46 10s. 10d.
Symon Hopper   per annum.
Isaac Staggins
John Myre
William Clayton
John Twiss
John Bannister
Edward Dyer

Richard Tomlinson
Thomas Farmer
Robert Strong   Each to receive
John Twiss   £46 12s. 3d.
Giles Stephens   per annum.
James Bannister
Geoffrey Bannister

Thomas Greeting   £57 14s. 2d. per annum.
Thomas Pursell, composer, £42 15s. 0d.

Wind musick (5 in number).

Dr. William Child
Thomas Blagrave   Each to receive
Thomas Laniere   £46 10s, 10d.
Henry Gregory   per annum.
Jeffrey Aylworth

Private musick (15 in number).

Richard Hart
John Singleton   To receive
John Young   £56 2s. 6d. each.

Thomas Pursell
Frederick Stiffkin   £46 10s. 10d. each.
Henry Brockwell

William Gregory - -   £46 0s. 0d. per annum.
Thomas Purcell - -   £36 2s. 6d.   ″
John Hingston - -   £50 0s. 0d.   ″
Edward Hooton - -   £110 0s. 0d.   ″

Christopher Preston, musician in ordinary for the virginalls £46 per annum and for his other place £40 per annum.

John Hingston, tuner and repairer of the wind instruments £60 per annum.

Claude de Grange £110 per annum.

Henry Brockwell, keeper of his Majesty's instruments £18 per annum.

L. C. Papers, Bundle 19.

1679, *December* 22.

Warrant to admit Jeoffery Aleworth as musician for the violin in ordinary with fee, in the place of Humphrey Madge, deceased.

Warrant to admit John Crouch as musician in ordinary with fee, for the wind instruments, in the place of Humphrey Madge, deceased.

L. C. Vol. 747, *p.* 432, *and L. C. Vol.* 480, *p.* 104.

1679, *December* 23.

Account for liveries due to Jervice Price, his Majesty's sergeant trumpeter, and to John Mawgridge, his Majesty's drum-major.

L. C. Vol. 205, *entries* 107d *and* 108d.

1679, *December* 24.

Account for a black felt and black castors for Coningsby, a Chappell boy gone off.

In April, 1680, an account for Spanish cloth for him.

L. C. Vol. 206, *entries* 25a *and* 30a.

1679, *December* 27.

Warrant for the payment of £240 to the following musicians for their riding charges and other expenses while attending his Majesty at Windsor for the space of 80 days, at 5s. a day to each of them, from 30 June to 17 September, 1679 :—

William Clayton,	Robert Ashton,
Thomas Farmer,	Isaack Staggins,
John Twist,	Henry Brockwell,
Jeoffery Aleworth,	Joseph Fashion,
Richard Thomlynson,	Theophilus Fittz,
John Crouch,	Edmund Flower.

Followed by a like warrant for the payment of £40 10s. to them for attendance at Newmarket for the space of 18 days, from 26 September to 13 October, 1679, at 5s. by the day.

L. C. Vol. 747, *p.* 435.

1679.

List of salaries payable out of the treasurys of the chambers office and registered upon different branches of the revenue.

Musicians.

	£	s.	d.
To Hen. Gregory on an order registered* on the hearth money No. 1044	81	10	6
To Isaac Staggins on an order registered on the fee-farm rents No. 65 - -	34	18	1
To John Singleton on the same order -	77	6	4
To Dr. Child on the same order - -	46	10	10
To Wm. Clayton on the same order - -	46	8	0

L. C. Papers, Bundle 23.

* Probably means " charged upon."

1679-80, *January* 12.

Warrant for clothing for Augustine Benford and Searle, Chappell boys dismist.

Warrant for seven yards of Spanish cloth for John Waters, a Chappell boy gone off.

L. C. Vol. 804, pp. 97d and 104.

1679-80, *January* 17.

Warrant for the payment of £124 to Albion Thompson and John Christmas, two of his Majesty's trumpeters, for their attendance on the Right Hon. Lawrence Hyde, esquire, master of his Majesty's robes, (who was sent as ambassador unto the King of Poland), for the space of 248 days, viz., from 9 June, 1676 to 12 February next following.

L. C. Vol. 747, p. 450.

1679-80, *January* 17.

Order to pay Gervas Price, his Majesty's sergeant trumpeter, the sum of £12, for a pair of new kettle-drums provided by him for his Majesty's troop of Horse, under the command of Captain Legg.

L. C. Vol. 747, p. 451.

1679-80, *January* 28.

Warrant for the payment of £60 to Jervas Price for the supply of two trumpeters and a ketttle-drummer that are to attend his Grace the Duke of Grafton at sea.

L. C. Vol. 747, p. 456.

1679-80, *February* 6.

Warrant to admit Robert King as musician in ordinary for the private musick, with fee, in the place of John Bannister, deceased.

L. C. Vol. 747, p. 459, and L. C. Vol. 480, p. 103.

1679-80, *February* 6.

Petition of Symon Beale, one of his Majesty's trumpeters, against Joseph Walker, trumpeter. Walker to appear upon the nynth of February instant.

L. C. Vol. 656.

1679-80, *February* 7.

Warrant to pay Charles Evans, harper for the Italian harp, the sum of £5 for strings for the harp for one year, ending at Christmas, 1679.

L. C. Vol. 747, *p.* 459.

1679-80, *February* 17.

Warrant to admit Joseph Fashion as musician in ordinary for the private musick in the place of Henry Hawes, deceased.

L. C. Vol. 747, *p.* 461, *and L. C. Vol.* 480, *p.* 104.

1679-80, *February* 23.

Assignment by John Myer, one of his Majesty's musicians, to Edward Gilbert, of the sum of £6 15s. od., to be paid out of the salary due to the said John Myer as musician aforesaid.

L. C. Vol. 747, *p.* 464.

1680, *March* 25.

Payments of £10 were made on this and the three following Feast days, St. John Baptist, Michaelmas and Christmas to John Blow, master of the children of the King's Chappell for keeping and teaching two singing boys.

L. C. Vols. 157 *and* 465.

1680, *March* 26.

Account for ribbon for James Cutler, a Chappell boy gone off. Further references to James Cutler in June and August, 1681.

L. C. Vol. 206, *entry* 54b; *L. C. Vol.* 206, *entry* 106b; *L. C. Vol.* 206, *entry* 120b and 127b; *also* 82c; *also Vol.* 207, *entries* 14b, 27b, 34b, 35b, 36b, 41b, 42b, 44b.

1680, *April* 24.

Warrant to admit John Bannister musician in ordinary to his Majesty for the violin, in the place of John Bannister his father, deceased, with wages of 1s. 8d. a day and an allowance of £16 2s. 6d. yearly for his livery.

L. C. Vol. 747, *p.* 528.

1680, *May* 3.

Warrant for liveries for Jervas Price, sergeant trumpeter and sixteen trumpeters and a kettle drummer.

L. C. Papers, Bundle 3.

1680, *May* 26.

Henry Gregory for teaching two boys, Midsummer 1677, £29 16s. 8d.

L. C. Vol. 715, *p.* 38.

1680. *Pentecost. May* 30.

Payment of £19 17s. 8d. each to the following trumpeters to the late King Charles I. for their pensions :—

Robert Ramsay.
Samuel Markland.
Henry Peacock.

L. C. Vol. 465, *p.* 72.

1680, *June* 4.

Warrant for the payment of £40 to Jervas Price, his Majesty's sergeant trumpeter, for the present supply of two trumpeters to attend the Earl of Mulgrave to Tangier.

L. C. Vol. 747, *p.* 506. *See also Vol.* 205, *entry* 124.

1680, *St. John Baptist.*

Payment of £29 16s. 8d. to Henry Gregory, musician to the King, for clothing, and educating two boys in the art of music for half a year.

L. C. Vol. 465, *p.* 76.

1680, *June* 26.

To William Child, musician, £16. 2. 6. for livery due St. Andrew, 1676.

L. C. Vol. 715, *p.* 38.

1680, *July* 14.

Assignment by Nicholas Staggins, master of the King's musick, to Mr. Charles Colman, one of his Majesty's musicians, of four debentures for liveries due to him, viz. :—two for the year 1677, and two for 1678, amounting together to £64. 10s.

L. C. Vol. 196, *p.* 8*d.*

1680, *July* 16.

Warrant for the payment of £12 to Jervas Price, his Majesty's sergeant trumpeter, for a pair of kettle-drums bought by him for his Majesty's service.

L. C. Vol. 747, *p.* 538.

1680, *July* 22.

Warrant to admit William Hall in the place and quality of musician in ordinary for the violin in the private musick, with fee, in the place of John Young, deceased.

L. C. Vol. 747, *p.* 539, *and L. C. Vol.* 775, *p.* 1.

1680, *July* 22.

Further order to pay to William Hall, musician in ordinary for the viol de Gambo, £40 per annum, and £16 2s. 6d. yearly during his Majesty's pleasure.

L. C. Vol. 775, *p.* 1.

1680, *July* 22.

To Alphonso Marsh, musician, £16. 2. 6. for livery due
St. Andrew, 1676.

L. C. Vol. 715, *p.* 38.

1680, *July* 24.

Account for shoes for Gilbert Coningsbey and Richard Elmes,
boys of the Chappell Royall, gone off.

A black castor for the latter, and 12 black castors and
12 black felts for the 12 children of the Chappell.

L. C. Vol. 206, *entries* 55a *and* 61a.

1680, *Michaelmas.*

Account for gloves for Gilbert Cunisbey, a Chappell boy,
whose voice is changed and gone off.

Other references to Coningsby and Elmes in February
following.

L. C. Vol. 206, *entries* 125a, 139a, 133a, *and* 33b.

Accounts ending Michaelmas, 1680.

Accounts for liveries for the following musicians :—

John Hingston	John Goodgroome
William Gregory	William Clayton
Thomas Lanier	John Blow
John Harding	Edward Hooten
Alphonso Marsh	William Turner
John Gamble	Francis Cruys
Thomas Purcell (3 liveries)	Edward Dyer
John Clement	John Mosse
Charles Coleman	Edmund Flower
Theophilus Fittz	

Nicholas Staggins, master of music, in the place of Lewis
Grabu.

Nicholas Staggins in the place of Robert Hudson.

Accounts for annual pensions to Robert Ramsay, Samuel
Markland and Henry Peacock, trumpeters to the late King
Charles I.

Account paid to Henry Gregory for clothing, and educating
two boys in the art of music.

Account paid to John Blow, master of the boys of the
Chappell Royall, for the keep of two boys and for teaching them
singing.

L. C. Vol. 69 ; *and L. C. Vol.* 157.

1680, *October* 15.

Certificate allowing Robert Mawgridg, his Majesty's drummer in ordinary, to continue the office of kettle-drummer to his Majesty's troop of Horse, commanded by Captain Legge, he providing a sufficient man to perform the duty in his place of drummer.

L. C. Vol. 183, pp. 38 and 42, also p. 2.

1680, *October* 23.

Warrant to pay Theophilus Fittz, musician in ordinary to his Majesty, £36 for his riding charges at Windsor for 144 days, from 19 April to 9 September, 1680, at the rate of 5s. by the day.

L. C. Vol. 749, p. 116.

1680, *October* 30.

Order to deliver to Dr. John Blow, master of the children of his Majesty's Chappell Royall, twelve in number, winter liveries for the said children.

L. C. Vol. 775, p. 16 ; L. C. Papers, Bundle 10.

1680, *November* 17.

Account for Spanish cloth for Elmes, a child of the Chappell, gone off.

L. C. Vol. 206, entry 101a.

1680, *November* 26.

Petition of Edward Wharton, one of the drummers in ordinary against Mr. John Mawgridge, his Majesty's drum major, for deteyning his clothes.

Mr. Mawgridge to appear and pay, 29 November instant.

L. C. Vol. 656.

1680. *St. Andrew. November* 30.

Payment of £16 2s. 6d. each to the following musicians of the King for their livery :—

John Hingston	William Child
William Gregory	Francis Cruys
Thomas Lanier	John Goodgroome
John Gamble	Theophilus Fitz
John Harding	Charles Colman
Alphonso Marsh	William Clayton
John Clements	John Blow
Thomas Purcell (in the place of Henry Lawes)	Edward Hooten
	William Turner
Thomas Purcell (in the place of Dr. John Wilson)	Edward Dyer
	John Moss

Thomas Purcell (in the   Edmund Flower
place of George Hudson)
Nicholas Staggins (master of music in the place of Lewis
Grabu)
Nicholas Staggins (in the place of Richard Hudson)

Payment of £29 16s. 8d. to Henry Gregory for clothing,
and educating two boys in the art of music for half a year.

L. C. Vol. 465.

1680-1, *January* 26.

Richard Robinson appointed instrument-keeper in the place
of Henry Brockwell, surrendered.

L. C. Vol. 480, *p.* 104.

1680-1, *February* 10.

Account for making 38 surplices for the Gentlemen of the
Chappell Royall at 5/- each, and 38 surplices for the Children
of the Chappell Royall at 2/6 each.

L. C. Vol. 206, *entry* 8*b.*

1680-1, *February* 10.

Warrant to pay Dr. William Holder, sub-dean of the
Chappell, the sum of £12, for some parts of anthems and
services written in the books, belonging to his Majesty's
Chappell Royall, from 12 February, 1676 to 25 December, 1680,
and for books and ruled paper for the children of the Chappell.

L. C. Vol. 206, *entry* 18*b.*

1680-1, *March* 10.

Claudius des Granges, his Majesty's sworne servant in the
quality of musician in ordinary to his Majesty with fee. A new
certificate dated as above.

L. C. Vol. 480, *p.* 102.

1681, *March* 25.

Payments of £10 to John Blow, master of the boys of the
Chappell Royall, for keeping and teaching two singing boys,
were made on this and the three following Feast days,
St. John Baptist, Michaelmas and Christmas.

L. C. Vols. 465, 466.

1681, *May* 18.

Warrant for summer liveries for the children of the
Chappell.

L. C. Papers, Bundle 10.

1681, *May* 23.

Warrant for two black castors and two black felts for
Francis Smith and Edward Buckler, two Chapel boys gone off.

L. C. Vol. 804, *p.* 131.

1681, *May 22. Pentecost.*

Payment of £19 17s. 8d. each to the following trumpeters to the late King Charles I. for their pensions,

> Robert Ramsay
> Samuel Markland
> Henry Peacock.

L. C. Vol. 465, *p.* 121.

1681, *May 30.*

Bernard Smyth appointed organ-maker in the place of James Farr, deceased.

L. C. Vol. 480, *p.* 105.

1681, *St. John Baptist.*

Payment of £29 16s. 8d. to Henry Gregory, musician to the King, for clothing, and educating two boys in the art of music for half a year.

L. C. Vol. 465, *p.* 125.

1681, *August 2.*

John Lenten appointed musician for the violin in the place of Dorney, deceased.

L. C. Vol. 480, *p.* 104.

1681, *August 29.*

Petition of William Cooke against James Bannister, violin, late a tennant to the petitioner and refuseth to pay rent plaintiff in the Temple.

Lett James Bannister have notice of this petition and appeare before mee upon the 30th August instant.

L. C. Vol. 656; *L. C. Vol.* 775, *p.* 32.

1681, *Michaelmas.*

Account for "woolsted hose" for Coningsby, Elmes and Cutler, Chappell boyes gone off.

L. C. Vol. 206, *entry* 130b.

Accounts ending Michaelmas, 1681.

Accounts for liveries for :—

Musicians.

John Hingston	John Goodgroome
William Gregory	William Clayton
Thomas Laneir	John Blow
John Harding	Edward Hooten
Alphonso Marsh	William Turner
John Gamble	Francis Cruys
John Clement	Edward Dyer
Thomas Purcell (3 liveries)	John Mosse

Charles Coleman   Edmund Flower
Theophilus Fitz
Nicholas Staggins master of music in the place of Lewis
Grabu.

Nicholas Staggins, in the place of Robert Hudson.

Account for annual pensions for the trumpeters to the late
King Charles I. :—Robert Ramsay, Samuel Markland and
Henry Peacock.

Account paid to Henry Gregory for clothing, and educating
two boys in the art of music.

Account paid to John Blow for the keep of two boys and for
teaching them singing.

L. C. Vol. 70 ; *L. C. Vol.* 157.

1681, *November* 8.

Warrant to pay Theophilus Fittz, musician in ordinary to
his Majesty, £30. 10. for his riding charges at Windsor for
122 days from 28 April to 27 August, 1681, at the rate of 5s.
by the day.

L. C. Vol. 749, *p.* 116.

1681, *November* 28.

Petition of John Smyth against James Bannister.   Debt.

L. C. Vol. 656.

1681, *November* 28.

Warrant to deliver to Dr. John Blow, master of the children
of the Chappell being twelve in number, the materials for
winter liveries for the said children.

L. C. Papers, Bundle 2.

1681, *St. Andrew.*

Payment of £16 2s. 6d. to each of the following musicians
to the King for their livery :—

John Hingston.
William Gregory,
Thomas Laneir.
John Gamble.
John Harding.
John Clements.
Thomas Purcell (in the place of Henry Lawes).
Thomas Purcell (in the place of Dr. John Wilson).
Thomas Purcell (in the place of George Hudson).
William Child.
Francis Cruys.

John Goodgroome.
Theophilus Fittz.
Charles Coleman.
William Clayton.
John Blow.
Edward Hooten.
William Turner.
Nicholas Staggins (master of music in the place of Lewis Grabu).
Nicholas Staggins (in the place of Richard Hudson).
Edward Dyer.
John Mosse.
Edmund Flower.

Payment of £29 16s. 8d. to Henry Gregory musician to the King, for clothing, and educating 2 boys in the art of music for half a year.

L. C. Vol. 466.

1681, *December* 20.

John Abell appointed musician for the lute and voice in the place of Alphonso March, deceased.

John Abell appointed musician for the violin in the place of Richard Dornye, deceased.

L. C. Vol. 480, *p.* 104.

1681.

Estimates for the liveries of the sergeant trumpeter, 16 trumpeters, and one kettledrummer, £1,800; and for the drum major, 4 drummers, and a phife, £300.

L. C. Vol. 545.

1681-2, *January* 5.

Mathias Show (also "Shore") appointed trumpeter in the place of Joseph Walker, deceased.

L. C. Vol. 480, *pp.* 188 *and* 189.

1681-2, *January* 29.

Warrant to prepare a new silver trumpet for John St. Amant, trumpeter in the 2nd troop of Horse Guards under the Duke of Ormond.

L. C. Vol. 602, *p.* 294. *See also p.* 340d

1681-2, *March* 1.

Thomas Barwell appointed trumpeter in the place of Milbert Meurs. [Name "Thomas Barwell" crossed out in original.]

L. C. Vol. 480., *p.* 188.

1681-2, *March* 7.

Warrant to prepare a new silver trumpet for John Seignior, trumpeter in the 3rd Troop of Guards under Lord Rivers.

L. C. Vol. 602, *p.* 284.

1681-2, *March* 8.

Augustin Buckler appointed trumpeter in the place of Thomas Barwell, in Captain Legg's troop.

L. C. Vol. 480, *p.* 188.

1682, *March* 25.

Payments of £10 to John Blow, master of the children of the Chappell Royall, for keeping and teaching two singing boys, were made on this and the three following Feast days, St. John Baptist, Michaelmas and Christmas.

L. C. Vol. 466.

1682, *April* 29.

Account for livery, banner, etc., for Alexander Lewis, appointed new trumpeter to the Duke of Albemarle.

L. C. Vol. 206, *entry* 134*b*, *also entries* 127*b*, 128*b*, 130*b*, 136*b*, 140*b*, 144*b*, *and* 80*c.*

1682, *Pentecost, June* 4.

Payment of £19 17s. 8d. to each of the following trumpeters to the late King Charles I. for their pensions :—

Robert Ramsay.
Samuel Markland.
Henry Peacock.

L. C. Vol. 466, *p.* 28.

1682, *June* 5.

£12 to be paid to Sergeant Price for a new pair of kettle-drums, provided by him for his Majesty's service, a pair of kettle-drums having been lately lost at sea.

L. C. Vol. 775, *p.* 91*d.*

1682, *June* 8.

Robert Mawgridge admitted kettle-drummer in ordinary in the place of Walter Vanbright, deceased.

L. C. Vol. 775, *p.* 66, *and L. C. Vol.* 480, *p.* 188.

1682, *St. John Baptist.*

Payment of £29 16s. 8d. to Henry Gregory, musician, for clothing, and educating two boys in the art of music, for half a year.

L. C. Vol. 466, *p.* 32.

1682, *July* 5.

Order to deliver to Jervas Price, his Majesty's sergeant trumpeter, four silver trumpets of the same fashion, quantity and proportion as have formerly been delivered . . . to replace four trumpets lost at sea.

L. C. Vol. 775, *p.* 91*d.*

1682, *July* 5.

John Crouch appointed musician in ordinary for the violin, in the place of Thomas Greeting, deceased.

L. C. Vol. 775, *p.* 92*b, and L. C. Vol.* 480, *p.* 104.

1682, *July* 7.

Received of Mr. Ramsay, trumpeter, for his debenture 1680, 1681 and 1682.

L. C. Vol. 458.

1682, *July* 18.

Order to deliver to Dr. John Blow, master of the children of the Chappell Royall, being 12 in number, their summer liveries.

L. C. Vol. 775, *p.* 101.

1682, *July* 27.

John Crouch appointed musician in ordinary for the violin and sackbut, in the place of Thomas Greeting, deceased ; wages 2s. 4d. a day and £16 2s. 6d. yearly for livery.

L. C. Vol. 775, *p.* 117.

1682, *August* 16.

Warrant for two black casters for Coningsby and Elmes, Chapel boys gone off.

L. C. Vol. 804, *p.* 163.

1682, *Michaelmas.*

Payments to be made out of His Majesty's Great Wardrobe.

For two suits 2 hats 4 shirts 4 half shirts 6 bands and cuffs 6 handkerchers 4 pairs of stockings 4 pairs of shoes 4 pairs of gloves for John Thatcher a chapel boy whose voice is changed £18 0. 0.

L. C. Vol. 545.

1682, *November* 10.

Warrant to pay Theophilus Fittz, musician in ordinary to his Majesty, £31. 10. for his riding charges at Windsor for 126 days, from 22 April to 25 April, 1682, at the rate of 5s. by the day.

L. C. Vol. 749, *p.* 116.

1682, *November* 17.

John Goodwin appointed musician in ordinary for the private musick, in the place of Thomas Purcell, deceased, to wayte among the violins.

L. C. Vol. 480, *p.* 104.

1682, *November* 20.

Nathaniell French appointed musician in ordinary for the private musick, in the place of Thomas Purcell, deceased, to wayte among the violins.

L. C. Vol. 480, *p.* 104.

1682, *St. Andrew.*

Payment of £16 2s. 6d. to each of the following musicians of the King for their livery,

John Hingston	Charles Colman
William Gregory	William Clayton
Thomas Laneir	John Blow
John Gamble	Edward Hooton
John Harding	William Turner
John Clements	Edward Dyer
Francis Cruys	John Moss
John Goodgroome	Edmund Flower
Theophilus Fittz	William Child

Nicholas Staggins (master of music in the place of Lewis Grabu).

Nicholas Staggins (in the place of Richard Hudson).

Payment of £29 16s. 8d. to Henry Gregory, musician to the King, for clothing, and educating 2 boys in the art of music for half a year.

L. C. Vol. 466.

1682.

A list of his Majesty's servants abovestairs that are to attend his Majesty at Windsor Castle this year 1682, includes:—

Musicians.
Trumpeters.
Drum major and drummers.

L. C. Vol. 547, *p.* 75.

1682-3, *January* 23.

Warrant to provide a new silver trumpet for Mr. William Shore, his Majesty's serjeant trumpeter, he having left his own with Mr. St. Amant who succeeded him upon his promotion to be serjeant trumpeter.

L. C. Vol. 602, *p.* 303 ; *see end of Vol. also.*

1682-3, *February* 16.

Michael Meire appointed trumpeter in ordinary in the place of Albion Thompson, deceased.

L. C. Vol. 480, *p.* 189.

1682-3, *February* 26.

Henry Heale appointed musician for the violin in the place of John Myers, deceased.

L. C. Vol. 480, *p.* 104.

1683, *March* 25.

Payments of £10 to John Blow, master of the children of the Chappel Royall, for keeping and teaching two singing boys, were made on this and the three following Feast days, St. John Baptist, Michaelmas and Christmas.

L. C. Vol. 466.

1683, *April* 16.

Will of Henry Peacock, pentionary trumpeter, of the parish of St. Martin in the fields, dated 16 April, 1683. With a certificate to the effect that he was buried at St. Martin in the fields on 30 October, 1684.

L. C. Vol. 196, *p* 27.

1683, *Pentecost.*

Payment of £19 17s. 8d. to each of the following trumpeters to the late King Charles I. for their pensions, Samuel Markland, Robert Ramsay and Henry Peacock.

L. C. Vol. 466, *p.* 64.

1683, *St. John Baptist.*

Payment of £29 16s. 8d. to Henry Gregory, musician to the King, for clothing, and educating two boys in the art of music for half a year.

L. C. Vol. 466, *p.* 69.

1683, *July* 28.

Warrant to deliver to Dr. John Blow the clothing " unprovided on my Lord Chamberlain's warrant dated 15 December 1680 " for Mr. James Cutler, one of the children of the Chapel, whose voice had changed and who had left the Chapel.

L. C. Papers, Bundle 2.

1683, *October* 26.

Account for clothing for John Thatcher, a Chappell boy whose voice is broken and gone from the Chappell.

L. C. Vol. 207, *entry 22a.*

Accounts ending Michaelmas, 1683.

Accounts for liveries for the musicians :—

John Hingstone	John Goodgroome
William Gregory	William Clayton
Thomas Lanier	John Blow
John Harding	Edward Hooten
Alphonso Marsh	William Turner
John Gamble	Francis Cruys
John Clement	Edward Dyer
Thomas Purcell (3 liveries)	John Mosse
Charles Colman	Edmund Flower
Theophilus Fittz	

Nicholas Staggins, master of music in the place of Lewis Grabu.

Nicholas Staggins, in the place of Robert Hudson.

Account for annual pensions for the trumpeters Robert Ramsay, Samuel Markland and Henry Peacock.

Account paid to Henry Gregory for clothing, and educating two boys in the art of music.

Account paid to John Blow for the keep of two boys and for teaching them singing.

L. C. Vol. 71.

1683, *November* 13.

Warrant for the allowance of winter liveries for the twelve children of the Chappell to be delivered to Dr. John Blow, master of the said children.

L. C. Papers, Bundle 15.

1683, *November* 28.

Warrant for clothing for Francis Piggot, late child of the Chappell.

L. C. Papers, Bundle 21.

1683, *St. Andrew.*

Payment of £16 2s. 6d. each to the following musicians to the King for their liveries :—

John Hingston	Edward Hooton
William Gregory	William Turner

Thomas Laneir
John Gamble
John Harding
John Clements
Francis Cruys
John Goodgroome
Theophilus Fittz
Charles Colman
William Clayton
John Blow

Nicholas Staggins (master
of music in the place of
Lewis Grabu)
Nicholas Staggins (in the
place of Richard Hudson)
Edward Dyer
John Moss
Edmund Flower
William Child

Payment of £29 : 16 : 8 to Henry Gregory, musician to the King, for clothing two boys and educating them in the art of music for half a year.

L. C. Vol. 466.

1683, *December* 17.

Appointment of Henry Purcell to be organ-maker and keeper, etc., in the place of Mr. Hingston, deceased.

L. C. Vol. 480, *p.* 104.

1683, *December* 22.

Robert Carr appointed musician for the violl in the place of Mr. Hingston, deceased.

L. C. Vol. 480, *p.* 104.

1683, *December* 25.

Order to pay to John Hingston, keeper and repairer of his Majesty's organs, £124 for repairing and keeping and mending the organs, harpsicords and pedalls, for setting up organs against Maundy Thursday, for portage of instruments, for blowing the organ, for rent of a room to keep the instruments in and for other services during the past five years :—

Layd out in his Majesty's service since the 24th of June 1678 unto the 25th of December 1683, being five yeares and a halfe, by John Hingston, keeper and repairer of all his Majesty's organs in his Chappells at Whitehall, Windsor, Hampton Court ; and also of all pedalls, harpsicords and other instruments in the Privy Lodgings.

	£	s.	d.
For repairing and mending severall harpsicords at severall tymes for ye practice of ye private musick in ye hall and in ye privy lodgings - -	7	15	0
For preparing and setting up an organ in ye banquetting house against Maundy Thursday, 1679 - -	2	5	0
For setting up an organ in ye banquetting house against Maundy Thursday, 1680 - - - -	2	5	0
For setting up an organ there against Maundy Thursday, 1681 - -	2	5	0
For setting up an organ there against Maundy Thursday, 1682 - -	2	5	0
For setting up an organ there against Maundy Thursday, 1683 - -	2	5	0
For strings for ye harpsicord and pedalls for $4\frac{1}{2}$ years - - - - -	3	10	0
For portage of instruments for $5\frac{1}{2}$ years -	6	15	0
For ye organ blower for blowing ye organ at Whitehall for $5\frac{1}{2}$ years -	42	0	0
For rent of a large roome to keep ye instruments in for $5\frac{1}{2}$ years - -	44	0	0
For mending and tuning ye great organ in ye chappell at Whitehall at severall tymes - - - -	5	15	0
For my charges to Windsor with an organ maker and two men to tune ye organ there in His Majesty's chappell - - - - - -	3	0	0
	£124	0	0

1683, *December* 27.

John Skyrme appointed drummer in the place of Edward Wharton, deceased; wages 12d. by the day and £16 2s. 6d. yearly for livery.

1683.

Report in obedience to the King's warrant of 27 April, 1683, as to moneys and accounts relative to his Majesty's servants. The following musicians' names appear in the list, with the dates of the years for which liveries were due :—

Thomas Purcell, 1679 to 1681.
Nicholas Staggins, as master of the music, and as musician, 1679 to 1682.
Thomas Bates, 1677.
John Clements, 1678 to 1682.
Charles Coleman, 1680 to 1682.
Theophilus Fitz, 1679 to 1682.
William Clayton, 1677 to 1682.
William Gregory, 1679 to 1682.
John Gamble, 1676 to 1682.
John Goodgroome, 1676 to 1682.
John Harding, 1677 to 1682.
John Hingston, 1676 to 1682.
Edward Hooton, 1678 to 1682.
John Jenkins, 1677.
John Lyllie, 1677.
Mathew Lock, 1676.
John Mosse, 1679 to 1682.
Edmund Flower, 1678 to 1682.
Thomas Laneir, 1678 to 1682.
Anthony Robert, 1676 to 1678.
Humphrey Madge, 1677 to 1678.
Alphonso Marsh, 1679 to 1681.
William Turner, 1679 to 1682.
Francis Cruys, 1679 to 1682.
Edward Dyer, 1677 to 1682.

L. C. Vol. 713, p. 11.

1683.

Account of Henry Gregory, musician, for 7 liveries due to him, and also for keeping and teaching two boys from 1679 to 1682, amounting together to £208 16s. 8d.

L. C. Vol. 713, p. 11 and p. 27.

1683.

Account of Dr. John Blow, musician, for liveries due to him 1669 to 1673, and 1678 to 1682, also for keeping and teaching two boys for four years and a half from Michaelmas, 1678 to Lady Day, 1683, at £40 a year, amounting together to £341 5s.

L. C. Vol. 713, p. 11d and p. 27.

1683.

Account of the pentionary trumpeters for their liveries due to them for the years specified :—

> Robert Ramsey, 1679 to 1682.
> Samuel Markland, 1678 to 1682.
> Henry Peacock, 1679 to 1682.

L. C. Vol. 713, *p.* 11*d.*

1683-4, *January* 12.

Petition of Robert Maugridge, one of his Majesty's drummers in ordinary, against John Maugridg, drum major, for deteyning his liveryes.

Let John Maugridg have notice of this petition and appear before me upon Thursday morning next by nyne of the clock.

L. C. Vol. 656.

1683-4, *January* 25.

Robert Carr appointed musician in ordinary for the violls, in the place of John Hingston, with wages of £50 per annum.

L. C. Vol. 749, *p.* 9.

1683-4, *January* 31.

Will of Robert Ramsay, pentionary trumpeter, of the city of Westminster, dated 31 January, 1683-4. And a certificate to the effect that he died 1 March, 1683-4, and was buried on 4 March at St. Margaret's Church, Westminster.

L. C. Vol. 196, *p.* 26.

1683-4, *February* 13.

John Stevenson made trumpeter in ordinary in the place of Milbert Meares, deceased.

L. C. Vol. 749, *p.* 22, *and L. C. Vol.* 480, *pp.* 188 *and* 189.

1683-4, *February* 15.

Petition of Rebecca Flower against Edmund Flower upon promise of marriage.

L. C. Vol. 656.

1683-4, *February* 16.

Henry Purcell appointed "keeper, maker, repairer and mender and tuner of all and every his Majesty's musicall wind instruments; that is to say all regalls, virginalls, organs, flutes, recorders and all other kind of wind instruments whatsoever, in the place of John Hingston, deceased." Wages £60 per annum, together with the money necessary for the "workinge, labouringe, makeing and mending any of the instruments aforesaid." "And also lycence and authority to the said Henry Purcell or his assigns to take up within ye realme of England all such mettalls, wyer, waynscote and other wood and things as shalbe necessary to be imployed about the premisses, agreeing, paying and allowing reasonable rates and prices for the same. And also in his Majesty's name and upon reasonable and lawfull prices, wages and hire, to take up such workmen, artificers, labourers, worke and store houses, land and water carriages and all other needefull things as the said Henry Purcell or his assignes shall thinke convenient to be used on ye premisses. And also power and authority to the said Henry Purcell or his assignes to take up all tymber, strings, and feathers, necessary and convenient for the premisses, agreeing, paying and allowing reasonable rates and prices for the same, in as full and ample manner as the said John Hingston . . . . formerly had."

L. C. Vol. 749, *p.* 23.

1683-4, *February* 22.

Order to pay £5 to Charles Evans, harper, for strings for the Italian harp for one year ending Christmas, 1683.

L. C. Vol. 749, *p.* 27.

1683-4, *February* 22.

Liveries ordered for Jervas Price, esquire, his Majesty's sergeant trumpeter, and for 16 trumpeters and a kettle-drummer. (For each a violet coat trimmed with silk and silver lace.)

L. C. Vol. 749, *p.* 27, *also L. C. Papers, Bundle* 15.

1683-4, *February* 22.

Liveries ordered for his Majesty's drum-major, four drummers and a fife, similar to the liveries of the trumpeters.

L. C. Vol. 749, *p.* 27.

1683-4, *March* 5.

£30 to be paid to Dr. John Blow, master of the children of the Chappell Royall, every year during the King's pleasure, for the maintenance of Francis Pigott, late a child of the Chappell, whose voyce is changed and is gon from the Chappell. Two suits of clothes, etc., also provided.

L. C. Vol. 749, *p.* 36.

1684, *March* 25.

Payments of £10 to John Blow, master of the children of the Chappell Royall, for keeping and teaching two singing boys, were made on this and the three following Feast days, St. John Baptist, Michaelmas and Christmas.

L. C. Vol. 466.

1684, *St. John Baptist.*

Payment of £29 16s. 8d. to Henry Gregory, musician to the King, for clothing, and educating two boys in the art of music for half a year.

L. C. Vol. 466.

1684, *July* 30.

Warrant to repair a silver trumpet, the same being now broken and unserviceable, and to deliver it to Mr. William Shore, one of His Majesty's trumpeters.

L. C. Vol. 602; *p.* 47, *see also pp.* 280 *and* 282.

1684, *August* 27.

Letter of assignment from Gyles Stephens of Egham, appointing Richard Robinson, one of the musicians to his Majesty, his true and lawful attorney.

L. C. Vol. 199, *p.* 13*d.*

1684, *September* 20.

Will of Samuel Markland, pentionary trumpeter, citizen and weaver of London, dwelling in the parish of St. James's, Clerkenwell. He nominates his wife, Elizabeth Markland, as his sole executrix, and leaves " to my loving son in law John Low 12d., to my loving grandson Samuel Low 2s. 6d. . . . . . and to my cousin John Sadler 12d."

L. C. Vol. 196, *p.* 28.

Accounts ending Michaelmas, 1684.

Accounts for liveries for the following musicians :—

John Hingstone	Edward Hooten
William Gregory	Nicholas Staggins, Master
Thomas Lanier	of music in the place of
John Harding	Lewis Grabu
John Gamble	Nicholas Staggins in the
John Clement	place of Robert Hudson
Charles Colman	William Turner
Theophilus Fittz	Francis Cruys
John Goodgroome	Edward Dyer
William Clayton	John Mosse
John Blow	Edmund Flower

Account for pensions for the trumpeters to the late King Charles I.:—Robert Ramsey, Samuel Markland and Henry Peacock.

Account paid to Henry Gregory for clothing, and educating two boys in the art of music.

Account paid to John Blow, master of the boys of the Chapel Royal, for the keep of two boys and for teaching them singing.

L. C. Vol. 72.

1684, *November* 1.

Order to pay to Dr. John Blow, master of the twelve children of the Chapel, £134 17s. 8d. for the following items :—

	£	s.	d.
For ye children's learning on ye lute -	30	0	0
For ye violin - - - - -	30	0	0
For ye theorbo - - - - -	30	0	0
For fire and strings for ye musicke roome in ye chappell - - - - -	20	0	0
For ruled paper and penns and inke, etc.	2	10	0
For strings for ye lutes and theorboe -	2	10	0
For 6 days travelling to Lyncolne and bringing a boy - - - - -	6	0	0
For a nurse for one of ye children -	3	12	0
For burying Edward Frost - - -	7	5	8
	£131	17	8

L. C. Vol. 749, *p.* 105.

1684, *November* 24.

Dr. William Child and Michael Wise mentioned as musicians in ordinary for the cornet. Wages 20d. a day and £16 2s. 6d. a year for livery.

L. C. Vol. 749, *p.* 113.

1684, *November* 26.

John Bowman appointed musician in ordinary to the King for the private musick, in the place of John Harding, deceased.

L. C. Vol. 749, *p.* 114, *and L. C. Vol.* 480, *p.* 104.

1684, *St. Andrew.*

Payment of £16 2s. 6d. to each of the following musicians to the King, for their livery,

William Gregory	William Clayton
Thomas Laneir	John Blow
John Gamble	Edward Hooton
John Clements	William Turner
Francis Cruys	Edward Dyer
John Goodgroome	John Moss
Theophilus Fittz	Edmund Flower
Charles Colman	William Child

Nicholas Staggins (master of music in the place of Lewis Grabu).

Nicholas Staggins (in the place of Richard Hudson).

Payment of £29 : 16 : 8 to Henry Gregory, musician to the King, for clothing two boys and educating them in the art of music for half a year.

L. C. Vol. 466.

1684, *December* 5.

" I doe hereby certifie that Mr. Francis Gwyn having promised in his petition to provide a roome for ye musicians to practise in ; (the other roomes belong to the sergeants at arms and sewers of the chamber and are not of soe greate necessity ; theire attendance being not but once a weeke and seldome made use of by the two societyes.) Soe that if the Lords Commissioners of the Treasury shall please to grant leave unto Mr. Gwyn to build there, I am content therewith (and that those roomes before mentioned may be pulled down).

Arlington [Lord Chamberlain].

[N.B.—This musicians' room was probably for Whitehall : a later entry mentions some building being carried on there by Mr. Gwyn.]

L. C. Vol. 749, *p.* 121.

1684 (*December* 5).

Order for winter liveries for the children of the Chapel, through Dr. John Blow, master.

L. C. Vol. 749, *p.* 122.

1684, *December* 8.

Petition of James Mercy, joyner, against James Bannister, musician, £41 10s. od. debt for meat, drink, and lodging of plaintiff in Maypole Alley Newmarket.

L. C. Vol. 656.

[1684].

Abstract of yearly provisions made in the office of the Great Wardrobe.

Furnishing the organ lofts at the King's Chappells with silk curtains.

Furnishing each Chappell boy as he goes off thence upon the change of his voice with 2 suits and double proportion of linen and all other necessaries.

Similar entries in the years 1692, 1694 and 1698.

L. C. Vol. 545.

1684-5, *January* 20.

Order to admit Richard Lewis, one of his Majesty's private musicians in ordinary without fee, to the first vacancy with fee.

L. C. Vol. 749, *p.* 146, *and L. C. Vol.* 480, *p.* 104.

1684-5, *January* 26.

Order to the following musicians of the King to attend at his Majesty's theatre royal to practice music for a ball, which is to be before his Majesty there ; viz : —

Mr. William Clayton	James Bannister
John Crouch	John Bannister
Robert King	Henry Heale
John Goodwyn	John Lenten
Theophilus Fittz	Edmund Flower

To Dr. Staggins, master of his Majesty's music.

L. C. Vol. 749, *p.* 147.

1684-5, *January* 27.

Warrant to pay Mr. John Gostling, one of the Gentlemen of his Majesty's Chappell Royall, £36. 18. for his rydeing charges and other expenses in his attending upon his Majesty at Windsor in 1683 and 1684, for 123 days at the rate of 6s. by the day.

L. C. Vol. 749, *p.* 148.

1684-5, *January* 27.

Appointment of Charles Staggins to be musician in ordinary for ye tennor hoboy with fee, and to be musician in ordinary for the violin in the place of his father Isaac Staggins, deceased.

L. C. Vol. 480, *p.* 104 ; *and Vol.* 749, *p.* 149 (*with date* 3 *December*, 1684).

1684-5, *February* 11.

Order to deliver to Mr. Jervas Price, His Majesty's sergeant trumpeter, and to 16 trumpeters and kettledrummers 8 yards of black cloth each for mourning for the funeral of King Charles II.

L. C. Vol. 561.

1685, *March* 25.

Dr. Nicholas Staggins, admitted in the place and quality of master of the musick in ordinary to His Majesty King James II., to enjoy all fees, wages and profits, etc.

L. C. Vol. 185, *p.* 22, *and L. C. Vol.* 481, *p.* 101, *and Vol.* 484.

1685, *March* 31.

Certificate of the appointment of Dr. Nicholas Staggins in the place and quality of master of the musicke in ordinary to his Majesty King James II.

L. C. Vol. 199, *p.* 1.

1685, *May* 16.

Gervace Price appointed Sergeant Trumpeter at his Majesty's accession to the Crown.

John Senner, and William Bounty, appointed trumpeters.

L. C. Vol. 481, *p.* 103, *also L. C. Vol.* 484.

1685, *May* 16.

Warrant for the appointment of Gervice Price, esquire, servant in ordinary to King James II., as sergeant of all trumpeters, drummers and fifes in England and other dominions of his Majesty.

L. C. Vol. 199, *and L. C. Vol.* 185, *p.* 41.

1685, *May* 16 *to June* 12.

Appointment of the following as trumpeters in ordinary to his Majesty King James II. : —

John Senior, William Bounty, sworn May 16 ; William Shore, junior, Jervas Walker, John Stevenson, Daniel Leffebre, sworn May 18 ; Simon Pearson, Richard Marsh, sworn May 20 ; Hugh Fisher, Henrick Davant, sworn May 23 ; Benedict Ragois, Thomas Barwell, Mathias Shore, William Bull, sworn May 25 ; Peter Monsett, and Michaell Maire, sworn June 12.

L. C. Vol. 185, *p.* 41.

1685, *May* 18.

Appointment of William Shore, John Stevenson and Daniel Le Febre as trumpeters.

L. C. Vol. 481, *p.* 103, *also L. C. Vol.* 484.

1685, *May* 18.

Jervace Walker appointed trumpeter.

This was Sergeant Price's man, which he permitted to be sworn into the void place, making the number sixteen.

L. C. Vol. 481, *p.* 103, *also Vol.* 484.

1685, *May* 20.

Appointment of Simon Pearson and Richard Marsh as trumpeters.

L. C. Vol. 481, *p.* 103, *also Vol.* 484.

1685, *May* 22.

Warrant for seventy six surplices for the gentlemen and musicians, eight and thirty surplices for the children of the Chapel.

L. C. Vol. 804, *p.* 211.

1685, *May* 23.

Hugh Fisher and Henrick Davant appointed trumpeters.

L. C. Vol. 481, *p.* 103, *also Vol.* 484.

1685, *May* 25.

Benedict Ragoies, Thomas Barwell, Mathias Shore and and William Bull appointed trumpeters.

L. C. Vol. 481, *p.* 103, *also Vol.* 484.

1685, *June* 12.

Michael Maire and Peter Moussett appointed trumpeters.

L. C. Vol. 481, *p.* 103, *also Vol.* 484.

1685, *August* 31.

Warrant to swear the following as musicians for his Majesty's private musick in ordinary with fee and salary :—

Countertenors.

These were at sea

- Thomas Farmer
- Jeoffrey Ayleworth
- Edward (Edmund) Flower
- James Peasable
- Joseph Fashion, his father drowned at sea.
- Edward Greeting, his father drowned at sea.

John Twist
Robert King
John Crouch
John Bannister
William Clayton
William Hall
Robert Carr
Nathaniel French
Richard Tomlinson
John Goodwyn
Edward Hooton
Henry Hele
Theophilus Fitz
Charles Staggins, junior
John Lenton

The vocall part
- John Abell
- William Turner

Bases.

Gosling
Bowman

For the Flute.

Monsieur Mario

Tenor.

Thomas Heywood

Base Viol.

Coleman

Harpsicall.

Henry Purcell

Composer.

Dr. Blow

Bases.

Reading
Henry Eagles
Mons. Le Rich

Keeper of the Instruments.

Henry Brockwell

L. C. Vol. 481, *p.* 101 ; *Vol* 484 ; *and Vol.* 750, *p.* 18.

1685, *September* 10 *to October* 22.

Certificates of the appointments of the following musicians for the private music in ordinary to his Majesty King James II. :—

September 10. John Crouch, John Bannester, Robert Carr, John Goslin, Francis Mariens, John Blow, and Balthazar Reading.

September 18. Theophilus Fittz.

September 23. Nathaniel French.

October 7. John Goodwin and Henry Heale.

October 8. Edmund Flower, Robert King, William Hall, Richard Thomlinson, Thomas Farmer, Thomas Heywood, and Francis le Riche.

October 9. Henry Purcell.

October 10. Jeoffery Aleworth, Joseph Fashions, Edward Greetinge, John Twist, William Clayton, John Lenton, John Abell, William Turner, Soloman Eagles, and Henry Brockwell.

October 11. Charles Coleman.

October 22. James Peaseable and John Bowman.

L. C. Vol. 199.

1685, *October* 15.

Order for winter liveries for the tenn children of the Chappell Royall, to be delivered to Dr. John Blow, master of the said children.

L. C. Vol. 776, *p.* 23.

1685, *November* 12.

Warrant for allowance of riding charges to musicians attending the King and Queen on their progress att Windsor and Hampton Court; 5s. a day to the master of the musick, and 3s. a day to each of the musicians for the first week, and half that sum for the remainder of the time spent in attendance.

"And forasmuch as Dr. Nicholas Staggins, master of the musick,

Thomas Farmer	Henry Brockwell
William Clayton	Henry Heale
Jeoffrey Ayleworth	James Peaseable
Robert Carr	John Lenton
John Crouch	Joseph Fashion
Nathaniell French	Soloman Eagles
Edward Hooton	Monsieur La Rich
Richard Tomlinson	

musicians to his Majesty, did attend his Majesty the last sumer most part of the tyme of his Majesty's residence at Windsor Castle, according to ye particular duty of theire places," it is requested that the sum of 5s. by the day be paid to Dr. Staggins, and 3s. by the day to each musician abovenamed for the space of 52 days from 16 August to 6 October, 1685.

L. C. Vol. 751, *p.* 10.

1685, *December* 11.

John Abell, musician in ordinary, to receive 3s. a day for his riding charges in attendance on the King at Windsor Castle, for the space of 64 days, from 4 August to 6 October, 1685.

L. C. Vol. 751, *p.* 48.

1685-6, *January* 13.

Warrant for payment of £75 . 14 . 3½ to the executors of John Baker, late trumpeter to his Majesty, arrears of livery for the year 1676.

L. C. Vol. 711, *p.* 63d.

1685-6, *February* 20.

Received Simon Peirson's trumpett, broke to peeces, weight 27 oz.

Received Thomas Barwell's trumpett, all broke to peeces, which was Culthrop's, weight 16 oz.

These two above mentioned trumpetts delivered to Mr. Bull, February 20, to be new made.

Received by me, Wm. Bull.

The trumpets were returned 12 May, 1686.

L. C. Vol. 440.

1685-6, *February* 25.

Arrears due to severall of the servants of his late Majesty King Charles II. ; accounts of liveries due to the following musicians :—

To Nicholas Staggins, master, 6 liveries, 1679 to 1684.

    Nicholas Staggins, as musician, 6 liveries, 1679 to 1684.
    John Gamble, 1676 to 1684.
    John Clements, 1662, 1664 to 1667, 1678 to 1684.
    Charles Coleman, 1666, 1667, 1670, 1680 to 1684.
    Theophilus Fitz, 1665 to 1667, 1670, 1679 to 1684.
    William Clayton, 1670, 1677 to 1684.
    William Gregory, 1679 to 1684.
    John Goodgroome, 1664 to 1667, 1670, 1676 to 1684.
    Thomas Laneir, 1660 to 1667, 1678 to 1684.
    Edward Hooten, 1678 to 1684.
    John Mosse, 1679 to 1684.
    William Turner, 1679 to 1684.
    Francis Cruys, 1679 to 1684.
    Edmond Flower, 1678 to 1684.
    Edward Dyer, 1677, 1679 to 1684.
    Doctor John Blow, 1669 to 1673, 1678 to 1684.
    Doctor William Child, 1662, 1665 to 1667, 1679 to 1684.

Account due to the drum major, 4 other drummers and a fife for 1676.

To the drum-major from 1679 to 1684.

To the serjeant trumpeter from 1680 to 1684.

Account due to Dr. John Blow for 5 years and three quarters keeping and teaching two boys at £40 per annum, ending Christmas, 1684.

Account due to Henry Gregory for half a year's keeping and teaching of two boys, ending at Midsummer 1665, and from 1679 to 1684.

L. C. Vol. 713, *pp.* 26 *and* 27.

1685-6, *March* 5.

Order for liveries for six trumpettors and a kettle-drummer, that attend the Earl of Clarendon, Lord Lieutenant of Ireland.

L. C. Vol. 751, *p.* 87.

1685-6, *March* 19.

Letter from James Bannester, one of his Majesty's musicians in ordinary, and to his late Majesty, appointing as his true and lawful attorney his wife, Mary Bannister, to demand and receive all sums of money due to him as salary.

L. C. Vol. 199, *p.* 6.

1686, *April* 21.

Order for liveries for the sergeant trumpettor, 16 trumpettors, and one kettledrummer, for 1686.

L. C. Vol. 751, *p.* 117.

1686, *April* 23.

Assignment by Jane Fisher, widow and administratrix of Hugh Fisher, late of the parish of St. Martin's in the Fields, one of the trumpetts in ordinary to his late Majesty, King Charles II., and to his present Majesty, of the sum of £8, to Charles Fisher, of the parish of St. James', Westminster, out of every £20 paid to her in respect of her late husband's service as aforesaid.

L. C. Vol. 196, *p.* 59.

1686, *April* 23.

Order for liveries for 1686, for the kettledrummer attending his Majesty's Troop of Guards, commanded by the Duke of Northumberland ; for the kettledrummer to the Troop of Guards commanded by Lord Churchill ; for the kettledrummer attending his Majesty's Troop of Horse in the Earl of Oxford's regiment, commanded by Sir John Parsons.

L. C. Vol. 751, *p.* 119.

1686, *May* 3.

Bill of Henry Brockwell, keeper of his Majesty's instruments :—

	£	s.	d.
From Our Lady Day 1685 to Our Lady Day 1686, for mending his Majesty's instruments	5.	0.	0.
For strings for 1 yeare for ye base violins ...	2.	0.	0.
For one yeare removing ye instruments ...	5.	0.	0.
For bowes and bridges for one yeare ...		5.	0.
For three new cases for ye base violins ...	6.	0.	0.
(Signed) Nicholas Staggins.	£18.	5.	0.

L. C. Vol. 751, *p.* 132.

1686, *May* 6.

Warrant to swear and admit Thomas Brady kettle-drummer in ordinary to his Majesty King James II., to attend the Earl of Clarendon, Lord Lieutenant of Ireland, to enjoy the said place with salary and profitts belonging thereto.

L. C. Vol. 481, *p.* 108; *Vol.* 484; *and Vol.* 751, *p.* 130.

1686, *May* 6.

Warrants to swear and admit Vandenand Cornelius and Robert Maugridge kettle-drummers in ordinary to his Majesty King James II., to enjoy all wages and profitts thereto belonging.

L. C. Vol. 481, *p.* 108 ; *Vol.* 484 ; *and Vol.* 751, *pp.* 131, 132.

1686, *May* 13.

Liveries for the year 1686 ordered for his Majesty's drum major, four drumes and a fife.

L. C. Vol. 751, *p.* 146.

1686, *May* 13.

Letter of assignment by Thomas Lanier, one of his Majesty's musicians, appointing Mrs. Francis Emps, his true and lawful attorney.

L. C. Vol. 196, *p.* 38.

1686, *June* 3.

Warrant to provide clothing for William Norris, late child of the Chappell whose voice is changed.

L. C. Papers, Bundle 11.

1686, *June* 4.

Order to pay to Dr. Nicholas Staggins, master of his Majesty's musick, £18 for hire of a room for the musick to practice in the last year 1685, in Windsor Castle.

L. C. Vol. 751, *p.* 151 ; *and Vol.* 775, *p.* 145.

1686, *June* 6.

Order that two of his Majesty's old trumpetts be new made, of the same quantity they were before, and to add to them what silver is wanting for his Majesty's service.

L. C. Vol. 751, *p.* 152 ; *and Vol.* 775, *p.* 147.

1686, *June* 20.

Warrant to swear and admit James Castles trumpettor in ordinary to his Majesty, King James II., to attend upon the Lord Lieutenant of Ireland for the tyme being, to enjoy all wages and profitts of the said place.

L. C. Vol. 481, *p.* 107 ; *Vol.* 484 ; *and Vol.* 751, *p.* 154.

1686, *July* 1.

Warrant to swear and admit Alexander Jackson, junior, trumpettor in ordinary to his Majesty, King James II., to attend upon the Lord Lieutenant of Ireland for the tyme being, to enjoy the said place with the wages and profitts thereto belonging.

L. C. Vol. 481, *p.* 107 ; *Vol.* 484 ; *and Vol.* 751, *p.* 154.

1686, *July* 10.

Letter from Nathaniel French of the parish of St. Martin's in the feilds, appointing Nicholas Staggins, of Little Chelsey in the parish of Kensington, doctor of musick, his certaine and lawful attorney.

L. C. Vol. 199, *p.* 8.

1686, *July* 14.

Delivered to Mr. Simon Pierson (also Pearson) one silver trumpet, weighing 33 oz. 12 dwt.

L. C. Vol. 440.

1686, *July* 17.

Letter from William Child, of Windsor Castle, doctor of musick, appointing Thomas Blagrave, one of the gentlemen of the Kings Majesty's Chappell his certaine and lawful attorney.

L. C. Vol. 199, *p.* 11.

1686, *July* 25.

Letter of assignment by Dr. William Child, one of his Majesty's musicians, appointing Thomas Haynes his true and lawful attorney.

L. C. Vol. 196, *p.* 38*d.*

1686, *August* 2.

Delivered to Mr. Thomas Barwell, one silver trumpet, weighing 31 oz. 1 dwt.

L. C. Vol. 440.

1686, *August* 3.

For embroidering 5 badges with " I.R." and knott and tassells for 5 drum cases at 18/- each, £4. 10s.

L. C. Vol. 208, *entry* 61.

1686, *August* 18.

Letter of assignment by Francis Cruys, appointing Mr. Charles Coleman as his true and lawful attorney. Witnessed by Nicola Matteis and Thomas Shemman.

L. C. Vol. 196, *p.* 37*d.*

1686, *September* 5.

Order to the master of the jewell house for foure silver trumpetts for the trumpettors of the Lord of Dover's Troop of Guards, such as his Majesty's trumpettors have.

L. C. Vol. 751, *p.* 174 ; *L. C. Vol,* 602, *p.* 100.

1686, *September* 5.

Liveries ordered for four trumpeters, two kettle-drummers, and two hautboys, in the 4th troop of Guards, commanded by Lord Dover.

L. C. Vol. 751, *p.* 174.

1686 *September* 6.

Winter liveries for the year 1686, to be provided for the children of the Chappell, and delivered to Dr. John Blow, master of the Children of the Chapple.

L. C. Vol. 751, *p.* 186.

1686, *September* 14.

Letter of assignment from Benedict Ragois, one of his Majesty's trumpeters, appointing his wife, Magdalen Ragois, his true and lawful attorney.

L. C. Vol. 199, *p.* 79.

1686, *September* 21.

Warrant addressed to Richard, Viscount Preston, master of his Majesty's Great Wardrobe for the payment of the following sums :—

" Whereas it appears that £2,484. 16s. 3d. remains due to the respective musicians to his late Majesty whose names follow, for the arrears of their liveries incurred during his late Majesty's reign :—after making such retrenchment throughout as was intended by his late Majesty and is commanded by his present Majesty to be observed in cases of arrears of this nature, these are to desire your Lordship, out of the money which is or shall be imprested to you at the receipt of the Exchequer of the new imposition on tobacco and sugar, to pay all the sums due to the said musicians " :—

Nicholas Staggins, master of musick, 1679 to 1684, £193 : 13.

John Gamble, 1676, 1679 to 1684, £112 : 17 : 6.

John Clements, 1662, 1664 to 1667, 1678 to 1684, £179 : 11.

Charles Coleman, 1666-67, 1670, 1680 to 1684, £129.

Theophilus Fitz, 1665 to 1667, 1670, 1679 to 1684, £161 : 5.

William Clayton, 1670, 1677 to 1684, £145 : 2 : 6.·

William Gregory, 1679 to 1684, £96 : 15.

John Goodgroome, 1664 to 1667, 1670, 1676 to 1684, £225 : 15.

Thomas Laneir, 1660 to 1667, 1678 to 1684, £170 : 10.

Edward Hooten, 1678 to 1684, £112 : 17 : 6.

John Mosse, 1679 to 1684, £96 : 15.

William Turner, 1679 to 1684, £96 : 15.

Francis Cruys, 1679 to 1684, £96 : 15.

Edmund Flower, 1678 to 1684, £112 : 17 : 6.

Edmund Dyer, 1677, 1679 to 1684, £112 : 17 : 6.

John Blow, 1669 to 1673, 1678 to 1684, £193 : 10.

William Child, 1662, 1665 to 1667, 1679 to 1684, £161 : 5s.

John Blow, for custody and teaching of two boys, £40 a year from 1679 to 1684, £230.

Henry Gregory, for custody and teaching of two boys, 1665, and 1679 to 1684, £139 : 4 : 5.

L. C. Vol. 805, *p.* 140; *L. C. Papers, Bundle* 14 *and Bundle* 21.

1686, *September* 29.

Liveries ordered for twelve hautboyes, and six drummers, for the 1st, 2nd, and 3rd Troops of Guards, to be made ready against his Majesty's birthday.

L. C. Vol. 751, *p.* 180.

Accounts ending Michaelmas, 1686.

Accounts for liveries for :—Jervis Price, the King's chief trumpeter. John Maugridge, the King's chief drummer.

L. C. Vol. 73.

1686, *October* 12.

Delivered to Mr. Sebastian Van Heisel, one silver trumpet, weighing 37 oz. 1 dwt.

His signature attached to the receipt of same. Note in margin " Lord Dover's trumpet."

Delivered to Mr. Eustace Gilliard, one silver trumpet, weight 36 oz. 1 dwt. 2 grs.

His signature attached to receipt of same.

Delivered to Mr. Elias le Fevre, one silver trumpet, weight 37 oz. 1 dwt. 2 grs. His signature attached to receipt of same.

Delivered to Mr. Charles Burgesse, one silver trumpet, weight 37 oz. 1 dwt. His signature attached to receipt of same.

L. C. Vol. 440.

1686, *October* 15.

Order that the sum of £10 be paid to John Abell, musician in ordinary to his Majesty, for a guytar by him bought for his Majesty's service in his bedchamber.

Order that John Abell, musician in ordinary, receive payment at 3s. by the day for his riding charges in attending the King at Windsor Castle, for 141 days, from 14 May to 1 October, 1686.

L. C. Vol. 751, *p.* 194.

1686, *November* 9.

Riding charges of 5s. by the day to be paid to Dr. Nicholas Staggins, master of his Majesty's musick, and 3s. by the day to each of his Majesty's musicians, for 141 days, for their attendance on the King at Windsor Castle, from 14 May to

1 October, 1686 ; amounting to £35. 5s. for the master, and
£21. 3s. to each of the following musicians :—

Jeoffery Aleworth	Theophilus Fittz
John Crouch	James Peaseable
William Clayton	William Hall
Thomas Farmer	Valentine Reading
Nathaniell French	Edward Flower
Edward Hooton	Edward Heale
John Lenton	Richard Thomlynson
Solomon Eagles	John Twist
Robert Carr.	

L. C. Vol. 751, *p.* 221.

1686, *November* 9.

These are to pray and require you to pay unto Dr.
Nicholas Staggins, master of his Majesty's musick, the sum of
£19. 11s. 6d. for faire writeing of a composition for his
Majesty's coronation day from the originall in score the 6 parts,
for drawing ye said composition into forty severall parts for
trumpetts, hautboyes, violins, tennors, bases, pricker's dyett
included, for ruled paper, penns, inke and chamber rent, and
disburst in providing severall musitians for ye coronation day
who were not his Majesty's servants.

L. C. Vol. 751, *p.* 213.

1686, *November* 17.

Warrant to swear and admit Nicholas Castles trumpeter in
ordinary to his Majesty, King James II., to attend the
Earl of Clarendon, Lord Lieutenant of Ireland, and to enjoy
all ways and fees of the said office.

L. C. Vol. 751, *p.* 227.

1686.

Fee of £6 received of Dr. John Blow, being £3. for his
debenters, 1669 to 1673, and 1678 to 1684 ; and £3 for his
quarterly debenters for keeping and teaching 2 boys for 5
yeares 3 quarters ending at Christmas, 1684.

Fee of £1 : 10 received of Mr. Turner, musician, for his 6
debenters, 1679 to 84.

Fee of £2 : 5 received of Mr. Clements, musician, for his
9 debenters, 1666, 1667, and 1678 to 1684.

Fee of £1 : 17 : 6 received of Mr. Colman for his own
debenters for the years, 1666, 1667 and 1670 ; and for Mr. Cruys
his debenters for 1681 to 1684 ; and for entering a letter of
attorney.

Fee of £1 : 15 received of Mr. Hooton for his 7 debenters, 1679 to 1684, as a musician.

Fee of £2 : 12 : 6 received of Serjeant Haynes for Dr. Child's debenters for 1662, 1665 to 1667, 1679 to 1684, and for entering the letter of attorney.

Fee of 10s. received of Mr. Gregory, musician, for his debenter due at St. Andrew, 1680.

Fee of £1 : 10 received of Dr. Staggins for his 12 debenters as master of music and musician, 1679-1684.

L. C. Vol. 458.

1686-7, *January* 24.

Letter of assignment from William Gregory, one of the private musick to his late Majesty King Charles II., appointing Thomas Whitefeild of the parish of St. Martin's in the feilds, his true and lawful attorney.

L. C. Vol. 199, *p.* 18*d.*

1686-7, *February* 11.

Liveries ordered for his Majesty's sergeant trumpeter, sixteen trumpeters and a kettle-drummer.

Also for his Majesty's drum major, four drummers and a fife, for the year 1687.

Also for the kettle drummer attending the Troop of Guards, commanded by the Duke of Northumberland; the kettle-drummer to the Troop of Guards commanded by Lord Churchill; and the kettledrummer attending the Troop of Horse commanded by Sir John Parsons.

L. C. Vol. 751, *pp.* 282, 283.

1686-7, *February* 18.

Memorandum that there remains due to the executrix of Thomas Purcell, deceased, upon account of his liveries of £40 per annum, due to him at every Feast of All Saints, as one of the grooms of the Robes, to his late Majesty, as also upon account of his livery of £16. 2s. 6d. per annum due to him at every Feast of St. Andrew as one of his said Majesty's musicians, to the Feast of St. Michael, 1671, the sum of £220. 12s. 6d., whereof he hath received from the said wardrobe by talley and order of loan upon the fee-farm rents the sum of £173. 7s. 3d.; which talley and order, if not yet discharged in the Exchequer, there still remains due to him as abovesaid the said sum of £220. 12s. 6d.

L. C. Vol. 711.

1687, *April* 2.

Petition of Henry Brockwell and Edmond Flower, musicians to his late Majesty, for payment of £111 : 6 : 8, due to them.

L. C. Vol. 713, *p.* 47.

1687, *April* 22.

Anthony Ragoies (also called Ragway) appointed trumpeter in ordinary to the King in the place of Benedict Ragoies (also " Ragway "), deceased.

L. C. Vol. 481, *p.* 103 ; *Vols.* 484 *and* 751, *p.* 323.

1687, *April* 25.

Warrant to swear and admit Samuel Akeroyde musician in ordinary to his Majesty, in the place of John Twist, deceased.

L. C. Vol. 751, *p.* 324.

1687, *May* 29.

" I doe hereby order that noe person presume to go into ye organ roome in his Majesty's Chappell Royall but ye musick who are to officiate their."

L. C. Vol. 751, *p.* 306.

1687, *July* 17.

Lewis appointed musician in ordinary to the King for the private musick in the place of Jeoffrey Ayleworth, deceased.

L. C. Vol. 776, *p.* 38.

1687, *August* 1.

Order to pay £23. 5s. to Henry Brockwell, keeper of his Majesty's instruments :—

From Lady Day, 1686, to Lady Day, 1687, for one yeares mending his Majesty's instruments, £5.

For strings for one year for the base violins, £2.

For one yeares removing the instruments to Windsor and back again, £4.

For a new base violin, with a new standing case, hinges, lock and key, £12.

For bowes and bridges, 5s.

Nicholas Staggins.

L. C. Vol. 776, *p.* 44.

1687, *August* 3.

Warrant to admit Charles Powell as musician in the place of Jeoffrey Ayleworth, deceased.

L. C. Vol. 481, *p.* 100 ; *L. C. Vol.* 484.

1687, *August* 8.

Charles Powell appointed musician in ordinary to his Majesty, of the private musick, in the place of Jeoffrey Ayleworth, deceased.

L. C. Vol. 776, *p.* 54.

Accounts ending Michaelmas, 1687.

These include the accounts for the liveries due by warrant of 21 September, 1686 (*see* under this date for amounts) to the chief trumpeter, chief drummer and other musicians to the late King Charles II.

L. C. Vol. 74.

1687, *October* 5.

Gervase Price, sergeant trumpeter, deceased, and Mathias Shore appointed in his place.

L. C. Vol. 481, *p.* 103 ; *L. C. Vol.* 484.

1687, *October* 5.

Mathias Shore appointed sergeant of the trumpeters, drummers, and fifes in ordinary, to his Majesty.

L. C. Vol. 752, *p.* 17.

1687, *October* 5.

Francis Loyscoean (also " Loiscan ") appointed trumpeter in ordinary in place of Mathias Shore.

L. C. Vols. 481, *p.* 103 ; *Vols.* 484 *and* 752.

1687, *October* 13.

Order to deliver winter liveries for 1687 to Dr. John Blow, master of the children of his Majesty's Chappell, they being tenn in number.

L. C. Vol. 752, *p.* 26.

1687, *October* 17.

Richard Lewys appointed keeper of the instruments in the place of Henry Brockwell.

L. C. Vol. 481, *p.* 101 ; *L. C. Vol.* 484.

1687, *October* 17.

Warrant to swear and admit Richard Lewis overseer and keeper of his Majesty's musical instruments in ordinary to his Majesty.

L. C. Vol. 752, *p.* 27.

1687, *October* 21.

" *To Dr. Staggins, master of his Majesty's musick.* Whereas you have neglected to give order to ye violins to attend at ye Chappell at Whitehall where Her Royal Highnesse ye Princesse Ann of Denmarke is present, these are therefore to give notice to them that they give theire attendance there upon Sunday next and soe to continue to doe soe as formerly they did."

L. C. Vol. 752, *p.* 31.

1687, *November* 10.

Letter of assignment from Nathaniel French, one of the musicians to his Majesty King James II., to Thomas Cooke, saylsman, of the sum of £25 : 12.

L. C. Vol. 199, *p.* 81.

1687, *November* 23.

Suit of clothes ordered for Charles Husband, late child of his Majesty's Chappell Royall, whose voice is changed and is gone from the Chappell. Also £20 for one year to be paid to him.

L. C. Vol. 752, *p.* 47. *L. C. Papers. Bundle* 78.

1687, *December* 8.

Certificate that John Smith was one of his late Majesty's private musick from the time of his said Majesty's happy restoration until midsummer, 1673, and that there is due in arrear to him the sum of £252. 17. 6.

The said John Smith alledges that he was forced to retire on account of his religion, the laws being at that time so severe against those of that religion, but that his Majesty having directed the payment of arrears to others who were obliged to retire on account of their religion it is agreed that his case may be represented to his Majesty for his directions.

On the back of the same document is a memorandum "that Mr. Grabu received all his arrears as master of the music to his late Majesty although not actually in his said Majesty's service at the time of his decease, Nicholas Staggins being admitted into that place many years before."

L. C. Papers. Bundle 20.

1687, *December* 19.

Musicians' riding charges for attending the King and Queen in their progresses at Windsor, Hampton Court, or elsewhere, at the rate of 3s. each by the day for the first week if lodged in the House, and half that sum for the rest of the time spent in attendance, due to forty-one persons, gentlemen and musicians and other officers of his Majesty's Chappell, viz.:—

Seignr. Fede, master.	Mr. Pordage
Seignr. Grande	Mr. Anatean
Seignr. Sansoni	Mr. Abell

Gregorians.

One organist	Mr. La Grange
Mr. Nicolson	Mr. Desabaye
Mr. Sherburn	Mr. Pawmester
Mr. Reading	Mr. Arnould
Mr. Curkaw	Seignr. Albrei

Instruments.

Mr. Hall	Mr. Carr
Mr. Farmer	Mr. Peasable
Mr. Hooden	Mr. Finger
Mr. Crouch	Mr. Neydenhanger
Mr. Goodwyn	

One organ-blower.

Two sacristarres.

Two vergers.

One master and eight children of the Chappell.

One keeper of the tribune, and

One cushion man.

The above attended his Majesty at Windsor Castle last summer for 113 days, and had no lodging in the House, but that the master and eight children of his Majesty's Chappell had lodging in the House. They are to be paid 3s. by the day each, the master and eight children to receive 3s. each for the first week of residence in the Castle, and 1s. 6d. each for the remainder of the time.

The time of his Majesty's residence was from 19 May to 16 August, and from 17 September to 11 October, 1687.

Total, £623. 8s.

L. C. Vol. 752, pp. 54 to 56.

1687, *December* 30.

Account for one pair of kettle drummes, heads and sticks at £10 for his Majesty's service in Ireland.

L. C. Vol. 208, entry 28b.

1687-8, *February* 1.

Warrant to swear and admit John Shaw musical instrument maker in ordinary to his Majesty.

L. C. Vol. 752, p. 100.

1687-8, *February* 7.

Warrant to admit John Shaw as musical instrument maker.

L. C. Vol. 481, p. 100 ; L. C. Vol. 484.

1687-8, *February* 28.

Liveries ordered for four trumpeters in Lord Dover's Fourth Troop of Guards, and for one kettle-drummer.

L. C. Vol. 752. p. 121.

1687-8, *March* 7.

The following musicians attended his Majesty during his residence at Windsor Castle for 117 days, from 19 May to 16 August, and from 13 September to 11 October, 1687. They are to be paid at the rate of 3s. each by the day, and 5s. to Dr. Staggins; *i.e.*, £16. 11s. for each musician and £29. 5s. for the master :—

Dr. Nicholas Staggins, master of musick,	Edward Greeting, Richard Tomlynson,
William Clayton,	Samuell Acroyd,
John Bannister,	John Lenton,
Robert King,	Sollaman Eagles,
Nathaniel French,	La Rich,
Theophilus Fitz,	Charles Powell,
Henry Heale,	Charles Staggins,
Edmund Flower,	Joseph Fashion,

Henry Brockwell.

L. C. Vol. 752, p. 147.

1687-8, *March* 8.

Account for rings, and tape, and making 4 curtains for the organ loft in the Princess's Chappell.

L. C. Vol. 208, entry 15c.

1687-8, *March* 10.

Letter of assignment from Francois le Rich, one of his present Majesty's private musique, to John Peters of St. Margarets, Westminster, of two sums of £10.

L. C. Vol. 199, p. 25.

1687-8, *March* 21.

Liveries for the year 1688 ordered for the kettle-drummers in the Duke of Northumberland's troop of Guards, in Lord Churchill's troop of Guards, and in the Duke of Berwick's troop of Horse.

L. C. Vol. 752, p. 134.

1687-8, *March* 21.

Order for liveries for the year 1688 for his Majesty's sergeant trumpeter, sixteen trumpeters and a kettle-drummer.

L. C. Vol. 752, p. 135.

1687-8, *March* 23.

Certificate that Mr. John Clements had a livery of £16. 2. 6 payable to him yearly, as one of his late Majesty's musicians, and hath received the same unto St. Andrew, 1684.

L. C. Vol. 183, p. 52.

1688, *March* 30.

John Shaw (also Shore) appointed trumpeter in ordinary to his Majesty in the place of William Bounty, deceased.

L. C. Vol. 481, p. 103 ; Vol. 484 ; and Vol. 752, p. 142.

1688, *March* 30.

Aaron Lake, Francis Castles and John Burton appointed trumpeters in ordinary to King James, to attend upon the Lord Lieutenant of Ireland.

L. C. Vol. 481, *p.* 107 ; *Vol.* 484 *and Vol.* 752, *pp.* 142, 143.

1688, *April* 10.

Warrants to swear and admit John Mawgridge, esquire, drum-major in ordinary to the King, in the place of John Mawgridge, deceased ; Robert Mawgridge, Devereux Clothier, Turtullian Lewys, and John Skyrme, drummers in ordinary ; and Clement Newth, fife in ordinary to his Majesty.

L. C. Vol. 481, *p.* 108 ; *Vol.* 484 ; *and Vol.* 752, *pp.* 151, 152, 154.

1688, *April* 14.

Liveries for the year 1688 ordered for his Majesty's drum-major, four drummers and a fife.

L. C. Vol. 752, *p.* 155.

1688, *April* 24.

Received Will Shore's trumpett, and delivered it at the same tyme to Mr. Bull, to be new made, it being broke, weight 30 oz. 1 dwt.

Received by me, William Bull. This trumpet returned 14 May, 1688.

L. C. Vol. 440.

1688, *June* 16.

" These are to pray and require you to make stop of ye payments of ye money for ye ryding charges of ye musicians, allowed them by my warrant for ye last Progress, untill you shall receive further order from me."

L. C. Vol. 752, *p.* 220.

1688, *June* 17 *and* 18.

Order to deliver £20 for one year and a suit of plain clothes, to Vaughan Richardson, late child of his Majesty's Chappell Royall, whose voyce is changed and is gon from the Chappell.

L. C. Vol. 752, *p.* 221. *L. C. Papers. Bundle* 78.

1688, *June* 25.

Order to pay £4 : 19 to Edmund Flower, musician in ordinary to his Majesty, the sum of 3s. by the day, riding charges, for 33 days, from 16 August to 17 September, 1687, for his attendance upon the King, according to the perticuler duty of his place, from Windsor to Portsmouth, Bath, Glocester, Worcester, Ludlow, Shrewesbury, Whitchurch, Chester, Newport, Leithfield, Coventry, Bambury, Oxford, Cirencester, Bath, and back again to Windsor.

L. C. Vol. 752, *p.* 223.

1688, *July* 6.

Delivered to Mr. Bull, for the use of Mr. Daniel Le Fever, one silver trumpet, weight 36 oz.

Received by me, Wm. Bull.

This trumpet returned 4 January, 1691-2.

L. C. Vol. 440.

1688, *August* 19.

" I do hereby order that a number of his Majesty's musitians shall attend the Queenes Majesty's maids of honour to play whensoever they shall be sent to, at the homes of dancing, at such homes and such a number of them as they shall desire. And hereof the master of the musick and the musitians are to take notice that they observe this order."

L. C. Vol. 776, *p.* 72.

1688, *September* 13.

Warrant to provide Common Prayer books in folio for the Gentlemen of the Chappell, and twelve Common Prayer books, in octavo, for the children of the Chappell.

L. C. Vol. 837.

1688, *October* 10.

Warrant to demand of the executors of Jervice Price, deceased, late serjeant trumpeter, the mace and trumpet that were in his custody at the time of his death, that they may be returned into the office for his Majesty's immediate service.

L. C. Vol. 603, *p.* 19.

1688, *October* 15.

Winter liveries ordered for the ten children of the Chappell, to be delivered to Dr. John Blow, master of the children.

L. C. Vol. 752, *p.* 267.

1688, *October* 18.

Letter of assignment by John Smith, of London, one of his late Majesty's musicians, appointing Thomas Townsend of Westminster, his true and lawful attorney.

L. C. Vol. 196, *p.* 55*d.*

1688, *October* 20.

Warrant for the payment, from 24 July to 20 September, 1688, to the following gentlemen, musicians and officers of the Chapel Royal, of the sum of 6s. each for going to Windsor on the 24 July and returning to London on the 20 September ; and to each of them 1s. 6d. a day during the said term :—

Seignior Fede,	Mr. Hooden,
Mr. Signor Grande,	Mr. Cruch,
Segnir Sansoni,	Mr. Goodwyn,

Mr. Abell,
Mr. Pordage,
Mr. Anatean,
One organist,
Mr. Nicolson,
Mr. Sherborne,
Mr. Reading,
Mr. Cuckow,
Mr. La Grange,
Mr. Desabay,
Mr. Powmester,
Mr. Arnould,
Seigneur Albreis,
Mr. Hall,
Mr. Farmer,

Mr. Carr,
Mr. Peasable,
Mr. Tringer
Mr. Newdenhaeser,
Seignor Filiber,
Mr. Merchants,
Mr. Keelin,
Mr. Jones,
Mr. Flower,
Seignr Francisco,
Seignor Bernardo,
Mr. Le Rich,
One organ-blower,
Two sacristanes,
Two virgers,

One master and eight children of the Chappell, and one keeper of the tribune.

L. C. Vol. 752, *p.* 341.

1688, *October* 20.

Warrant to pay John Shaw, musical instrument maker in ordinary, the sum of £5. 10s. for mending the King's instruments from Michaelmas, 1687 to Michaelmas, 1688 : £12. 10s. for a base violin and case; £1 for catleens; £4 10s. for strings for one year; and £2 for bows, bridges and pins for one year, Michaelmas, 1687 to Michaelmas, 1688. The account is signed by Nicholas Staggins.

L. C. Vol. 752, *p.* 342.

1688, *October* 20.

Riding charges of the following musicians :—

Dr. Staggins, master of
            the musick
William Clayton
John Banester
Robert King
Nathaniell French
Theophilus Fitz
Henry Heale
Charles Coleman

Richard Tomlinson
Samuel Akeroyde
John Lenton
Solomon Eagles
Francis Mariens
Charles Staggins
Joseph Fashions
Charles Powell
Richard Lewys

10s. to be paid to Dr. Staggins, and 6s. to each musician, by the day, for attending the King to Windsor 24 July, 1687 and back to London 20 September, 1687. Also 2s. 6d. by the day to the master and 1s. 6d. to each musician, for 57 days, from 25 July to 19 September.

L. C. Vol. 752, *p.* 316.

[1688, *November.*]

The list of his Majesty's servants who are appointed to attend his Majesty in his progresses :—

Mathias Shore, Esq., sergeant trumpeter.

For the King's Chappell.

Mr. Pedley   Mr. Abell

L. C. Vol. 752, *p.* 283.

1688, *November* 28.

Warrant for payment of the riding charges of Mr. Pedley, one of the gentlemen of the King's Chappell Royall, for attendance on the King to Salisbury, from 17 to 26 November, 1688.

L. C. Vol. 752, *p.* 355.

1688, *December* 8.

John Abraham appointed bowmaster in the place of Thomas Farmer, deceased.

L. C. Vol. 481, *p.* 100; *L. C. Vol.* 484.

1688, *December* 20.

Warrant for the payment of the riding charges (6s. each) from London to Windsor and back of Mr. Gally, Mr. Ronchi, senior, Mr. Ronchi, junior, Mr. Mansuet, Mr. Lacrig, Mr. Naish, Mr. Ruga, Mr. Sacheller, senior, Mr. Sacheller, junior, and Mr. White, gentlemen of her Majesty's Chappell, and eight other belonging to her Chappell and in the nature of yeomen, who attended on the Queen last summer whilst she was in residence at Windsor Castle, and 1s. 6d. a day each whilst they were in attendance, viz., from 25 July to 19 September, 1688.

L. C. Vol. 752, *p.* 351.

1688-9, *March* 12.

Order to deliver to Dr. John Blow master of the children of his Majesty's Chappell Royall, winter liveries for the year 1688, for the tenn children of the Chappell Royall.

L. C. Vol. 753, *p.* 19.

1688-9, *March* 16.

Warrant to provide liveries with their Majesties' cyphers embroydered thereon, for the serjeant trumpettor, 16 trumpetts and a kettle drummer, in all particulars as was provided unto them at the last coronation, for the coronation of William and Mary.

The same for his Majesty's drum major, 4 drummers and a fife.

A later warrant of March 28, to provide the same for 3 kettledrummers.

L. C. Vol. 429, *pp.* 8 *and* 19.

1688-9, *March* 22.

Scarlet mantles to be made for the Master of the Musick and 38 musicians, that are to attend at their Majesties' coronation.

L. C. Vol. 429, *p.* 10.

1688-9, *March* 22.

Warrant to swear and admit Richard Medlicott overseer and keeper of his Majesty's musicall instruments.

L. C. Vol. 486, *p.* 67 ; *and Vol.* 753, *p.* 38.

1689, *March* 25.

A list of such of the King's servants as receive their salaries in the treasury of the chamber's office, with an account of what was owing in arrears to each of them at Lady day, 1689 :—

Mathias Shore, sergeant trumpeter, £80.
Dr. Staggins, master of the musick, £100.

Musicians, £30 each.

M. Farmer,	Edward Hooton,
Charles Powell,	Henry Heale,
Edmund Flower,	Theophilus Fitz,
James Paisible,	Charles Staggins,
Thomas Fashon,	John Lenton,
Edward Greeting,	John Abel,
Samuel Akeroyde,	William Turner,
Robert King,	John Gostling,
John Crouch,	John Bowman,
John Bannister,	Francis Mariens,
William Clayton,	Charles Coleman,
William Hall,	John Blow,
Robert Carr,	Balthazer Redding,
Nathaniel French,	Francis Le Rich,
Richard Tomlinson,	Richard Lewis,
John Goodwynn,	Solomon Eccles.

L. C. Papers. Bundle 21.

1689, *March* 28.

Scarlet cloth for coronation liveries for the Master of the children and 12 children of the Chappell.

> *L. C. Vol.* 429, *p.* 15 *; L. C. Papers. Bundle* 79.

1689, *April* 10.

Order to prepare and deliver unto the Sergeant Trumpeter one mace guilt and a coller of SS of the same quantity and fashion as heretofore.

> *L. C. Vol.* 753, *p.* 84.

1689, *April* 11.

Accounts for liveries for the coronation of William and Mary :—

For five yards of scarlet cloth for the Master of Musick, also for twenty-four yards for twelve Chappell boyes.

Several different items for the Chappell boyes.

Eighty yards of scarlett cloth for twenty gentlemen of the Chappell, and also 140 yards for thirty-five musicians.

Liveries for 16 trumpettors, 4 kettle-drummers, 4 drummers and a phife; also for the serjeant trumpettor and for the drum major.

> *L. C. Vol.* 428.

1689, *May* 4.

Warrant to swear and admit Bernard Smyth organ-maker in ordinary to his Majesty.

> *L. C. Vols.* 485, *p.* 99 *;* 486, *p.* 68 *;* 487, *p.* 23 *;*
> 488, *p.* 31 *; and* 753, *p.* 119.

1689, *May* 24.

Warrant to provide for the 2nd Troop of Guards commanded by the Duke of Ormond a silver trumpett of the same fashion, weight and proportion as other his Majesty's trumpetts.

> *L. C. Vol.* 602, *p.* 149 *; Vol.* 753, *p.* 145.

1689, *July* 1.

Warrant to provide four new silver trumpetts for his Majesty's Troop of Guards commanded by Lord Overkirke, Master of the Horse.

> *L. C. Vols.* 602, *p.* 153, *and* 603, *p.* 6.

1689, *July* 4.

Dr. Nicholas Staggins, master of the private musick.

John Lenton appointed musician for the private musick.

> *L. C. Vol.* 486, *p.* 101.

1689, July 5.

Warrant to pay to Symon Corbett, late child of his Majesty's Chappell Royall, whose voyce is changed and is gon from the Chappell, £20 for one year, and to provide him with clothing.

L. C. Vol. 753, p. 214; L. C. Papers. Bundle 79.

1689, July 5.

Warrant to swear and admit George Bingham, and Joseph Manship musicians for the private musick, and Robert Kinge one of his Majesty's private musicke and composer in ordinary.

L. C. Vol. 486, p. 101 ; and Vol. 753, pp. 176, 177.

1689, July 7.

Thomas Richardson appointed to the vocall musick.

L. C. Vol. 487, p. 26 ; Vol. 488, p. 34.

1689, July 11.

Moses Snow appointed musician for the private musick.

L. C. Vol. 486, p. 101.

1689, July 11.

Moses Snow appointed to the vocall musick.

L. C. Vol. 487, p. 26 ; Vol. 488, p. 34.

1689, July 16.

Anthony Robert appointed to the vocall musick.

L. C. Vol. 487, p. 26 ; Vol. 488, p. 34.

1689, July 16.

Thomas Clayton and William Clayton appointed musicians for the private musick in ordinary to his Majesty.

L. C. Vol. 486, p. 101 ; and Vol. 753, p. 187.

1689, July 17.

Leonard Woodson appointed to the vocall musick.

L. C. Vol. 487, p. 26; Vol. 488, p. 34.

1689, July 17.

Order to pay £20 for one year to Thomas Richardson, late child of his Majesty's Chappell Royall, whose voyce is changed and is gone from ye Chappell, and to provide him with suit of clothing.

L. C. Vol. 753, p. 184 ; L. C. Papers. Bundle 4.

1689, July 17.

Anthony Robert, Richard Lewis, Henry Eagles, Leonard Woodson, and Solomon Eagles appointed musicians for the private musick.

L. C. Vol. 486, p. 101; Vol. 753, pp. 181, 186.

1689, *July* 18.

Warrant to swear and admit Mr. Alexander Damascene composer in his Majesty's private musick in ordinary.

L. C. Vol. 486, *p.* 101 ; *and Vol.* 753, *p.* 183.

1689, *July* 18.

Edward Hooton and Theophilus Fitz appointed musicians for the private musick in ordinary.

L. C. Vol. 486, *p.* 101 ; *and Vol.* 753, *p.* 186.

1689, *July* 18.

Mr. Jonas Bourchier (also called " Josiah Boucher ") appointed one of his Majesty's private musick in ordinary.

L. C. 486, *p.* 101 ; *and Vol.* 753, *pp.* 189, 190.

1689, *July* 18.

Alexander Damasceen appointed to the vocall musick.

L. C. Vol. 487, *p.* 26; *Vol.* 488, *p.* 34.

1689, *July* 19.

Appointment of Mr. John Gosling, clerk, to the vocall musick.

L. C. Vol. 487, *p.* 26; *Vol.* 488, *p.* 34.

1689, *July* 19.

John Gostling, John Goodwyn, Morgan Harris, Francis Cruys, Frederick Steffkin, John Davenport, and Christian Steffkin appointed musicians for the private musick.

L. C. Vol. 486, *p.* 101 ; *Vol.* 753, *pp.* 189, 190.

1689, *July* 20.

Dr. John Blow appointed composer for the vocall musick.

L. C. Vol. 487, *p.* 26 ; *Vol.* 488, *p.* 34.

1689, *July* 20.

Edmond Flower, Alphonso Marsh, Richard Thomlynson, William Turner, Dr. John Blow, composer in his Majesty's private musick, John Bowman, William Hall, Charles Coleman and Samuel Acroyd, appointed musicians for the private musick.

L. C. Vol. 486, *p.* 101 ; *and Vol.* 753, *pp.* 189, 190.

1689, *July* 22.

John Bannester, Robert Carr, Henry Heale, Charles Powell, Henry Purcell, musician composer, and Robert Strong, appointed musicians for the private musick.

L. C. Vol. 486, *p.* 101 ; *and Vol.* 753, *pp.* 189, 190.

1689, *July* 22.

Order for two silver trumpetts for his Majesty's service in the troop commanded by the Rt. Hon. the Lord Viscount Lumbley.

L. C. Vol. 602, *p.* 155 ; *and Vol.* 753, *p.* 182.

1689, *July* 23.

William Turner appointed to the vocall musick.

L. C. Vol. 487, *p.* 26 ; *Vol.* 488, *p.* 34.

1689, *July* 24.

Warrant to swear and admit Dr. Nicholas Staggins master of their Majesties' musick.

L. C. Vol. 753, *p.* 196.

1689, *July* 27.

Alexander de la Tour appointed musician for the private musick.

L. C. Vol. 486, *p.* 101 ; *and Vol.* 753, *pp.* 189, 190.

1689, *August* 7.

Order that his Majesty's drum-major do order that drums and fife do attend his Majesty's First regiment of Foot Guards, commanded by Lord Viscount Sydney, as they did heretofore.

L. C. Vol. 753, *p.* 207.

1689, *August* 8.

Letter of assignment from Richard Medlycott, keeper of his Majesty's musicall instruments in ordinary, to John Moseley, of all his salaries, profitts, etc., due to him since his appointment.

L. C. Vol. 199, *p.* 122.

1689, *August* 9.

Warrant to swear and admit John Mosley overseer and keeper of his Majesty's musicall instruments in ordinary in the place and upon the surrender of Richard Medlicott.

L. C. Vols. 485, *p.* 99 ; 486, *p.* 67 ; 487, *p.* 24 ; 488, *p.* 31 ; *and* 753, *p.* 212.

1689, *August* 13.

Delivered to Matthias Shore, esquire, sergeant trumpeter to their Majesties, for the use of Francis Giddins and Richard Marsh, trumpeters in the 1st troop of Guards under the Lord Lumley, two silver trumpets, weighing 33 oz. 1 dwt. and 33 oz. 0 dwt. 2 gr. Mr. Marsh returned 4 January, 1691-2, lost 16 oz.

L. C. Vol. 440.

1689, September 21.

Warrant to swear and admit John Mawgridge, esquire, in the place and quality of drum-major generall of all his Majesty's forces.

L. C. Vol. 753, *p.* 251.

1689, September 21.

Warrant to swear and admit Matthias Shore serjeant trumpeter in ordinary to the King. The like warrants of same date to admit the following trumpeters :—

William Bull	Henrick Davant
John Stephenson	Anthony Ragways
Thomas Barwell	Daniell la Faver
John Seignier	John Doorescourt
Jervace Walker	Bernard Van Batom
William Shore	Francis Giddins
Robert Maugridge,	Richard Marsh
kettledrummer	Christian Perll

Nicholas Dewell.

L. C. Vol. 753, *p.* 243 ; *L. C. Vols.* 485, *p.* 101 ; 486, *p.* 69 ; 487, *p.* 24.

1689, September 21.

List of trumpeters :—Mathias Shore, sergeant trumpeter, William Bull, John Stephenson, Thomas Barwell, John Seignier, Jervas Walker, William Shore, Henry Davant, Anthony Bagwayes, Daniell La Faver, John Doorescourt, Bernard Van Batom, Francis Giddons, Richard March, Christian Pearle, Nicholas Dewell (also Dewett).

Drummers :—John Maugridge, drum-major general of all his Majesty's forces ; Deavereux Clothier, Turtullian Lewis, John Skyrme, and Robert Maugridge, kettledrummer.

L. C. Vol. 186 (*Opposite end of book*) ;
L. C. Vols. 485, *pp.* 101, 103 ; 486, *pp.* 69, 71.

Accounts ending Michaelmas, 1689.

Account for clothing for Thomas Richardson and Simon Corbett, two boys who are dismist from the Chappell.

Account of liveries given to Dr. John Blow, master of the children of the Chappell Royall, for ten boys of the Chappell Royall.

L. C. Vol. 76.

1689, October 21.

Order to provide Dr. John Blow, master of the children of his Majesty's Chappell Royall, they being tenn in number, with their winter liveries for this present year 1689.

L. C. Vol. 753, *p.* 271 ; *L. C. Papers. Bundle* 9.

1689, *November* 2.

Order to prepare a bill for his Majesty's signature conteyning a grant unto Matthias Shore of the office of serjeant of all trumpettors, drummers and fifes in ordinary to their Majesties, to enjoy the place in like manner as Jervice Price, deceased, or any other serjeant of trumpettors. The first payment to commence the Annunciation last past.

L. C. Vol. 753, *p.* 299.

1689, *November* 7.

Warrant to swear and admit John Shaw musical instrument maker in ordinary to his Majesty.

L. C. Vols. 485, *p.* 99 ; 486, *p.* 68 ; 753, *p.* 310.

1689, *St. Andrew.*

Payment of £16. 2. 6. to each of the following musicians to the King and Queen for their liveries :—

Nicholas Staggins, master of the music	Daniel Short
	Robert Strong
William Clayton	Christian Steffken
John Goodwin	Henry Eccles
Edward Hooton	Solomon Eccles
Robert Carr	Francis Cruys
John Banister	John Lenton
William Hall	Charles Powell
Robert King	Francis Cruse ("vacat.")
Henry Heale	Alexander de Latour
Theophilus Fittz	Richard Lewise
George Bingham	Charles Colman
Morgan Harris	Edmund Flower

Fredrick Steffkin.

L. C. Vol. 467.

1689, *December* 7.

Clothing for the tenn children of the Chappell Royall to be provided through Dr. John Blow, master of the children of his Majesty's Chappell Royall.

L. C. Vol. 753, *p.* 345. *L. C. Papers. Bundle* 9.

1689—90, *January* 1.

Letter of assignment from Mary Preston of York, widow of Christopher Preston, late musician to King Charles II. for the virginalls and private musick, appointing Mr. Allan Chambers, her true and lawful attorney.

L. C. Vol. 199.

1689—90, January 19.

Charles Hobson appointed drummer in ordinary without fee, to come in ordinary with fee, upon the first avoidance.

L. C. Vol. 486, p. 71.

1689—90, January 20.

Warrant to admit Maurice Reignolds harper in ordinary to his Majesty, with fee.

L. C. Vols. 485 p. 99; 486, p. 68; 487, p. 24; 488, p. 31; and Vol. 754, p. 5.

1689—90, February 6.

Order to Bernard Smith to view all their Majesties' organs and to keep the same in repair, and to see the same be not embezlled or destroyed, and all persons who have any of their Majesties' organs in their custody are hereby required not to molest or disturb you in the execution of this your office.

L. C. Vol. 754, p. 16.

1689—90, March 9.

Warrant to provide livery for Francis Brabant, kettledrummer attending his Majesty's Troop of Guards, commanded by the Duke of Ormond, Cornelius Vandenand, kettledrummer to the Troop commanded by the Earl of Marlebrough, John Bullard, kettledrummer to the Troop commanded by Lord Overkirke, and to John Brookes, trumpeter, attending his Majesty's Troop of Guards commanded by the Duke of Ormond.

L. C. Vol. 754, p. 36.

1690, April 7.

Letter of assignment from William Child, of Windsor Castle, doctor in musick, appointing Edward Bradocke, gentleman, of the city of Westminster, his true and lawful attorney.

L. C. Vol. 199, p. 51d.

1690, April 9.

Certificate that Nicholas Staggins, doctor of musick and one of the servants of the late King Charles II., has taken the oathes and made the declaration contained in the Act of Parliament entitled an "Act for abrogating the oathes of supremacy and allegiance," etc.

L. C. Vol. 805, p. 254.

1690, April 10.

Will, dated 5 June, 1686, with codicil of 11 September, 1687, and probate (10 April, 1690) of Gervase Price, of the parish of St. Martin's in the Fields; he desires to be buried near to the body of his late dear wife in the Cathedral Church of St. Peter's, Westminster.

L. C. Vol. 196, pp. 65—69.

1690, *April* 12.

John Ashbury appointed fife, in the place of Clement Newth, deceased.

L. C. Vol. 186 *and Vols.* 485, *p.* 102 ; 488, *p.* 32.

1690, *April* 15.

Warrant to pay to Dr. Nicholas Staggins the sum of £25. 16s., in part of what is due to him as one of the musicians to the late King Charles II., provided that he has taken the necessary oaths.

L. C. Vol. 805, *p.* 253*d*.

1690, *April* 15.

Warrant to pay to John Blow, the sum of £30. 13s. 4d., in part of what is due to him as one of the musicians to the late King Charles II., provided he has taken the necessary oaths.

L. C. Vol. 805, *p.* 265.

1690, *April* 15.

Account for liveries for Dr. Nicholas Staggins, John Blow, and Henry Gregory, musicians to his late Majesty King Charles II.

Account for the residue of the liveries due to Jervisy Price, keeper of the bows and chief trumpeter, and to John Mawgridge, chief drummer to his late Majesty King Charles II. to be paid to their executors.

L. C. Vol. 77.

1690, *April* 28.

Letter of assignment from Frederick Wilhelm Steffkin, musician to his late Majesty, King Charles II., appointing William Parkes of the city of Westminster, gentleman, his true and lawful attorney.

L. C. Vol. 199, *p.* 35.

1690, *April* 30.

Petition of William Franklyn against Dr. Nicholas Staggins, master of his Majesty's musick, for monies due a long time since. All parties concerned to appear.

L. C. Vol. 657.

1690, *May* 8.

Letter of assignment from Giles Stevens, of Egham, one of the musicians in ordinary for the violins to his late Majesty King Charles II., to Richard Robinson, of London, of arrears due to Giles Stevens, in payment of a sum of £100.

L. C. Vol. 199, *p.* 64.

1690, *August* 2.

Warrant to Bernard Smyth, their Majesty's organ maker in ordinary, to provide a new organ for the Chappell Royall at Hampton Court.

L. C. Vol. 754, *p.* 130.

1690, *September* 25.

Warrants to pay to William Smyth and James Townsend, late children of his Majesty's Chappell Royall, whose voyces are changed and are gone from the Chappell, the sum of £20 each for one year, and to provide them with one suit of plain cloth, one hat and hatband, two holland shirts, two cravatts, two paire of cuffs, two handkerchiefs, two paire of stockings, two paire of shoes, and two paire of gloves each.

L. C. Vol. 754, *p.* 149 : *L. C. Papers. Bundle* 4.

Account ending Michaelmas, 1690.

Account for payment of £60 for liveries to Mathias Shore, chief trumpeter.

L. C. Vol. 77.

1690, *October* 31.

Petition of Christian Smyth against Bernard Smyth, organist. Bernard Smyth to appear.

L. C. Vol. 657.

1690, *November* 6.

Letter of assignment from Thomas Richardson, late one of the children of their Majesties' Chappell, appointing Thomas Richardson, gentleman, of their Majesties' Chapell Royall, his true and lawful attorney.

L. C. Vol. 199, *p.* 55.

1690, *November* 26.

Letter from Elizabeth Hart, widow of Richard Hart, deceased, lately one of the musick to his late Majesty King Charles II., appointing Jonas Watson of Whitehall, gunner, her lawful attorney.

L. C. Vol. 199, *p.* 57d.

1690, *November* 29.

Warrant to pay to Dr. Nicholas Staggins, master of his Majesty's musick, and to William Hall, John Goodwyn, Robert Carr, Edward Hooton, Henry Heale, Samuel Akroyd, Theophilus Fitz, Richard Lewis, Richard Tomleson, Charles

Powell, Solomon Eagles and John Lenton, musicians in ordinary to their Majesties, the several sums hereafter mentioned, vizt. :—

To Dr. Staggins, the sum of 5s. by the day for the space of 11 days, from 30 September to 4 October, 1689, inclusive, for his ryding charges and other expenses in attending his Majesty at Newmarkett, and to each of the said musicians the sum of three shillings by the day for the said time for their like attendance, amounting to the sum of £22. 11s.

L. C. Vol. 754, *p.* 185.

1690, *St. Andrew.*

Payment of £16. 2. 6. to each of the following musicians to the King and Queen for their liveries :—

Nicholas Staggins	Robert Strong
William Clayton	Christian Steffken
John Goodwin	Henry Eccles
Edward Hooton	Solomon Eccles
Robert Carr	John Lenton
John Banister	Charles Powell
William Hall	Francis Cruys
Robert King	Alexander De Latour
Henry Heale	Richard Lewise
Theophilus Fittz	Charles Colman
George Bingham	Edmund Flower
Morgan Harris	Fredrick Steffkin
Daniel Short	

L. C. Vol. 467.

[1690, *December* 8.]

A list of His Majesty's servants above stairs, who are to attend His Majesty in his voyage unto Holland, and who are paid in the Treasury Chamber :—

Trumpeters.

Mathias Shore, sergeant trumpeter	John Stevenson
	John Shore
William Bull	James Truelove (this name
Thomas Barwell	crossed out and "William
Jarvis Walker	Shore" inserted)

John Maugridge, kettledrummer.

Musicians.

Dr. Nicholas Staggins, master	Edward Hooton
John Bannister [altered to	Christian Stephkins
" Francis Cruys "]	Morgan Harris
Robert King [altered to	Edmund Flower
" Henry Eagles "]	Richard Tomlinson
Bingham	Frederick Stephkins
William Hall [altered to	Solomon Eagles
" Samuel Akeroyde "]	John Lenton
Robert Carr	Richard Lewin
John Goodwyn	Charles Powell
Henry Heale	and five Hooboys

John Mosley, Keeper of the instruments.
William Brown, Chamberkeeper to the music.

L. C. Vol. 754, *p.* 189.

1690, *December* 10.

Warrant to prepare three new silver trumpets for His Majesty's expedition into Holland to replace three that were lost in Ireland and elsewhere.

L. C. Vol. 602, *p.* 176.

1690, *December* 10.

Certificate that Matthias Shore, sergeant trumpeter, William Bull, Thomas Barwell, Jervas Walker, John Stephenson, John Shore, William Shore, are appointed trumpeters to attend His Majesty in his voyage unto Holland, and John Maugridge, kettledrummer, and are to have the liveries provided for the voyage.

L. C. Vol. 754, *p.* 190.

1690, *December* 24.

Warrant to pay to Mathias Shore, sergeant trumpeter in ordinary to his Majesty, for himself and William Bull, Thomas Barwell, Jervis Walker, John Stevenson, John Shore and William Shore, trumpeters, and John Maugridge, kettle-drummer, appointed to attend His Majesty in his voyage unto Holland, the several sums of money allotted to them by the Treasury.

L. C. Vol. 754, *p.* 199.

1690, *December* 24.

Warrant to pay to Francis Cruys, Henry Eagles and Samuel Akeroyde, musicians appointed to attend his Majesty in his voyage unto Holland in place of John Bannister, Robert King and William Hall, such sums of money as the said Bannister, King and Hall were to have received.

L. C. Vol. 754, *p.* 199.

1690, *December.*

Warrant to pay to Dr. Nicholas Staggins, master of the musick, the sum of £120, whereof £100 is to be paid by him to the five hautboyes, £20 to each of them, appointed to attend the King his intended voyage into Holland, and the other £20 to William Browne, chamber-keeper to the musick, for his expenses in his voyage to Holland.

L. C. Vol. 724.

1690.

Will, dated 21 November, 1687, of John Mawgridge, of St. Pawle's, Covent Garden; he appoints his wife Sarah Mawgridge his sole executrix.

L. C. Vol. 196, *p.* 70d.

1690—1, *February* 21.

Letter of assignment from William Turner, one of the gentlemen of their Majesties' Chappell Royall, appointing Thomas Whitfield of St. Martin's in the Feilds, gentleman, his true and lawful attorney.

L. C. Vol. 199, *p.* 83.

1691, *April* 17.

Warrants for the payment of £25 : 16 to Dr. Nicholas Staggins, and £30 : 13 : 4 to John Blow, part arrears due to them as musicians to the late King Charles II.

L. C. Vol. 805, *p.* 360.

1691, *April* 20.

Letter of assignment from Henry Heale, one of his Majesty's musicians, appointing Mary his wife, his true and lawful attorney.

L. C. Vol. 199, *p.* 95.

1691, *April* 26.

Warrant for liveries for two trumpeters, a kettledrummer and four hautboys, attending the Guards commanded by the Duke of Ormond.

L. C. Vol. 754, *p.* 242.

1691, *April* 26.

Warrant for the allowance of a livery to Jeremiah Clarke, late child of the Chappell, whose voice is changed.

L. C. Papers. Bundle 8.

1691, *May* 9.

Warrant to prepare two new silver trumpets for his Majesty's 2nd Troop of Guards commanded by his Grace the Duke of Ormond.

Warrant to provide one new silver trumpet for his Majesty's 3rd Troop of Guards commanded by the Earl of Marlborough.

L. C. Vol. 602, *pp.* 180, 181.

1691, *May* 22.

Warrant for liveries for three trumpeters, a kettledrummer and four hautboyes, and two drummers for the Granadeers belonging to the same Troop, attending the Troop of Guards commanded by the Duke of Ormond.

L. C. Vol. 754, *p.* 256.

1691, *June* 23.

Warrant to pay to Dr. Nicholas Staggins, master of his Majesty's musick, Edward Hooton, John Goodwin, Robert Carr, Henry Heale, Henry Eagles, George Bingham, Morgan Harris, Christian Stephkins, Solomon Eagles, Francis Cruys, John Lenton and Charles Powell, musicians in ordinary to his Majesty; La Rush, George Sutton, Greenville, Baptist, and one more hautboyes, the several sums following, vizt. :—

To Dr. Staggins 5s. by the day for the space of 103 days, from 1 January, 1690 to 13 April, 1691, for his ryding charges and other expenses in attending his Majesty unto Holland, amounting to £24. 15s., and to each of the said musicians and hautboyes 3s. by the day for the said tyme, amounting to the sum of £15. 9s. each.

L. C. Vol. 754, *p.* 269.

1691, *June* 24.

Warrant for liveries for three trumpeters, a kettledrummer, four hautboyes and two drummers, attending the Troop of Guards commanded by the Earl of Marleborough.

L. C. Vol. 754, *p.* 268.

1691, *July.*

Account for 8 hautbois and 4 drummers' liveries, to the Grenadeeres of the 1st, 2nd and 3rd troopes of Horse Guards. Paid 26 March, 1692.

L. C. Vol. 209, *entry* 26.

1691, *July* 10.

Warrant to pay to Matthias Shore, Esq., his Majesty's sergeant trumpeter, William Shore, Thomas Barwell, William Bull, John Stevenson, Jarvis Walker, and John Shore, trumpeters, and John Maugridge, kettledrummer, the several sums of ryding charges following, vizt.:—to the sergeant trumpeter, 10s. by the day, and to each of the trumpeters and kettledrummer, 5s. by the day, for the space of 103 daies from 1 January, 1690 to 13 April, 1691, for ryding charges and other expenses in attending on his Majesty in the voyage unto Holland.

L. C. Vol. 754, *p.* 273.

1691, *July* 19.

Letter from John Gostling of the parish of St. Gregory by by St. Paul's, London, one of their Majesties' private musick, appointing Dr. John Blow, his lawful attorney.

L. C. Vol. 199, *p.* 117.

1691, *August.*

Account for the livery of Charles Allanson (also " Allison "), a Chappell boy whose voice is changed and gone off. Paid March 26, 1692.

L. C. Vol. 209, *entries* 42, 47 *and* 70.

1691, *August* 20.

Letter of assignment from Elizabeth Hart, widow of Richard Hart, lately one of the musicians to his late Majesty King Charles II., to William Bushell of Tuttle Fields, Middlesex, of the sum of £28, arrears due to the late Richard Hart.

L. C. Vol. 199, *p.* 114.

1691, *August* 21.

" Whereas the Queenes Majesty hath been graciously pleased to give the great organ which is in the Great Chappell of Whitehall, which heretofore the Papist possessed, unto the parish of St. James, to be set up in the parish church, I do therefore hereby authorise Dr. Tennison to remove the said organ and to employ whosoever he shall think fit to do the same."

L. C. Vol. 754, *p.* 292.

Accounts ending Michaelmas, 1691.

Account of residue of livery owing to Doctor Nicholas Staggins, John Blowe and Henry Gregory, musicians to his late Majesty, King Charles II. Sums of £25 : 16; £30 : 13 : 4 and £43 : 15 : 1 respectively.

Account of residue of livery paid to the executors of Jervise Price, chief trumpeter and keeper of the bows and crossbows of the late King Charles II., and to the executors of John Mawgridge, chief drummer to the late King.

Account of £40 paid for livery for John Mawgridge, chief drummer.

Accounts for liveries for eight hautbois and four drummers to the Grenadeers of the 1st and 3rd troops of Horse Guards.

Account paid for livery for Charles Alleson, a boy who has left the Chappell, whose voice has changed.

Payment of £42. 16. 4. to Dr. John Blow, master of the Chappell Royall, for winter liveries for the children of the Chappell for the years 1690 and 1691, also £10 : 10s. for summer liveries.

L. C. Vol. 78.

1691, *October* 6.

Letter of assignment from Edmund Flower, one of the musicians attending on their Majesties, appointing William Brown, servant and attendant on their Majesties' musicians in ordinary, his true and lawful attorney.

L. C. Vol. 199, *p.* 121.

1691, *October* 15.

Warrant for the allowance of a livery to Hugh Braddock, late child of the Chappell whose voice is changed.

L. C. Papers. Bundle 8.

1691, *October* 16.

Warrant to pay to John Shaw, musicall instrument maker to His Majesty, the sum of £35. 5s. for mending His Majesty's instruments, for musick, for bridges, bowes and strings, and for other service by him done in the years 1689 and 1690.

L. C. Vol. 754, *p.* 309.

1691, *St. Andrew.*

Payment of £16. 2. 6. to each of the following musicians to the King and Queen for their liveries :—

Nicholas Staggins, master of the music	Daniel Short
	Robert Strong
William Clayton	Christian Steffken
John Goodwin	Henry Eccles
Edward Hooton	Solomon Eccles
Robert Carr	John Lenton
John Banister	Charles Powell
William Hall	Francis Cruys
Robert King	Alexander De Latour
Henry Heale	Richard Lewise
Theophilus Fittz	Charles Colman
George Bingham	Edmund Flower
Morgan Harris	Frederick Steffkin.

L. C. Vol. 467.

1691, *December* 8.

Warrant for the allowance of a livery to Charles Monson, late child of the Chappell whose voice is changed and is gone from the Chappell.

Like warrant for John Barrett.

L. C. Papers. Bundle 8.

1691, *December* 10.

Warrant by the Earl of Dorset addressed to Dr. Blow, and whosoever he shall appoynt to keep the seats in the organ loft in Their Majesties' Chappell at Whitehall :—

" I do hereby order that the seat in the organ loft appoynted for my use in the Chappell Royall at Whitehall be kept only for the Right Hon. the Countess of Northampton or whome she shall appoynt to sitt there and none others and you are hereby required carefully to observe this order."

L. C. Vol. 754, *p.* 356.

1691, *December* 18.

Warrant to permit Dr. Tennison, bishop elect of Lincoln, or whoever he shall appoint, to take down the wainscot that did belong to the organ which belonged to the Popish Chappell in Whitehall, with all other necessaries belonging to the said organ.

L. C. Vol. 754, *p.* 344.

1691, *December* 30.

Warrant to provide a new silver trumpet for John Stevens, trumpeter in ordinary, he delivering into your office his old trumpett.

L. C. Vol. 602, *p.* 188.

1691.

Order that the King's Chappell shall be all the year through kept both morning and evening with solemn musick like a collegiate church.

L. C. Vol. 626.

1691.

A bill amounting to £22 10. 8., spent on necessaries for the children of the Chappell Royall, signed by John Blow.

L. C. Papers. Bundle 8.

1691-2, *January* 9.

Warrant to provide for Daniel Le Fever, trumpeter to his Majesty's Third Troop of Guards under the command of the Earl of Marleborough : Anthony Ragway, trumpeter to the First Troop of Guards under the Earl of Scarbrough, and Joseph Williams, trumpeter, who is put into the First Troop in place of Richard March, unto each of them one silver trumpet for his Majesty's service, each delivering their old trumpets to the Treasury Office.

L. C. Vol. 754, *p.* 357.

1691-2, *January* 11.

Delivered to Mr. Le Fever, one of his Majesty's trumpetts, one silver trumpet, weight 35 oz. 2 dwt. His signature attached to receipt of same.

L. C. Vol. 440.

1691-2, *January* 16.

Appointment of James Castle, senior trumpeter for Ireland.

L. C. Vol. 487, *p.* 26; *Vol.* 488, *p.* 33.

1691-2, *January* 16.

List of Trumpetters for Ireland.

James Castle, seignier trumpeter	Nicholas Castle
	John Burton
Aron Lake	William Cooper, kettle-drummer
Francis Castle	
Alexander Jackson	

L. C. Vol. 485, *p.* 107; *Vol.* 486, *p.* 104.

1691-2, *January* 16.

Warrant to prepare and deliver to James Castles, sergeant trumpeter for Ireland, 6 new silver trumpettes for the 6 trumpetters that are to attend the Lord Lieutenant, Lord Deputy, and Lord Justices of the Kingdom of Ireland.

L. C. Vol. 602, *p.* 187.

1691-2, *January* 22.

Delivered to Mr. John Stephenson, one of the trumpeters of their Majesties' second troop of Guards, one silver trumpet with mouth piece, 36 oz. 2 dwt. Received by me, John Stevenson.

L. C. Vol. 440.

1691-2, *January* 22.

Petition of Henry Robinson against Jacob Langley, drummer, for lodging money, £3 2s. All parties concerned to appear.

L. C. Vol. 657.

1691-2, *January* 25.

Delivered to Mr. Anthony Rague, one of their Majesties' trumpetts, one silver trumpet with mouth piece, weight 35 oz. 3 dwt. Received by me for his use, Wm. Bull.

Delivered to Mr. Joseph Williams, one of their Majesties' trumpetts, one silver trumpet with mouth piece, weighing 35 oz. 3 dwt. His signature attached to receipt of same.

L. C. Vol. 440.

1691-2, *February* 27.

A list of the private Musick payd in the Treasury Chamber, by warrant of 27 February, 1691-2 :—

Nicholas Staggins,
 master of the musick
John Goodwyn
Edward Hooton
Henry Heale
Robert Carr
George Bingham
Morgan Harris
Henry Eccles (also
  " Eagles ")
Solomon Eccles (also
  " Eagles ")
Fredrick Stepkins
Christian Stepkins
John Lenton
John Mosley, instrument keeper.

Charles Powell
Richard Lewis
Francis Cruys (also
  " Cruse ")
Edward Flower
John Bannister
Robert King
William Hall
Theophilus Fitz
William Clayton
Robert Strong
Daniell Short
Alexander de la Tour
Charles Coleman

L. C. Vol. 186 ; *Vol.* 485, *p.* 97 ; *Vol.* 486, *p.* 66.

1691-2, *February* 27.

Whereas his Majesty in the establishment of the payments of the office of the Treasury Chamber hath ordered that there shall be a master of the musick, four and twenty musicians, and a chamberkeeper: these are to certifie that I have nominated and appoynted these persons hereafter named to be the persons who are to be settled and payd according to the establishment, vizt. :—

Nicholas Staggins, master, John Goodwyn, Edward Hooton, Henry Heale, Robert Carr, George Bingham, Morgan Harris, Henry Eacles, Solomon Eacles, Fredrick Stephkins, Christian Stephkins, John Lenton, Charles Powell, Richard Lewis, Francis Cruse, Edward Flower, John Bannister, Robert King, William Hall, Theophilus Fitz, William Clayton, Robert Strong, Daniel Short, Alex. Delatour, Charles Coleman and John Mosley, instrument keeper, and I do hereby pray and require you to pay unto the respective persons aforesaid their respective allowances in the said establishment accordingly.

L. C. Vol. 186 ; *and Vol.* 755, *p.* 32.

1691-2, *February* 27.

Thomas Clayton, son of William Clayton appointed as musician for the first vacancy.

L. C. Vol. 486, *p.* 67.

1691-2, *March* 15.

Delivered to sergeant trumpeter Shore, six trumpets white, for the kingdom of Ireland, weighing 221 oz. 15 dwt.

Received by me, Matthias Shore.

L. C. Vol. 440.

1692, *April* 26.

Petition of Mr. Dardon and Needham, against Robert Carr, musician, indebted to both, £32 12s. All to appear.

L. C. Vol. 657.

1692, *May* 19.

Warrant for the allowance of liveries to the following :—

John Brookes, trumpeter attending his Majesty's Troop of Guards commanded by the Duke of Ormond.

Cornelius Van Dennande, kettle-drummer attending his Majesty's Troop of Guards commanded by Lord Colchester.

John Bullard, kettle drummer attending his Majesty's Troop of Guards commanded by Lord Overkirke.

L. C. Papers. Bundle 8.

1692, *June* 15.

Warrant for the allowance of a livery for Richard Henman, late child of the Chappell Royall, whose voice is changed.

L. C. Papers. Bundle 8.

1692, *June* 24.

Warrant to swear and admit John Walsh musicall instrument maker in ordinary to his Majesty, in the place of John Shaw, surrendered.

L. C. Vols. 485, *p.* 99 ; 486, *p.* 68 ; 487, *p.* 24 ; 488, *p.* 31 ; *and* 755, *p.* 91.

1692, *August* 17.

Warrant to pay to Dr. Nicholas Staggins, master of his Majesty's musick, the sum of £59. 6s. for fair writing and pricking severall compositions, for ruled paper, penns and inke, and for the prickers' dyett, and chamber rent, and for other service by him done in the years 1690 and 1691.

L. C. Vol. 755, *p.* 120.

1692, *August* 17.

Warrant to pay to Dr. Nicholas Staggins, master of his Majesty's musick, the sum of £52. 2s. 6d. for fair writing and pricking of compositions for the Coronation Day and the Queen's Birthday, and for paper, penns and inke, for other service by him done in the year 1689.

L. C. Vol. 755, *p.* 120.

Accounts ending Michaelmas, 1692.

Account of part residue of liveries paid to the executors of Jervise Price, chief trumpeter and keeper of the bows to the late King Charles II, and to the executors of John Mawgridge, chief drummer to the late King.

Account of liveries for four hautbois and two drummers to the Grenadeers of the 2nd troop of Horse Guards.

Account for residue of liveries for Dr. Nicholas Staggins, Dr. John Blow and Henry Gregory, musicians to the late King Charles II.

Account paid to Dr. John Blow, master of the boys of the Chappell Royall, for the liveries of the children of the Chappell.

Account for cloth for Charles Allanson, a boy who has left the Chappell Royall.

L. C. Vol. 79.

1692, *November* 9.

Warrants to pay to William Richardson and Thomas Christmas, late children of his Majesty's Chappell Royall, whose voyces are changed, and are gone from the Chappell, £20 each for one year, and to provide each with a suit of clothing.

L. C. Vol. 755, p. 150.

1692, *November* 24.

Whereas John Goodwyn one of His Majesty's private musick hath abused Dr. Richard of the Treasury Chamber, with scandalous and menaceing language, I do therefore hereby suspend him his place and all profitts thereto belonging until I shall give further order.

Signed " Dorset."

L. C. Vol. 657.

1692, *St. Andrew.*

Payment of £16. 2. 6. to each of the following musicians to the King and Queen, for their liveries :—

Nicholas Staggins	Daniel Short
William Clayton	Robert Strong
John Goodwin	Christian Steffken
Edward Hooton	Henry Eccles
Robert Carr	Solomon Eccles
John Banister	John Lenton
William Hall	Charles Powell
Robert King	Francis Cruys
Henry Heale	Alexander De Latour
Theophilus Fittz	Richard Lewise
George Bingham	Charles Colman
Morgan Harris	Edmund Flower

Fredrick Steffkin.

L. C. Vol. 467.

[1692.]

The names of His Majesty's musick :—

Dr. Nicholas Staggins, master
Dr. Nicholas Staggins, composer

William Clayton	Christopher Steffkins
John Goodwin	Henry Eccles
Edward Hooton	Solomon Eccles
Robert Carr	John Lenton
John Bannister	Charles Powell
William Hall	Francis Cruse
Robert King	Alexander d'Lature
Henry Heale	Richard Lewis
Theophilus Fittz	Charles Coleman
George Bingham	Edmund Flower
Morgan Harris	Frederick Steffkin
Daniel Short	Robert Strong

(Signed)   NICHOLAS STAGGINS.

L. C. Vol. 755, *p.* 188.

1692.

Account for making 4 surplices at 8s. each, for the Lord Sidney, Lord Lieutenant of Ireland, his Chappell there.

Account for making 64 surplices for the gentlemen at 5s., and 36 surplices for the children of the Chappell Royall at 2s. 6d. each, £20. 10s.

Account for making 4 surplices for Sir William Beeston, Governor of Jamaica, and Mr. Godard, Governor of Bermudoes, their Chappells there.   Accounts paid 5 April, 1693.

L. C. Vol. 209, *entries* 14*b*, 16*b*, *and* 35*b*.

1692-3, *February* 10.

Order for a bill for the Signet enabling the master of the Great Wardrobe to furnish the master of his Majesty's musick, and composer, and six and twenty other musicians, with such liveries as have been formerly supplied to them.

L. C. Vol. 755, *p.* 188.

1692-3, *March* 2.

Warrant to pay to John Moseley, keeper of his Majesty's musicall instruments, the sum of £17. 11s. for his charges to Newmarket in the year 1690, and also for his charges for carriage of the said instruments into Holland and charges there and going and coming back, £25. 15s., in the year 1691, and also the sum of £46 for mending the said instruments, and for bowes, bridges and strings for the instruments for two years and three quarters, and for two new pennons and a new scarf for the said musician, and for other services.

L. C. Vol. 755, *p.* 196.

1693, *May* 3.

John Castle, appointed trumpeter for Ireland in the place of Nicholas Castle, surrendered.

L. C. Vol. 486, *p.* 104.

1693, *July* 8.

Thomas Clayton appointed musician for the private musick, in the place of John Goodwin, deceased.

L. C. Vol. 486, *p.* 101 ; *Vol.* 755, *p.* 32.

1693, *July* 19.

Petition of John Strachan and Hans Marchant against Richard Lewis, musician, debt of £7. 8s. interest. Lewis to appear.

L. C. Vol. 657.

1693, *July* 30.

Warrant to pay Dr. John Blow, master of the children of our Chappell Royall, for forty pair of stockings, forty pair of gloves, twenty hatts, eight pieces of ribbon, sixty pair of shoes, twenty pair of drawers, and for cloth, buttons, silk and thread for mending the cloths and linen several times, for the ten children of our said Chapel in lieu of their winter liveries, for the years 1690 and 1691, £42. 16s. 4d. To him more for sixty pair of waxt leather shoes for the said children, their summer liveries, £10. 10s.

L. C. Vol. 806.

Accounts ending Michaelmas, 1693.

Accounts for liveries for each of the following musicians to the King and the Queen :—

Dr. Nicholas Staggins, master of the music.

William Clayton	Robert Strong
John Goodwin	Christopher Steffkins
Edward Hooton	Henry Eccles
Robert Carr	Solomon Eccles
John Bannister	John Lenton
William Hall	Charles Powell
Robert King	Francis Cruse
Henry Heale	Alexander D'Lature
Theophilus Fitz	Richard Lewise
George Bingham	Charles Coleman
Pelagio Harris	Edmund Flower
Daniel Short	Frederick Steffkins

Account for livery for Mathias Shore, chief trumpeter.

Account for livery for John Mawgridge, chief drummer.

Accounts for liveries for 12 hautbois and a drummer to the Grenadiers.

Account paid to Dr. John Blow, master of the children of the Chapel Royal, for liveries for ten children.

Account for cloth, &c., for William Richardsone, Thomas Christian and Hugh Braddock, three boys dismist from the Chapel Royal, whose voices have changed.

L. C. Vol. 80.

1693, *St. Andrew.*

Payment of £16. 2. 6. to each of the following musicians to the King and Queen, for their liveries :—

Nicholas Staggins, master of music.

William Clayton	Christian Steffken
John Goodwin	Henry Eccles
Edward Hooton	Solomon Eccles
Robert Carr	John Lenton
John Banister	Charles Powell
William Hall	Francis Cruys
Robert King	Alexander De Latour
Henry Heale	Richard Lewise
Theophilus Fittz	Charles Colman
George Bingham	Edmund Flower
Morgan Harris	Fredrick Steffken
Daniel Short	Thomas Clayton
Robert Strong	

L. C. Vol. 467.

1693, *December 4.*

Warrants to pay for the use of Ralph Allinson and John Pennington, late children of his Majesty's Chappell, whose voices are changed, and are gone from the Chappell, the sum of £20 each for one year, and also to supply them with clothes.

L. C. Vol. 755, *p.* 284.

1693.

Accounts for certain liveries for William Richardsone, Thomas Christian, and Hugh Braddocc, three Chappell boys gone off.

Account for the livery of John Mawgridge, drum major, for the year 1691, amounting to £40.

Account for 16 yards of red baise for drumme cases, £2. 8s.

Account due to Dr. John Blow, master of the children of their Majesties' Chappell for £20. 13. for their liveries for the year 1693.

Accounts paid 10 May, 1694.

L. C. Vol. 209, *entries* 14c, 24c, 33c, 42c *and* 71c.

1693-4, *January* 6.

Will, dated 3 July, 1693, of John Godwin of Westminster, late one of their Majesties' private musick. He desires to be buried in the cloisters at Westminster Abbey; among other items he bequeathes to his uncle, Anthony Blagrave, of the city of Norwich, the sum of £20, and to his two sons Richard and John Blagrave £10 each, to Theophilus Fittz of Hampton £5, and to the poor of the parish of St. Margaret's, Westminster, the sum of £5. [Probate dated as above].

L. C. Vol. 196, *p.* 86*d.*

1693-4, *January* 27.

Warrant to supply one new silver trumpett to William Shore, trumpettor to his Majesty's first Troop of Horse Guards, being robbed of his trumpett this last campaigne in Flanders, as is certified by the Earl of Scarbrough.

L. C. Vol. 602, *p.* 212 ; *and Vol.* 755, *p.* 308.

1693-4, *March* 2.

Delivered to Mr. William Shore, one of his Majesty's trumpeters to the first troop of Guards, having been robbed of his trumpett in the campagne in Flanders, one silver trumpet with crook and mouth piece, weighing 36 oz. 1 dwt.

Received by me, Wm. Shore.

L. C. Vol. 440.

1693-4, *March* 6.

Warrant to repair a trumpett belonging to Francis Giddings, trumpeter in the 1st Troop of Guards, commanded by the Earl of Scarbrough.

L. C. Vol. 602, *p.* 213.

1693-4, *March* 9.

Petition of Dr. Fisher Littleton, against Solomon Eccles, musitian, disbursed and lent, £400. All to appear.

L. C. Vol. 657.

1693-4, *March* 13.

Warrant to pay to Dr. Nicholas Staggins, master of his Majesty's musick, the sum of £61. 6s. for pricking and faire writing severall compositions, for prickers' dyett, and chamber rent, and for several other services in the year 1692.

Warrant to pay to Dr. Nicholas Staggins the sum of £57. 15s. for faire writing and pricking severall compositions, for ruled paper, penns and inke, for the prickers' dyett, and chamber rent, and for other services in the years 1693 and 1693-4.

L. C. Vol. 755, *p.* 331.

1693-4, *March* 19.

Delivered to Mr. Francis Gibbons, one silver trumpet, new made, weight 35 oz. 3 dwt.

Received by me, Francis Gibbons.

L. C. Vol. 440.

1693-4, *March* 22.

Warrant to provide a livery for William Shore, trumpeter to the first troop of Horse Guards, under the Earl of Scarbrough, he being robbed of his livery this last campaigne.

L. C. Vol. 755, *p.* 338.

1694, *April* 14.

Warrant to repair a trumpett belonging to John Stevenson, trumpeter in the 2nd regiment of Horse Guards, commanded by the Duke of Ormond.

L. C. Vol. 602, *p.* 213.

1694, *April* 18.

Delivered to Mr. William Bull, for the use of Mr. John Brooke, his trumpet new made. One silver trumpet, weight 36 oz. 1 dwt.

L. C. Vol. 440.

1694, *April* 23.

Petition of William Bull, trumpeter, to take his course at law against Robert Maugridge, kettle drummer, for scandalous words.

L. C. Vol. 657.

1694, *May* 24.

Mr. Webb, attorney, and Richard Hipwell for proceeding at law against Dr. Staggins without leave. Both to appear.

L. C. Vol. 657.

1694, *June* 13.

William Pink, drugster, against William Green, violyn, for £20.

L. C. Vol. 657.

1694, *June* 22.

Richard Lewis appointed musician in ordinary without fee, to come in ordinary with fee upon the first avoydance.

L. C. Vol. 485, *p.* 98.

1694, *June* 22.

Richard Bradley appointed musician in the place of Robert Strong, deceased, Robert Lewis in the place of Charles Colman, deceased, and John Eccles in the place of Thomas Tollett.

L. C. Vol. 183, *p.* 74; *L. C. Vol.* 485, *pp.* 97 *and* 98.

1694, *September* 28.

Warrant to appoint John Ridgley one of the twenty-four musicians in ordinary to their Majesties, in the place and upon the surrender of Richard Lewis, to enjoy all wages and liveries thereof.

L. C. Vol. 186, *p.* 7 *; Vol.* 485, *p.* 97.

Accounts ending Michaelmas, 1694.

Account for liveries to Dr. John Blow, master of the children of the Chapel Royal.

Account for liveries to Dr. Nicholas Staggins, master of the music to the King and Queen and to the following musicians :—

William Clayton	Christopher Stepkins
Edward Hootten	(also Steffkins)
Robert Carr	Henry Eccles
John Bannister	Solomon Eccles
William Hall	John Lenton
Robert King	Charles Powell
Henry Heale	Francis Cruse
Theophilus Fitz	Alexander D'Lature
George Bingham	Charles Colman
Pelagio Harris	Edmund Flower
Daniel Shorte	Frederick Steffkins (also
Robert Strong	(Stepkins)
	Richard Lewis

L. C. Vol. 81.

1694, *St. Andrew.*

Payment of £16. 2. 6. to each of the following musicians for their liveries :—

Nicholas Staggins, master of the music

William Clayton	Henry Eccles
John Goodwin	Solomon Eccles
Edward Hooton	John Lenton
Robert Carr	Charles Powell
John Banister	Francis Cruys
William Hall	Alexander De Latour
Robert King	Richard Lewise
Henry Heale	Charles Colman
Theophilus Fittz	Edmund Flower
George Bingham	Fredrick Steffkin
Morgan Harris	Thomas Clayton
Daniel Short	John Ridgley
Robert Strong	Richard Bradley
Christian Steftken	William Gorton

John Shore (crossed out and " vacatur " entered).

L. C. Vol. 467 *; L. C. Papers. Bundle* 78.

1694, *December* 12.

Warrant to pay £20 for one year to Mr. John Gerrard for the use of Alexander Gerrard, late one of the children of their Majesties Chappell Royall, whose voyce is changed and is gone from the Chappell.

L. C. Vol. 776, p. 7b.

1694.

Warrant to the Great Wardrobe to deliver to Dr. John Blow the liveries for the ten children of the Chappell, as usual, for the year 1694.

L. C. Vol. 209, entry 39d.; and Vol. 776, p. 4b.

1694-5, *January* 10.

James Truelove appointed trumpeter for Ireland in the place of Aron Lake.

L. C. Vol. 485, p. 107.

1694-5, *January* 10.

Warrants for the providing of mourning for the late Queen :
To the first regiment of footguards, 25 covers for drumms and 6 banners for the hautboyes.
To the 16 Gentlemen of the Chappell Royall.
To the sergeant trumpett, 16 trumpeters and a kettle-drummer.
To Dr. Staggins, master of the musick.

L. C. Vol. 561, pp. 112 to 119.

1694-5, *January* 10.

Warrant to deliver to Mr. John Gerrard the usual supply of clothing for the use of Alexander Gerrard, late child of the Chappell, whose voice is changed.

L. C. Papers. Bundle 78.

1694-5, *January.*

Account for 20 yards of black baize to cover five drum cases, at 3. 6d. per yard, £3. 10s.
And for 8 yards ditto to cover one pair of kettle-drums at 3s. 6d. per yard, £1. 8s.

L. C. Vol. 209, entry 44e.

1694-5, *February* 10.

Warrant to appoint James Burton trumpeter in ordinary to his Majesty, to attend the Lord Lieutenant, Lord Deputy or Lord Justices for Ireland for the time being, in the place of Francis Castle, late one of his Majesty's trumpeters, with all salaries and liveries thereto attached.

L. C. Vol. 186, p. 16 ; L. C. Vol. 485, p. 107.

1694-5, *February* 21.

Warrant to appoint Mr. Robert Lewis one of the twenty-four musicians in ordinary to his Majesty, in the place and upon the decease of Charles Coleman, to enjoy all salaries and liveries thereof.

L. C. Vol. 183, *p.* 74 ; *L. C. Vol.* 186, *p.* 14.

1694-5, *March* 13.

Warrant to provide four new silver trumpets for the fourth troop of Guards commanded by Lord Overkirke, the old ones being broke and unserviceable.

L. C. Vol. 755, *p.* 409.

1695, *March* 27.

Mr. Thomas Tollett, musician in ordinary without fee, to come in ordinary with fee on the first vacancy of any of the 24 musicians, and then to enjoy all salaries.

L. C. Vols. 186 *and* 485.

1695, *March* 28.

Mr. John Eccles, musician in ordinary without fee, to come in ordinary with fee next after Mr. Thomas Tollett upon the first vacancy of any of the twenty-four musicians, and then to enjoy all salaries.

L. C. Vols. 186 *and* 485.

1695, *March* 28.

John Seignier appointed trumpeter in the place of John Seignier his father.

L. C. Vol. 186, *p.* 19 ; *L. C. Vol.* 485, *p.* 101.

1695, *March* 29.

Mr. John Shore, musician in ordinary without fee, to come in ordinary with fee next after Mr. Tollett and Mr. Eccles upon the first vacancy of any of the twenty-four musicians, and then to enjoy all salaries.

L. C. Vols. 186 *and* 485.

1695, *March* 30.

Mr. William Williams, musician in ordinary without fee, to come in ordinary with fee next after Mr. Tollett, Mr. Eccles and Mr. Shore, upon the first vacancy of any of the twenty-four musicians, and then to enjoy all salaries.

L. C. Vols. 186 *and* 485.

1695, *April* 4.

Delivered to Mr. Sergeant-trumpeter, four trumpetts for the use of John Descoate, Christian Perll, Nicholas Dewitt, and Mr. Vanbarten, all in the Lord Overkerk's fourth troop of Guards weighing 145 oz.

Received by me, Matthias Shore.

L. C. Vol. 440.

1695, *April* 8.

Warrant to pay £45. 5s. to Dr. Nicholas Staggins, master of musick, for pricking and faire writing several compositions, for prickers' dyett, and chamber rent, and for several other services performed by him in November, 1694 and January, 1694-5.

L. C. Vol. 776, *p.* 15*b.*

1695, *June* 10.

Warrant to pay to Thomas Chaville and John Ober, for themselves and four other hautboyes, the sum of £6 : 10. to each of them amounting to £39, for playing four times at the practice and once at the ball on his Majesty's birthday at night the 4 November, 1694.

L. C. Vol. 776, *p.* 31*b.*

1695, *October* 18.

Petition of Mr. William Shore, trumpeter, against Mr. George Bingham, musician, £10 bond.   Both to appear.

L. C. Vol. 657.

1695, *October* 25.

Delivered to Mr. Bull, Mr. Semor's trumpett to be new made.   Without mouth piece or crook, weight 28 oz. 2 dwt.

Received by me, Wm. Bull.

L. C. Vol. 440.

1695, *November* 2.

Thomas Parkinson, musician in ordinary without fee, to come in ordinary with fee next after Mr. Tollet, Mr. Eccles, Mr. Shore and Mr. Williams, upon the first vacancy of any of the twenty-four musicians, and then to enjoy all salaries.

L. C. Vols. 186 *and* 485 ; *Vol.* 488, *p.* 30.

1695, *November* 30.

Appointment of Dr. John Blow and Mr. Bernard Smith, as tuners of the regalls, organs, virginalls, flutes and recorders, and all other kind of wind instruments, in ordinary to his Majesty, in the place of Mr. Henry Purcell, deceased.

The place between them, and the survivor to enjoy the whole place.

L. C. Vols. 186, *p.* 53 ; 485, *p.* 102 ; 487, *p.* 24 ; 488, *p.* 31.

1695, *St. Andrew.*

Payment of £16. 2. 6. to each of the following musicians to the King for their liveries :—

John Ridgley	Edmund Flower
Robert Lewis	Robert King
Richard Bradley	Henry Heale

Nicholas Staggins
William Clayton
John Goodwin
Edward Hooton
Robert Carr
John Banister
William Hall

Theophilus Fittz
George Bingham
Morgan Harris
Daniel Short
Francis Cruys
Fredrick Steftkin

L. C. Vol. 467 ; L. C. Papers. Bundle 78.

1695, *December* 12.

Delivered to Mr. Bull, Mr. William's trumpett broke, to be new made. Without mouth piece and crook. Weight 25 oz. 1 dwt.

Received by me, Wm. Bull.

L. C. Vol. 440.

1695.

Account for mourning linen for Ralph Allison, John Penington and Alexander Gerrard, 3 Chappell boys gone off.

L. C. Vol. 209, entries 24e, 39e, 40e and 44e.

1695-6, *January* 7.

Warrant to pay Mary Saunderson, seampstress, for making six holland shirts, six muslin cravatts, six pairs of cuffs and six pockethandkerchiefs, for William Richardson, Thomas Christian and Hugh Braddock, three Chappell boys gone off, their voices being broken.

Warrant for three yards of cloth colour serge for Hugh Braddock, a Chappell boy gone off.

Warrant for Spanish cloth for Charles Allanson, a Chappell boy gone off.

Warrant for fifteen yards, three quarters of crimson cloth for liveries for four Hautbois and two drummers belonging to the Grenadiers of the 2nd Troop of Horse Guards.

Warrant for six yards of cloth coloured shalloone to line coats for William Richardson and Thomas Christian, two boys gone from our Chappell Royall.

L. C. Vol. 806.

1695-6, *January* 9.

Warrant to appoint Thomas Tollett one of the twenty-four musicians in ordinary to his Majesty, in the place and upon the decease of Robert Carr, to enjoy all wages and liveries thereof.

L. C. Vol. 186, p. 55.

1695-6, *January* 14.

Petition of William Clayton, one of the Musick, against Edward Kinnaston, one of his Majesty's comedians, for articles of agreement for £100, made in May, 1676. Mr. Kinnaston to have notice of petition.

L. C. Vol. 657.

1695-6, *January* 14.

Mr. John Gaspar Keiling, musician in ordinary without fee, to come in ordinary with fee next after those already sworn.

L. C. Vols. 186 *and* 485.

1695-6, *February* 3.

Order, but not warrant : Mr. Evan Maylan appointed harper without fee, to come in ordinary with fee upon the first vacancy of one of the 24 musicians.

L. C. Vol. 485.

1695-6, *February* 10.

Warrant to provide a new silver trumpet, the old one being broke, for Daniel Le Fever, one of his Majesty's trumpettes in the 3rd Troop of Guards commanded by the Earl of Rivers.

L. C. Vol. 602, *p.* 244.

1695-6, *February* 14.

Petition of William Holland against Robert Mawgridge, kettle drummer, £4 by bond.   Both parties to appear.

L. C. Vol. 657.

1695-6 *February* 27.

Delivered unto Mr. Williams, one of his Majesty's trumpeters, his old trumpett new made.   Weight 28 oz.   His signature attached to receipt of same.

L. C. Vol. 440.

1695-6, *March* 2.

Delivered to Daniel Le Fever, one of his Majesty's trumpetts in the third troop of Guards, under the Earl of Rivers, one silver trumpet new, with mouth piece and crooke, weight, 36 oz. 2 dwt.

His signature attached to receipt of same.

L. C. Vol. 440.

1695-6, *March* 23.

Petition of Mr. Anthony Nurse, brewer, against Dr. Nicholas Staggins, £120, " beare and ale."   All to appear.

L. C. Vol. 657.

1696, *April* 4.

Warrant to appoint Mr. William Gorton one of the twenty-four musicians in ordinary to his Majesty, in the place and upon the surrender of Mr. George Bingham, to enjoy all wages and liveries thereof.

L. C. Vol. 186, *p.* 56; *Vol.* 485, *p.* 97.

1696, *September* 2.

Warrant to appoint Mr. John Eccles one of the twenty-four musicians in ordinary to his Majesty, in the place and upon the decease of Mr. Thomas Tollett, to enjoy all wages and liveries thereof.

L. C. Vol. 183, *p.* 74; *L. C. Vol.* 186, *p.* 59.

1696, *September* 14.

Mr. William Pike, trumpeter in ordinary without fee, to come in ordinary with fee upon the first vacancy of any of the sixteen trumpetters in ordinary to his Majesty.

L. C. Vol. 485.

Accounts ending Michaelmas, 1696.

Accounts for liveries for each of the following musicians to the King and Queen:—

Dr. Nicholas Staggins, master of the music	Pelagio Harris
	Daniel Shorte
William Clayton	Christopher Stepkins
Edward Hooten	Henry Eccles
Robert Carre	Solomon Eccles
John Banister	John Lenton
William Hall	Charles Powell
Robert King	Francis Cruise
Henry Heale	Alexander D'Lature
Theophilus Fittz	Edmund Flower
George Bingham	Frederick Stepkins

Account for livery for Mathias Shore, chief trumpeter to the King.

Account for livery for John Maugridge, chief drummer to the King.

Account paid to Dr. John Blowe, master of the children of the Chapel Royal, for the liveries of the children.

L. C. Vol. 82.

1696, *November* 27.

Letter of assignment by Richard Lewis of London, late musician in ordinary to his Majesty, appointing John Langly of the parish of St. Giles in the Fields, Middlesex, his true and lawful attorney.

L. C. Vol. 196, *p.* 82d.

1696, *St. Andrew.*

Payment of £16. 2. 6. to each of the following musicians to the King for their liveries :—

Nicholas Staggins, master of music	Daniel Short
	Robert Strong
William Clayton	Christian Steffken
John Goodwin	Henry Eccles
Edward Hooton	Solomon Eccles
Robert Carr	John Ridgley
John Banister	Richard Bradley
William Gorton	John Eccles
William Hall	John Lenton
Robert King	Charles Powell
Henry Heale	Francis Cruys
Theophilus Fittz	Alexander De Latour
George Bingham	Richard Lewis
Edmund Flower	Charles Colman
Robert Lewis	Fredrick Steffkin
Morgan Harris	Thomas Clayton

L. C. Vol. 467; *L. C. Papers. Bundle* 78.

1696, *December* 18.

Andrew Games appointed musician in ordinary without fee.

L. C. Vol. 485.

1696.

John Mawgridge, drum major, craves allowance of £40 for his livery for the year 1692.

L. C. Vol. 209, *entry* 23*f.*

1696.

Mathias Shore, sergeant trumpeter, claims £60 for his livery for the year 1692.

L. C. Vol. 209, *entry* 25*f*; *L. C. Papers. Bundle* 16.

1696-7.

Warrant for nine yards of coloured cloth, nine yards of shalloone, for three suits and making the three suits, etc., for Jeremiah Clarke, Richard Henman and Jacob Wood, three Chapel boys whose voices are broken and gone off.

L. C. Vol. 806; *L. C. Papers. Bundle* 3.

1696-7, *January* 4.

Mr. Herbert Clinch appointed musician in ordinary without fee, to come in ordinary with fee upon the next vacancy.

L. C. Vol. 485.

1696-7, January 28.

Warrant to appoint Mr. John Shore one of the twenty-four musicians in ordinary to his Majesty, in the place and upon the decease of William Clayton, to enjoy all wages and liveries thereof.

L. C. Vol. 183, p. 75 ; L. C. Vol. 186, p. 65.

1696-7, February 26.

Mr. Anthony Robert appointed musician in ordinary without fee.

L. C. Vol. 485.

1696-7, February 27.

Mr. Thomas Williams appointed musician in ordinary without fee, to come in ordinary with fee upon the next vacancy.

L. C. Vol. 485.

1696-7, March 3.

Warrant to make choice out of the sixteen trumpeters of his Majesty's household in ordinary, of four of the best trumpeters to attend in his Majesty's liveries, on his Majesty's Ambassadors and Plenipotentiaries for the Treaty of Peace, as formerly on like occasions.

L. C. Vol. 755, p. 459.

1696-7, March 8.

Warrant to pay to William Shore, Jervas Walker, John Stephenson and William Pyke, the four trumpeters chosen to attend his Majesty's Ambassadors and Plenipotentiaries for the Treaty of Peace, the sum of £80 towards their charges and expenses.

L. C. Vol. 755, p. 459.

1696-7, March 23.

Dr. John Blow admitted musician in ordinary to his Majesty for the virginalls, in the place of Mr. Giles Tompkins, deceased.

Dr. William Turner admitted one of the private musick in ordinary to his Majesty for lute and voice, in the place of Captain Cooke, deceased.

Mr. John Gostling admitted one of his Majesty's private musick for the voice, in the place of Mr. John Harding, deceased.

Mr. John Howell admitted one of the private musick for the voice, in the place of Mr. Alphonso Marsh, deceased.

A warrant to be prepared for the allowance of yearly liveries to the above-named musicians, to commence 25 March, 1689.

L. C. Vol. 186, p. 68.

1697, *March* 27.

Warrant to provide a new silver trumpet for John Stephenson, one of the sixteen trumpeters in ordinary of his Majesty's Household, appointed to attend on his Majesty's Ambassadors extraordinary for the Treaty of Peace.

L. C. Vol. 602, *p.* 256.

1697, *March* 28.

Warrant to provide a new silver trumpet for Anthony Ragway, one of the trumpeters in his Majesty's 1st Troop of Guards commanded by the Earl of Scarborough.

L. C. Vol. 602, *p.* 272 ; *Vol.* 756, *p.* 74.

1697, *March* 31.

Warrant for 9 yards of black cloth for suits, and 15 yards of black serge to line them, for Ralph Allison, John Pennington and Alexander Gerrard, three Chappell boys whose voices are changed.

L. C. Vol. 806

1697, *April* 6.

Warrant to give notice to William Shore, Jervas Walker, John Stephenson and William Pike, that they be in readiness to attend on their Excellencies the Ambassadors for the Treaty of Peace.

L. C. Vol. 755, *p.* 460.

1697, *April* 8.

Warrant to provide forthwith a new silver trumpet for William Pike, one of the 16 trumpeters in ordinary of his Majesty's Household, appointed to attend on his Majesty's Ambassadors extraordinary and Plenepotentiary for the Treaty of Peace.

L. C. Vol. 602, *p.* 262.

1697, *April* 12.

Delivered to William Pike, one of his Majesty's trumpeters of the Household, one silver trumpet, weighing 37 oz. 0 dwt. 2 grs. His signature attached to receipt of same.

L. C. Vol. 440.

1697, *April* 26.

Delivered to Mr. John Stevenson, one of his Majesty's trumpeters of the Household, one silver trumpett, weighing 37 oz. 1 dwt. His signature attached to receipt of same.

L. C. Vol. 440.

Accounts ending Michaelmas, 1697.

Accounts for liveries for the following musicians to the King and Queen :—

Dr. Nicholas Staggins, master of the music

William Clayton	Christopher Steffkins
Edward Hotton	Henry Eccles
John Banister	Solomon Eccles
William Hall	John Lenton
Robert King	Charles Powell
Henry Heale	Francis Cruyse
Theophilus Fitz	Alexander de la Toure
Pelagio Harris	Edmund Flower
Daniel Shorte	Frederick Steffkins

Account paid to Dr. John Blow, master of the boys of the Chapel Royal for their liveries, and for clothes for Jeremiah Clarke and Richard Henman, two boys who have been dismissed from the Chapel on account of their voices having changed.

L. C. Vol. 83 ; *L. C. Papers. Bundle* 15.

" The Bill No. 66, for clothes for two children, their voices being broken and gone off, the names are mistaken.

Pray insert James Townsend and William Luddington instead of Clarke and Henman."

L. C. Papers. Bundle 15.

1697, *November* 6.

Mr. William Williams appointed musician in ordinary to his Majesty, in place of Mr. Morgan Harris, deceased.

L. C. Vols. 183, *p.* 73*d ;* 487, *p.* 23 ; 488. *p.* 30.

1697, *St. Andrew.*

Payment of £16. 2. 6. to each of the following musicians for their liveries :—

Nicholas Staggins, master of music

William Clayton	John Lenton
John Goodwin	Charles Powell
Edward Hooton	Francis Cruys
Robert Carre	Alexander De Latour
John Banister	Richard Lewis
William Hall	Charles Powell
Robert King	Edmund Flower
Henry Heale	Fredrick Steffkin
Thomas Fittz	Thomas Clayton
George Bingham	John Ridgley

Morgan Harris ("vacatur.	Richard Bradley
mort. ante diem ")	Robert Lewis
Daniel Short	John Eccles
Robert Strong	William Gorton
Christian Steffken	William Williams
Henry Eccles	John Shore
Solomon Eccles	

L. C. Vol. 468 ; L. C. Papers. Bundle 78.

1697, *December* 16.

Delivered to Mr. Thomas Barwell, one silver trumpet new made, weight 33 oz. 3 dwt. His signature attached to receipt of same.

L. C. Vol. 440.

1697, *December* 23.

Delivered to Mr. Gervas Walker, one silver trumpet, weighing 38 oz. 1 dwt. His signature attached to receipt of same.

L. C. Vol. 440.

Delivered to Mr. Hendrick Davent, one silver trumpet, weighing 38 oz. 1 dwt. His signature attached to receipt of same.

L. C. Vol. 440.

[1697.]

Instrumental Musick (24).

Each, £40.

Nicholas Staggins, Master of the musick, £200.

Thomas Clayton	Francis Cruys, " for life "
Edward Hooton	Edward Flower
Henry Heale	John Bannister
William Gorton	Robert King
Morgan Harris	William Hall
Henry Eacles	Theophilus Fitz
Solomon Eacles	Daniel Short
Frederick Stepkins	Alexander De La Toure
Christian Stepkins	Richard Bradley
John Lenton	Robert Lewis
Charles Powell	John Eccles
John Ridgely	John Shore

Keeper of the instruments.

John Mosley

Musical instrument maker.

John Walsh

Organ maker.

Bernard Smith

Tuner of the regalls, organs, virginalls, flutes, etc.

Dr. John Blow and Mr. Bernard Smith, and the longer liver.

Harper.

Maurice Reynolds.

Trumpeters (16).
Each, £91 5s.

Matthias Shore, Esquire, sergeant trumpeter, £100.

William Bull	John Doores Court
John Stephenson	Bernard Van Baton
Thomas Barwell	Francis Giddens
Jervas Walker	Richard March
William Shore	Christian Perle
Henrick De Vant	Nicholas Dewell
Anthony Bagways	John Seigneor
Daniel La Faver	

Trumpetters for Ireland.

James Castle, senior trumpetter.

Alexander Jackson	John Burton
James Burton	James Truelove

William Cooper, kettledrummer for Ireland.

L. C. Vol. 487, *pp.* 23 *to* 26.

1697.

Warrant for the payment of £120 to each of the following musicians, the amount due to them for liveries for the years 1689 to 1696 :—

Dr. John Blow, musician for the virginalls in the place of Giles Tomkins, deceased.

Dr. William Turner, private musician in ordinary for the lute and voyce, in the place of Captain Henry Cooke, deceased.

John Gostlin, private musician in ordinary for the voyce in the place of John Harding, deceased.

John Howel, private musician for the voyce in the place of Alphonso Marsh, deceased.

L. C. Papers. Bundle 15.

1697-8, *March* 5 .

Appointment of sergeant trumpeter and trumpeters, and drum major and drummers, among others of the King's servants, to attend the Swedish Ambassador.

L. C. Vol. 756, *p.* 68.

1698, *April* 19.

Delivered to Mr. Richard Marsh, one of his Majesty's trumpets of the Household, one silver trumpet, weighing 40 oz. 7 dwt. His signature attached to receipt of same.

L. C. Vol. 440.

1698, *May* 12.

Appointment of sergeant trumpeter and trumpeters, drum major and drummers to attend, among others of the King's servants, at the entertainment of Count Tallard, Ambassador from France.

L. C. Vol. 756, *p.* 86.

1698, *June* 3.

Fee of £2 : 5 received of Mr. Edmond Flower, musician, for his several debenters for his liveries due at St. Andrew, 1689 to 1697.

L. C. Vol. 458.

1698, *June* 3.

Warrant to admit Mr. George Chocke as one of his Majesty's instrumental musick in extraordinary.

L. C. Vols. 487, *p.* 23 ; 488, *p.* 30 ; *Vol.* 757, *p.* 7.

1698, *June* 4.

Letter of assignment by Edmund Flower, of Corsham in the county of Wilts, one of his Majesty's musicians in ordinary, appointing William Browne of St. Margaret's, Westminster, his true and lawful attorney.

L. C. Vol. 196, *p.* 82.

1698, *June* 10.

Warrant to pay to Mr. Edmond Flower, one of his Majesty's musicians, the sum of £23 for a tennor Cremona violin and a bass violin, which Dr. Nicholas Staggins, master of his Majesty's instrumental musick, has certified he has bargained for at the said price for his Majesty's service.

L. C. Vol. 756, *p.* 97.

1698, *June* 22.

Warrant to pay to Dr. Nicholas Staggins, master of his Majesty's musick in ordinary, the sum of £45. 8s. 6d. for pricking and fair writing several compositions, for prickers' dyett, and chamber rent, and for severall other services by him performed in October and November, 1697.

L. C. Vol. 756, *p.* 105.

1698, *June* 28.

Warrant to pay to Mrs. Sarah Spalding the sum of £20 for the year 1697, for the use of her son Richard Spalding, late one of the children of his Majesty's Chappell Royall, whose voice is changed and gone from the Chappell.

Warrant to supply her with a suit of clothing for his use.

L. C. Vol. 756, *p.* 107.

1698, *October* 10.

William Pike appointed trumpeter in place of Christian Perle, deceased.

L. C. Vols. 487, *p.* 23*d*; 488, *p.* 32.

1698, *St. Andrew.*

Payment of £16. 2. 6. to each of the following musicians to the King for their liveries :—

Nicholas Staggins

William Clayton
(" vacatur : mort. ante diem ")

William Williams

Edward Hooton

John Eccles

John Banister

William Hall

Robert King

Henry Heale

Richard Bradley

William Gorton

Edmund Flower

Morgan Harris
(" vacatur : mort. ante diem ")

Daniel Short

Robert Lewis

Christian Steftken

Henry Eccles

Solomon Eccles

John Ridgley

Charles Powell

Francis Cruys

Alexander De Latour

Fredrick Steffkin

John Lenton

Henry Eccles

Theophilus Fittz

John Shore

Thomas Clayton

L. C. Vol. 468.

1698, *December* 2.

Warrant to provide and set up in the new Chappell at Whitehall an organ, which the Bishop of London, Dean of his Majesty's Chappell, has certifyed is wanting there.

L. C. Vol. 756, *p.* 139.

1698, *December* 2.

Warrant to provide William Shore, one of his Majesty's trumpeters, with a new silver trumpet, the Sergeant Trumpeter having certified that his own is worn out.

L. C. Vol. 756, *p.* 140.

1698, *December* 7.

Warrant to pay to Mr. Bernard Smith, his Majesty's organ maker, the sum of £200 which is to be advanced to him for making an organ for his Majesties Chappell at Whitehall.

L. C. Vol. 756, *p.* 140.

1698-9, *January* 6.

Warrant to prepare two silver trumpets for the second Troop of Guards commanded by the Duke of Ormond.

L. C. Vol. 602, *p.* 283; *and Vol.* 756, *p.* 151.

1698-9, *February* 20.

To Mr. Thomas Betterton and the rest of his Majesty's comedians acting in Lincoln's Inn Fields :—

Several persons of quality having made complaint to me that the musick belonging to your theatre behave themselves disrespectfully towards them, by wearing their hats on, both in the Playhouse and upon the Stage, these are therefore to require you to give orders that for the future they take care to be uncovered during the time they are in the House.

The like warrant verbatim was sent to the Patentees for his Majesty's Company of comedians acting in Dorset Garden or Drury Lane.

L. C. Vol. 756, *p.* 163.

1699, *April* 10.

Warrant to pay Dr. John Blow, master of the children of our Chappell Royall, for 60 pair of strong waxt leather shoes for the said children of our Chappell Royall, their liveries for the year 1696. A like warrant dated June 9.

L. C. Vol. 806.

1699, *April* 24.

Warrants to provide clothes for William Crofts and William Robert (also called " Robarts "), late children of the Chappell Royall, whose voices are changed, and gone from the Chappell, and to pay them the sum of £20 each for the year 1698.

L. C. Vol. 756, *pp.* 183, 184; *Vol.* 826, *pp.* 21, 22.

1699, *April* 25.

Mr. Charles Smith appointed to the instrumentall musick in the place of Mr. Charles Powell, deceased.

L. C. Vols. 487, *p.* 23 (*gives date* 26 *April,* 1700), *and* 488, *p.* 29d.

1699, *April* 29.

Warrant to swear and admit John Clothier one of the drummers of his Majesty's most Honble. Household in ordinary, in the room of Tertullian Lewis, deceased.

L. C. Vol. 757, *p.* 17; *and Vol.* 488, *p.* 32.

1699, *May* 5.

Warrant to fit up a shed in Whitehall for Mr. Smith, his Majesty's musicall instrument maker to work in during the time he is preparing an organ for his Majesty's Chappell at Whitehall.

To Sir Christopher Wrenn, surveyor generall of his Majesty's works.

L. C. Vol. 756, *p.* 187.

1699, *May* 30.

Warrant to provide a new silver trumpet for Francis Giddins, one of the trumpetts in his Majesty's First Troop of Horse Guards, commanded by the Earl of Albemarle.

L. C. Vol. 602, *p.* 288; *and Vol.* 756, *p.* 199.

1699, *June* 1.

To Dr. John Blow, composer of his Majesty's musick, and Mr. Bernard Smith, his Majesty's organ maker :—

His Majesty having been graciously pleased upon the petition of the minister and churchwardens of St. Ann's, Westminster, to grant to them the organ now remaining in the Chappell of St. James's, commonly call'd the Queen Dowager's Chappell ; these are therefore to require you to deliver to the said minister and churchwardens the said organ.

L. C. Vol. 756, *p.* 199.

Accounts ending Michaelmas, 1699.

Accounts for liveries for the following musicians to the King and Queen :—

Doctor Nicholas Staggins, master of the music.

Edward Hooton	Henry Eccles
John Bannister	Solomon Eccles
William Hall	John Lenton
Robert King	Charles Powell
Henry Heale	Francis Cruise
Theophilus Fitz	Alexander de la Tour
Daniel Short	Edmund Flower
Christopher Steffkin	Frederick Steffkins

Account for liveries for the musicians :—

John Ridgley	William Gorton
Richard Bradley	John Eccles
Robert Lewis	John Shore
William Williams	

Account for livery for Thomas Clayton, musician to the King and Queen.

Account for cloth, etc., for William Croft, William Robert and Richard Spalden, three boys who have been dismissed from the Chapel on account of their voices having broken.

Account paid to Dr. John Blow, master of the boys of the Chapel Royal, for their liveries.

L. C. Vol. 84.

1699, *October* 17.

Warrant to deliver to Dr. Blow, certain liveries for the children of his Majesty's Chapple for the year 1699.

L. C. Vol. 826, *p.* 32.

1699, *October* 23.

Warrant to pay to John Colmack, Stephen le Fevre, Thomas Chevalier, John Paulain, John Aubert, Peter la Tour and John Shore, musicians to Her Royall Highness the Princess Ann of Denmark, the sum of £22. 11s. 6d. for their performance in musick at two balls and a play at Whitehall on his Majesty's birthday, which service Dr. Staggins, master of his Majesty's musick has certified was duly performed.

L. C. Vol. 756, *p.* 220.

1699, *St. Andrew.*

Payment of £16. 2. 6. to each of the following musicians to the King for their liveries :—

Nicholas Staggins	Daniel Short
William Clayton	Robert Lewis
John Eccles	Christian Steffkins
Edward Hooten	Henry Eccles
John Shore	Solomon Eccles
John Bannister	John Ridgley
William Hall	Charles Powell
Robert King	Francis Cruys
Henry Heale	Alexander de la Tour
Richard Bradley	Fredrick Steffkin
William Gorton	John Lenton
Edmund Flower	Theophilus Fitz
Morgan Harris	Thomas Clayton

L. C. Vol. 468.

1699, *December* 22.

Warrant, upon the certificate of Dr. John Blow, master of his Majesty's musick, for the allowance of a suit of clothing to John Reading, late child of the Chappell, whose voice is changed, and is therefore removed from the service of the Chappell. Also for the sum of £20 to be paid to him, being the usual allowance.

L. C. Vols. 756, *p.* 239 *and* 826, *p.* 61 ; *L. C. Papers. Bundle* 78.

[1699.]

Instrumentall Musick (24).
Each, £40.

Nicholas Staggins, master of the musick, £200.

Thomas Clayton	Robert King
Edward Hooton	William Hall
Henry Heale	Theophilus Fitz
William Gorton	Daniel Short
Henry Eacles	Alexander de la Toure
Solomon Eacles	Richard Bradley
Frederick Stepkins	Robert Lewis
Christian Stepkins	John Eccles
John Lenton	John Shore
Charles Powell	William Williams
John Ridgeley	Thomas Parkinson,
Francis Cruys, patent for life	extraordinary
Edward Flower	George Chocke, extra-
John Bannister	ordinary

John Mosley, keeper of the instruments
John Walsh, musical instrument maker
Bernard Smith, organ maker

Dr. John Blow and Mr. Bernard Smith, and the long liver, tuner of the regalls, organs, virginalls, flutes, etc.

Maurice Reynolds, harper.

Trumpeters (16).
Each, £91 : 5.

Matthias Shore, Esquire, sergeant trumpeter, £100.

William Bull	Bernard van Batom
John Stephenson	Francis Giddens
Thomas Barwell	Richard Marsh
Jervas Walker	Nicholas Dewell
William Shore	John Seigneor
Henrick de Vant	William Pike
Anthony Ragway	Robert Maugridge,
Daniel la Fevre	kettledrummer
John Dorescourt	John Ashbury, fife, £24

Drummers.
Each, £24.

John Maugridge, drum major, £30.

Devereux Clothier	Robert Maugridge
John Skyrme	John Clothier

Trumpetters for Ireland.

James Castle, senior trumpetter.

Alexander Jackson   James Burton
John Burton   James Trewlove
William Cooper, kettledrummer for Ireland

Vocall Musick.

Dr. John Blow, composer   Anthony Robert
Thomas Richardson   Alexander Damasceen
Moses Snow   Leonard Woodson
Mr. John Gosling, clerk   William Turner

L. C. Vol. 488, *pp.* 30 *to* 34.

1699.

Bill for 31 yards of crimson mantua for curtains to draw round the organ loft in the banqueting house used for the Chapel at Whitehall.

L. C. Papers. Bundle 16.

1699-1700, *January* 5.

Mr. John Gotfrid Ernst appointed trumpeter in the room of Mr. Thomas Barwell, who surrendered.

Mr. John Conrade Richter appointed trumpeter in the room of Mr. William Bull, who surrendered.

Mr. Joseph Williams appointed trumpeter in the room of Mr. Richard Marsh, who surrendered.

L. C. Vol. 488, *pp.* 31, 32 ; *and Vol.* 757, *pp.* 30, 31.

1700, *May* 21.

William Shore, esquire, appointed serjeant trumpeter in the room of Matthias Shore, esquire, deceased.

L. C. Vol. 488, *p.* 31 ; *and Vol.* 757, *p.* 42.

1700, *June* 3.

Mr. Abrahall appointed to the instrumentall musick in the room of Mr. William Hall, deceased.

June 30 : John Eccles appointed Master of the Musick, in the room of Dr. Staggins, deceased.

July 16 : Thomas Parkinson appointed to the instrumentall musick, in the room of Mr. John Eccles, made master.

L. C. Vol. 488, *p.* 30.

Accounts ending Michaelmas, 1700.

Accounts for liveries for the following musicians to the King and Queen :—

Dr. Nicholas Staggins, master of the music

Edward Hootton	Henry Eccles
John Banister	Solomon Eccles
William Hall	John Lenton
Robert King	Charles Powell
Henry Heale	Francis Cruise
Theophilus Fitz	Alexander D' la Tour
Daniel Shorte	Edmund Flower
Christopher Stepkins	Frederick Steffkin

Accounts for livery for the musicians :—

Thomas Clayton	William Gorton
John Ridgley	John Eccles
Richard Bradley	John Shore
Robert Lewis	

L. C. Vol. 85.

Accounts ending Michaelmas, 1700.

Account paid to Dr. John Blow, master of the children of the Chapel Royal, for the liveries for ten children.

Account for cloth, &c., for John Reading and Anthony Young, two boys of the Chapel, who have left on account of their voices having broken.

L. C. Vol. 85 ; *and Vol.* 210, *entries* 22, 62.

NOTES ON MUSICIANS AND OTHER PERSONAGES MENTIONED IN THESE RECORDS.

ABELL, JOHN.—A celebrated alto singer, and performer on the lute. In 1679 he is appointed in place of Antony Roberts, at a salary of £40 per annum. On p. 355 we learn that he took the place of Alphonso Marsh for the lute and voice, and the place of Richard Dornye for the violin. In 1686 he is paid £10 for a guitar bought by him for use in James the Second's bedchamber. In 1688 he is commanded, with Mr. Pedley, to attend the King in his progresses. Grove says he was dismissed from the Chapel Royal in 1688 on account of his Romanism.

ALBRIGI, VINCENT.—Composer and organist, born at Rome in 1631. He was at one time in the service of Christina, Queen of Sweden. He then went to Dresden, and in 1682 he was summoned to a post at Prague. He, together with two others of his family, is only mentioned once in these records, and that is on the occasion of being awarded by Charles II. three gold chains and medals for himself and company. Concerning such gifts, there is a note in Hawkins' History of Music to the following effect:—
" A golden medal and chain was the usual gratuity of princes to men of eminence in any of the faculties. It seems that the medal and chain once bestowed as a testimony of family favour was ever after a part of the dress of the person thus honoured, at least on public occasions." The name of Albrei, or Albreis, which occurs in the reign of James II., looks much akin to Albrigi, but it seems very doubtful whether the same family is intended.

BALTZAR, THOMAS.—Grove mentions that he was born at Lübeck in 1630, and that he was the finest violinist of his time, and the first really great performer heard in England. In the list of musicians of 1660 he is entered as having a "a new place." In 1661 he is paid £34 : 13 : 4 for two violins bought by him for the King's service. In 1661 he is appointed violinist in the private music, at a salary of £110 yearly. In 1662 he is paid £6 : 13 : 4 for strings for one year, also in 1663. In 1667, Thomas Fitz is appointed in his place, and at the same rate of payment, such payment to commence from the June quarter-day. On p. 207 we read "Thomas Fitz succeeds one Mr. Baltzar, the *Swede*."

BANISTER, JOHN.—An English violinist of considerable repute, born in the year 1630. In the lists given by these records for 1660 and 1661 "vacatur" is written against his name. In April, 1662, he is to have the ordering and direction of twelve violinists attending Charles II. to Portsmouth "or elsewhere, for the reception of his dearest consort the Queen." In the same year he is mentioned as succeeding Davies or Daniel Mell, at a salary of £110 yearly. In October of this year, he is paid £40 for two Cremona violins for the King's service. On p. 159 we find his name, in conjunction with Matthew Lock and George Hudson, as a composer. In August, 1663, he is appointed to choose twelve out of the regular company of twenty-four violinists to form a select band to wait on the King, and for this service, and considering the smallness of the present wages, he and the twelve are to receive the magnificent sum of £600 yearly, this regal payment to commence on the March quarter-day, 1662, so that he at once draws more than sufficient for a present *comfortable* maintenance, provided the money is regularly paid. On p. 182 we can see the names of the full band of violinists "which was made choyce of by Mr. Banister and appointed by the Lord Chamberlain," and they are twenty-six in number. In 1666 the sum of £464 is paid to Banister and seven others for riding charges and etceteras, the riding occupying the space of 232 days, and extending to Oxford and Hampton Court. In the same year he and the seven receive some further £140 by way of an advance "to fitt and enable them to attend the Queene to and at Tunbridge." In 1666—and this was a knock-down blow for Banister—there is the order that Mr. Banister and the twenty-four violinists shall obey the directions of Mons. Louis Grabu, master of the private music. In 1666-7, to crown the indignity which he considered was put upon him, Grabu takes his place at the head of the select band of violinists, still twelve in number, and therefore the £600 passes to Grabu. In 1668 Banister is still in the company of the twenty-four violinists, and his so continuing was doubtless a matter of pecuniary necessity, for in 1668-9 he is put down as having a yearly salary of £110. In 1674 we find him playing under the leadership of Mons. Combert. He seems never to have recovered from the misfortunes which overtook him through the advent of foreigners, and in May of 1679 we notice that leave to travel for six months or longer is granted to him. On p. 336 comes the brief notice "Obiit. 3 Oct., 1679." In November of the same year he is succeeded by his son. There are some very interesting particulars respecting Banister and his fall from favour in Sir Frederick Bridge's excellent little work on Pepys and his musical friends. Pepys himself says that Banister "was furious at the advent of Grabu."

BARTHOLOMEW, Mr.—In Evelyn's Diary, under date Nov. 20, 1679, he writes: "I din'd with Mr. Slingsby, Master of the Mint, with my wife, invited to hear musiq, which was exquisitely performed by four of the most renowned masters," and amongst these he enumerates, "Signor Bartolomeo, an Italian, on the harpsichord." On Feb. 7, 1682, he writes, "My daughter Mary began to learn musick of Signor Bartolomeo." And on March 10, 1685, when his daughter was sick of the smallpox, referring to her death on the 14th, he says: "She had an excellent voice, to which she play'd a thorough bass on the harpsichord, in both which she arrived at that perfection, that of the schollars of those two famous masters Signiors Pietro and Bartolomeo she was esteem'd the best."

BATTEN, ADRIAN.—A lay-vicar of Westminster Abbey, at the time of the death of James I. He was afterwards vicar-choral of S. Paul's, and organist, jointly with John Tomkins. This was in the time of Laud. He is said to have composed seven services and fifty anthems.

BEAUPUIS, Mr.—A famous French opera-singer, who made his "debut" under the direction of Lulli in 1672. He seems to have been specially engaged for the masque at Whitehall in 1674.

BIRDE, WILLIAM.—Mentioned as being at the funeral of Queen Elizabeth, and his name occurs amongst the household of Queen Anne, wife of James I. There is reference to an anthem by Bird, "O God, the proud," on p. 306. The Thomas Byrd mentioned on pp. 5 and 7 is evidently the father of this worthy, who is described in the Cheque Book as "William Bird, a Father of Musick."

BLOW, JOHN.—On p. 120 he is spoken of as "Master of his Majesty's musick," although on p. 178 he is described as being still under the tutelage of Captain Cooke, but it will be noticed that the date given to the former reference is queried as being evidently not quite trustworthy. In 1668–9 Blow is appointed to the virginalls in place of Giles Tompkins. In the list of those who attended at Windsor in 1671 he is mentioned twice as organist (p. 236). On July 23, 1674, he is appointed Master of the Children and composer in the King's private music for voices in the place of Pelham Humfryes. On p. 288 he is said to have succeeded Captain Cooke in private musick for the voices. On pp. 305 to 307 we find in a long list of services and anthems Blow's Services in A and G, and his Benedicite, and the anthems, "Turn thou us," "Behold how good," "O Lord I have sinned," "Lord how are they increased," "O how amiable," "God is our hope," "O God wherefore art thou absent," and "Save me O God." In 1676 he is paid £143 for, "inter alia," charges and expenses for going to Windsor, Oxford, Gloucester, Hereford, and Worcester, to fetch boys for the quires for the King's Chapel, and for nurse and chamber rent and firing for one of the Children who was sick of the spotted fever (p. 312); and in 1677 there is amongst his charges an item "For the cure of a broaken legg of one of the Children" (p. 327). On p. 372 we have him as Composer under James II., and in 1689 he is still Master of the Children, "they being tenn in number." He is further mentioned during the reign of William and Mary (p. 399), and in 1695 is appointed with Bernard Smith tuner of virginalls and wind instruments in place of Henry Purcell. He and Smith are to share the place between them and the survivor is to enjoy the whole benefit. On p. 425 it is stated that he is appointed to the virginalls in place of Giles Tompkins, though this has already been mentioned on p. 211, nearly thirty years previously, so this may be a confirmation of the previous appointment, or a discrepancy, of which these records afford various instances. We leave him on p. 437 still alive. Pepys mentions in his Diary that Blow went with Loggins, who is mentioned on pp. 191 and 194, to sing in his presence, and Pepys was not at all pleased with their broken voices. The Cheque Book says, "Dr. John Blow, Organist, Composer in ordinary to His Majesty, and Master of the Children, dyed Oct. 1st, 1708, and had his full pay for both places to Xmas."

BOWER, RICHARD.—The Household Book of Edward VI. has the following entry: " To Richard Bower, for playing before the King's Majestie with the Children of the Chappell, in rewarde, vj*li*. xiij*s*. iiij*d*." (This means a payment of £6 : 13 : 4.) Bower probably succeeded William Crane as Master of the Children, and his tombstone in old Greenwich Church recorded that he was Master under Henry VIII., Edward VI., Mary, and Elizabeth.

BRADDOCK, EDWARD.—The Cheque Book of the Chapel Royal mentions that he was Clerk of the Cheque from 1689 to 1706. Canon Sheppard in his " Memorials of S. James' Palace " mentions that the office of serjeant and yeoman of the vestry and that of clerk of the cheque were originally held by the same person, and that the two former are now held by one person, while the office of clerk of the cheque is joined to that of the sub-dean. Dr. Rimbault says that the duties of the clerk were to keep an account of the attendance and to note the absence of the priests and gentlemen, to attend all admissions into Chapel appointments and to keep a record of the same. No salary was attached to the office, but there were certain fees. It is possible that this is the Mr. Braddock, whose daughter, Elizabeth, was married to Dr. Blow, also that Hugh Braddock, mentioned as a Child of the Chapel, is Edward Braddock's son.

BRIDGES, PAUL FRANCIS.—In the Calendar of State Papers (Domestic Series) we find in 1660 the entry: " Francis Bridges. For appointment as Musician to the Chamber and Chapel, having left his service at Brussels on His Majesty's promise to that effect "— also " Certificate by the Earl of Worcester and six others that Paulus Franciscus Bridges, musician to the King of Spain at Brussels, often brought his companions to play for the King, or played for him alone, and has left his service to serve him in England." On p. 169 of these records there is an account paid to Mr. Perkins in Hatton Grounds for lodging " Mr. Briges of the musique " at 5/- per week, and on p. 207 his yearly salary in the private music is stated to be £56 : 2 : 6. In 1671 a widow, Sarah Glascock, is to take her course at law against Bridges for a debt of £10, unless it be paid within a month. In 1673 he surrenders his place to John Young, this to take effect from June 24.

CAMBERT, or COMBERT, Mons.—Cambert was organist of S. Honoré in Paris, as well as " sur-intendant de la musique " to

Anne of Austria. About the year 1672 he was driven out of France by the machinations of Lulli, and it is recorded by French authentics that he was appointed " sur-intendant " of music at the Court of Charles II. Favoured by this monarch, he produced one of his operas, " Pomone," here, but with indifferent success. It is reported that he died of grief and vexation in 1677. His death is thus accounted for by Bourdelot in " L' Histoire de la Musique et ses Effets." " It was the spirit of envy, a not unknown companion to merit, that shortened his days. The English do not care for a foreigner to interfere with their own amusements, much less to instruct them. This poor fellow therefore died in England a little sooner than he would have died elsewhere."

CHEVALIER, THOMAS.—A member of the chamber-music under Henry IV. and Louis XIII. of France, he is said to have been one of the most skilful composers of instrumental music, more especially of music for the ballet.

CHILD, WILLIAM.—In the year 1660 he takes Alphonso Ferra-bosco's place. On p. 119 those curious in such matters may see a detailed account of the materials for his actual livery. On p. 123 he is mentioned as taking the place of Clement Lanier, deceased, for the cornet. In 1664 we find him in the place of Henry Ferabosco, also deceased (p. 169). In 1670 he has a petition against the rest of his fellows for detaining six and a half years' board wages on the pretence of his not attending the service. On p. 269 he is mentioned as organist. On p. 295 we note that he has written from Windsor asking that the rest of his livery may be paid to the bearer, a certain serjeant Haynes. On pp. 305 to 307 he figures as composer of a Benedicite, an Evening Service in G, a Te Deum to his Benedicite, a Service in E flatt, a Service in A re, and the following anthems: " O pray for the peace of Jerusalem," " The earth is the Lord's," " Thou art my King," " O let my mouth be filled," " Behold how good and joyful," " Let God arise," " O sing unto the Lord," and " O Lord, rebuke me not." On p. 317 Thomas Haynes, Serjeant of the King's Vestry, is mentioned again, this time as his true and lawful attorney. The last notice of him in these records is the appointing (because the faithful Thomas Haynes is now dead) of Edward Bradocke, gentleman, of Westminster, as his true and lawful attorney. This is in the year 1690 ; he is supposed to have died in 1697, and was evidently blessed with a good constitution, as Grove gives the date of his birth as 1606. [As mention has been made here of a Serjeant of the Vestry, it may not be out of place to consider the duties which attached to that office. As to this particular individual, the Cheque Book says that Thomas Haines was sworn Serjeant in 1685 and that he departed this life in 1687. The Cheque Book mentions the following as the daily duties of the Serjeant—To open the vestry, to keep it clean, to assist the Sub-dean in putting on his surplice, to walk before the Dean, Bishops, and Sub-dean with his virge, and to place the velvet cover on the lesson desk. On Sundays and holy days to put the white linen cover on the communion table, and to mark the places in the Prayer Book. He is also to provide new books and surplices, and to attend to the washing of the surplices. When new surplices are ordered he is to procure from the Great Wardrobe the finest and best holland allowed, and to cause two to be made for each gentleman, each marked with the initials of the name, and he is to take special care that the surplices are long and large enough and fit in the neck.]

CLARKE, JEREMIAH.—A chorister under Blow, he was afterwards the original composer of the music to Dryden's Ode "Alexander's Feast." He was associated with Henry Purcell in writing music for various operas. So far as these records are concerned, he is only mentioned as having a livery on leaving the Chapel Royal, but a note on p. 427 says that even in this particular a mistake has been made, and that the name of Townsend must be substituted for that of Clarke, though on p. 400 Townsend is stated to be leaving the Chapel in 1690, and the livery alluded to above is of the date 1697. Probably there was some carelessness in making out these accounts.

COLEMAN, Dr. CHARLES.—Chamber musician to Charles I. After noting the appearance of his name twice in lists of musicians belonging to the Court of Charles I., we find that in 1660 he was appointed for a "viall" in Mr. Thomas Ford's place (p. 114). Dr. Coleman's son, also named Charles, seems to have been appointed with his father to share Ford's place. In 1662 he (the Doctor) is paid £10 for a viol, by him sold and delivered for the King's service. In Nov., 1662, he is appointed in the place of Henry Lawes as composer. In July, 1664, Henry Cooke is appointed, at Dr. Coleman's decease, to take his place, with apparently the same wages, £40, to commence from June 24, 1664. In the next year Charles Coleman is appointed to succeed his father, appointment to date from Sept. 29, 1664.

COLEMAN, CHARLES, Junr.—In Sept., 1672, he is admitted as musician for the viol in the private music, and his name may be noted as being amongst the base violls for the Mask of 1674. In 1685 he is still occupying the same position, and in 1689 he is appointed to the private music under William and Mary. In 1694 one Robert Lewis takes his place, he being deceased, though his name is still retained in a list bearing date 1696. Grove places his death about 1694, but adds that information as to his existence was advertised for in the *London Gazette* of April 12–15, 1697. Although, as will be seen, there are so many entries in these records with regard to this name, most of them give no further information than the including of his name in the several lists of Court musicians of the time. Neither the Doctor nor his son Charles are mentioned in the Cheque Book.

COLEMAN, EDWARD.—Another son of Dr. Coleman. His wife, Mrs. Coleman, is mentioned by Pepys, and is said to have been one of the first actresses who appeared on the English stage. In 1660 Edward is appointed in "the place of John Lanier for a voyce." In a list bearing date S. Andrew, 1669, "mort ante diem" is written against his name, and the Cheque Book says "Mr. Edward Coleman departed this life at Greenwich on Sunday, August 26, 1669."

COOK, CAPT. HENRY.—He first appears in these records in 1660, and is then enjoying the following emoluments :—£60 per annum for lute and voice (in place of Duvall), £20 per annum for strings, £24 for "breeding" a boy for vocal music, and £10 each for two boys in quarterly payments from 1660 to 1672. His succeeding to Dr. Coleman's place has been before mentioned. He is first mentioned as Captain in the entry of April 6, 1661. He is to have the same livery as Thomas Day as Master of the Children, and the same as Duvall as musician in ordinary. On September 17, 1661, £19 : 10 : 0 is to be paid to him for the attendance of himself and the Children on the King at Windsor, and a further sum of £2 : 16 : 0 is to be paid for torches and lights used whilst practising the Coronation music. Later in the same year his name is mentioned in connection with the materials for the clothing of the Children, their summer and winter liveries; and there is a further sum of £45 to him for sums expended to masters during the space of one year in teaching the Children to write and to learn and to speak Latin. In 1662-3 thirteen Prayer Books are delivered to him for the use of the *thirteen* Children in the Chapel. In 1663 he is paid £30 for the Children's learning of the violins and organ. In 1663-4 he is paid £20 for yearly cost of firing for the music room at the Chapel, and for strings for the "base voyall" and other Chapel instruments. In 1664 he is paid £60 for "learning Latin" to the children and teaching them the lute and organ for nearly one year, also £10 for firing and strings for the half-year, £7 for strings for virginals and lutes, £11 : 6 : 0 for coach hire and other expenses to Windsor and Canterbury. In 1665 he is paid £115 : 10 : 6 for having the Children taught Latin as well as to write, to play on the violin, organ, and lute; for stringing and *penning* their harpsichords; for firing and strings; for clothes for Michael Wise; for going into the country and looking for boys, and for nursing three boys sick of the smallpox. In 1665 he is to be paid £40 yearly for the maintenance of Pelham Humphreys, £30 for John Blow, and £30 for John Blundivile. In 1666 thirteen more Prayer Books are delivered to him for the Children, but in this instance the New Testament is bound in with the Prayer Book. In 1668-9 his yearly fees are mentioned as totalling £188. In 1669 there is an order to repair his lodgings at the further end of the Old Bowling Alley, Hampton Court, and for the erection of chimneys there. In 1671 he is given a sum of money for, amongst other things, doctors' and nurses' fees; for looking after several children when sick; and for going to Westchester, Lichfield, Canterbury, and Rochester, to look for boys. In the same year he is paid £431 : 12 : 0 for the attendance at Windsor during May, June, and July, of the Gentlemen of the Chapel, the organist, and two base violists. A further account seems to show that the Children (now twelve in number) were at Windsor during all or part of this period. He departed this life on July 13, 1672. His will, with its characteristically quaint provisions, will be found "in extenso" on pp. 245–6. He is immediately succeeded by one of his pupils, Pelham Humphreys. (Bumpus, in his "History of English Cathedral Music," says that his death was caused through jealousy of Humphreys.) In 1675 we have the certificate of his burial in the cloister at Westminster on July 17, 1672. From the

Cheque Book we learn that Cook acted as steward at the annual Chapel feast in 1663, but he only accepted the office on condition that it created no precedent, as he did not think it "meete or convenient for the Master of the Children to have that office." On May 28, 1666, in conjunction with Thomas Purcell and other Gentlemen of the Chapel, Cook petitioned " on behalf of themselves, the pages of the Chapel, and boys whose voices have changed, for payment, there being no money assigned to the Treasurer of the Chamber for that purpose." We may supplement this fact with a notice from Pepys' Diary bearing the date of Dec. 19, 1666. (Sir Frederick Bridge has already given this passage in his Pepysian volume, but it will bear repeating, especially in this context.) Pepys says, " Talked of the King's family with Mr. Hingston, the organist" (see " Hingston " in these notes). " He says many of the musique are ready to starve, they being years behindhand for their wages : nay, Evens, the famous man upon the Harp, having not his equal in the world" (he is mentioned in these records), " did the other day die from mere want." With regard to Pepys' appreciation of Cook, he writes in his Diary under date Sept. 14, 1662, " To White Hall Chapel, where sermon almost done, and I heard Captain Cooke's new musique—I could discern Capt. Cooke to overdo his part at singing, which I never did before " ; and on Dec. 21, 1663–4, he writes, " To my Lord Sandwich's, where I find him with Capt. Cooke and his boys, Dr. Childe, Mr. Madge " (this would most likely be the Humphrey Madge of these records) " and Mallard, playing and singing over my Lord's anthem, which he hath made to sing in the King's Chapel." Pepys elsewhere states his opinion that Cook was a good singer, but a " vain coxcomb." Elias Ashmole says that at the festival of S. George at Windsor in 1661 " the hymn was composed and set with verse and chorus by Capt. Cook—by whose direction some instrumental loud musick was at that time introduced, namely, two double sackbuts and two double courtalls—one sackbut and courtal before the four petty canons who began the hymn, and the other two immediately before the prebends of the College." Cook in the Civil War was on the Royalist side, and obtained a captain's commission. We have a glimpse of the Captain during the Commonwealth in Evelyn's Diary, as follows :—" Nov. 28, 1654. Came Lady Langham, a kinswoman of mine, to visit us; also one Captain Cooke, esteem'd ye best singer after the Italian manner of any in England; he entertained us with his voice and theorba."

CORBETT, MR. FRASICO.—Francesco Corbetti was born at Pavia about 1630. The Duke of Mantua sent him to Louis XIV., and from the French Court he came to England. Charles II. appointed him to an office in the Queen's Household, and it is said even provided him with a wife. He was esteemed to be the best guitarist of his time, and it may be noted that he appeared in the Whitehall Mask of 1674. He eventually returned to France.

CORNYSH, WILLIAM.—The second known Master of the Children of the Chapel. It is said that he had some renown as a poet, and that he was a great favourite of King Henry VIII. Under Cornish's direction the Gentlemen of the Chapel were accustomed to act plays before the King and Court. In 1504 he was committed to the Fleet prison, but afterwards came again into Royal favour.

CRANE, WILLIAM.—Crane succeeded Cornish in the Mastership. In the Household Book of Henry VIII. we have an entry similar to the one referred to under " Bower " :—" to Maister Crane, for playing before the king with the children of the chappell, in rewarde, v*jli.* xiij*s.* iiij*d.*" In a book of Receipts and Payments of the Exchequer, 18 Henry VIII., he is mentioned as " Will? Crane, Magister Puerorum Capellae Dom. Regis."

CUTTING, THOMAS.—Cutting was an excellent performer on the lute. In 1607 he was in the service of Lady Arabella Stuart, but she, at the instance of Ann, wife of James I., and sister of Christian IV. of Denmark, sent him to Denmark to replace Dowland. Cutting stayed in Denmark but little more than four years, for he appears as being in the service of Henry, Prince of Wales, in 1611.

DAVIES, Mrs.—Mary Davis, sometime comedian in the Duke of York's company of players, is the Moll Davis so frequently alluded to by Pepys. She seems to have been noted as a singer, and appeared in the Masque of 1674, as Father Thames in the prologue, and as Sylvia in the pastoral scenes. Her attainments as a dancer are thus referred to by the celebrated diarist :—" 1666-7, March 7. To the Duke's playhouse.—Little Miss Davis did dance a jigg after the end of the play, and then telling the next day's play, so that it come in by force only to please the company to see her dance in boy's clothes." And again :—" 1667. August 5. Miss Davis, dancing in a shepherd's clothes, did please us mightily."

EAGLES, SOLOMON.—According to Grove, this strange character was born in 1618, and was noted as a teacher of the virginals and viols. About 1660 he became a Quaker, broke his instruments, burned them, together with his music books, and turned shoemaker. There seems to be no direct evidence to connect this individual, despite his fanaticism, with the crazy prophet who has been immortalized by Ainsworth in his account of the great Fire of London, although there are undoubted points of similarity. The only information we gain from these records is that in 1693 he was in debt to the amount of £400, and that in 1700 a certain Solomon Eccles (a glance at the various references will show that the name Eccles and Eagles seems to describe one and the same person) was still amongst the Court musicians. There is one Eagles mentioned in the 1674 Masque, and this is more likely to have been Solomon than Henry, though one cannot pronounce with certainty. If the date given in Grove for Solomon's death—viz., 1683, be correct, then we are confronted with a difficulty, and can only suppose that Eccles and Eagles must be separately identified, but it is not easy to discern any break in the continuity. Solomon's eldest son, John, here set down as John Eccles, was appointed Master of the Musick in 1700, and Henry, his second son, also had a place amongst the Court musicians.

EVESEEDE, Mr. (See Oveseede, in Index).—Mr. Henry Eveseede is set down in the Cheque Book as one of the Yeomen of the Vestry. He is dismissed, after his petition being considered, " for a foule disease in his groine," for drunkenness, for blasphemy, and for actual violence, in 1620-1. "On S. Peter's Day last, beinge the day of our feast—Mr. Eveseed did violently and sodenly without cause runne upon Mr. Gibbons, took him up and threw him down upon a standard wherby he received such hurt that he is not yet recovered from the same." A " standard " was a large chest generally used for holding plate, &c., but sometimes for linen.

FERABOSCO, ALPHONSO.—It seems doubtful whether this is the eldest Ferabosco who was in this country, as Grove says that he left England in 1578, whereas the first notice in these records of this Alphonso is in the year 1603. Fétis makes the following remarks on the earlier Ferabosco. " He was born in Italy about 1515, and appears to have established himself in England about

1540. Amongst the English writers there is a misty uncertainty as to the actual residence of this musician in England, and they are not even of one mind as to the orthography of his name." In our records, in 1627, another Alfonso is mentioned as succeeding his father, whilst Henry Ferabosco also appears as a brother of the second Alfonso, and there is a note on p. 63 to the effect that the father having had a musician's, a composer's, a violl's and an instructor's place to the Prince of Wales, the benefit of these places descends to his sons by the King's special grant. In 1630 there is a warrant for a livery for John Ferabosco, and on p. 78 we have all three brothers mentioned, Alfonso for the violin, Henry for the voices, and John for the wind instruments. John last appears on p. 107, in the years 1641–2, and Grove says that he was appointed organist of Ely Cathedral in 1662. Alfonso seems to have surrendered his place before 1660, and Henry is in that year spoken of as already deceased. On p. 127 we have the entry, "Thomas Bates, in the place of Alphonso Ferabosco, junr, which his father, Alfonso Ferabosco, enjoyed as instructor to his late majesty (Charles I.), when Prince of Wales, £50 per annum, and in the place of Henry Ferabosco, deceased, £40 more."

FINGER, Mr.—A Moravian, who came to England in 1685. He appears in these records in the years 1687 and 1688. In 1693 he composed the music for Parsons' Ode to S. Cecilia. The *London Gazette* for Feb. 1 of that year makes the following announcement : "At the Consort in York Buildings on Monday next the 5th inst., will be performed, Mr. Finger's St. Cecilia's Song, intermixed with a variety of new musick, at the ordinary rates." In 1702 Finger received the appointment of Chamber musician to Sophia Charlotte, Queen of Prussia.

FITZ, THEOPHILUS.⎫ On p. 315 these two musicians are men-
FITZ, THOMAS. ⎭ tioned as "Fitz the elder" and "Fitz the younger," and they seem to have followed each other so closely during their lives that they may well be included in one notice. As violinist under Charles II., Theo. (it will be a convenience to shorten their names) has 1/8 per diem, besides his livery. On p. 124 Tom is described as musician of the violins in ordinary. In 1662, Theo. is amongst those attending on Charles II. to receive the Queen, and in 1664 he is to attend at His Majesty's Theatre, with others, when-ever required by Mr. Killigrew. In 1665 he is appointed to the post

of double sackbutt, and in the same year we find him in Banister's company of violinists. In 1666 he is ordered to attend the Queen at Tunbridge. In 1666-7 he is transferred from Mr. Banister to Mons. Grabu. In 1667 he is appointed with another to "wait" during the allowed absence of Henry Comer, and in the same year he is to attend with three others at the Chapel Royal, Whitehall, whenever Captain Cook should so require. In this year also Tom is appointed to the violins in the private musick in the place of Baltzar. In 1668 he takes Richard Hudson's place—a place for life—with a fee of £46:12:8. In 1669 he is paid £21:10:0 for riding charges in attending Charles II. at Newmarket, Bagshot, Portsmouth, and Audley End. In 1670 they are both to attend at the Chapel, and in the same year Tom is amongst the twenty-four violinists who attended the King at Dover for twenty days. In 1674 the two are to be paid £24 for two violins bought by them for the Chapel. In the same year Theo. with five others is in attendance on the Queen at Hampton Court for thirty-six days, whilst at about the same time Tom is in attendance with six others on the King at Newmarket. They both figure amongst the violinists in the Mask of 1674, and in 1674-5 they are amongst those attending in the Chapel at Windsor for one-hundred-and-nine days. In 1675 "Mr. Fitzz" (this is evidently Theo.) is paid £12:10:0 for a "sagbutt." In 1677 we hear of the death of Tom, and in this same year we find Theo. petitioning with others against their dismissal from the playhouse by Mr. Killigrew, the Master of the Revels. In 1684-5 Theo. is to attend with others at the King's Theatre to practise music for a ball to be held there. In 1688 he is amongst those attending James II. to Windsor. In 1689 he is appointed to the private music under William and Mary. In 1693-4 John Godwin, of Westminster, bequeaths to Theophilus Fitzz, of Hampton, £5. In the year 1700 we leave Theo. still living.

FLEURI, NICHOLAS.—Fétis says that François Nicholas Fleuri was born about 1630, that he acquired remarkable skill on that difficult instrument, the theorbo; that in 1637 he entered the service of the Duc d'Orleans, and in 1678 was still in the same service. There must, however, have been some break in this engagement, as we find him in England in 1663, as one of Charles II.'s French musicians in ordinary, and this is the only notice he has in these records.

GAMBLE, JOHN.—His first appearance in these records is in the year 1660. In 1661 a livery is allowed him against the King's coronation, and in 1662 he has the livery formerly granted to Jerome Lanier, now deceased. In 1666 the sum of £7 is lent to him. In 1670 he is to attend in the Chapel with others, also in 1671 and 1672. In 1671-2 he assigns to one Parrott his livery due out of the King's Great Wardrobe. In 1674 he is to practise with others under Mons. Combert in the theatre at Whitehall, and in the same year he is waiting on the King at Windsor from July 11 to Sept. 1. We find him named amongst the violinists in the Masque of 1674. In 1675-6 he assigns to J. Talcott, apothecary of Westminster, one debenture for livery due Nov. 30, 1674. In 1676 he receives payment for attendance, with seven others, in the Chapel at Windsor from July 7 to Sept. 11, 1675. In 1676 there is a letter of assignment from John Gamble, of the Parish of S. Giles-in-the-Fields, appointing J. Spicer, of S. Martin's-in-the-Fields, his true and lawful attorney. He last appears in 1686. Grove says he performed at one of the theatres, and was a cornet player in the Royal Chapel.

GIBBONS, ORLANDO.—This well-known character is mentioned as privy organist in the list of King James' household. In the same list is Dr. W. Heather, who took his Doctor of Music degree at the same time as Gibbons, and Gibbons is said to have written Heather's exercise as well as his own. Grove says that he married Elizabeth, daughter of J. Patten, Yeoman of the Vestry. He died in 1625. It is related that Henry Eveseed, a drunken Groom of the Vestry, did him serious hurt five years before his death, and he does not seem to have recovered well from the shock, which may have accelerated his end.

GIBBONS, Dr. CHRISTOPHER. — This was the second son of Orlando, and he was born in 1615. In 1660 he is appointed to Warwick's place (Warwick had succeeded his father) for the virginals—" the virginall in the Presence "—and in the same year he is approved by the King at Baynards Castle, and it is ordered that an organ be built for him. In 1672 Dr. Gibbons and Mr. Pickering are to provide mourning for trumpeters, drummers, and fife at the funeral of Lord Sandwich. In 1676 C. Preston succeeds the Doctor, he being now deceased. Grove mentions that he was in the Royalist Army, and that, besides being organist of the Chapel Royal and private organist to the King, he was also organist of Westminster Abbey.

GILES, NATHANIEL.—According to Antony à Wood, he was " noted as well for his religious life and conversation (a rarity in musicians) as for excellence in his faculty." His last entry in these records bears the date 1628. Grove says that the inscription on his grave at Windsor says that he was Master of the Children there for forty-nine years, and at the Chapel Royal (presumably at Whitehall) for thirty-eight years.

GOSLIN, JOHN.—He takes Mr. John Harding's place, and is mentioned as Clerk on p. 436. He was later appointed precentor of Canterbury, and Sub-dean of S. Paul's. Henry Purcell wrote the bass solos in his anthems for this noted singer.

GRABU, LOUIS.—In the list of 1600 the name of Nicholas Lanier, Master, is crossed out, and Grabu's name inserted, and on p. 126 it is stated that Nicholas Lanier, Master of Musick, is dead, and that Grabu is Master in his place. In 1665 he is appointed composer in the King's music. (Many details concerning Grabu will be found under the name of Banister.) In Lanier's place he has £200 per annum—this, with the £600 taken from Banister, makes the respectable total of £800 per annum ! In 1668 he is paid £165 : 9 : 6 for " fayre writing severall dances, aires, and other musick," &c., &c. ; and in the same year he is to have the teaching of two boys, not, let us be sure, without due payment. He has also a yearly livery of £16 : 2 : 6 during the King's pleasure, and this is apparently in addition to the sums already mentioned. In 1671-2 he is paid £117 : 4 : 6 for " fayre writing and pricking severall sorts of musick," &c., at various times in 1668-9, and for other services. In the same year he has £20 for riding and other charges in attending the King to Dover during the space of twenty days in 1670. This he assigns, with another sum of £137 : 4 : 6, to Walter Lapp, citizen and mercer of London, the same tradesman who, in 1647, made the wreaths for the King's musicians for the theatre at Whitehall. In 1674 there is a warrant to deliver to Grabu, or his representative, the scenery from Whitehall for the use of the French opera in Bridges Street, the same to be returned after fourteen days. This bears date March 27, and on April 27 there is a warrant to deliver to Sir Christopher Wren, the King's Surveyor General of Works, the said scenery. In the list of 1674, against Grabu's name is written " vacatur," and Mr. Staggins is in his place. (From the course of events we can only suppose this to be an enforced and compulsory resignation of his many emoluments, owing to the Royal countenance being turned against him.) In 1674-5 Mr. Staggins is to enjoy Grabu's £200 per annum, commencing from September 29, 1674. In 1675 there is still a warrant to pay Grabu his livery, and in 1676-7 certain violinists are ordered to practise some of his music, so his downfall was not a swift and sudden flight, but a little managed—" un peu adouci " expresses it. The real extent of his ill-luck can only be appreciated when we come to his pitiful petition on p. 317. In this he speaks of being a menial servant to the King, and asks for help for his distressed family, and to be kept from arrests. The King refers the whole petition to the Lord Chamberlain. This is in 1667, and in June of the same year Lord Arlington finds that there is due to Grabu out of the Exchequer the sum of £450, out of the office of the Treasury Chamber, £145 : 4 : 6, and out of the Great Wardrobe £32 : 5 : 0— making in all the sum of £627 : 9 : 6, and he further finds that Grabu's condition is " very poor and miserable." (This seems one of the saddest histories we have to deal with in these records.) On the back of a document bearing the date, Dec. 8, 1687, in the reign of James II., there is a memorandum that " Mr. Grabu received all his arrears as master of the music to his late Majesty, although not actually in his said Majesty's service at the time of his decease," so that as Grabu passes from our sight we have the pleasant reflection that justice was after all rendered to this strangely-fortuned individual. Grove says that Grabu came to England in 1666, but these records point to an earlier date—also that in 1690 he composed the music to one of Beaumont and Fletcher's pieces, but according to the information given above, Grabu was in 1687 already regarded as dead.

GREETING, THOMAS.—He is appointed in 1662. He figures in the band of twenty-four violins of the time of Charles II. In 1673-4 he is appointed to the violin and sackbut for the Chapel Royal at 2/4 " per diem." He is amongst the violinists in the Mask of 1674. In 1682 one Crouch takes his place. Grove mentions that he was a teacher of the flageolet, and that amongst his pupils were Mr. and Mrs. Pepys.

GUALTIER, JACQUES.—In 1637 this musician is paid £10 for a treble lute to be used in masques. In 1660 we find that P. Rogers, also a lutenist, took his place, and as the said Rogers is appointed at a salary of £100 per annum, we may infer that Gaultier received the same payment. Grove says that Denys Gualtier and Gaultier " le vieux" were the last two members of a celebrated family of " lutheriens " who lived in Paris during the reign of Louis XIII. It is possible that the " le vieux " is identical with the above-named Jacques, and this same person, in the course of a correspondence with a certain Huygens respecting the sale of a " luth de Bologne," wrote, " After being thirty years in the service of so illustrious a king and queen, I have nothing to show for it save this lute ; moreover I am encumbered with a wife."

HARDING, JOHN.—In the Cheque Book, under date 1671, there is this entry :—" It is ordered that the old bookes and surplices shall be to the use of the Gentlemen of His Majesties Chapell Royall, paying to the Serjeant of the Vestry 12*d.* for the old bookes and 10/- apiece for their old surplices. Upon the testimony of Mr. John Harding, Gentleman for fifty years standing."

HINGSTON, JOHN.—In 1660 he is appointed to the viol in place of A. Ferabosco. He also takes Norgate's place as repairer of organs. In 1662 he is paid £155 for organs and harpsichord for the King's Chapel and the organ for the Queen's private chapel. In the same year he is paid £76 : 5 : o for repairing the organs in the Chapel Royal, Whitehall, for a " base violl," and for erecting an organ in the Banqueting House at Whitehall. In the same year there is a direction given for enlarging the organ-loft at Whitehall, at Hingston's discretion. In 1663 he is paid £67 : 11 : o for removing and setting up the organ in Her Majesty's Chapel at S. James', for removing another organ from Whitehall to S. James' " for the French musick", and for " portage " of a larger organ from Mr. Nicoe's to S. James', and setting it up there. In 1663 there is a warrant for a new organ-loft at Whitehall in the place where formerly the great double-organ stood—the rooms over the bellows-room to be rebuilt two stories high, as formerly ; the lower story for the sub-dean, the upper story, with two rooms, one for the organist-in-waiting, the other for Hingston—each room to have a chimney and boxes and shelves. In the same year he is paid £83 : 15 : o for taking down the organ in the Queen's chapel at S. James' and remounting it in the "new musique room"; for mending organs and harpsichords; for mending the Queen's harpsichord "that stands in her own chamber " ; for mending a " claricon " ; and for erecting an organ in the Banqueting House. In 1668 he is described as "tuner and repayrer of the wind instruments and organs under the Broad Seal," and in another list is put down as "organ maker." In 1669 he is paid for, amongst other items, stringing, penning, and repairing harpsichords. In 1673 he is paid £45 : 3 : 6 for keeping, repairing, and "amending" the King's organs, harpsichords, and "pedalls," for the rent of a room to keep them in, for strings for "base violls," for a "base violl" bought by him, and various other services during the space of two years. In 1673 Henry Purcell is appointed as his assistant and successor. On pp. 298 to 300 there is a very interesting account presented by Hingston for work done from 1673 to 1675. We may note in it the following—"Repairing and amending two harpsichords and carrying them to the playhouse "— "Repairing and setting up organ in the Banqueting House for Maunday Thursday "—"Twenty yards of saile cloth to cover and secure the organ (at Windsor) from the weather and dust "—"For a grate harpsichord with three ranks of strings for His Majesties musick in the hall and in the privy lodgings." (In this account the name of Bernard, better known as Father, Smith, frequently occurs.) In 1678 we come across another account, a much shorter one, and lacking the interest of the first one, inasmuch as it repeats many of the previous items. In 1683 there is still another account, much resembling the previous one; from this it is evident that an organ was set up in the Banqueting House at Whitehall every Maunday Thursday. In 1683-4, Henry Purcell succeeds Hingston.

HOLDER, Dr. W.—On p. 306 two of his anthems are mentioned, "Thou, O God," and "O prayse our God." In 1680-1 there is a warrant to pay to Dr. Holder, Sub-dean of the Chapel, £12 for some parts of anthems and services written in the Chapel books, and for books and ruled paper for the Children. Grove says he was sworn Sub-dean in 1674, and that he resigned before Christmas, 1689— that he was also Sub-almoner. He married a sister of Sir Christopher Wren. Hawkins says that from being very exact in the performance of choral service, and frequently reprimanding the choirmen for their negligence in it, Michael Wise used to call him Mr. Snub-dean.

HUMPHRYES, PELHAM.—In 1666 he is bracketed with T. Purcell and Matthew Lock as composer. In 1665-6 he is appointed for the lute in the place of Nicholas Lanier. On p. 254 there is a bill for teaching the Children for half a year, and to it is appended this note: " In this warrant was nothing for fetching children from several cathedrals, as is sometymes." In 1673 we have articles of agreement between Humfryes and J. Lilly, of S. Andrew's, Holborn, one of his Majesty's musicians in ordinary, for teaching and instructing four of the Children in the viol and theorbo, for which service Humfryes is to pay £30 yearly out of his salary. Humfryes departed this life on July 14, 1674, at the early age of twenty-seven years, and was succeeded by Blow. (It is strange that in the list of 1673 "mortuus" is written against his name.) The service alluded to on p. 305 is probably his full Service in E minor. On p. 307 six of his anthems are mentioned, including the well-known " Lord, teach us to number our days." Pepys tells us that Humfryes, on his return from a stay on the Continent, greatly decried everything English, though at the same time he mightily abused Louis Grabu; also that, when quite young, he was a pretty boy.

JENKINS, JOHN.—He is mentioned in 1660 for the theorbo, and in 1661 for the flute. We have also an entry as to the probable date of his decease—" Died October, 1678." Grove says he was born at Maidstone in 1592, and that he resided for some time in the family of Sir Hamon l'Estrange. North has this passage:—" His talents lay in the use of the lute, and Base or rather Lyra-Viol. In most of his friends' houses there was a chamber called by his name. He kept his places at Court, as I understood, to the time of his death, and then he for many years was incapable to attend; the Court musitians had so much value for him that advantage was not taken; but he received his salary, as they were payd."

LANIER.—As will be seen by the Index, we have here to deal with a very numerous and intermarried family, and the information conveyed to us in these records concerning the various members is of the most meagre description. It is difficult to establish the exact relationships, but the most practical way of attempting an elucidation is to set down the individuals mentioned with their respective dates as given in the records. John Lanier, who is first in chronological order, is first mentioned in 1564, for the sackbut, and Edward Coleman succeeds him in 1662. Nicholas (the flute-player) is first mentioned in 1566. In 1603 we have the first mention of three members of the family, Alphonso, Jerome, and Innocent. Andrea appears in 1618 for the flute, in place of his father, Nicholas; then Clement, in 1625; and Nicholas (the singer) in 1625. Another Nicholas comes to light in these records in 1625, and he is the best known of all the Laniers, but it seems doubtful whether here two persons have not been rolled into one, and possibly an error may have been made in indexing the luter and the Master as identical. However, there are indications, as will be seen below, of the correctness of such identity. This Nicholas appears as Master of the Music in 1626, but in 1660 his name is crossed out, and he is announced as dead. In 1665-6 we have probate of the will of Nicholas Lanier, of East Greenwich, in Kent, "dyed and buried there February 24th, 1665-6." In 1666 Humfryes succeeds him for the lute, and Grabu as Master. The erasure of his name some time before his death would appear to point to a dignified retirement to the pleasant village where he eventually died. In the " Life of Inigo Jones," printed for the Shakespeare Society in 1848, there are some reproductions of sketches of costumes for Masques made by that artist. On one of these sheets of drawings (it must be said that they are very roughly and hastily executed, though one can detect the master-hand) we find depicted "a damsell," a dwarf, and, as a third figure, a man of more than average height, stalwart, and mustachioed, in a standing posture, and evidently engaged in plucking the strings of a harp. Over against this figure is written the word "Lanier." Mr. Cunningham, the editor of the above-mentioned work, informs us that Nicholas Lanier sang and composed the music for Ben Jonson's masque of " Lethe " after the Italian manner, " stylo recitativo." Nicholas was an artist as well as a musician, and sometimes assisted in painting the very scenes before which he figured. This same volume contains a hitherto unprinted Masque, or, more properly, Show, which is of rather a peculiar character, since it was written for the sake of introducing and terminating a supper, upon some occasion which has not been recorded. It is called the " Masque of the Four Seasons," and it is considered probable that Nicholas played the part of Orpheus in this Show, and that the sketch with the harp represents his costume on that occasion. We next have Henry Lanier, who appears in 1629, and is announced as deceased in 1633. During his lifetime Mrs. Emilia Lanier has a petition against him, showing that unanimity was not always a prevailing note in this family. In 1633 Mrs. Jone Lanier, the widow of Henry, petitions to dispose of her child, William, to be trained in music. (William's dates in these records are from 1637 to 1660.) Thomas, the last member of this family to come before our notice, is the son of Mrs. Joyce Lanier. He also is trained by Andrea, and in 1660 he takes his place on his decease, and acts as executor for him. In 1663 there is an order for his arrest at the suit of a blind man. He is last mentioned in 1686.

LAWES, HENRY.—He is first mentioned as a Gentleman of the Chapel in 1628, and he takes the place of Richard Marsh as musician for the lutes and voices. In 1635-6, Henry and William have two lutes at £10 each on the certificate of Mr. Lanier. On p. 114, Henry is described as composer in the private music for lutes and voices in Mr. T. Ford's place. On Nov. 16, 1662, T. Purcell is composer for the violin in place of Henry, and in the same year Dr. Coleman succeeds Henry for the voices. From the Cheque Book it appears that Henry was sworn in "Pisteller" in 1625, and Gentleman in November of the same year.

LAWES, WILLIAM.—In 1635 he takes the place, as musician in ordinary, of J. Lawrence. In 1662 John Clement takes William's place (owing to William's death) for the lutes, viol, and voices, at £40 per annum. Grove says that on May 5, 1611, he resigned his place to Ezekiel Wade, but that on Oct. 1 he was re-admitted "without paie." (The Cheque Book gives May 1 as the date of resignation, and quotes his actual words in resigning.) William joined the Royalist Army, and was killed at the siege of Chester in 1645. Hawkins mentions that the King was so affected at his loss that he wore a particular suit of mourning for him.

LOCK, MATHEW.—In 1660 he takes the place of John Coperario. On p. 123 he is in the place of Alphonso Ferrabosco as composer for the wind music; on p. 124 he has "a new place" amongst composers for the violin, and on p. 126 he is bracketed amongst composers with T. Purcill and P. Humfryes. In 1661-2 he is appointed composer to the King's private band. On p. 169 there is an account paid to Margaret Pothero for lodging Mr. Lock, organist, and his servants, at 10/- per week. On p. 207 it is stated that his yearly salary as composer is £46 : 10 : 0, but on p. 210 it is put down at £40. On p. 307 an anthem by Mr. Lock, "Not unto us, O Lord" is mentioned. On p. 318 he is mentioned as being deputy to Mr. Staggins. In 1677, Henry Purcell takes his place amongst the violins, and in the same year Ed. Dyer takes his place as composer. North, in his "Memoires of Musick," gives us considerable information about Lock, and the following passages may here be appropriately quoted:—" He was organist at Somerset House Chappell as long as he lived "—(this statement is rather too ample)—" but the Italian masters that served there did not approve of his manner of play, but must be attended by more polite hands, and one while one Sabinico" (mentioned in these records) " and afterwards Sig. Baptista Draghi used the great organ, and Lock (who must not be turned out of place, nor the execution) had a small chamber organ hard by, on which he performed with them the same services." Also—" He " (Lock) " set most of the psalms to musick in parts, for the use of some vertuoso ladies in the city; and he composed a magnificent consort of four parts after the old style, which was the last of the kind that hath been made, so we may rank him with Cleomenes, king of Sparta, who was styled 'ultimus Nerooum.'" What dear old-fashioned sonorousness! We can fancy that even Lock himself would be rather startled to hear such magniloquent parallelism, not to mention the vocal adaptability of the Latin appellation.

MATTEIS, N.—This name only comes before us once in these records, and that is in 1686, when he witnesses a letter of assignment by F. Cruys. Grove says he was an eminent Italian violinist who came to England about 1672. In 1696 he composed an Ode for S. Cecilia's Day, but this, according to North, was never printed. Pepys thus alludes to him:—" By all that I have knowne of him and other musick of Italy, I cannot but judge him to have bin second to Corelli."

NIGHTINGALE, R.—Hawkins has a brief note about this musician, in which he says that he was distinguished as a singer, that he was one of the Chapel Gentlemen under Charles I., that he became a clergyman, and that at the Restoration, though then advanced in years, he was again appointed a member of the Royal Chapel.

NOTARI, A.—He first appears in 1625. In 1633 he is in debt. In 1660, Henry Purcell is put in his place, but see entry on p. 124. In 1662, Henry Purcell is appointed for the lute "in the same place " with Notari. In 1663 (?) he is written down as " mort," and in 1664, John Goodgroome is appointed in his place. Fétis says that he was an Italian musician who established himself in London in the beginning of the 17th century. About 1614 he printed a collection of pieces under the following title, "Prime musiche nuove a 1, 2, e 3 voci, per cantar con la tiorba ed altri stromenti. Londres, 1616."

PORDAGE, Mr.—In Evelyn's Diary, under date Jan. 27, 1685, we have the following entry: "I din'd at Lord Sunderland's, being invited to heare that celebrated voice of Mr. Pordage, newly come from Rome; his singing was after the Venetian recitative, as masterly as could be, and with an excellent voice both treble and basse—Pordage is a priest, as Mr. Bernard Howard told me in private."

POWNELL, N.—The Cheque Book says that Mr. R. Sandie (see Index) and Mr. N. Pownall had in 1630 an admonition given them to be more industrious and studious. This was when Laud was Bishop of London and Dean of the Chapel Royal.

PURCELL, HENRY.—In 1660 he is amongst the composers for the violin in the place of Angelo Notari; this is afterwards crossed out, and the name of John Goodgroome is written over Purcell's name, with the date August 20, 1664. This is confirmed on pp. 170 and 173, and is stated to be in consequence of Purcell the elder's death, though in 1662, Henry is appointed for lute and voice *in the same place* with Notari. On June 10, 1673, Henry Purcell, apparently the son, is appointed keeper of organs, &c., and assistant to John Hingston, and in December, 1673, clothing and £30 per annum is to be provided for a certain Henry Purcell, late Child of the Chapel, whose voice has changed. Also in January, 1674, there is an account for fine holland and a felt hat for this same Henry; in February and at Michaelmas bills for handkerchiefs; and in 1676 there is an order for four whole shirts, four half shirts, bands and cuffs. (Bumpus says that Henry, the younger, was born in 1658, so that he was fifteen years old when he left the Chapel—are we therefore to believe that at this age he was appointed to a responsible post?) About 1674, Henry's name is substituted in the list of musicians for that of Matthew Lock, and on Sep. 10, 1677, he is appointed composer in ordinary with fee for the violin, in the place of Lock, now deceased. In 1683, Henry is appointed organ-maker and keeper, in place of Mr. Hingston, deceased. (Possibly this may point to his previously being under the tutelage of

Hingston, and perhaps in a manner apprenticed to him.) For the full terms of the warrant, allowing him the same powers and privileges as his predecessor, and the same salary (£60 per annum), and this quite apart from any sum for necessary expenses, see p. 364. On August 31, 1685, in the list of James II.'s musicians, we have the entry, "Harpsicall, Henry Purcell." On p. 394 he is described as "musician composer," and on Nov. 30, 1695, Dr. Blow and Mr. Bernard Smith succeed him on his decease. Henry lost his father when he was only six years old, and was left to the guardianship of his uncle, Thomas Purcell. It will be seen that unfortunately Henry the younger only lived for thirty-seven years.

PURCELL, THOMAS.—In Nov., 1662, he is appointed musician in ordinary in the place of Henry Lawes, deceased. On p. 124 he is put amongst composers for the violin in place of Henry Lawes, and on p. 155 is in the receipt for lutes and voices in the private music, in the place of Henry Lawes, of £36 : 2 : 6 per annum, the lowest amount mentioned in the list on p. 207. On p. 252 he is mentioned as Groom of the Robes. In 1673 he is appointed with Humfryes in the place of George Hudson, deceased, as composer for the violins—and payment to both is to be at the rate of £42 : 5 : 10 during their natural lives, and to be continued for the longest liver, but the next entry (p. 257) mentions the sum of £200 per annum, and the longest liver. In 1674 he receives three liveries, in the places respectively of Henry Lawes, Dr. John Wilson, and George Hudson. He receives £40 annually as Groom of the Robes (p. 289). In Oct., 1675, he is paid £410 : 8 : 0 for attendance of himself and organist on Charles II. at Windsor for seventy-two days. In 1676 he is appointed to the private music in the place of Dr. Wilson at £20 per annum. In 1679 he appears in the list of the Gentlemen who attended at Windsor in 1678. (Amongst the Children who were there at the same time is one Daniel Purcell. Grove says that Daniel was the youngest son of old Henry Purcell.) On p. 381 there is a memorandum of monies owing on the decease of Thomas Purcell.

SEBENICO, G.—On p. 222 this musician is with another of his countrymen mentioned in conjunction with Mr. Killigrew under the heading of "Italian Musitians," a curious circumstance, and evidently a clerical error in the inclusion of Mr. Killigrew. In 1673 "a chayne or medall of gold of about the value of £70 " is to be given to him. Sebenico was a professor of singing, a good tenor, also a composer. He was born at Venice towards the middle of the seventeenth century. A note in North's Memoirs speaks of him as an obscure musician who came to this country with Mary d'Este, Princess of Modena. Some of his compositions are preserved in the Oxford Music School.

SHORE.—Of this family we have four members mentioned in these records. There is a John Shore, trumpeter, who appears in 1688, and in 1690 is appointed to attend King William to Holland, being paid for such service 5s. "per diem." In 1695 there is a John Shore, musician, who in 1696-7 is appointed one of the musicians in ordinary under William and Mary. The last mention of him is in 1700. Mathias Shore, serjeant trumpeter, appears in 1681-2. As serjeant he has £80 per annum. In the time of William and Mary he attends the King to Holland at the wages of 10d. a day. In 1696 he claims £60 for his livery for 1692. In 1697 he is in the enjoyment of £100 per annum. It is said that the daughter of Mathias married the celebrated actor, Colley Cibber. William Shore appears in 1679. In 1690 he is to attend King William to Holland. In 1693-4 there is an order for a new livery for him, he having been robbed whilst campaigning. In the same campaign, in Flanders, he also seems to have been robbed of his trumpet. In 1696-7, in company with three other trumpeters, he attends the Ambassadors for the Treaty of Peace. In 1700 he is appointed serjeant trumpeter in the place of Mathias, although previous to this date he is once mentioned (evidently in error) as serjeant. The title of Serjeant Trumpeter lapsed when the late Thomas John Harper retired (see *Athenæum*, Jan. 2, 1909). As the notes under this name deal with trumpeters, it may now be mentioned that in the case of Henry Peacock, who is many times mentioned in these records as a " pentionary trumpeter," we find the following in the Calendar of State Papers (Domestic Series):—" 1660. Henry Peacock, His Majesty's Trumpetere (Petition to the King) for restoration to the place which he held under him as Prince, and not confirmed therein in Scotland. Lost £1,500, all he had, in the Royalist cause, was dangerously wounded at the battle of Worcester, and imprisoned. With note that he is to bring a certificate to the Lord Chamberlain for serjeant trumpeter."

SMYTH, BERNARD.—The real name of the family is Schmidt. Bernard came to England at the time of the Restoration. He is said to have been called " Father " Smith to distinguish him from his two nephews. In 1674 he is spoken of as " the organ maker." In 1681 he is appointed organ-maker in the place of Farr. On p. 398 there is a special warrant to Bernard. In 1690 he is to provide a new organ for the Chapel at Hampton Court. In 1695 he is appointed with Blow as tuner of various instruments. In 1698, £200 is to be advanced to him for the organ at Whitehall Chapel. In 1699 he is to deliver to the minister and wardens of St. Ann's, Westminster, the organ in S. James' Chapel. He last appears in these records in 1699.

STAGGINS.—Of this family no less than six members are mentioned in these records, but of these six, three are only distinguished by a solitary reference, giving us the following dates: James, 1660-1 ; John and Thomas, 1676. Isaac, the father of Nicholas, appears in 1660, and in 1684, Charles, another son, takes Isaac's place. In 1671, Nicholas is appointed for the violin in the place of W. Young, and in 1673 takes Young's place for the flute. In 1674 he is appointed to be master of the violinists, and in this year appears to have taken Grabu's place. On pp. 297-8 there is a very interesting bill from Nicholas for £93 : 2 : 0. In 1678-9, Dr. Staggins and the violinists are to attend the King every night a play is acted at Court. In 1685 Dr. Nicholas Staggins is re-appointed Master of the Music under James II. On p. 280 we have another bill from Dr. Nicholas in connection with expenses incurred at the coronation of James II. On p. 383 there is an admonition to the Doctor. Later, we find that the Doctor attended King William to Holland. In 1695-6 (be it mentioned with bated breath) he owes the brewer £120 (!) for " beare and ale." In 1700, John Eccles is appointed Master, on the Doctor's decease.

TESTA, ANDREA.—In the Calendar of State Papers (Domestic Series) we have under date of 1668 a petition of Andrea to the King for a pension promised by His Majesty, " as formerly granted to Gerolamo Zenti, harpsicall maker, whose place he supplies, being sent over by Zenti, who went to Paris, and died in the French King's service.

TINKER, PHILIP.—In 1661 a Rev. Philip Tinker was Confessor of the Household. It was " the duty of the Clerk of the Closet or

Confessor to the Sovereign, who was usually a Bishop, to attend at the right hand of the Sovereign in the Royal Closet during Divine Service."

TOMKINS.—All of the family who are mentioned in these records appear to have been sons of a Rev. Thomas Tomkins, of Gloucester Cathedral. Thomas, who appears in 1625, was sworn as organist of the Chapel Royal in 1621, and died in 1656. John is mentioned in 1628, and in 1633 was organist on Charles the First's journey to Scotland. Giles succeeds Richard Deering, and is co-organist with his brother in 1633. He is appointed to the virginals in 1660, and is inscribed as dead in 1668, Blow being his successor. Robert is in 1641 amongst the King's musicians.

TURNER, WILLIAM.—In the time of Charles II. he is under Captain Cooke, who is to have £30 per annum for keeping him after he left the Chapel, his voice being changed. This is to commence in 1666. In 1671 he is amongst the Gentlemen at Windsor. In 1672 he is appointed for the lute and voice in the place of his master, now deceased. A warrant on page 264 shows that he had £30 yearly from 1666 to 1670. In 1674 he is singing in " The Tempest" at His Royal Highness' Theatre, and is to remain in town (even in the King's absence) all the week for that purpose, only taking the week-end at Windsor. In 1674 he is apparently engaged in the masque at Whitehall. Three of his anthems are mentioned on page 307—" Lord, what is man," " O Lord God of hosts," and " O Lord, Thou hast been our refuge." In 1689 he is appointed to the vocal music. " He had the singular honour," says Boyce, " of being a Gentleman of the Royal Chapels to seven kings and queens successively." He was eighty-eight years old when he died. Grove says that he died in 1739-40, having survived his wife, with whom he had lived nearly seventy years, only four days, and they were buried in one grave in the cloister of Westminster Abbey. A charming instance of wedded constancy, and a good trait in one who was the guardian of young Henry, his nephew!

WALSH, JOHN.—In 1692 he is appointed " Musical Instrument Maker in Ordinary to His Majesty," in the place of John Shaw, surrendered. He last appears in 1699. He was one of the most eminent music-publishers of his day, and is said to have amassed a fortune of £20,000. He died in 1736.

WARWICK, THOMAS.—He first appears in 1628, and is mentioned in 1641 for the virginal. In 1660, Christopher Gibbons takes his place. " Mr. T. Warrick in 1630 received a check of his whole paye for the month of March because he presumed to playe verses on the organ at service tyme, being formerly inhibited by the Deane from doinge the same, by reason of his insufficiency for that solemne service." (Cheque Book.)

WHITE, BLASE.—" 1675. Mr. Blasius White was by the Sub-deane discharged from His Majestie's service in obedience to His Majestie's pleasure so signified in this following letter from Mr. Vice-Chamberlain." (Cheque Book.) No reason is assigned in the letter for such discharge.

WILSON, DR. JOHN.—He was born in 1594, and first appears in these records in 1635. He is said to have been a Gentleman of the Chapel. His name is not found in the Cheque Book, but he is there described in a warrant of April 17, 1641, as being amongst " Musicians for the Waytes." He died at Westminster in 1673, and was buried in the cloisters of the Abbey, and on p. 266 we have the certificate of his burial. In 1673-4, Thomas Purcell takes his place. He is said to have been a fine lutenist, and Charles I. greatly admired his singing.

WISE, MICHAEL.—In 1644, James Farr is to be paid £30 yearly for the maintenance of Wise, whose voice has changed ; to commence from September last, 1663. In 1665, Captain Cooke is to be paid for his disbursements for clothes for Wise. In 1678, £30 is to be paid yearly to Wise during Charles the Second's pleasure. In 1684 Wise is mentioned with Dr. W. Child as musician in ordinary for the cornet, with wages of 20d. a day, and usual livery. Bumpus says that in 1668 he succeeded Giles Tomkins as organist of Salisbury, and that in 1675 he succeeded Courteville (mentioned in these records) at the Chapel Royal. Grove gives particulars respecting his somewhat tragic end.

WOODWARDE, RICHARD.—He appears in these records in 1546-7. In 1563 he is mentioned as " musician to the lady the Queen " (Elizabeth). There is evidently some confusion here, as details given by Grove relate to R. Edwards, and yet they seem in part to fit this personage, who does not appear to have been really a bagpiper, as he is only once so mentioned. Possibly there should have been two separate entries in the Index, but the question presents difficulties.

NOTES ON REFERENCES TO COSTUME
IN THESE RECORDS.

PAGE 1.—" Sarsynett "= sarcenet. A thin silk, first used in the thirteenth century. In Henry II.'s time we find this material mentioned as being in use for trumpet banners.

PAGE 10.—" Sloppes "= slops. The wide Dutch breeches mentioned by Chaucer, and again introduced during the reign of Elizabeth.

PAGE 10.—" Cassock." A long loose coat, or gown, worn by both sexes. White and green were the Tudor colours.

PAGE 119.—" Chamblett "= camlet. A mixed stuff of wool and silk, used for gowns in the time of Elizabeth and James I. It was originally manufactured from camel's hair, and, though expensive, was said to be of lasting wear.

PAGE 119. — " Budge." Lambskin with the wool dressed outwards. It is still used for trimming livery gowns. (Budge Row is so named because of this fur, and of the skinners who dwelt there.) In an account made out for Lord Burghley about 1585 there appears the following :—

> " Allowance of Apparrell for a Musician out of
> the Gardrobe."
> " Chamlett, 14 yardes, at 3s. 4d. the yarde -   - 46s. 8d."
> " Velvet, 6 yardes, at 15s. the yarde, amounteth to 4l. 10s."
> " Damask, 8 yardes at 8s. the yarde -   -   - 3l. 4s."
> " One furre of Budge, pryce   -   -   -   -   4l."
> " Lyneing and making   -   -   -   -   -   20s."
> Summa 15l. 0s. 8d."

The above sum was the usual livery in the time of Elizabeth, and it is said (I cannot vouch for the accuracy of the statement) to be equal to fifty or seventy pounds in our present monetary system. The usual provision for the livery, as will be seen in our records, was the sum of £16 : 2 : 6.

PAGES 136-7.—" Bastard." A term applied to several articles. Bastard cloth is mentioned as an English manufacture in the time of Richard III.

PAGE 153.—" Perfumed gloves." These were brought as presents from Italy in the sixteenth century, a custom that continued till the middle of the eighteenth century.

PAGE 229.—" Shalloon." A woollen stuff, first imported from Chalons, where it was originally manufactured, and of which its name is a corruption.

PAGE 285.—" Avinnion." A stuff upon which metallic colour was printed, chiefly used for fancy dresses, and named from Avignon, in Southern France, the place of its original manufacture.

PAGE 285.—" Tabby." A thick silken stuff with a soft nap. In 1487 " white and grey tab " is mentioned for carriage awnings in the wardrobe accounts of Henry VII.

PAGE 285.—" Taffata." A thin silk used in the sixteenth century for various articles of dress, and considered as a luxury. It was used for doublets and pages' dresses in the ensuing century.

PAGE 286.—" Tinsell." A kind of satin.

PAGE 288.—" Castor " = the beaver. The name was hence applied to beaver hats.

For most of the above information I am indebted to the Glossary appended to Fairholt's " Costume in England " (Bohn's Artists' Library.)

NOTES ON COURT MASQUES, PARTICULARLY THE WHITEHALL MASQUE OF 1674.

It will be noticed that in the years 1674-5 we have a vast amount of detail concerning the production of a masque at Whitehall. There is given a list of singers and musicians who took part in the masque, further on we have bills showing cost of dresses furnished for some of the musicians, with accounts as to materials and making, and lastly a bill to be paid to the Master of the Music for labours entailed in attending to the proper supplying of the music for the masque. I was at first inclined to consider this masque, which was evidently a function of considerable importance, as being an adaptation of some French opera of the time. But when I carefully read the chapter in Canon Sheppard's " History of Whitehall," which treats of this form of entertainment, I could come to no other conclusion, so identical were many of the particulars, that this is none other than Crowne's masque, " Calisto, or the Chaste Nymph." I should advise everyone to read the chapter referred to, as it really supplements all that is set down in these records.

Before speaking of this particular performance, I should like to mention three masques that were presented at Court in the reign of James I., and that may be fitly included in this section. They call for attention, because amongst those employed, we find the names of some musical worthies who live again in these records.

The Masque of Hymen, produced in 1605-6, was the work of Jonson and Jones. The music was composed by " Master Alphonso Ferrabosco," and the dances made and taught by " Master Thomas Giles." The Masque in celebration of the " Lord Viscount Haddington's marriage at Court on the Shrove Tuesday at night " (1607-8)—the Carnival season seems to have been a favoured time for these performances — was called " The Hue and Cry after Cupid " (an admirable title for a modern play). Of the four dances in it, two were made by Thomas Giles, two by " Master Heer Herne," and, as before, the tunes were by " Master Alphonso Ferrabosco."

The Masque, " Love freed from Ignorance and Folly " (a rather cumbersome naming), was presented at Christmas, 1610-11. The Bill of Costs has been discovered among the Pell Records. Amongst " Rewards to the persons imployed in the Maske " are the following items :—" To Mr. Alfonso, for making the songes, £20; to Thomas Lupo " (mentioned in our records) " for setting the dances to the violins, £5; to the twelve musicians that were priests, that songe and played, £24; to the twelve other lutes that suplied, and wth flute, £12; to the ten violencas that continually practized to the Queen, £20; to four more that were added at the Maske, £4; fifteen musitions that played to the pages and fooles, £20; to eighteen hoboyes and sackbutts, £10."

Before giving any account of " Calisto," I here introduce two maxims which attracted my attention on reading through the " Mountebank's Maske," by John Marston. The one is, " He cannot be a cuckold that weares a Gregorian, for a periwigg will never fitt such a head." On p. 384 of our records it will be noticed that several musicians are classified under the heading " Gregorians." I do not mean to say that the above quotation has a note of explanation in it. I cannot imagine that in describing musicians any term of political significance would be used ; rather, looking at the period in which this term occurs, must we conclude that it refers to the modal character of the music which they sang. The other maxim is somewhat in the nature of a pun, and I commend it as a motto : " Musicians cannot but be helthfull, for they live by good aire."

With regard to John Crowne, the writer of " Calisto," it will be sufficient to say that he was the son of an Independent minister " in that part of America which is called Nova Scotia "—that he was considered superior to Dryden as a writer of comedies—that he contributed a song or two, set to music by Henry Purcell, to the " Gentleman's Journal, or Monthly Miscellany," edited by Motteux in 1691-2—and that he got the nickname of " Starch Johnny Crowne " from the " stiff and unalterable primness of his long cravat."

It was owing to the influence of the Earl of Rochester that Crowne was selected to compose this Masque, for the task ought naturally to have fallen to Dryden, as Poet-Laureate. Dryden appears to have gracefully waived his rights, and was good-natured enough to write an Epilogue, but this, through the above-named influence, was rejected, a somewhat unnecessary insult.

The Masque, which was printed in 1675, is dedicated to " Her Highness the Lady Mary, Eldest Daughter of His Royal Highness the Duke." Crowne, in his " Preface to the Reader," says that he was only allowed a month to write the play, prologue, and songs. " I was also confined in the number of the persons ; I had but seven allowed me—those seven to be all ladies, and of those ladies two only to appear in men's habits " : " I have in the Prologue represented the river Thames by a woman, and Europe by a man, contrary to all authority and antiquity. I know no sexes in lands and rivers, nor of any laws in poetry, but the fundamental one to please,—and the graceful motions and admirable singing of Mrs. Davis " (mentioned in our records) " did sufficiently prove the discretion of my choice. And Thames, Peace, and Plenty, being represented by women, I was necessitated to make Europe a man—otherwise I must either have made those parts of the world men, and one a woman ; or worse, representing them all by women, have spoiled the music by making it consist all of trebles."

Turning to the list of names in our records on pp. 280-1, the following can be identified with characters represented in the Masque : Mrs. Davies, the River Thames ; Mrs. Knight, Peace ; Mrs. Butler, Plenty ; Mr. Hart, Europe ; Mr. Richardson, Asia ; Mr. Marsh, jun., Africa ; Mr. Ford, America ; Mr. Turner, the Genius of England. These were all in the Prologue, and the only words that came from the three continents, in response to Europe saying " I will my thanks in offerings proclaim," were the following :—(Asia) " I'll lend you spice ; " (America) " I gold ; " (Africa) " I the same ; " so that these were not exacting parts !

In the " Choruses betwixt the Acts " the following were employed:—Mr. Hart, Strephon ; Mrs. Turner, Coridon ; Mrs. Davis, Sylvia ; Mrs. Knight, Daphne ; Mrs. Butler and Mrs. Hunt, two " African Women, or Blacks." These interludes break up the several acts of the Masque, filling up the time usually allowed for the " entr'actes." They are conceived in a pastoral vein, as the names of the characters will show, and whilst they formed a sort of explanatory undercurrent to the play, they afforded opportunities for singing and dancing. They have some points of resemblance with the Spanish "entreméses." In the Prologue and the Masque itself there were also various dancing entries ; for instance, in the Prologue one stage direction is : " Here the Princesses and the other ladies danced several sarabands, with castanets " (the saraband being really a Spanish measure). "A minuet was also danced by his Grace the Duke of Monmouth." At the end of Act I., there is the direction : " An entry of Basques " (probably to exhibit some quaint dance of the Pyrenean region). We find also at the end of the other acts respectively : " An entry of gypsies," " An entry of satyrs," " An entry of Bacchuses." In the Prologue we meet with this naïve direction : " The following stanza is properly part of the Genius's speech—but being set extremely pleasantly, and for a treble voice, it was sung by Thames."

As a specimen of the lyrical merit of the songs, we cull the vocal number at the conclusion of the Prologue. " Enter two, who sing this following song—

> Now for the play, the prologue is done,
> The dancing is o'er, and the singers are gone.
> The ladies so fine, and so fair, it surpasses,
> Are dress'd, and have all tak'n leave of their glasses.
> Where are the slaves that should make ready the stage ?
> Here, here are the slaves should make ready the stage.
> An Entry of Carpenters."

In praising and thanking the performers, Crowne mentions "the singers, and the composer of all the musick, both vocal and instrumental.—Mr. Staggins has not only delighted us with his excellent composition, but with the hopes of seeing in a very short time a master of music in England equal to any France or Italy have produced." (See Mr. Staggins' bill in connection with charges for the music of the Masque on p. 290 of our records.)

The Masque proper is taken from that incident in the Second Book of Ovid's Metamorphoses which shows the meeting of Jupiter with Calisto, a daughter of the King of Lycaonia. Crowne dexterously avoids the natural and realistic sequence of the story by making Calisto triumph by her chastity over the amorous advances of the monarch of Olympus, who presents himself to her affrighted gaze first in the guise of Diana and then in his own shape. Crowne also introduces an underplot of his own imagining in which he makes

Mercury fall in love with one of Diana's attendants, Psecas, "an envious nymph," who assists Juno against Calisto, and is rewarded with the jealous queen's friendship.

The characters in the Masque were represented by the following Royal and noble personages:—Calisto, H.H. the Lady Mary; Nyphe, friend to Calisto, H.H. the Lady Anne; Jupiter, the Lady Henrietta Wentworth; Juno, the Countess of Sussex; Psecas, the Lady Mary Mordant; Diana, Mrs. Blagge; Mercury, Mrs. Jennings. "The Nymphs who danced in the prologue and in the several entries in the play were, the Countess of Derby, the Countess of Pembroke, the Lady Katharine Herbert, Mrs. Fitzgerald, Mrs. Frazier." "The Persons of Quality of the men that danced were, His Grace the Duke of Monmouth, the Viscount Dunblaine, the Lord Daincourt, Mr. Trevor, Mr. Harpe, Mr. Lane."

The Princess Mary, afterwards Queen Mary, was born at S. James' Palace on April 30, 1662, and was therefore nearly thirteen years old when she acted in this Masque. Princess Anne, afterwards Queen Anne, was born Feb. 10, 1664, and was therefore nearly eleven years old at the end of 1674. Mrs. Jennings, Maid of Honour to the Duchess of York, subsequently married John Churchill, and was famous as the "confidante" and adviser of Queen Anne. Mrs. Frazier was a Maid of Honour to the Queen.

Evelyn mentions that Mrs. Godolphin, when Margaret Blagge, performed the character of Diana in this Masque, and "had on that day near twenty thousand pounds value of jewells," also that during the performance she lost a diamond lent to her by the Countess of Suffolk. The stage was swept and diligent search made, but it was probably stolen in "the infinite crowd." However, the King or the Duke sent sufficient money to repair the Countess' loss. "For the rest of that days triumph I have a particular account still by me of the rich apparel she" (Mrs. Blagge) "had on her, amounting besides the Pearles and Pretious Stones, to above three hundred pounds, but of all which she immediately disposed her selfe soe soone as ever she could get clear of the stage. Without complimenting any creature or trifling with the rest who staid the collation and refreshment—away she slips like spiritt to Berkley House to her little oratorye: whither I waited on her, and left her on her knees thanking God that she was delivered from this vanity, and with her Saviour againe; never, says she, will I come within this temptation more whilst I breath."

I extract the following from the particulars given by Canon Sheppard concerning the Masque in his Whitehall book :—" All the Women's Accounts of their Habits delivered into his Ma^{ty.} Great Wardrobe, Madam Knight, Pease, £4 : 10 : 0; a Shephardess, £3 : 10 : 0 ; Madam Butler, Plenty, £3 : 15 : 0; Afrycan Lady, £3 : 3 : 0 ; Madam Hunt, shepherdess, £5 : 1 : 6 ; Mrs. Maistres and Mrs. Pearse, £4 : 1 : 6; Mrs. Hunt, £3 : 15 : 0." Also, these further charges, which may be compared with those that are to be found on pp. 286-7 of our records :—" Mascarading Habitts made by John Allan, 10 violins, £5 ; made by William Watts, 10 violins at 10/- each, £5. Four gittar men at 18/- each, £3 : 12 : 0. Made by W. Watts, 3 trumpets at £1 : 14 : 6 each, £5 : 3 : 6; made by T. Allan, one trumpeter and one kettle drum, £3 : 9 : 0."

There is a large amount of useful information concerning this Masque in Vol. I. of the Dramatic Works of John Crowne, published by Sotheran in 1873, and I am indebted to this work for many of the particulars above given.

Evelyn in his Diary gives December 15 and 22, 1674, as the dates on which " Calisto " was presented at Court. On the first occasion he calls it " a comedie," and on the second " the Pastoral."

NOTES ON SOME GENERAL
REFERENCES IN THESE RECORDS.

PAGE 1.—" Mynstralls." The word "minstrel" does not appear to have been in use in this country before the Norman conquest. By a Record of the 9th year of Edward IV. it is recited to be the duty of minstrels to pray in the King's Chapel, " and particularly for the departed souls of the King and Queen when they shall die." " The minstrels derived their knowledge from the schools of the monasteries. They learnt something of the theoretical principles of music, the practical part of singing, and the elements of grammar, including perhaps as much knowledge of poetry as was sufficient for the composition of a song or ballad." North, in alluding to the reign of Henry VIII., says: " There was small show of skill in music in England, except what belonged to the cathedral churches and monasteries (when such were), and for that reason the consortiers wherever they went were called Minstels, and then the whole faculty of music—The Minstrelsie."

PAGE 2.—" Shalmoyes." "' Chalmy,' ' Shawm' in Old English, is a clarinet of low pitch." (Burney.)

PAGES 7 and 8.—In comparing the list of names given on these pages with a somewhat similar list given in Burney, and with another list (almost similar to Burney's) given in Hawkins, we may note that the following names correspond with those found in these records. [In any variation of the name, such variation is added in brackets.] " William Hychyns (Huchins), Robert Philipps, Thomas Byrde, Richard Bower (Bowyer), Robert Perrye (Perry), William Barber, Robert Richemound (Richemount), Thomas Whayt (Wayte), Thomas Talys, Nicholas Mellowe, Thomas Wright." From the same sources we have some particulars as to various payments, which may be compared with those on pp. 38 and 39. Though the sums mentioned in our records belong to a somewhat later date, there will in some instances be observed a striking similarity, notwithstanding the fact that they have another origin. I quote those that deserve attention, placing on the left side details derived from the writers I have mentioned, and on the right side details which we find in the records.

" Sergeant trumpeter £24 6 8 " " Sergeant trumpetor £24 6 8 "

" Trumpeters, in number 16, every of them having by the yere   -   - £24 6 8 "

" Trumpetors 16, fee amongst them   £389 6 3 "

" Sagbutts, in number 6, whereof 5 havinge   -   - £24 6 8 by the yeere, and one at -   -   - £36 10 0 "

" Sagbuttis 6, fee to 5 of them   -   - £24 6 8 to one -   -   - 20 0 0 "

" Vyalls in number 8, whereof 6 at   -   30 8 4 the yeere, and another at   -   - £18 5 0 and one at   -   - £20 0 0 "

" Vyalls 8, fee to 6 of them a piece   - £30 8 4 to one -   -   - £20 0 0 and the other   - £10 5 0 "

" Dromslades in number 3, whereof Robert Bruer, Mastet Drummer £18 5 0 Alexander Pencax, same, and John Hodgkin   -   -: £18 5 5 "

" Drumslads 3, fee to every of them - £18 5 0 " (The three names appear on p. 9.)

" Players   on   the flutes, Olivier Rampous   -   - £18 5 0 Pier Guye   -   - £34 8 4 "

" Players oh the flute 2, fee to eyther of them   -   -   - £18 5 0 " (P. Guy, *see* Index.)

" Players   on   the virginals, John Heywoode   -   - £50 0 0 Anthony de Chounte £30 8 4 Robert Bowman   - £12 3 4 "

" Players   on   the virginalles 3, fee to every of them   - £50 0 0 " (H. de Countie, *see* Index.)

" Musicians Straungers,   Augustine Bassano   -   - £36 10 0 William Trosses   - £38 0 0 William Demirat   - £38 0 0 "

" Musicions straungers 4, to the 4 brethren Venetians, amongst them   -   -   - 183 6 8 "

"The 4 brethren Venetians, viz., John, Anthonye, Jasper, and Baptiste (Bassanie) - £16 6 8"

(Bassanie and Trochies, *see* Index.)

"Players of interludes, in number 8 £26 13 4"

"Players of interludes 8, fee to every of them per annum - £66 0 0"

"Makers of instruments, William Beton, organ-maker - - - £20 0 0

"Makers of instruments 2, fee to one per annum - - £20 0 0

William Treforer, regal-maker - - £10 0 0"

fee to the other - £10 0 0"

"Gentlemen of the Chappell, 32, every of them 7d. a day."

"Gentlemen of the Chappell 32, fee to every of them per diem, 7½d."

PAGE 44.—The list of Gentlemen of the Chapel, given on this page of the records, when compared with the list given in the Cheque Book for the year 1604, gives as a result the dual occurrence of the following names (the variations in the Cheque Book version being signified by enclosure in brackets) : " Doctor Ball, Nathaniel Giles, William Birde, Richard Canwell (Granwell), Drue (Crue) Sharpe, William Randall (Randoll), Edmond Browne, Thomas Woodison (Woodson), Robert Stone, Henry Oveseed (Henrie Eveseede), Robert Allison, John Stephens, John Howlett (Hewlett), Thomas Gold (Goolde), Richard Plumley, Peter Wright (Wryght), William Lawrence, James Davis (Davies), John Amery (Amerye), John Baldwell (Baldwin), Francis Wilbroughe (Wyborow), Arthur Cocke, George Woodison (Woodson), Edmund Hoop (Hooper)." A list given in the Cheque Book for the year 1603 does not agree so well with our records, but in one for the Coronation of James I. the names are almost the same as in these records.

PAGE 59.—" Black cloth for liveries." In the Cheque Book there is this notice :—" At the funeralls of Kinge James—Natha. Giles, Dr. and Mr. of the Children ; William Heather, Dr. ; T. Hewlett, Clerk of the Check ; John Steephens, Recorder of Songes ; and Orlando Gibbons, senior Organist, had the lyke allowance of nine yards apiece for themselves as the ministers had, and two yards apiece for their servauntes. The rest of the gentlemen, being 17, had for their blacks every one seven yards, and for every of their servauntes two yards apiece."

PAGE 64.—The Masque here mentioned is probably " Pan's Anniversary," a Masque presented at Court before King James I. in 1625, the inventors being Inigo Jones and Ben Jonson.

PAGE 88.—There is a mention of two treble lutes for the Masque at Shrovetide. This would appear, from the date, to have been ' The Temple of Love," a Masque at Whitehall, presented by the Queen and her ladies on Shrove Tuesday, 1634, by Inigo Jones and William Davenant.

PAGE 94.—" Chayre " = choir.

PAGE 113.—The entries in the Cheque Book of the Chapel Royal cease in 1640, and re-commence in 1660. In these records, as will be seen, the entries stop at the beginning of 1644, and begin again about the middle of 1660. The gap is caused by the Commonwealth epoch.

PAGE 120.—We have an account of the amount of scarlet cloth given to, respectively, the Children, the wind musicians, the com-posers, and the violinists, for the Coronation of Charles II., and there is a similar reference on p. 392. This scarlet cloth was for the purpose of being made into mantles, according to the following directions : " These mantles were made like a Rocolo (but without a cape, button, or buttonhole), gathered and bound round with a silk Ferrit, to tye before with a Bow Not ; and a silk button and loop stitched round to fasten it round the neck like a Rocolo. The length of the Mantle must be so as to reach the ground behind." This word " Rocolo " is evidently a somewhat misspelt form of an Italian word, and would seem to imply that these mantles were to be made on the model of a rochet. In Fairholt's " Costume in England " a Rochette is defined as a loose upper garment, and a clerical gown, and a Rochet as a cloak without a cape.

PAGE 134.—On this page we find a warrant for taking up all trumpeters, drummers, and fifers, who sound with trumpets, or beat drums, or blow fifes, at plays, dumb shows, or " models," without license from the serjeant-trumpeter. On p. 206 there is a similar order, with this addition—it empowers the serjeant to take fees from show-mongers. On p. 217 there is a warrant for apprehending seven persons for keeping playhouses, and sounding trumpets, drums, and fifes, at dumb shows, and " modells," without paying the fee to the serjeant—the said fee being 12*d*. per day, to be paid by every playhouse when there are performances, the King's players excepted. On p. 225 there is a similar notice regarding the penalties attaching to dumb shows, &c. On pp. 232-3 there is set out in full the form of warrant used for apprehending these offenders. There are other references in these records, which, though they have to do with the Corporation of Music, and not with the Serjeant-Trumpeter, may here conveniently be noticed. On p. 169, " all persons professing the art and science of musick, who play at playhouses, gamehouses, taverns, victualling houses, or any place in the city of London and Westminster, without the approbation and lycense of the Marshall and Corporation of musique" are to be apprehended. On p. 217 we notice that five persons, amongst them Cæsar Duffill, one of the King's violinists, are arrested for " teaching, practising, and executing music, in companies and otherwise," without approbation or license. On p. 221 there are the names of five other persons so arrested. On p. 231 there are the names of four others. On p. 241 we have the text of a warrant for apprehending four musicians (names given); on p. 246 another body of five are to be arrested; and on p. 249 we read that no less a number than seventeen are to be arrested, although it should be stated that some of the names have occurred previously, and are only here repeated. Lastly, on p. 257 there are the names of seven persons to be arrested on similar charges. Grove points out that so early as 1469, Edward IV. granted a charter to his " beloved minstrels " empowering them to constitute themselves into a guild ; that at the opening of the sixteenth century there is a mention of a new guild, a " Fellowship of Minstrels and Freemen of the City of London ; " that this Fellowship was reconstituted under a charter of James I., which brought into existence the Company of Musicians. (For further information respecting the history of our Musicians' Company, I refer interested readers to the admirable hand-book issued by the Company some few years ago.) The main object of these respective bodies was always one and the same, viz., to safeguard their privileges, and to prevent the unlawful exercise of their calling by those not properly qualified for the same. Whether the Corporation of Music, above alluded to, is identical with the Company seems a question open to some doubt, but the use of the term

in this case, the gowns are not to be so full, and are to have short sleeves to the elbow ; it was probably found that the former habits seriously interfered with the playing of the violins ; on p. 263 there is evidently a similar order ; on p. 266 we have a like order, and again the gowns are to have short sleeves. On p. 269 we find still another order, " after the same manner and fashion as formerly." I think, looking at the date of the first of these entries, that it refers to the representation at the King's Theatre in Drury Lane, in January, 1664, of " The Indian Queen," a tragedy in heroic verse, by Sir Robert Howard and Mr. Dryden. With regard to Mr. Killigrew and the two theatres here mentioned, I must make a necessary digression, which, though not belonging strictly to the art of music, concerns a sister art, and may be interesting to a general reader. These particulars are taken from Dr. Doran's " Annals." Charles II., in 1663, granted patents for two theatres in London. Under one patent, Killigrew, at the head of the King's Company, opened a new theatre in Drury Lane in August, 1663 : under the second patent, Davenant and the Duke of York's company found a house, first at the Cockpit, and then in Salisbury Court, Fleet Street. This second house was destroyed in the fire of 1666, but before the great conflagration Davenant and his troop went to the old Tennis Court. In 1671, after Davenant's death, his company migrated to a house designed by Wren, and decorated by Grinling Gibbons ; this was the Duke's Theatre, in Dorset Gardens. It is worth remembering, for this presents a note of similarity with the Chapel Royal establishment, that the actors in Killigrew's company were sworn at the Lord Chamberlain's office to serve the King. Of these gentlemen, ten were enrolled in the Royal Household establishment, and provided with liveries of scarlet cloth and silver lace. In the warrants of the Lord Chamberlain they were styled " Gentlemen of the Great Chamber." It may not be inappropriate to quote here, with respect to the above-mentioned dresses for musicians, the following passage from North's " Memoires of Musick " : " In the reign of King James the First musick had the greatest encouragement, for the masques at Court, which were a sort of Balles, or Operas, found imployment for very many of them, and in the Theaters at Court they were adorned with liverys, that is divers coloured silk mantles and scarfs with rich capps, and the master in the shape of an Apollo, for decoration of the same." The office of Master of the Revels is also alluded to on p. 176, and a word of explanation may not be amiss. Hone's "Every-Day Book" (vol. i., p. 1243) has the following: "The late T. C. Crowle was master of the revels. In that quality he claimed a seat in any part of the theatres, and being opposed by the manager of the little theatre in the Haymarket, maintained his right. He was also trumpet-major of England, to whom every one who blows a trumpet publicly (excepting those of the theatres-royal) must pay a certain sum, and therefore the office has jurisdiction of all the merry-andrews and jack-puddings of every Fair throughout England. The office of master of the revels was created under Henry VIII., in 1546." "Sir Henry Herbert established his office of Master of the Revels, in Tothill Street."

PAGE 182.—"Band of Violins." "During the rage for French fashions in music which obtained in Charles the Second's reign, the '24 violons' were imitated here, in the King's music, and became the 'four and twenty fiddlers all of a row' of nursery rhyme. The 'vingt-quatre violons' were formed under Louis XIII., and dissolved by decree of Louis XV." (Grove.) Antony à Wood, speaking of this same band, says: "Before the Restoration of Charles the Second, and especially after, viols begun to be out of fashion, and only violins used, as treble violin, tenor, and bass violin; and the King according to the French mode, would have 24 violins playing before him while he was at meals, as being more airie and brisk than viols." Pepys, on Oct. 1, 1667, writes: "To White Hall; and there in the Boarded Gallery did hear the musick with which the King is presented this night by Monsieur Grebus, the Master of his Musick: both instrumental (I think twenty-four violins) and vocall: an English song upon Peace. But, God forgive me! I never was so little pleased with a concert of music in my life." Possibly the presence of Grabu had something to do with the disgust here expressed.

PAGE 202.—"The prickers." There are many allusions through-out these records to the "pricking" of music. "Prick" is a Saxon word signifying a "small mark or point." A musical note was formerly called a "prick" (hence the term "prick-song"), and a dot, following a note, was called a "prick of addition." We find in the Cheque Book the phrase, "An admonition with a prick was sett upon his head." This means that a small mark or dot, equivalent to a bad mark, was set against his name. Grove defines

" prick-song " as " the name given by old writers upon music to divisions or descant upon a Plain-Song or Ground, which were written, or pricked down, in contradistinction to those which were performed extemporaneously." " The term ' pricking of music-bookes ' was formerly employed to express the writing of them. Payments for so doing are frequently found in the accounts of cathedral and college choirs."

PAGE 219.—There is possibly an error in judgment in having admitted the last entry on this page as a purely musical item—the same remark may apply to the entry concerning bits and stirrups on p. 206, but neither entry is lengthy enough to offend against any canon of precision.

PAGE 254.—" Fetching children from cathedrals." An ancient custom existed in the Chapel Royal of " pressing " men and boys with good voices for the service of the choir. This practice may be traced as far back as the time of Richard III. Commissions " to take up well-singing boys for furnishing the Royal Chapels " are frequent among the Patent Rolls of the sixteenth and the early part of the seventeenth centuries. One of the latest, granted to Dr. N. Giles, Aug. 26, 1626, has these words : " Provided always, and we straightly charge and command, that none of the said Choristers or Children of the Chappell, soe to be taken by force of this Commission, shall be used or imployed as Comedians, or Stage Players, or to exercise or acte any Stage plaies, Interludes, Comedies, or Tragedies ; for that it is not fitt or desent that such as should sing the praises of God Almighty should be trained or imployed in such lascivious and prophane exercises." A reference to p. 271 will show that these pious sentiments were sometimes more honoured in the breach than in the observance, and possibly they were in 1626 an almost unconscious reflection of that Puritanic spirit which was then taking its birth. Queen Elizabeth kept in full force during her whole reign the prerogative of issuing placards or writs for impressing singing boys for her Chapel, as well in the Capital as at Windsor, at least so says Burney.

PAGE 297.—" Scaramoucha." In this same year, 1675, Evelyn writes in his Diary, under date Sept. 29 : " I saw the Italian Scaramucchio act before the King at Whitehall, people giving money to come in, which was very scandalous, and never so before at Court diversions. Having seene him act before in Italy, many yeares past, I was not averse from seeing the most excellent of that kind of folly." To connect this with the item mentioned in the text is purely conjecture, but it seems to me reasonable to do so, both from similarities of name and date.

PAGE 321.—The will, transcribed out of the French, of Anthony Robert. He desires to be buried in Somerset Chapel, where he served the Queen Mother (Queen Henrietta Maria) as music master for forty years. If he cannot be buried there, he must in any case be buried with the full rites of the Roman Church, and he directs that a hundred masses should be said for the repose of his soul. Hare in his " Walks in London " says that " the building which projects into the grounds of Marlborough House and which is entered from the roadway into the Park on the left of S. James' Palace, is interesting as the Roman Catholic Chapel built by Charles the First for his Queen." Canon Sheppard, in his " Memorials of S. James' Palace," writes: " The Queen's Chapel was designed and built by Inigo Jones. As it was originally intended for the Infanta, the Spanish Ambassador laid the first stone in 1623. Its completion was due to the importunities of Queen Henrietta Maria." In the " Life of Inigo Jones" it is said that he " designed the Chapel for the Infanta at Somerset House. The front of the Chapel faced the Thames, and presented an harmonious elevation of a rustic arcade with five arches, and five well-proportioned windows between Corinthian pilasters, duplicated at the other end." Another passage in the same " Life " says that Inigo " is said to have been the architect of the Queen's Chapel, at St. James." Mr. W. B. Donne places the chapel assigned to Queen Henrietta Maria in Somerset House, which in 1616, James I., in honour of his Danish Queen, commanded to be called Denmark House. Stowe's Chronicle, under date 1616, has the entry, " Queen Anne feasted the King at her Pallace in the Strand, formerly called Somerset-House, and then the King commanded it should no more be so called, but that it should from henceforth be called Denmarke-House." These somewhat conflicting testimonies seem to prove that Queen Henrietta Maria originally had her Chapel at S. James' Palace, and that on the advent of Queen Catherine of Braganza, she moved it to Somerset House.

PAGE 347.—There is here an allusion to the old chimney tax, or, as it was called, hearth-money. On March 8, 1689, Evelyn writes : " In the mean time to gratify the people, the Hearth Tax was remitted for ever, but what was intended to supply it, besides present great taxes on land, is not named."

PAGE 383.—Order for attendance of the violinists at the Chapel at Whitehall. On p. 9 of the Chapels Royal Register of Births, Marriages, and Deaths, there is the following order, given by the Lord Chamberlain to the Closet Keeper of the Chapel, and dated 1685. It runs: " It is His Ma^{tyes.} pleasure that H.R.H. Princess Anne of Denmark do sit in His Ma^{tyes.} Closet at his Chappell Royall at Whitehall upon one side of His Ma^{tyes.} chayre, which might remayne in its place and not turn'd," and goes on to say that no one is to enter when the Princess is there, except the Clerk of the Closet or his deputy, or the Lord Chamberlain, and the Vice-Chamberlain. This is confirmed by Evelyn's statement that the Princess, " since his Majesty came to the Crown, allways sate in the King's closet, and had the same bowings and ceremonies applied to the place where she was, as his Majesty had when there in person."

PAGE 422.—Edward Kinnaston. He was originally one of the boys belonging to Davenant's company. It is said that Kynaston made " the loveliest lady " for a boy, ever beheld by Pepys. Kynaston was twice thrashed, the second time being cudgelled, for his impertinent mimicry of Sir Charles Sedley. He remained on the stage from 1659 to 1699. " Even at past sixty," Cibber says, "his teeth were all sound, white, and even as one would wish to see in a reigning toast of twenty." He died in 1712, and was buried in the churchyard of S. Paul's, Covent Garden. " So exalted was his reputation that it has since been disputable among the judicious, whether any woman that succeeded him so sensibly touched the audience as he." " Kinaston the boy had the good turn to appear in three shapes : first, as a poor woman in ordinary clothes—then in fine clothes, as a gallant; and in them was clearly the prettiest woman in the whole house: and lastly, as a man; and then likewise did appear the handsomest man in the house." " To the King's playhouse, where ' The Heyresse,' notwithstanding Kinaston's being beaten, is acted : and they say the King is very angry with Sir Charles Sedley for his being beaten, but he do deny it. But his " (Kynaston's) " part is done by Beeston." " To the King's playhouse—and here we find Kinaston to be well enough to act again ; which he do very well, after his beating by Sir Charles Sedley's appointment." (Pepys.)

Page 431.—A new organ for the Chapel at Whitehall. "A new organ is set up in the Banquetting House Chappel, with a Dial in the middle of it, this being the first of that make ; the other is packt up in Boxes there, in order to be sent to Barbadoes." (*London Post*, October 4, 1699.)

Page 432.—"Mr. Thomas Betterton."—Mrs. Betterton played for thirty years the chief female characters, especially in Shakespeare's plays, with great success. When "Calisto" was to be played at Court in 1674, she was chosen as instructress to the Lady Mary and the Lady Anne. After Betterton's death, Queen Anne settled on her old teacher a pension of £500 per annum. Betterton himself, during a long career, played at Drury Lane, Dorset Gardens, Lincoln's Inn Fields, and the Opera House in the Haymarket. The highest salary he obtained was £5 per week, which included £1 by way of pension to his wife, after her retirement in 1694. Pepys on several occasions alludes to Betterton's acting, and his opinion of his talent may be summed up in the one sentence : "I only know that Mr. Betterton is the best actor in the world." With regard to this warrant about the wearing of hats, it must be remembered that in those days they were more frequently worn indoors than people are apt to imagine. Probably the "persons of quality," who complained about the musicians being covered in their presence, never thought for a moment of removing their own head-gear. It can be readily seen that what they wanted was to mark once and for all the social difference which they thought should exist between themselves and those who contributed to their amusement. As to the practice of wearing a hat in houses, and even in churches, these two references from Pepys will show the custom of the day : " To church, and heard a simple fellow upon the praise of Church musique, and exclaiming against men's wearing their hats on in the church." (Evidently the hat-wearing in church was a decaying remnant of the Puritan regime.) " Home to bed ; having got a strange cold in my head, by flinging off my hat at dinner, and sitting with the wind in my neck."

INDEX.

NOVELLO AND COMPANY, LTD., PRINTERS, LONDON.